The Encyclopedia of ANIMAL BEHAVIOUR

The Encyclopedia of ANIMAL BEHAVIOUR

JILL BAILEY

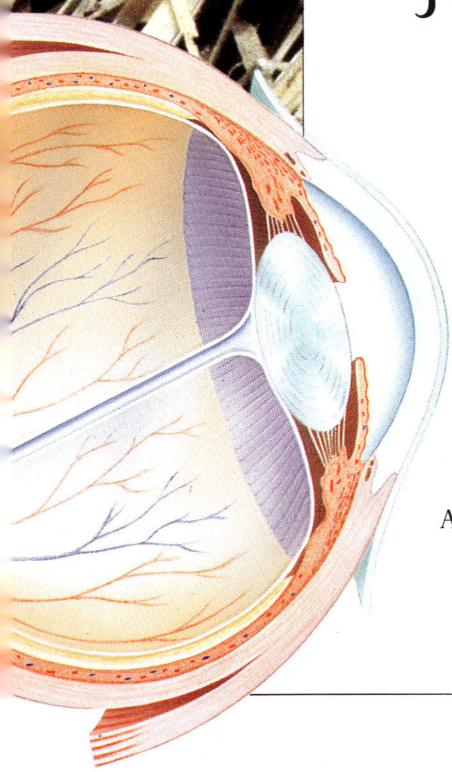

ANDROMEDA OXFORD

CONTENTS

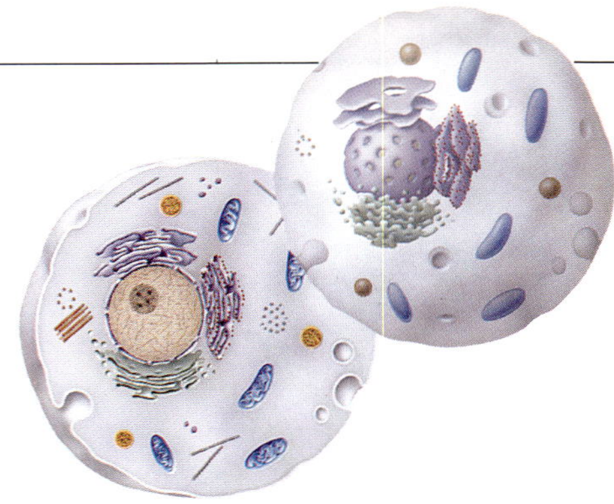

Introduction 6

Knowledge Map 8

Timechart 12

Biology Keywords 16

1 *The Great Variety* 48

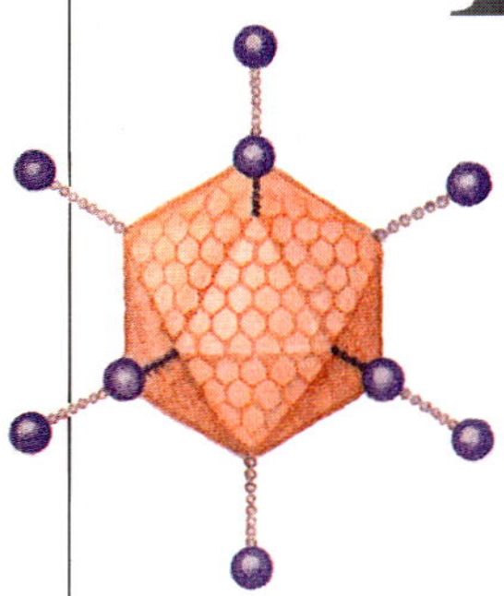

Soft-Bodied Animals 50

Shells and Spines 52

Jointed Legs 54

Animals with Backbones 56

One-Celled Wonders 58

2 *Life Processes* 60

Chemistry of Life 62

Building Blocks of Life 64

Processing Food 66

Waste Disposal 68

Circulation 70

Air Pumps 72

Chemical Control 74

Nervous Control 76

Controlling Heat and Water 78

Recovery and Repair 80

3 *Finding Food* 82

Diets Galore 84

Plant-Eaters 86

Flesh-Eaters 88

Hunting Techniques 90

Unfussy Feeders 92

Breakdown Specialists 94

Fussy Feeders 96

Living Off Others 98

Living Together 100

4 *Animal Movement* 102

Muscle-Powered Movement 104

Built for Movement 106

Walking, Running, Jumping 108

Crawling and Climbing 110

Moving Through the Air 112

Moving Through Water 114

Project editor	Peter Furtado
Editors	Lauren Bourque, John Clark
Editorial assistant	Marian Dreier
Art editor	Ayala Kingsley
Visualization and artwork	Ted McCausland/ Siena Artworks
Senior designer	Martin Anderson
Designer	Roger Hutchins
Picture manager	Jo Rapley
Picture research	Alison Floyd
Production	Clive Sparling

Produced and published by
Andromeda Oxford Ltd
9-15 The Vineyard
Abingdon
Oxfordshire OX14 3PX

First published in the United Kingdom 1995

Text pages 16–47

ISBN 1 871869 46 3

Printed in Spain by Graficromo SA, Cordoba

5 *Growth and Reproduction* *116*

Patterns of Growth *118*
Getting Together *120*
Animal Reproduction *122*
Egg to Embryo *124*
Growing Up *126*
Changing Shape *128*

6 *Animal Communication* *130*

Seeing the World *132*
Detecting Sound *134*
Taste and Smell *136*
Hidden Senses *138*
Insect Societies *140*
Mammal Societies *142*

Factfile *144*

Metric Prefixes *144*
Conversion Factors *144*
SI Units *145*
Classification of Animals *146*
Mammalian Hormones *148*
The "Fight-or-Flight" Response *149*
Minerals and Diet *150*
Vitamins and Human Diet *151*
Digestive Enzymes *151*
The Krebs Cycle *152*
Further Reading *152*
The Menstrual Cycle *153*
Nobel Prizewinners *154*

Index *156*
Acknowledgments *160*

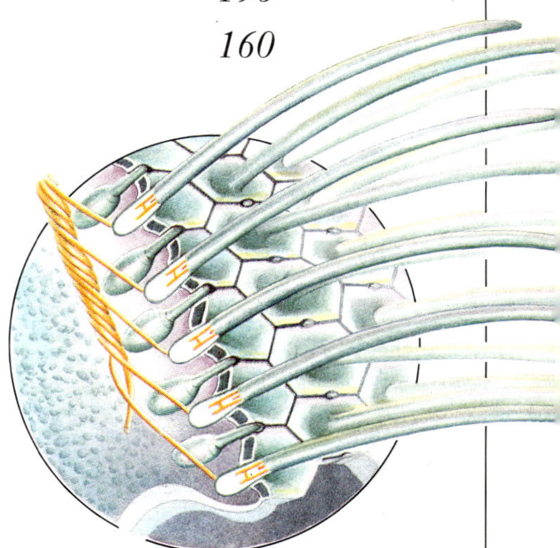

INTRODUCTION

THE ANIMAL KINGDOM today probably contains more than 10 million different species, the vast majority still unidentified by scientists. Some live for a day or less; others for more than a hundred years. Animals have adapted to every imaginable environment on Earth, from the ocean depths to the dryest, hottest deserts.

The appearance of these animals, the number and capability of their limbs and the structure of their internal organs seems infinitely varied. Yet, from the ameba to the zebra, all these life forms face the same problems of survival and rely on the same principles of existence. Their bodies are adapted in a wonderful range of ways to solve these problems. Feeding, evading capture, detecting changes in the immediate environment, maintaining chemical stability within the body, finding a mate, protecting the young: all these are common needs across the animal kingdom. Furthermore, every living creature collects food in the form of oxygen, sugars and proteins, and converts these through a similar set of chemical reactions in its cells into energy for growth and movement. Although the simplest animals are no more than single cells, whose behavior is based purely on chemical stimuli, even large thinking animals are made up of such cells, organized into complex, specialized tissues.

For more than two thousand years, scientists have tried to explain and classify this great variety. While the theory of evolution by natural selection has proved the most powerful way of explaining the diversity, the fundamental similarities between the most different animals can be seen by looking at the basic tasks every living animal needs to fulfil. Some of the great insights of 20th-century biology relate to the ever more detailed understanding of the biochemical activity that takes place in and between cells, and the relationship between the behavior patterns of a species and its need to survive in a competitive environment. In addition, physiological research in the present century into the workings of the human body has contributed to the understanding of the biology, not just of other mammals, but also of many other members of the animal kingdom.

This book begins with an introduction to the basic body plans of the largest categories – soft-bodied animals, mollusks, echinoderms, arthropods (including insects, the largest category of all), vertebrates, and one-celled animals. The various processes essential to the maintenance of life are reviewed next , with the important bodily organs that sustain these processes. The following sections cover the essential physical aspects of existence – feeding, moving and reproducing – to show how the requirements of different habitats, diets and threats from predators have led to the evolution of very different forms of bodies and behavior. The final thematic section covers the senses, through which animals communicate with the outside world and – in the case of social species – with one another.

THIS BOOK aims to make all this information available to the whole family, from students studying for examinations and projects to adults wanting to bring their scientific knowledge up to date. To achieve this, the book is organized in such a way as to provide readers with a quick answer to a specific query, or allow them to follow a more detailed account of a particular topic.

At the heart of the book is a 96-page thematic section, made up of 48 major narrative topics, each one richly illustrated to tell the story of a central theme of the book. The strong graphic presentation and the style of writing are designed to make this section the ideal point of departure for the less well-informed reader. Sets of keywords highlighted on each topic spread point the reader to the second major section of the book, a 32-page alphabetic mini-encyclopedia of the subject, containing some 400 entries. This section, too, leads the reader back to the thematic topics.

No region of modern science can be neatly detached from other fields. Biology merges into ecology and environmental studies on one side, chemistry on another and genetics in other respects. The Knowledge Map, immediately following this Introduction, maps out the entire field of modern science, shows how each area of science is related to another, and defines the major fields. This is followed by a brief Timechart, tracing the development of the subject through the great discoveries. Finally, to ensure that the volume is of genuine value for reference as well as browsing, the Factfile provides a wealth of hard data, tables and statistics.

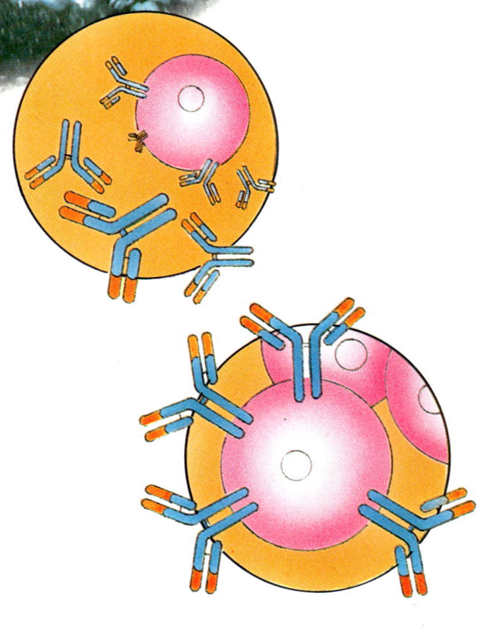

Knowledge Map

Key Fields of Modern Science

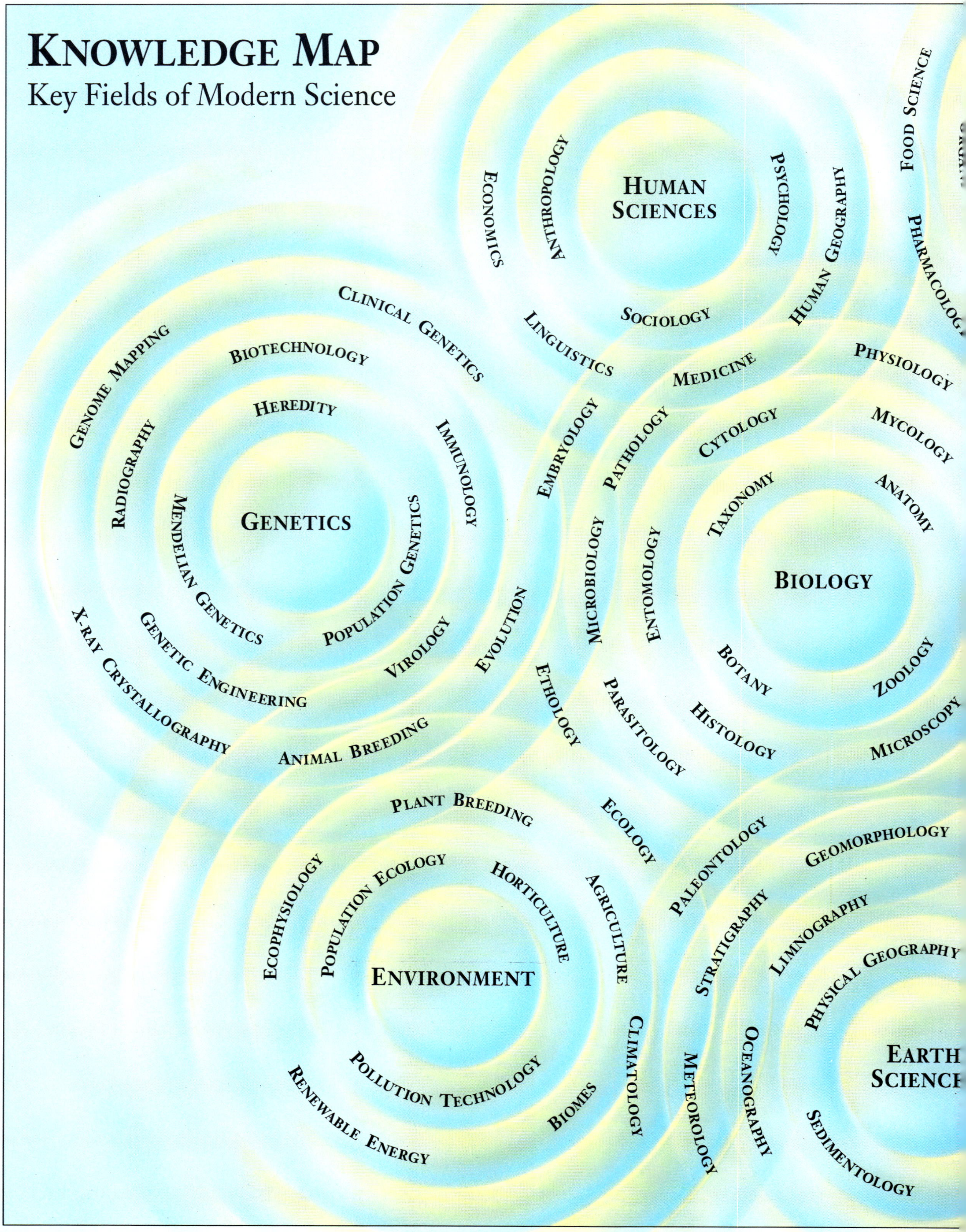

Chemistry
Analytical Chemistry
Physical Chemistry
Chromatography
Industrial Chemistry
Materials Science
Electrochemistry
Photochemistry
Spectrography
Inorganic
Periodic Table
Biochemistry
Biophysics
Astronomy
Stellar Evolution
Stellar Astronomy
Galactic Astronomy
Observational Astronomy
Celestial Mechanics
Space Exploration
Astrophysics
Grand Unified Theories
Lunar Studies
Cosmology
Relativity
Spectroscopy
Radioastronomy
Physics
Quantum Physics
Atomic Physics
Radioactivity
Electricity
Particle Physics
Mechanics
Solid State Physics
Nuclear Physics
Statics
Optics
Heat and Thermodynamics
Dynamics
Acoustics
Cryogenics
Recording
Gravity
Electromagnetism
Electronics
Tectonic Theory
Seismology
Mineralogy
Planetology
Mapping
Math and Computers
Robotics
Mensuration
Artificial Intelligence
Multimedia
Number Theory
Software Engineering
Logic
Algebra
Telecommunications
CADesign
Statistics
Geometry
Mathematical Analysis
Info Technology
Graphics
Applied Math
Spreadsheets
Word Processing

Knowledge Map

Modern Biology

BIOLOGY

The study of living organisms, their shape, structure, vital processes, origin, classification, distribution and behavior. Biology explains how organisms work, how they respond to their surroundings, why they live where they do, and how different organisms are related. Main fields are ANATOMY and ZOOLOGY.

TAXONOMY

The classification of living organisms into hierarchical groups, representing relationships between them. These groups derive from comparisons of physiology, shape, biochemistry and genes. There are several taxonomic schemes covering the natural world.

ANATOMY

The study of the shape and structure of plants and animals, at both the visible level (gross anatomy) and the microscopic level. Dissection and microscopy are commonly used to investigate internal structures. The comparative anatomy of related organisms is an important tool in determining evolutionary relationships. Anatomy is closely related to PHYSIOLOGY.

BOTANY

The study of plants, their shape, structure, vital processes, diseases, origin, classification and distribution. The term is often used to include the study of fungi, algae and fossil plants. An understanding of botany is important for agriculture, horticulture and forestry, and for plant breeding, which offers hope of expanding food production into unsuitable areas.

ZOOLOGY

The study of animals, their shape, structure, vital processes, reproduction and development, origin, classification, distribution and ecology. Zoology involves studying not only how animals work (PHYSIOLOGY), but also how they behave and interact with each other and how they are affected by each other and by their environment (ECOLOGY).

CYTOLOGY

The study of the appearance, structure and function of living cells, including their life history, multiplication, and the diseases which affect them. Cytology includes the study of the physical and chemical processes taking place inside cells, the interactions between cells, and their detailed microscopic structure. The culture of cells outside the body provides material for genetic research, and offers the potential for cures of certain hereditary diseases.

PHYSIOLOGY

The study of the vital processes of living organisms, including the functions and activities of cells, tissues and organs and the physical and chemical processes involved. These are studied both in the living organism and in external cell cultures. Physiology is fundamental to the understanding of diseases and disorders of the body. It is studied at many levels, from the microscopic compartments of cells to responses of the whole organism.

MICROBIOLOGY

The study of microorganisms, their shape, structure, vital processes, mode of life, ecology, origin, classification and distribution. Its subjects can only be seen with a microscope, and include viruses, algae, fungi, yeasts and protozoa. Microbiology has applications in biotechnology, medical and genetic research.

HISTOLOGY

The study of living tissues and cells, usually with the aid of a microscope. Histologists study the differences between the various types of animal and plant tissue; medical histology is the study of the pathology of tissues. Dead tissues are studied during a biopsy.

PARASITOLOGY

The study of the various parasites, internal and external, that affect humans, animals and plants, their anatomy, physiology, origin, development, and the ways in which medically and economically important parasites can be controlled. Major branches of the field include veterinary, medical and agricultural parasitology.

EMBRYOLOGY

The study of the formation and development of animal embryos, including the interaction of the embryo with its physical and chemical environment, and the factors which switch on and off the genes controlling development.

BIOPHYSICS

The study of the physical principles involved in the vital processes. It uses techniques of physics, such as X-ray diffraction, to study the nervous system, animal locomotion, navigation and communication.

MICROSCOPY

The investigation of the detailed structure of objects, including living and dead organisms, using a microscope. Objects may be viewed by means of light reflected from or passed through them, or through thin sections of their tissues (giving a magnification up to 2000 times); or they may be studied at higher magnification using beams of electrons.

PATHOLOGY

The study of the causes and nature of diseases, and their effects on the bodies of living organisms. The organisms studied in pathology range from large parasites to microscopic protozoans, bacteria, viruses, and fungi. Pathology studies the life cycles of these pathogens (disease-causing organisms), the mechanisms by which they exert their effects on the body, and the ways in which the body defends itself against them.

ETHOLOGY

The study of animal behavior. Ethology seeks to explain the behavior of animals in terms of evolution and development, and local factors acting on them. Ethologists make comparative studies of particular types of behavior across a range of animal groups.

ENTOMOLOGY

The study of insects, their shape, structure, vital processes, mode of life, ecology, origin, classification and distribution. As many important pests are insects, entomology is an important field of biology.

ECOLOGY

The study of the relationship between living organisms and their environment, including the effects of chemical and physical aspects of an organism's surroundings, and of the presence of other organisms, including predators and food sources. Ecology seeks to explain how the abundance of organisms is affected by these relationships.

MYCOLOGY

The study of fungi, their shape, structure, vital processes, mode of life, ecology, origin, classification and distribution. Mycology has many applications, from the study of fungus-induced diseases, to biotechnology, including the development of antibiotics, fermentation of wine and beer, baking and the production of dyes.

BIOCHEMISTRY

The study of the chemical compounds and chemical processes found in living organisms. It involves the analysis of the compounds involved in cell structure and metabolism, and the study of metabolic reaction sequences. This helps the understanding of many bodily processes, including the conversion of food to energy, the expression of hereditary information from the genes, and the building of body structures.

Timechart

Of all the sciences, biology offers the most immediate practical rewards. The earliest people must have known how useful it is to understand the variety and behavior of animals hunted for food. But, as with much else, it was the Greeks who first deliberately sought such knowledge and attempted to structure it systematically. Early Greek philosophers such as Alcmaeon and Empedocles were followed by Aristotle (384–322 BC), who aimed to assemble an organized encyclopedia that contained all existing knowledge. Central to his thinking was the idea that facts should always take precedence over what might seem to follow from general principles. As a naturalist, he observed – and dissected – creatures found in the seas around Lesbos, near the coast of Ionia (now Turkey).

Aristotle highlighted several problems that were to occupy scientists for the next 2000 years. Struck by the great variety of living creatures, he tried to classify these creatures into groups or classes. He established many of the principles of classification, placing animals on a hierarchical scale, extending from humans

First studies of the **STRUCTURE AND BEHAVIOR OF ANIMALS**, including the dissection of human bodies, by the Greek Alcmaeon of Creton (c500 BC)

Greek philospher **EMPEDOCLES** of Akragas recognizes that the heart is the center of the blood vessel system (c450 BC)

GREEK PHILOSOPHER ARISTOTLE establishes the basic philosophy of the biological sciences and outlines a theory of evolution. He classifies animals: 500 species are divided into eight classes (c350 BC)

Roman physician **GALEN** writes extensively on human physiology. His work dominates Western thought up to the Renaissance (cAD 135–201)

French naturalist **PIERRE BELON** publishes a classification of 200 species and compares the anatomy of birds and humans (1555)

Italian anatomist **REALDO COLOMBO** demonstrates that Galen was wrong to suppose that blood passed directly between the two chambers of the heart (1559)

Italian physician **HIERONYMUS FABRICIUS** describes the valves in the veins (1603). The following year he describes the blood circulation in the umbilical cord

English physician **WILLIAM HARVEY** shows that the blood circulates through the arteries and veins (1628)

Dutch microscopist **JAN SWAMMERDAM** is the first to see and describe red blood cells (1658)

Italian **MARCELLO MALPIGHI** observes capillaries in the lungs, completing Harvey's work on blood circulation (1661)

Englishman Robert Hooke describes **CELLS** for the first time (1665)

Dutchman **ANTON VAN LEEUWENHOEK** observes protozoa with simple hand-held microscope, which magnifies 200 times (1674)

English naturalist John Ray introduces a **CLASSIFICATION OF ANIMALS**. It follows Aristotle by using the divisions "bloodless" and "blooded" (1693)

Swedish biologist **CARL LINNAEUS** develops the modern system of naming and classifying animals and plants (1735)

ANATOMY
PHYSIOLOGY
BIOCHEMISTRY
HEALTH AND MEDICINE
ZOOLOGY

AD1 | 1500 | 1600 | 1700

downward through quadrupeds, birds, snakes, fish, insects, mollusks and molds. A comprehensive and systematic method of classifying the living world was finally devised by Carl Linnaeus in 1735.

Aristotle also studied the development of chicks in the egg, breaking open fertilized eggs, one each day, as the chick developed – a pioneering study in embryology. His work established the framework into which later biologists fitted much of their thinking. In the early 17th century Hieronymus Fabricius published the next important study of embryology and fetal development, adding detail to the work of Aristotle.

Aristotle pondered, too, the reason for the variety of living creatures. He believed that, in nature, everything has a purpose; and that if this purpose can be understood, the differences between the species of animals and plants can also be understood. This attitude persisted until the mid 1800s when Charles Darwin put forward a different interpretation of nature's variety: evolution by natural selection.

Swiss physiologist Albrecht von Haller publishes the first textbook on **PHYSIOLOGY** (1747)

Italian physicist Luigi Galvani discovers the electrical nature of **NERVE IMPULSES** (1771)

Spallanzani proves that semen is necessary for **FERTILIZATION** (1778)

French naturalist **JEAN-BAPTISTE LAMARCK** publishes a classification system for invertebrates and argues that species change with time (1801)

French naturalist Georges Cuvier founds the study of **COMPARATIVE ANATOMY** (1805)

Scottish anatomist and surgeon **CHARLES BELL** distinguishes, during his work on the brain, between sensory and motor nerves; he reports this in *New Anatomy of the Brain* (1811)

US Army doctor **WILLIAM BEAUMONT** shows that digestion is a purely chemical process (1833)

German biologist Theodor Schwann discovers the first **ENZYME**, pepsin (1836)

THEODOR SCHWANN proposes that all living matter is made up of cells (1839)

German-Swiss physiologist **GABRIEL GUSTAV VALENTIN** discovers that pancreatic juice breaks down food during digestion (1844)

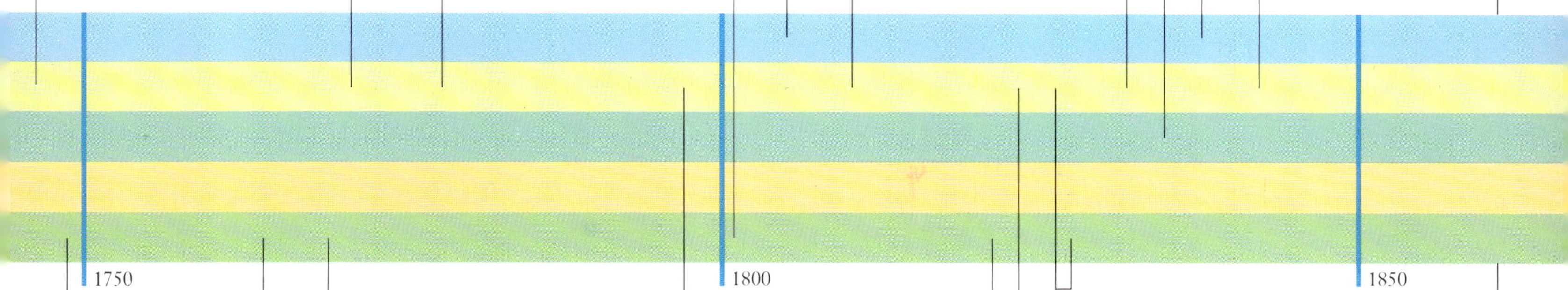

Frenchman the **COMTE DE BUFFON** begins publication of a 44-volume work, which takes him 55 years to complete, describing all that is known about animals and minerals (1749)

Swiss naturalist **CHARLES BONNET** develops his theory of "preformation"; according to this each creature is already preformed in miniature in the egg (1764)

Italian biologist Lazzaro Spallanzani demonstrates that the **SPONTANEOUS GENERATION** of micro-organisms does not take place in solutions that have been boiled and placed in sealed bottles (1769)

French pathologist **MARIE-FRANCOIS-XAVIER BICHAT** identifies 21 different types of tissue in animals, including bone, muscle and blood (1797)

JEAN LAMARCK distinguishes between vertebrates and invertebrates in his *Natural History of Invertebrates* (1822)

French anatomist and physiologist Pierre Flourens studies the **CENTRAL NERVOUS SYSTEM**, demonstrating that the cerebellum controls muscular movements (1824)

Russian biologist **KARL ERNEST VON BAYER** discovers that mammals develop from eggs (1827)

American naturalist **JOHN JAMES AUDUBON** starts publication of *Birds of America*, a collection of life-like drawings (1827)

Another breakthrough for biology was the development of the microscope, probably invented about 1590. The new instrument allowed Anton van Leeuwenhoek to see bacteria, protozoa and other tiny organisms. Robert Hooke used the microscope to observe regular structures, which he called cells, in cork. In 1839, German physiologist Theodor Schwann proposed that cells were the building blocks of all living material.

That life is essentially biochemical was recognized about 1830. German chemist Friedrich Wohler prepared the organic compound urea from nonorganic material, and US Army doctor William Beaumont showed that digestion is a purely chemical process by observing the stomach of a wounded soldier. Since that time the chemistry of life has been gradually mapped out.

In the 19th century, Charles Darwin's insights led the study of animal behavior onto a more scientific path. Darwin realized that animal behavior was part of the animal's adaptation to its environment and was as important for its survival as its anatomical structure. Therefore, behavior routines must be inherited and

ANATOMY
PHYSIOLOGY
BIOCHEMISTRY
HEALTH AND MEDICINE
ZOOLOGY

American biochemist Thomas Osborne demonstrates that there are a vast variety of proteins, some of which contain **AMINO ACIDS** which are essential for life (1859)

British biologist Charles Darwin puts forward the theory of **EVOLUTION BY NATURAL SELECTION** (1859)

German physiologist **KARL VON VOIT** reveals that food is converted to energy by a complex web of reactions (1865)

German Joseph Breuer identifies the feedback mechanisms involved in **RESPIRATION** (1868)

French entomologist Henri Fabre shows how large a part **INSTINCT** plays in insect life (1879)

German anatomist Walther Flemming studies **CELL DIVISION** and describes mitosis (1882)

French biochemist **LOUIS PASTEUR** establishes the chemical theory of immunity (1888)

German bacteriologist Paul Ehrlich does important work in **IMMUNOLOGY**, studying the diphtheria antitoxin (1890)

German biologist August Weismann observes **MEIOSIS**, and proposes germ-plasm theory of heredity (1892)

German chemist **EDUARD BUCHNER** discovers that an extract of yeast which he names zymase can convert sugar to alcohol (1897)

German biochemist Emil Fischer postulates the "lock-and-key" hypothesis to explain the specificity of **ENZYME ACTION** (1899)

British biochemist Frederick Gowland Hopkins discovers tryptophan, the first known **ESSENTIAL AMINO ACID** (1900)

1900

Russian physiologist **IVAN PAVLOV** formulates his law of learning by conditioning (1902)

British microbiologist Frederick Twort discovers the first virus infection of bacteria (**BACTERIOPHAGE**) (1915)

Austrian zoologist **KARL VON FRISCH** discovers that bees communicate by body movements (1919)

German pharmacologist **OTTO LOEWI** discovers neurotransmitters, the chemicals that pass messages between nerve cells (1921)

INSULIN is first extracted from the pancreas by Canadian physiologist Frederick Banting and American-Canadian physiologist Charles Best (1921)

naturally selected. This idea was the beginning of the science of ethology, the study of animal behavior in its natural setting.

German ornithologist Oskar Heinroth noticed that newly hatched geese regard the first thing that they see after hatching as their parent, a phenomenon now called "imprinting". In 1925, Austrian zoologist Konrad Lorenz established that imprinting of specific behavior routines occurred at different moments in an animal's life. Dutch zoologist Nikolaas Tinbergen continued the study of animal behavior, emphasizing the role of instinct. One of the cofounders of ethology, Austrian Karl von Frisch, specialized in bees, showing how they communicate the location of nectar sources by movements called "dances".

In 1964, the altruistic behavior of social ants and bees was explained by New Zealand biologist W. D. Hamilton as a mechanism for increasing the passage of their genes to the next generation. In 1975, US biologist E. O. Wilson developed the study of social insects and their behavior, especially the implications for animal behavior in general, into a new science.

German-British biochemist Hans Adolf Krebs discovers the **KREBS CYCLE**, the cycle of oxidation and energy production in living cells (1937)

French biologist Edouard Chatton identifies the simplest living cells, the **PROKARYOTES** (1937)

American biochemist **LINUS PAULING** determines the alpha-helix structure of proteins (1951)

Dutch zoologist Nikolaas Tinbergen emphasizesthe role of **INSTINCT** in animal behavior (1951)

Britons Alan Hodgkin and Andrew Huxley put forward the modern theory of **NERVE EXCITATION**, based on the movement of sodium and potassium ions in nerve cells (1952)

British biochemist Frederick Sanger determines the **AMINO-ACID SEQUENCE OF A PROTEIN** (1955)

German biologist William Hennig develops **CLADISTICS**, a classification system based on comparisons of physical characteristics of species (1960s)

J. Hughes discovers **ENDORPHINS**, morphine-like chemicals in the brain (1975)

American biologist Edward Osborne Wilson publishes *Sociobiology*, a study of social insects and their behavior, especially regarding the implications for animal behavior in general (1975)

1950

German chemist **GERHARD DOMAGK** discovers the first sulfa drug, Prontosil (1932)

Austrian zoologist Konrad Lorenz publishes the first of many major studies of **ANIMAL BEHAVIOR**, founding the discipline of ethology (1935)

American biologist Donald Griffin shows that bats use ultrasound in **ECHOLOCATION** (1938)

Britons **HUGH HUXLEY AND J. HANSON** propose the sliding filament theory of muscle contraction (1953)

Briton Francis Crick and American John Watson show the double-helix structure of **DNA**, the molecule of inheritance (1953)

Briton **MAX PERUTZ** demonstrates the structure of the hemoglobin molecule (1962)

New Zealand biologist **W. D. HAMILTON** explains the altruistic behavior of social bees and ants genetically (1964)

HIV, the virus causing acquired immunity deficiency syndrome (AIDS) is identified (1984)

THE FIVE-KINGDOM SYSTEM OF CLASSIFICATION of living creatures is put forward by R.H. Whittaker (1980s)

German **H. FRICKE** uses a submersible to study coelacanths in the Indian Ocean (1987)

Biology KEYWORDS

abdomen
The region of the body trunk below the **thorax** (chest) that contains the digestive organs. In insects and other arthropods, the abdomen is the lower part of the body, commonly separated from the thorax or cephalothorax by a narrow constriction, and is characterized by the absence of limbs and may be segmented. In mammals, the abdomen is separated from the thorax by the diaphragm.

absorption
The passage of a fluid or dissolved substance across a **cell membrane**. In animals, nutrients are absorbed into the circulatory system through the cells lining the intestine. Absorption may be a passive **diffusion** process, or substances may be actively taken into cells using energy from **adenosine triphosphate** (ATP).

accommodation
The ability of the **eye** to change its effective focal length to see objects clearly at varying distances. In humans and some other animals this is achieved by reflex adjustments to the shape of the lens.

acetylcholine
A **neurotransmitter** or chemical that serves to communicate **nerve** impulses between the cells of the nervous system across a **synapse**. It is also associated with the transmission of impulses between nerve cells and muscle cells.

acquired characteristics
Features of the body that develop during the lifetime of an individual, usually as a result of repeated use or disuse, such as the enlarged muscles of a weightlifter.There is no reliable evidence that acquired characteristics can be imherited, and no mechanism is known whereby bodily changes can influence the genes.

actin
A contractile protein that can form into long fibers. It was originally discovered in **muscles** in association with myosin, though it is now known to be widely distributed at sites of cellular movement.

action potential
A change in the potential difference (voltage, or difference in electrical charge) across the membrane of a **nerve** cell when an impulse passes along it. A local, transient change in potential (from about –60 mV to +45 mV) occurs, and the membrane is said to be depolarized. This is due to a change in the permeability of the membrane, which causes sodium ions to pass into the cell and potassium ions to move out.

active transport
The movement of dissolved substances across a cell membrane against a concentration gradient, therefore needing energy. It is a key process in maintaining the correct balance of potassium and sodium ions in muscle cells and nerve cells.

adaptation
Any change in the structure or function of an organism that allows it to survive and reproduce more effectively in its environment. Adaptation is thought to occur as a result of random variation in the genetic makeup of organisms (produced by mutation and recombination) coupled with natural selection. It produces individuals whose genetically determined characteristics allow them to survive and reproduce more effectively.

CONNECTIONS

CONTROLLING HEAT AND WATER **78**
FUSSY FEEDERS **96**
ANIMAL MOVEMENT **102**

adenosine triphosphate (ATP)
A molecule used to transfer energy from one part of the cell to another. Found in all cells, it can yield large amounts of energy, and is used to drive the numerous biological processes needed to sustain life., growth, movements and reproduction In animals, ATP is formed by the breakdown of glucose molecules, usually obtained from the carbohydrate component of a diet, in **respiration**.

adrenal glands
A pair of **endocrine glands** situated immediately above the kidneys. The cortex (outer part) secretes aldosterone, which controls salt and water metabolism, and other steroid hormones which regulate the use of carbo-

hydrates, proteins and fats. The medulla (inner part) secretes adrenaline and noradrenaline, which are the hormones that control the body's response to stress.

adrenaline
Also known as epinephrine, a hormone secreted by the adrenal medulla in response to stress.

aggression
Behavior used to intimidate or injure another organism, usually to gain or defend a territory, a mate, or food. It often involves an escalating series of threats made to intimidate an opponent without having to engage in potentially dangerous physical contact. Aggressive signals include snarling by dogs, the fluffing up of feathers by birds and the raising of fins by some species of fish.

aging
The period of deterioration of the physical condition of a living organism that leads to death. Three current theories attempt to account for aging. The first suggests that the process is genetically determined; the second that it is due to the accumulation of mistakes during the replication of **DNA** at cell division; and the third that it is actively induced by pieces of DNA that move between cells, or by cancer-causing viruses that become abundant in old cells and induce them to produce unwanted proteins or interfere with the control functions of their DNA.

aldosterone
A hormone secreted by the cortex of the **adrenal glands** that controls the excretion of sodium by the kidneys and thus maintains the balance of salt and water in body fluids.

algae
A group of photosynthetic plantlike organisms with a great variety of form, ranging from single-celled organisms to multicellular seaweeds of considerable size and complexity. Most algae live in aquatic habitats or in moist conditions on land. They belong to two kingdoms. Blue-green algae (cyanobacteria) have a primitive cell structure (*see* **prokaryote**) and are classified with bacteria in the kingdom Monera. Other algae belong to the kingdom Protoctista. They include red, brown and green seaweeds, diatoms, euglenas and several groups of pigmented single-celled flagellates. *See* **protoctist**.

alimentary canal
The digestive tract leading from the mouth to the anus. In humans it consists of the mouth, buccal cavity, pharynx, esophagus, stomach, intestines and anus. *See* **digestion**.

alternation of generations
A reproductive process in various organisms in which two forms occur alternately: diploid (having two sets of chromosomes) and haploid (one set of chromosomes). The diploid generation produces haploid spores by **meiosis** (a halving of the chromosomes), and is called the sporophyte, while the haploid generation produces **gametes** (male and female sex cells), and is called the gametophyte. The gametes fuse to form a diploid zygote, which develops into a new sporophyte; thus the sporophyte and gametophyte alternate. Alternation of generations is found in all plants and in many invertebrate animals such as corals and aphids. *See* **jellyfish**.

alveolus
One of the thousands of tiny air sacs at the end of each bronchiole in the lungs of mammals and reptiles that increases the surface area available for gas exchange. *See* **lung**.

ameba
One of the simplest living animals, with a body of colorless protoplasm consisting of a single cell, belonging to the kingdom Protoctista. Its activities are controlled by the nucleus and it feeds by phagocytosis: extending lobelike **pseudopods** to surround and engulf particles of organic debris.

amino acid
Any water-soluble organic molecule, mainly composed of carbon, oxygen, hydrogen, and nitrogen, containing a basic amino group ($-NH_2$) and an acidic carboxyl ($-COOH$) group. Two or more amino acids join to form peptides, which can link together to form polypeptides, which in turn combine to form **proteins**. Proteins are made of interacting polypeptides and are folded or twisted into characteristic shapes. All proteins living organisms are made up of the same 20 or so amino acids, joined together in varying combinations. Eight of these, the essential amino acids, cannot be synthesized by humans and must therefore be obtained from the diet.

AMEBA

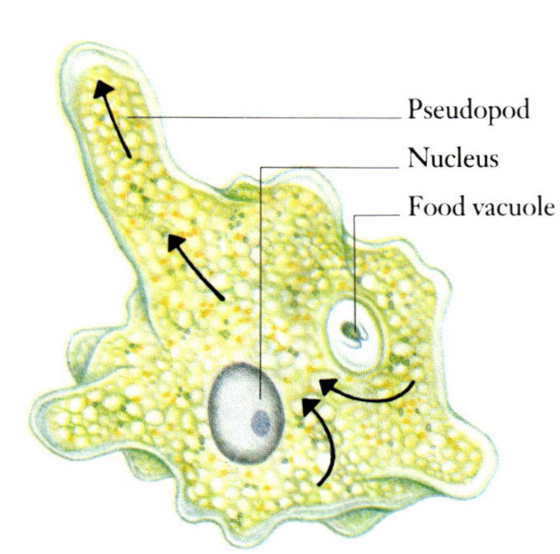

CONNECTIONS
CHEMISTRY OF LIFE **62**
PROCESSING FOOD **66**
DISPOSAL OF WASTE **68**
CHEMICAL CONTROL **74**

amnion
The innermost of three membranes that enclose the **embryo** within the egg (reptiles and birds) or within the uterus (mammals). It contains fluid that cushions the embryo.

amphibian
Any member of the vertebrate class Amphibia. Amphibians are cold-blooded. The skin of most species is soft, moist and covered in mucus. They usually spend their larval stage in fresh water, transferring to land at maturity and returning to water to breed. The aquatic larval stage possesses gills for respiration and undergoes metamorphosis to reach the adult form. Amphibians include frogs, toads, newts, salamanders and caecilians (worm lizards).

annelid worm
Any segmented worm of the phylum Annelida. Annelids include the earthworms, leeches and various marine worms. They have a distinct head end and soft body, divided into a number of segments separated from each other internally by membranous partitions, but there are no jointed appendages. They move by alternate contraction of circular and longitudinal muscles in the body wall.

antenna
An appendage ("feeler") on the head. Insects, centipedes and millipedes each have one pair of antennae, but there are two pairs in crustaceans, such as shrimps. Antennae generally have a sensory function, though they may be modified for other purposes such as swimming and defense.

antibody
A defensive protein molecule produced in the blood in response to the presence of foreign substances **(antigens)**. Antibodies bind specific foreign agents that invade the body, tagging them for destruction by phagocytes (white blood cells that engulf and destroy invaders) or activating a chemical system that renders them harmless.

BACTERIA

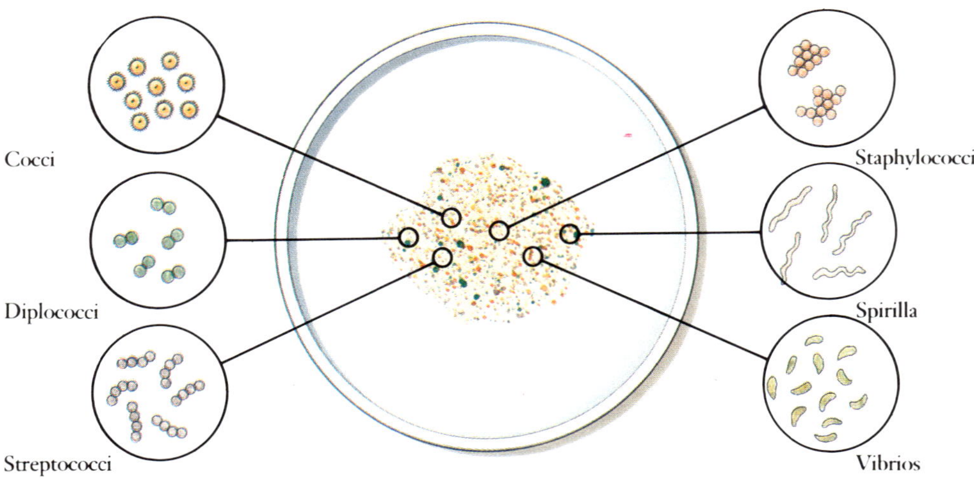

antidiuretic hormone (ADH)
A hormone secreted by the posterior pituitary gland that stimulates the absorption of water by the **kidneys** and thus helps to control the concentration of body fluids. Also known as vasopressin.

antigen
Any substance that causes the production of **antibodies**. Common antigens include the proteins carried on the surface of bacteria, viruses and pollen grains. The proteins of incompatible blood groups or tissues also act as antigens.

antitoxin
Any substance made by living cells that counteracts the effect of a specific toxin.

antler
One of two bony structures that grow from the head of male deer (and female reindeer). Unlike true horns, antlers are shed and regrown each year.

arachnid
Any arthropod of the class Arachnida, including spiders, scorpions and mites. Arachnids differ from insects in possessing only two main body regions, the cephalothorax and the abdomen. The cephalothorax bears a pair of grasping or piercing appendages, a pair of pedipalps used as sensory structures or for manipulation, and four pairs of walking legs. The abdomen may bear various sensory or silk-spinning appendages. Most arachnids are carnivorous, secreting enzymes to digest their prey externally or feeding on the body fluids of their prey. Ticks and some mites are parasitic.

artery
A vessel that carries blood from the heart to the rest of the body. Thick walls containing muscle and elastic fibers can withstand considerable pressure. When the heart muscles contract, arteries expand in diameter to allow for the sudden increase in pressure that occurs. Most arteries carry oxygenated blood; the pulmonary arteries convey deoxygenated blood from the heart to the lungs.

arthropod
Any member of the phylum Arthropoda; an invertebrate animal with jointed legs and a segmented body with a horny or chitinous casing (exoskeleton), which is shed periodically and replaced as the animal grows. Included are spiders and mites, crustaceans, millipedes, centipedes, and insects.

asexual reproduction
Any form of reproduction that does not involve the manufacture and fusion of gametes or the necessity for two parents. Asexual reproduction has the advantage that there is no need to search for a mate. However, only identical individuals are produced – that is, there is no variation. Asexual processes include binary fission, in which the parent organism splits into two or more "daughter" organisms, and budding, in which a new organism is formed as an outgrowth of the parent organism. *See also* **reproduction**.

assimilation
Following digestion, the process by which the breakdown products of food are converted into other substances (such as the conversion of **amino acids** into **proteins**).

autonomic nervous system
The part of the nervous system in mammals that controls the involuntary activities of the smooth muscles (of the digestive tract and blood vessels), the heart, and the glands. It consists of the sympathetic nervous system and the parasympathetic nervous system.

autotroph
Any living organism that synthesizes complex organic substances from simple inorganic molecules by using light or chemical energy. All green plants and many planktonic organisms are autotrophs, which convert carbon dioxide and water to oxygen and sugars by **photosynthesis**.

axon
A long thread-like extension of a **nerve** cell that conducts electrochemical impulses away from the cell body toward other nerve cells, or toward an effector organ such as a muscle. Axons end in synapses with other nerve cells, muscles or glands.

bacteria
A diverse group of microscopic single-celled organisms belonging to the kingdom Monera (*see* **prokaryote**). They usually reproduce by binary fission. Bacteria are classified biochemically, but their varying shapes provide a convenient system of classification.

balance
The sense by which an animal is able to maintain its correct bodily orientation with respect to gravity. Many animals have special

BALANCE

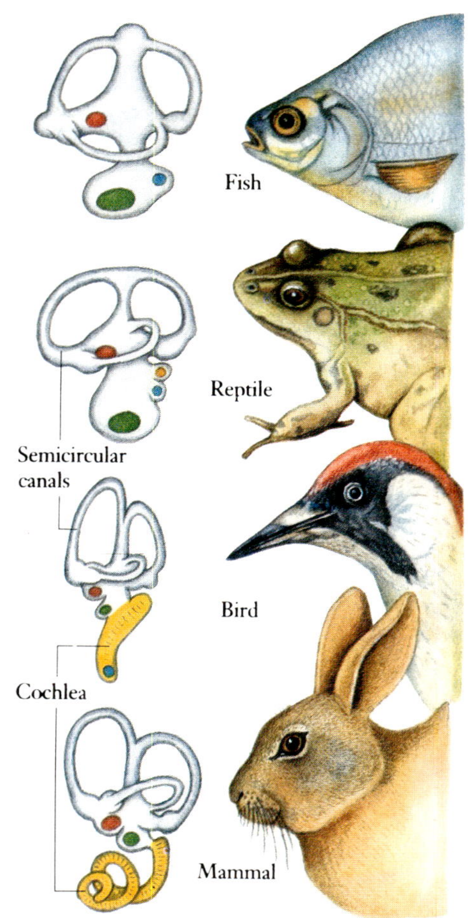

organs that are sensitive to gravity. The simplest is the statocyst, which consists of a fluid-filled cavity lined with ciliated cells. A dense mass of crystals (the statolith) bends the cilia when in contact with them under the influence of gravity, thus stimulating the sensory cells in a particular region. Statocysts are found in most invertebrates. In vertebrates gravity is detected by the labyrinth or inner ear, which consists of two otolith organs, the semicircular canals (which detect angular acceleration) and the cochlea (which detects sound). All of these organs work in a similar way to statocysts: the movement of a fluid in response to gravity results in the bending of the cilia of a sensory cell. Different cells respond to movements in different directions, signaling the animal's position with respect to gravity. Fish have an additional sensory system, the lateral line system.

baleen
A material found as fibrous plates hanging in rows from the roof of the mouth in whales; it is often known as whalebone.

beak
The keratin-covered projecting jaws of a bird or similar looking structures in other animals such as the tortoise or octopus. The beaks of birds are adapted by shape and size to specific diets.

CONNECTIONS
DIETS GALORE **84**
PLANT-EATERS **86**
FLESH-EATERS **88**
FUSSY FEEDERS **96**

bilateral symmetry
The type of symmetry in which one half of an organism is a mirror image of the other half if an imaginary line is drawn along its longest axis. An example is the left and right pair of arms and legs in humans. The majority of animals show bilateral symmetry, including insects, fish, mammals, and most crustaceans. *See also* **radial symmetry**.

bile
A brownish fluid produced by the **liver**. In most vertebrates, it is stored in the gall bladder and emptied into the small intestine as food passes through. Bile consists of bile salts, bile pigments, cholesterol and lecithin. Bile salts assist in the breakdown and absorption of fats. Bile pigments are the breakdown products of old red blood cells that are passed into the alimentary canal to be eliminated with the feces.

biochemistry
The study of the chemical composition of the various substances occurring in living organisms and the chemical reactions in which they are involved; a science on the boundaries of biology and organic chemistry Thetechniques used by biochemists include labeling with radioactive isotopes, and separation techniques such as chromatography and X-ray diffraction.

binary fission
A form of **asexual reproduction** whereby a single-celled organism, such as an ameba, divides into two smaller "daughter" cells. Common in bacteria, protozoans and algae, it can also occur in a few simple multicellular organisms, such as sea anemones, producing two smaller sea anemones of equal size. Binary fission is the most common form of reproduction by fission. *See also* **budding**.

binocular vision
The ability to focus both eyes on an object at the same time. Human eyes, which are about 7 cm apart, provide two slightly different images of the world, coordinated to give a three-dimensional perception that allows the brain to judge accurately the position and speed of objects up to 60 m away. The area over which an animal has binocular vision varies greatly according to how far apart its eyes are, the degree to which they can move to converge on an object, and the length of the nose or snout, which may interrupt the line of sight. Typical predators such as birds of prey and owls, whose eyes are directed forward, have a wide field of binocular vision allowing them to estimate the speed and position of their prey. Prey animals such as rabbits and grazing mammals have eyes at the sides of their heads and only a narrow field of binocular vision. But they have a much wider field of monocular (non-overlapping) vision, which enables them to detect the approach of a predator from almost any direction.

BINOCULAR VISION

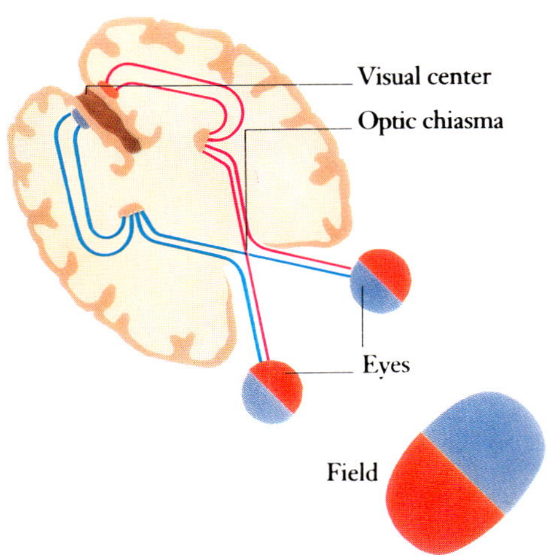

biological clock
The regular internal rhythm of activity in living organisms, produced by unknown mechanisms, and not dependent on external time signals. Such clocks are known to exist in almost all animals, and in many plants, fungi and unicellular organisms. In higher organisms, there appears to be a series of clocks of graded importance. For example, although body temperature and activity cycles in humans are normally "set" to 24 hours, the two cycles may vary independently. There are several kinds of clock: diurnal or 24-hour clocks, annual or seasonal clocks, and lunar clocks (in many marine animals activities are often correlated with phases of the Moon, and hence of the tides). Biological clocks are usually fine-tuned by signals such as the onset of night or day.

CONNECTIONS
CONTROLLING HEAT AND WATER **78**
ANIMAL REPRODUCTION **122**

bird
An animal of the class Aves, the biggest group of land vertebrates, with warm blood, feathers, wings, breathing through lungs, no teeth, a horny beak, and egg-laying by the female. Birds are bipedal, with the front limb modified to form a wing and retaining three digits. The heart has four chambers and the body is maintained at a high temperature. Most birds fly, but some groups are flightless, and others include flightless members. Typically the eggs are brooded in a nest and the young receive a period of parental care.

bivalve
Any marine or freshwater **mollusk** whose body is enclosed between two shells hinged together by a ligament on the dorsal side of the body. The shell is closed by strong adductor muscles. Ventrally, a retractile "foot" can be put out to assist movement in mud or sand. Two large gills are used for breathing and filtering small particles of food from the water. The bivalves form one of the five classes of mollusks, the Pelycypoda.

bladder
A hollow elastic-walled organ in the urinary systems of some fishes, most amphibians, some reptiles, and all mammals that acts as a receptacle for **urine** prior to excretion. Urine enters the bladder through two ureters, one leading from each kidney, and leaves it through the urethra.

BLOOD

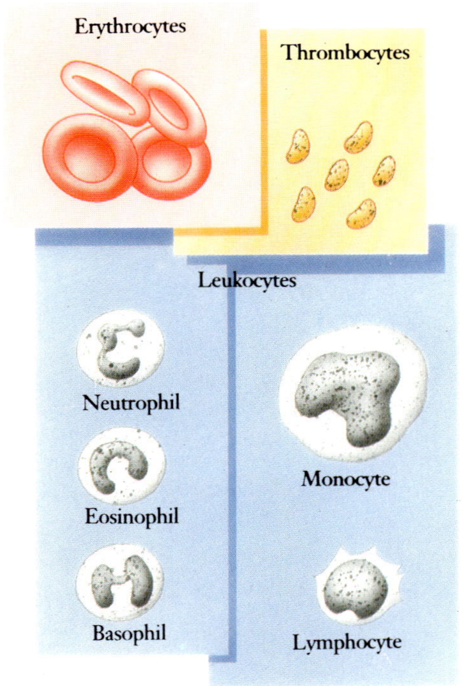

blood

Liquid circulating in the arteries, veins and capillaries of vertebrate animals. The term also refers to the fluid in the closed circulatory systems of some invertebrates (in animals with an open circulatory system it is known as hemolymph). Blood carries nutrients and oxygen to cells and removes waste products, such as carbon dioxide. It is also important in the immune response and in heat distribution over the body. Human blood makes up 5 percent of the body weight and consists of a colorless, transparent liquid called plasma, containing three main varieties of microscopic cells. Red cells (erythrocytes) form nearly half the volume of the blood. Their color is caused by hemoglobin. White cells (leukocytes) are of various kinds: some (phagocytes) ingest invading bacteria and protect the body from disease; others (lymphocytes) produce antibodies. The platelets (thrombocytes) assist in the clotting of blood. Salts, proteins, sugars, fats and hormones are dissolved in the plasma for transport round the body.

CONNECTIONS

CIRCULATION **70**
CONTROLLING HEAT AND WATER **78**
RECOVERY AND REPAIR **80**

blood pressure

The pressure exerted by blood as it flows through the major arteries of the body. It is at its greatest when the ventricles of the **heart** contract, forcing blood into the arterial system (systolic pressure). Pressure falls to its lowest when the heart is filling with blood (diastolic pressure).

bone

The hard connective tissue comprising the skeleton of most vertebrates. It consists of collagen fibers impregnated with mineral salts (largely calcium phosphate and calcium carbonate). Enclosed within this solid matrix are bone cells (osteocytes), blood vessels and nerves. Osteocytes are resting bone cells. When they become active they are called osteoblasts, and secrete bone collagen. Surrounding the bone is a tough sheath of connective tissues, the periosteum.The interior of the long bones of the limbs is filled with a soft marrow that produces blood cells. There are two types of bones: spongy bones develop by replacing **cartilage**, and membrane bones are formed directly from the skin of the developing embryo. Spongy bone consists of meshed bony struts with soft marrow in between. Membrane bones are usually platelike in shape and are found in the skull, jaws and shoulder girdle.

book lung

A thin, highly folded region of the body wall, similar to a fish's gill, found in certain arachnids. Book lungs permit the exchange of respiratory gases between the outside environment and the circulatory system.

brain

A concentration of interconnected nerve cells, forming the anterior part of the central **nervous system** in higher animals, whose activities it coordinates and controls. In vertebrates, the brain is contained by the skull. An enlarged portion of the upper spinal cord, the medulla oblongata, contains centers for the control of respiration, heartbeat rate and strength, and blood pressure. Overlying this is the cerebellum, concerned with coordinating complex muscular processes such as maintaining posture and moving limbs. The cerebral hemispheres (cerebrum) are paired outgrowths of the front end of the forebrain. In early vertebrates they are mainly concerned with the senses, but in higher vertebrates they are involved in the integration of all sensory input and motor output, and in intelligent behavior. In the brain, nerve impulses are passed across **synapses** by **neurotransmitters**, in the same way as in other parts of the nervous system. In mammals the cerebrum is the largest part of the brain, carrying the cerebral cortex. This consists of a thick surface layer of cell bodies (grey matter), below which fiber tracts (white matter) connect the various parts of the cortex to each other and to other parts of the **central nervous system**.

BRAIN

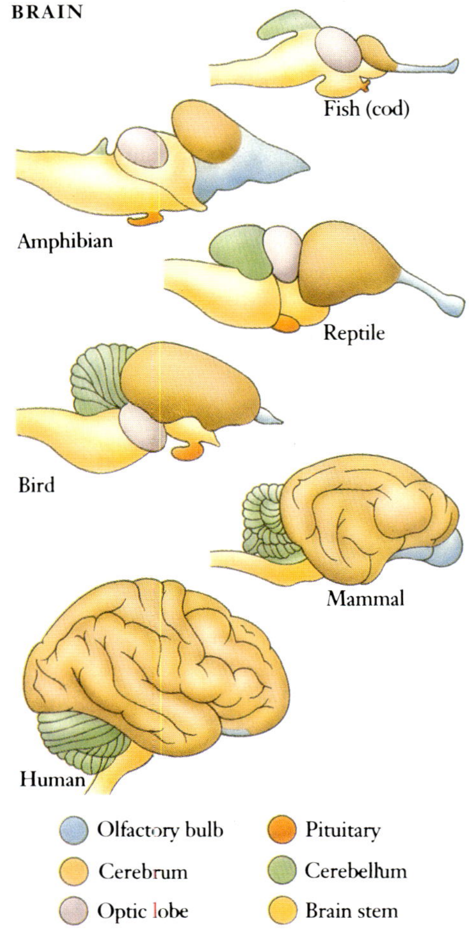

breathing

The muscular movements whereby air is taken into the body of an animal and then expelled. The **lungs** of vertebrates are specialized for gas exchange but are not themselves muscular, consisting of elastic spongy material. In humans, air is drawn into the lungs when the intercostal muscles raise the rib cage up and outward and the muscular diaphragm contracts and flattens. This action increases the volume of the thorax and reduces the pressure inside it, causing the lungs to expand and suck in air. Breathing out is achieved by lowering the ribs and relaxing the diaphragm.

bronchus

One of a pair of large tubes (bronchi) branching off from the **trachea** and passing into the vertebrate **lung**. Its cartilaginous rings give rigidity and prevent collapse during breathing movements. Numerous glands secrete a slimy mucus, which traps dust and other particles.

budding
A type of **asexual reproduction** in which an outgrowth develops from a cell or from part of the body to form a new individual. Single-celled creatures such as yeasts and a few cnidarians, such as hydra, multiply in this way. In reef-building corals, the new individuals fail to separate completely from the parent, and large interconnected colonies are formed.

buoyancy
The ability to float in a liquid. Animals achieve buoyancy in two ways: by increasing their surface area to volume ratio, and by lowering their density. Many tiny planktonic creatures have long, thin spines which increase their surface area. Some bony fish reduce their density by having a gas-filled **swim bladder**, the size of which can be varied according to the depth. Oil is less dense than water; many planktonic animals and fish eggs contain droplets of oil, whereas sharks, which have no swim bladders, have oil-rich livers.

camouflage
Body markings or structures that allow an animal to blend with its surroundings in order to avoid detection by other animals. Camouflage can take the form of matching the background color, of countershading (darker on top, lighter below, to counteract natural shadows), or of irregular patterns that break up the outline of the animal's body. In a more elaborate form of camouflage, the animal closely resembles a feature of the natural environment, as with the stick insect. Some animals, such as chameleons, are able to change their color to match that of the background. Special body postures may be used to reinforce the effect.

canine
Any of the long, often pointed teeth at the front of the mouth between the incisors and premolars of land-living carnivores. There are two in the upper jaw and two in the lower jaw. Canine teeth are used for catching prey, for killing and for tearing flesh. They are absent in herbivores such as rabbits and sheep, and are much reduced in humans.

capillary
The narrowest type of blood vessel in vertebrates, distributed as complex networks connecting arteries and veins. Capillary walls consist of a single layer of cells, and so nutrients, dissolved gases and waste products can easily pass through them. This makes the capillaries the main area of exchange between the fluid (lymph) bathing body tissues and the blood.

carapace
The **dorsal** part of the exoskeleton of some **crustaceans**, acting as a shield over several segments of the head and thorax. The domed dorsal part of the shell of turtles and tortoises which is formed by the fusion of the ribs and bony plates and covered by a horny epidermal layer is also known as a carapace. The ventral part of the shell is similar but flatter.

carbohydrate
Any chemical compound composed of carbon, hydrogen, and oxygen, with the basic formula $(CH_2O)_n$, and related compounds with the same basic structure but modified functional groups. In the forms of sugar and starch, carbohydrates form a major part of the human diet, contributing an important source of energy. The simplest carbohydrates are sugars (single sugar units or monosaccharides, such as glucose and fructose, and double sugar units as in disaccharides, such as sucrose). When these basic sugar units are joined together in long chains or branching structures they are known as polysaccharides, such as starch and glycogen, which serve as food stores in plants and animals respectively. There are even more complex carbohydrates, such as **chitin** and **cellulose**.

CONNECTIONS

LIFE PROCESSES 60
CHEMISTRY OF LIFE 62
BUILDING BLOCKS OF LIFE 64
PROCESSING FOOD 66
DISPOSAL OF WASTE 68

carbon dioxide
A colorless gas (CO_2), slightly soluble in water and denser than air. It plays an important part in the biosphere, that part of the Earth's surface and atmosphere inhabited by living things. Carbon dioxide is a waste product produced during **respiration** in plants and animals, and through the decay of organic matter. However, it is also used in all plants during photosynthesis and is thus a major contributor to the food of virtually all forms of life on Earth.

carnassial teeth
A powerful scissorlike pair of teeth, found in all mammalian carnivores except seals. Carnassials are formed from an upper premolar and lower molar, and shaped to produce a sharp cutting surface. Carnivores chew meat at the back of the mouth, where the carnassials slice up the food ready for swallowing.

CELL

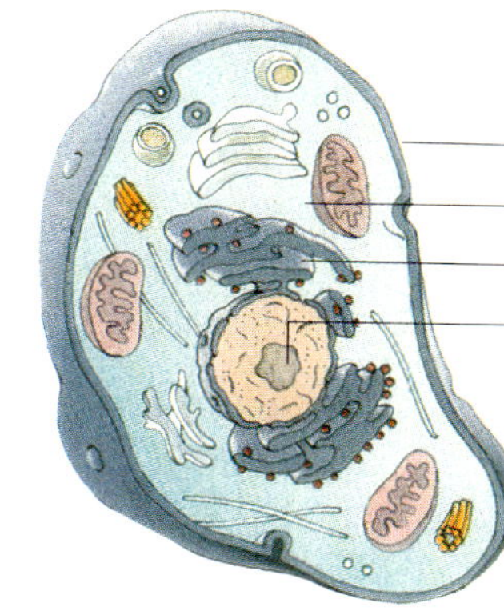

cartilage
Flexible connective tissue made up of the protein collagen formed by special cells called chondrocytes. In cartilaginous fish it forms the skeleton; in other vertebrates it forms the greater part of the embryonic skeleton, and is replaced by bone in the course of development, except in areas of wear such as bone endings, and the disks between the vertebrae. It also forms structural tissue in the larynx, nose and external ear of mammals. Rings of cartilage support the trachea and bronchi.

caterpillar
The larval stage of a butterfly or moth.

cell
The basic structural and functional unit of living organisms. All organisms (except viruses) consist of one or more cells: many microorganisms consist of single cells, whereas a human is made up of billions. Essential features of a cell are the membrane (*see* **cell membrane**), which encloses it and restricts the flow of substances in and out; the jelly-like material within (protoplasm); the **ribosomes**, which carry out protein synthesis; and the **DNA**, which forms the hereditary material. The composition of the protoplasm varies, but the products of its breakdown when the cell dies are mostly proteins. It also contains carbohydrates, fats and inorganic salts such as the phosphates and chlorides of calcium, sodium and potassium. The cell wall in most animal cells is not a substantial membrane, and the shape of the cell is maintained by surface tension or chemical action. In protozoa, fungi and higher animals and plants, DNA is organized into chromosomes and contained within a nucleus; this type of cell is known as a eukaryotic cell (*see* **eukaryote**). The only cells of the human body that have no nucleus

are the red blood cells. In bacteria and cyanobacteria (blue-green algae) the DNA forms a simple loop and there is no nucleus; this type of cell is known as a prokaryotic cell (*see* **prokaryote**).

CONNECTIONS
ONE-CELLED WONDERS **58**
BUILDING BLOCKS OF LIFE **64**
ANIMAL REPRODUCTION **122**

cell division
The formation of two daughter cells from a single mother cell. The cell nucleus first divides and this is followed by the formation of a cell membrane between the daughter nuclei. There are two forms of cell division. In **meiosis** (which is associated with sexual reproduction), the daughter nuclei contain half of the number of chromosomes, and therefore half the genetic information, of the mother cell. In **mitosis** (associated with growth, cell replacement or repair) the daughter nuclei are identical to the original nucleus.

cell membrane
A thin layer of protein and fat surrounding **cells** that controls substances passing between the cytoplasm and the intercellular space. The cell membrane is selectively permeable. Fat-soluble molecules can pass through the membrane in solution, whereas small molecules – such as water, glucose and amino acids – diffuse in through protein-lined pores. The substances that can pass through are controlled by the size of the pores and by the distribution of electrical charges across their lining. Certain molecules, such as those which are already present in greater concentration inside the cell than outside, are transported across the membrane by special carrier proteins, a process requiring energy from ATP (*see* **active transport**). On the outer surface of the cell are protein or glycoprotein molecules which are involved in the recognition of antigens, hormones and other cells. Certain reactions take place on the surface of membranes; the reactants can be arranged in a specific way on the membrane so as to speed up the reaction. Other membranes in the cell play a part in the active transport of nutrients, hormonal responses and cell metabolism.

CONNECTIONS
CHEMISTRY OF LIFE **62**
BUILDING BLOCKS OF LIFE **64**

cellulose
A complex **carbohydrate** composed of long chains of glucose units. It is the principal constituent of the cell wall of higher plants and a vital ingredient in the diet of many herbivores. Molecules of cellulose are organized into long, unbranched filaments called microfibrils that give support to the cell wall.

centipede
A jointed-legged, fast moving predator of the group Chilopoda, members of which have a distinct head and a single pair of long antennae. Their bodies are composed of segments (which may number nearly 200), each bearing a single pair of legs. Nocturnal, frequently blind and all carnivorous, centipedes live in moist, dark places, and protect themselves by a poisonous secretion. They have a pair of poison claws and strong jaws with venomous fangs.

cephalopod
Any predatory marine **mollusk** of the class Cephalopoda, with the mouth and head surrounded by tentacles. There are about 650 living species, including octopus, squid and cuttlefish, but there are over 7500 fossil forms. Cephalopods are the most intelligent, the fastest-moving, and the largest of all invertebrates. All are predators, seizing their prey with suckers on their arms or tentacles. They have a highly developed nervous and sensory system, the eye in some closely paralleling that found in vertebrates. Shells are rudimentary or absent in most cephalopods. Squid and cuttlefish swim by undulating fin-like extensions of the mantle but, like the octopus, they can also use jet propulsion to propel themselves backward by squirting water out of a siphon.

cerebral hemisphere
One of the two halves of the cerebrum. *See* **brain**.

chemical reaction
A change in the chemical composition of a substance or substances (called reactants) that results in the formation of another substance or substances (the products). In living things, reactions include anabolic reactions, such as the condensation of small molecules to form much larger ones, and catabolic reaction, such as the hydrolysis of large molecules to form smaller ones. Many biochemical reactions are mediated by **enzymes**, which are essential to make the reaction proceed at a useful rate.

chitin
A complex, long-chain nitrogen-containing derivative of glucose that forms the exoskeleton of insects and other arthropods. It combines with protein to form a covering that can be hard and tough, as in beetles, or soft and flexible, as in caterpillars and other insect larvae. It is insoluble in water and resistant to acids, alkalis and many organic solvents. In crustaceans such as crabs, it is impregnated with calcium carbonate for extra strength. Chitin also occurs in some protozoans and cnidarians (such as certain jellyfish), in the jaws of annelid worms, and in the cell walls of fungi.

chlorophyll
The green pigment that is present in most plants and responsible for the absorption of light energy during photosynthesis. The pigment absorbs the red and blue-violet parts of sunlight but reflects the green, thus giving plants their characteristic color. Chlorophyll is found within organelles called chloroplasts, present in large numbers in leaf cells. Algae, cyanobacteria (blue-green algae) and other photosynthetic bacteria also have chlorophyll, though of a slightly different type. Chlorophyll is similar in structure to hemoglobin, but with magnesium instead of iron as the reactive part of the molecule.

chordate
Any animal belonging to the phylum Chordata. All these animals, at some stage of their lives, have a cartilage supporting rod (notochord or backbone) running down their bodies, a dorsal hollow nerve cord, and gill clefts. They include the sea squirts, lancelets and vertebrates.

chromosome
A threadlike structure in the **cell** nucleus that carries the genetic information (genes). Each chromosome consists of a strand of highly folded and coiled **DNA**. The cells of animals contain two copies of each chromosome (diploid), except in the **gametes** (sperm and eggs), which contain only one copy (*see* **meiosis** and **mitosis**). In **eukaryote** cells, the DNA is enclosed in sheath of proteins called histones. Portions of the histone coat peel away to expose the DNA where a particular gene is active.

CONNECTIONS
CHEMISTRY OF LIFE **62**
GROWTH AND REPRODUCTION **116**
PATTERNS OF GROWTH **118**
ANIMAL REPRODUCTION **122**

chrysalis
See **pupa**.

cilia
Microscopic hairlike protrusions on the surface of certain animal and plant cells. Cilia usually occur in large clusters or rows, and they beat in a coordinated way to move fluids over the cell surface or to propel the cell.

CONNECTIONS
ONE-CELLED WONDERS 58
CIRCULATION 70
UNFUSSY FEEDERS 92

ciliate
A protoctist belonging to the phylum Ciliophora. Most ciliates are single-celled freshwater or marine organisms which swim and/or feed by means of cilia. Most have two different kinds of nuclei, one large and one small, in each ciliated cell. Some ciliates, such as paramecia, are free-swimming, whereas others, such as stentors and vorticellids, are trumpet-shaped and attached to a substrate.

circulation
The process by which oxygen- and nutrient-rich **blood** is transported throughout the body and deoxygenated blood is returned to the heart through a system of vessels (the circulatory system). All animals have a circulatory system apart from sponges and cnidaria.

CONNECTIONS
SHELLS AND SPINES 52
CIRCULATION 70
NERVOUS CONTROL 76

class
See **classification**.

CIRCULATION

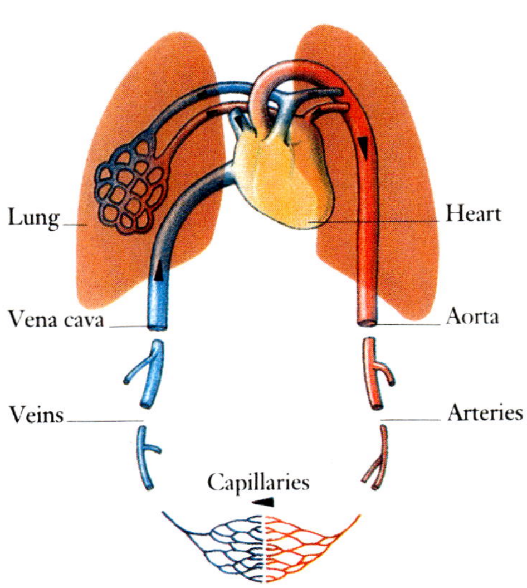

classification
The ordering of organisms into a hierarchy of groups on the basis of their similarities in biochemical, anatomical, physiological or other characteristics. The basic grouping is a species, several of which may constitute a genus, which in turn are grouped into families, and so on up through orders, classes, phyla, to kingdoms. The higher up the hierarchy, the fewer the number of similarities between members of group become. Such a classification is thus thought to mirror the evolutionary relationships between organisms. The science of biological classification is known as taxonomy.

claw
A hard, hooked, pointed outgrowth of the digits of mammals, birds and most reptiles. Claws are composed of keratin and grow continuously from a bundle of cells in the lower skin layer. Hooves and nails are modified structures with the same origin as claws.

cloaca
The posterior chamber of most vertebrates into which the digestive, urinary and reproductive tracts all open. It is found in most reptiles, birds and amphibians; many fish; and a few marsupial mammals. Placental mammals have a separate digestive opening (the anus) and urinogenital opening. The cloaca forms a chamber in which products can be stored before leaving the body via a muscular opening, the cloacal aperture.

clotting
The series of events that prevents excessive bleeding after injury. When platelets in the bloodstream come into contact with a damaged blood vessel, they and the vessel wall itself release the enzyme thrombokinase, which converts the inactive enzyme prothrombin into the active thrombin. Thrombin catalyzes the conversion of the soluble protein fibrinogen, present in blood plasma, to the insoluble fibrin. This fibrous protein forms a net over the wound that traps red blood cells and seals the wound. Calcium, vitamin K and a variety of other factors are also necessary for efficient blood clotting.

CONNECTIONS
CIRCULATION 70
RECOVERY AND REPAIR 80

cnidarian
Any member of the phylum Cnidaria, also called coelenterates. The group includes corals, jellyfish, hydroids and sea anemones. Cnidarians are the simplest form of animal that possesses differentiated cell layers. They lack the organ systems that characterize higher animals: they have a single body cavity which opens through the mouth; there are no blood vessels and only a simple nerve net. Cnidarians are carnivorous, and have stinging cells arranged on tentacles which surround the mouth. There are two forms, sedentary cup-shaped polyps and swimming jellyfish-like medusae. Some cnidarians are always medusae, some are always polyps, whereas in others both forms occur at different stages in the life cycle. *See* **jellyfish**.

CLASSIFICATION

Living organisms

Animalia	Kingdom
Chordata	Phylum
Mammalia	Class
Carnivora	Order
Felidae	Family
Panthera	Genus
tigris	Species

cocoon
A protecting covering for the eggs and/or larvae produced by many invertebrates. *See* **pupa**.

coelenterates
See **cnidarian**.

cold-blooded animal
Also called an ectotherm or poikilothermic animal, an animal in which the body temperature is dependent on the temperature of the air or water in which it lives. Only birds and mammals, which maintain their body temperature by internal heat generation and regulation, are warm-blooded. Cold-blooded animals regulate their body temperature by behavioral means.

color vision
The ability of the **eye** to recognize different frequencies in the visible spectrum as colors. In most vertebrates, color vision relies on the presence in the retina of three types of light-sensitive cone cells; each contains a different pigment and responds to a different primary color (red, green or blue). The degree of stimulation of the different kinds of cone cells is interpreted by the brain as different shades and intensities of color. Other species

of vertebrates may have different types of cone cells and see different ranges of color than humans do. Cone cells function best in bright light. The nerve fibers from several rods are linked together to a single nerve in the optic nerve, so that several weak signals can combine to give a stronger one; cones are individually linked to single fibers.

commensalism
A relationship between two species that is beneficial to one (the commensal) but does not affect the other. Certain species of millipede and silverfish inhabit the nests of army ants and live by scavenging on the refuse of their hosts.

compound eye
The type of eye found in crustaceans and insects. It consists of visual units called ommatidia – lenses with crystalline cones and light-sensitive cells underneath. The eye is convex, with the points of the cone pointing towards the optic nerve.

connective tissue
A type of strong tissue that binds together organs and other tissues. It consists of a matrix of intercellular material containing fibers, cells and, sometimes, vessels.

contour feather
The feathers that give a bird its streamlined shape and also protect the skin from damage and sunburn. They cover all parts of the body except the beak and the scaly parts of the legs and feet. The lower part of a contour feather is fluffy and helps to keep the body warm. The outer part may also be water-repellent. *See* **feather**.

contractile vacuole
A tiny organelle found in many single-celled freshwater organisms. It is involved in **osmoregulation**. The vacuole slowly fills with water, and then contracts, expelling the water from the cell. Marine protozoa do not have a contractile vacuole. *See* **vacuole**.

coral
A sedentary marine invertebrate of the class Anthozoa in the phylum Cnidaria, which contains about 6200 species. The coral animal is a cup-shaped polyp (rather like a sea anemone). Reef-building corals secrete a skeleton of calcium carbonate extracted from the surrounding water and produce large colonies by incomplete budding (*see* **budding**). They are found only in warm seas. They usually form a **symbiosis** with certain algae, without which reef-building is very slow or nonexistent. Because the algae need light for photosynthesis, reef corals need relatively shallow, clear water. Although most corals form large colonies, there are several species that live singly, and not all have hard skeletons.

counter-current flow
The system in the gills of bony fish by which water is pumped past the gill, flowing in the opposite direction to the blood flowing in the gill. This arrangement ensures that the oxygen and carbon dioxide concentrations in the blood and the water never reach equilibrium, because a concentration gradient is maintained along the whole length of the gill. A similar relationship is found between the arterioles leading to and venues leading out of the feet of seabirds, ensuring that maximum heat is retained.

courtship
The behavior exhibited by animals as a prelude to mating. Patterns vary considerably from one species to another, but are often ritualized and not obviously related to mating (such as courtship feeding in birds). Courtship ensures that copulation occurs with a member of the opposite sex of the right species. It álso synchronizes the partners' readiness to mate and allows each to assess the suitability of the other.

CONNECTIONS

GETTING TOGETHER **120**
ANIMAL REPRODUCTION **122**
ANIMAL COMMUNICATION **130**
MAMMAL SOCIETIES **142**

crinoid
Any **echinoderm** of the class Crinoidea, which comprises about 80 species (also known as sea lilies). They are the most primitive living group of echinoderms. In crinoids, the mouth and anus are both on the upper surface of the cup-shaped body. Most crinoids are attached to the substrate by a stalk at the base of the cup. Crinoids feed by sieving small particles of food from passing currents by means of many long tube feet. As a large surface area is required for effective food collection, crinoids may have up to 40 tube feet, forming a large crown (or calyx), surrounded by many branching arms which form a funnel along which mucus bearing food particles stream to the mouth. Many crinoids are covered in heavy plates.

crop
A thin-walled enlargement of the digestive tract between the esophagus and stomach found in birds. It is an effective storage organ, especially in seed-eating birds.

crustacean
A member of the **arthropod** class Crustacea, containing over 30,000 species distributed worldwide, mainly in marine and freshwater environments. Crustaceans include crabs, lobsters, shrimps, woodlice and barnacles. The segmented body usually has a distinct head (with mouthparts, compound eyes, and two pairs of antennae), thorax and abdomen, and is protected by an external skeleton made of protein and chitin hardened with calcium carbonate. Each segment bears a pair of appendages that may be modified as sensory feelers or as swimming, walking or grasping structures. Crustaceans are very important in the food chains of the sea.

cuticle
The hard noncellular protective surface layer of many invertebrates such as insects. The cuticle reduces water loss and, in arthropods, acts as an exoskeleton to which muscles are attached. Joints in the exoskeleton (where the cuticle is very thin and flexible) allow for the wide range of movement found in arthropods.

cytoplasm
The material making up all of the eukaryotic cell apart from the nucleus (*see* **cell**). It includes all the organelles (mitochondria, chloroplasts, and so on), but often cytoplasm refers to the jelly-like matter in which the organelles are embedded (correctly termed the cytosol). In some cells, the cytoplasm is made up of two parts: the ectoplasm (or plasmagel), a dense gelatinous outer layer concerned with cell movement, and the endoplasm (or plasmasol), a more fluid inner part where most of the organelles are found.

decapod
Any member of the class Decapoda, the largest order of **crustaceans**, which are distributed worldwide, living mainly in marine habitats. Swimming forms include shrimps and prawns. Crawling forms include crabs, lobsters and crayfish. All decapods are characterized by having five pairs of walking legs. In the crawling forms the first pair of legs is greatly modified into powerful grasping pincers. The carapace is fused with the thorax and head to form a cephalothorax.

decomposer
Any organism that breaks down dead matter. Decomposers play a vital role in the ecosystem by freeing important chemical substances, such as nitrogen compounds, locked up in dead organisms or excrement. They feed on some of the released organic matter, but leave the rest to filter back into the soil or pass in gas form into the atmosphere. The

principal decomposers are bacteria and fungi, but earthworms and many other invertebrates are often included in this group.

dendrite
Slender projections from the body of a nerve cell. They receive incoming messages from many other nerve cells and pass them on to the cell body. *See* **nerve**.

CONNECTIONS
SHELLS AND SPINES **52**
NERVOUS CONTROL **76**
RECOVERY AND REPAIR **80**

deoxyribonucleic acid
See **DNA**.

detritus feeder
Any organism that feeds on the particles of organic debris from the decomposition of dead animals, plants and other organisms.

CONNECTIONS
DIETS GALORE **84**
UNFUSSY FEEDERS **92**
BREAKDOWN SPECIALISTS **94**

diaphragm
A muscular sheet separating the thorax (chest) from the abdomen in mammals. In its relaxed state it curves up into the thorax, but when contracted it flattens, increasing the volume of the thorax. Its rhythmic contractions and relaxations help to cause the pressure changes in the lungs that result in **breathing**. The term diaphragm is also applied to any dividing structure in a body organ or organism.

diastema
A gap, with no teeth, in the jaw of a mammal (often a herbivore) which allows room for the tongue to manipulate leafy food.

differentiation
The process in developing tissues and organs whereby cells become increasingly different and specialized, giving rise to more complex structures that have particular functions. For instance, embryonic cells may develop into nerve, muscle or bone cells in the adult.

diffusion
The spontaneous movement of molecules or ions from areas where they are in high concentration to areas where they are in low concentration. The process continues until the concentration of the substance is equal throughout the container. In living organisms, the diffusion of gases, ions and other dissolved substances takes place across membranes and through membrane pores. Diffusion is the main transport mechanism over short distances in animals' bodies. *See also* **osmosis**.

CONNECTIONS
BUILDING BLOCKS OF LIFE **64**
DISPOSAL OF WASTE **68**
AIR PUMPS **72**

digestion
The process of breaking down complex food molecules eaten by an animal, either physically (by organs such as the teeth and muscles of the digestive tract) and chemically (by **enzymes** in the digestive tract), to produce simpler compounds that can be absorbed into the body and used as a source of energy. The digestive system in most higher animals consists of the mouth, stomach, intestine and associated glands. In mammals the food is broken down in the stomach and most nutrients are absorbed in the small intestine. Undigested material is stored and concentrated into feces in the large intestine. In birds, additional digestive organs are the crop and gizzard. In smaller, simpler animals such as jellyfish, the digestive system is simply a cavity (coelenteron or enteric cavity) with a "mouth" into which food is taken; the digestible portion is dissolved and absorbed in this cavity, and the remains are ejected back through the mouth. In some single-celled organisms, such as amebae, a food particle is engulfed by the cell and digested in a vacuole within the cell.

CONNECTIONS
PROCESSING FOOD **66**
PLANT-EATERS **86**
FLESH-EATERS **88**
BREAKDOWN SPECIALISTS **94**
FUSSY FEEDERS **96**
LIVING TOGETHER **100**

diploid
Any cell having two copies of each different chromosome, as in the normal body cells (not **gametes**) of animals. *See also* **meiosis** and **mitosis**.

dispersal of species
The spread of species to new areas.

diurnal
Activity associated with daylight hours as opposed to night (**nocturnal**). Crepuscular activity is associated with the hours around dawn and dusk.

diving mammal
Any aquatic **mammal** that has special adaptations for diving. Whales have comparatively small lungs; when they dive, air remains in the windpipe where gas exchange is much slower, enabling them to "hold their breath" for long periods. Their ribs collapse to cope with the pressure in deep water, and a layer of fat (blubber) insulates against the cold. Limbs are modified into flippers.

DNA
A large complex molecule that contains, in chemically coded form, all the information needed to build, control and maintain a living organism. DNA is a ladderlike double-stranded nucleic acid that forms the basis of genetic inheritance in virtually all living organisms. It is organized into **chromosomes** and contained in the cell nucleus. DNA is made up of two chains of nucleotide sub-units, with each nucleotide containing either a purine (adenine or guanine) or pyrimidine (cytosine or thymine) base. The

DNA

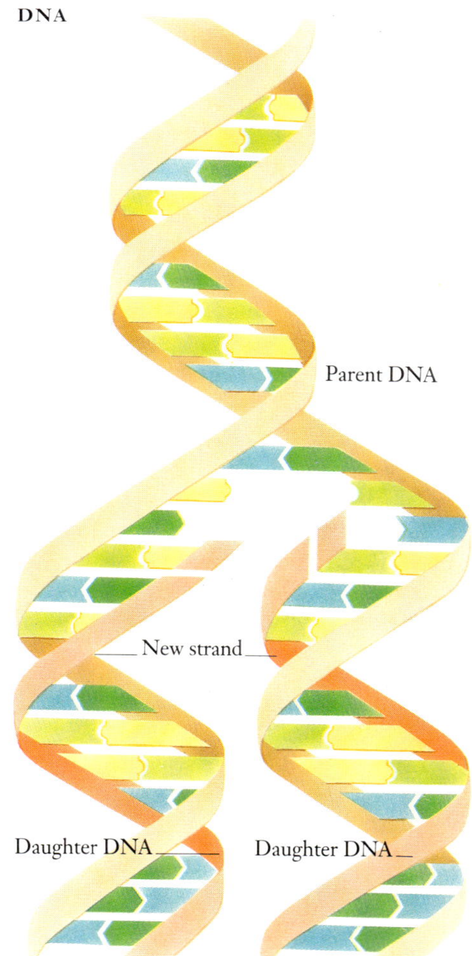

bases link up with each other (adenine linking with thymine, and cytosine with guanine) to form pairs that connect the two strands of the DNA molecule like the rungs of a twisted ladder.

CONNECTIONS

CHEMSITRY OF LIFE **62**
BUILDING BLOCKS OF LIFE **64**
CHEMICAL CONTROL **74**
FROM EGG TO EMBRYO **124**

dorsal
Relating to the upper surface of an animal – in a vertebrate, nearest the backbone.

ear
The organ of hearing in animals that responds to the vibrations that constitute sound, translating these into nerve signals and passing them on to the brain. A mammal's ear consists of three parts: outer ear, middle ear and inner ear. The outer ear is a funnel that collects sound, directing it down a tube to the ear drum (tympanum), which separates the outer and middle ear. Sounds vibrate this membrane, the mechanical movement of which is transferred to a smaller membrane leading to the inner ear by three small bones, the auditory **ossicles**. Vibrations of the inner ear membrane move fluid contained in the snail-shaped cochlea, which vibrates ciliated cells that stimulate the auditory nerve connected to the brain. Three fluid-filled canals of the inner ear detect changes of position; this mechanism, with other sensory inputs, is responsible for the sense of **balance**. When a loud noise occurs, muscles behind the eardrum contract, suppressing the noise to enhance perception of sound and prevent injury. The ear is usually on the head, but in some insects is on the legs, thorax or abdomen.

ear drum (tympanum)
See **ear**.

ecdysis
The periodic shedding of the exoskeleton, or cuticle, by insects and other arthropods to allow growth. Prior to shedding, a new soft and expandable layer is laid down underneath the existing one. The old layer then splits, the animal moves free of it and pumps itself up with air or water while the new layer expands and hardens. New tissue grows to fill the enlarged cuticle. *See* **molting**.

echinoderm
Any marine invertebrate of the phylum Echinodermata (which means "spiny-skinned"), characterized by a five-radial symmetry and the possession of tube feet – small, muscular, water-filled sacs that can be protruded or pulled back into the body at will. Tube feet may be used for locomotion or for feeding. There are some 6000 living species of echinoderms. They include starfish (sea stars), sea urchins, sea cucumbers, sea lilies (crinoids) and brittlestars. Most echinoderms are covered in a series of calcium carbonate plates which lie just below the epidermis and bear spines in some species. *See also* **symmetry**.

echolocation
A method used by certain animals, notably bats and dolphins, to detect the positions of objects by using sound. The animal emits a stream of high-pitched sounds, generally at ultrasonic frequencies (that is, out of the range of human hearing) and listens for the returning echoes reflected off objects in order to determine their exact location. The location of an object can be established by the time difference between the emitted sound and its differential return as an echo to the two ears.

ectoderm
The external layer of cells in the early stages of animal embryogenesis which will eventually develop into the nervous system and skin epidermis in the adult.

ectoparasite
A parasite that lives on the outer surface of its host's body.

ectothermic
See **cold-blooded animal**.

egg
The ovum or female **gamete** (reproductive cell). After fertilization by a sperm cell, it begins to divide to form an embryo. Eggs may be deposited by the female (ovipary) or they may develop within her body (vivipary and ovovivipary). In the oviparous reptiles and birds, the egg is protected by a shell, and well supplied with nutrients in the form of yolk.

egg tooth
A sharp projection on the upper beak of embryo birds and reptiles by which they break open the egg shell. The egg tooth is shed soon after hatching.

electric fish
Any of several fish that produce electricity, including the South American "electric eel", the electric ray and the electric catfish. Such fish often have electricity-detecting sensors in pores on their heads and special electroreceptor areas in the brain. One of the most powerful electric fishes, *Electrophorus electricus*, has lateral tail muscles modified to form electric organs capable of generating 650 volts. The current passing from tail to head is strong enough to stun another animal. Not all electric fishes produce such strong discharges; most use weak electric fields to navigate and to detect nearby objects.

electron transport chain
A sequence of reactions that forms the last stage of aerobic **respiration** (respiration in the presence of oxygen). It involves the transport of electrons or hydrogen atoms derived during the first stage of respiration (which can take place in the absence of oxygen) to molecular oxygen via a series of intermediate compounds, eventually forming water. During this process, energy released from the breakdown of food is trapped in the form of ATP. Electron transport also plays a similarly important role in photosynthesis, trapping energy absorbed from light rays.

embryo
The early developmental stage of an animal or a plant following fertilization of an ovum (egg cell) or activation of an ovum by **parthenogenesis**. In animals the embryo exists either within an egg (where it is nourished by food contained in the yolk) or, in placental and marsupial mammals, in the uterus of the mother. In placental mammals the embryo is fed through the **placenta**.

CONNECTIONS

ANIMALS WITH BACKBONES **56**
CIRCULATION **70**
FROM EGG TO EMBRYO **124**
GROWING UP **126**

endocrine gland
Any gland that secretes **hormones** into the blood to regulate body processes. Endocrine glands are most highly developed in vertebrates, but are found in other animals, notably insects. In humans the main endocrine glands are the pituitary, thyroid, parathyroid, adrenal, pancreas, ovary and testis.

endoderm
The internal layer of cells in the early stages of animal embryogenesis which eventually develop into the digestive glands and alimentary canal (intestines) in the adult. *See also* **ectoderm**.

endoparasite
Any parasite that lives inside the body of its host.

endoplasmic reticulum

A complex membranous network of tubes, channels and flattened sacs that form compartments within eukaryotic cells (*see* **eukaryote**). It stores and transports proteins within cells and carries **enzymes** needed for the synthesis of fats. The ribosomes that carry out protein synthesis are attached to parts of the endoplasmic reticulum.

endoskeleton

The internal supporting structure of vertebrates, made up of **cartilage** or **bone**. It provides support and acts as a system of levers to which muscles are attached to provide movement. Certain parts of the skeleton (the skull and ribs) give protection to body organs.

endothermic

See **warm-blooded animal**.

enzyme

A **protein** molecule produced by cells that acts as a catalyst for chemical reactions by converting one molecule (substrate) into another (product). Enzymes are large complex proteins, and are highly specific, each chemical reaction requiring its own particular enzyme. The enzyme fits into a "slot" (active site) in the substrate molecule, forming an enzyme-substrate complex that lasts until the substrate is altered or split, after which enzyme and products part company. The activity and efficiency of enzymes are influenced by various factors, including temperature and pH conditions. Each enzyme operates best within a specific pH range, and is denatured by excessive acidity, alkalinity and heat. Digestive enzymes include amylases (which digest starch), lipases (which digest fats) and proteases (which digest protein). Other enzymes play a part in the conversion of food energy into ATP; the manufacture of all the molecular components of the body; the replication of DNA when a cell divides; the production of hormones; and the control of movement of substances into and out of cells.

ENZYME

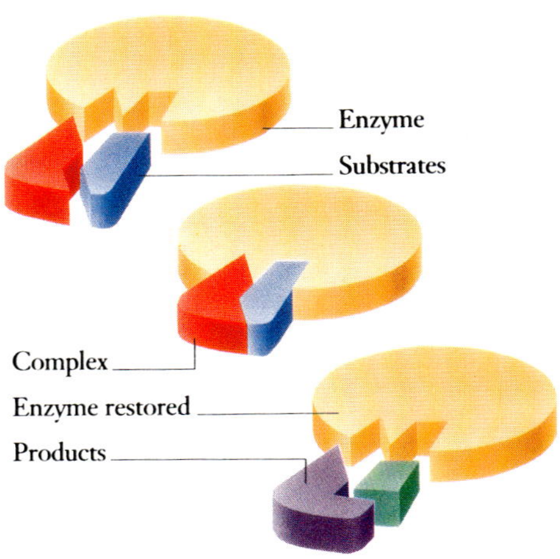

CONNECTIONS

CHEMISTRY OF LIFE **62**
BUILDING BLOCKS OF LIFE **64**
PROCESSING FOOD **66**
AIR PUMPS **72**
CONTROLLING HEAT AND WATER **78**
RECOVERY AND REPAIR **80**

epithelium

A sheet of closely packed cells with very little intercellular material. Many epithelia lie on a basement membrane. Epithelia cover the exposed surfaces of the body, and also line tubes and internal cavities. Many epithelia contain glandular cells which secrete enzymes or other substances. The lining of the alimentary canal and the blood vessels are examples.

erythrocyte

See **red blood cell**.

esophagus

The muscular tube by which food travels from the mouth to stomach. Its upper end is at the bottom of the pharynx, immediately behind the windpipe.

estivation

A state of inactivity and reduced metabolic activity, similar to **hibernation**, that occurs during a dry season or period or drought in species such as lungfishes and snails. In botany, the term is used to describe the way in which flower petals and sepals are folded in the buds. It is an important feature in plant classification.

estrogen

Any of a group of sex **hormones** produced by the ovaries of vertebrates; the term is also used for synthetic hormones that mimic their effects. (Some estrogens are secreted by the cortex of the adrenal glands.) The principal estrogen in mammals is estradiol. Estrogens promote the development of female secondary sexual characteristics, stimulate egg production and prepare the lining of the uterus for pregnancy in mammals.

estrus cycle

The hormonally regulated cycle that occurs in female mammals of reproductive age, during which the body is prepared for pregnancy through the control of **estrogen** and **progesterone**. At the beginning of the cycle, a Graafian (egg) follicle develops in the ovary and the inner wall of the uterus forms a soft spongy lining. The egg is released from the ovary and the lining of the uterus filled with blood vessels. If fertilization does not occur, the corpus luteum (remains of the Graafian follicle) breaks down, and the uterine lining breaks down and is shed.

eukaryote

One of the two major groupings into which all organisms are divided. Eukaryotes include all organisms, except bacteria and cyanobacteria (blue-green algae), which belong to the **prokaryote** grouping. The cells of eukaryotes have a defined nucleus, bounded by a membrane, within which **DNA** is formed into chromosomes. Eukaryotic cells also contain mitochondria, chloroplasts and other membrane-enclosed structures not found in the cells of prokaryotes.

evolution

The process by which life developed on Earth. Theories of evolution try to explain the origin of the different species through gradual changes in ancestoral groups. The idea of gradual evolution (as opposed to creationism) gained wide acceptance in the 19th century, following the work of Scottish geologist Charles Lyell, French naturalist Jean Baptiste Lamarck, English naturalist Charles Darwin and English biologist Thomas Henry Huxley. Darwin assigned the major role in evolutionary change to natural selection acting on randomly occurring variations. Natural selection occurs because those individuals better adapted to their particular environments are more likely to survive and reproduce, thus contributing their characteristics to future generations. The current theory of evolution, called Neo-Darwinism, combines Darwin's theory with Austrian biologist Gregor Mendel's theories on genetics and Hugo de Vries' discovery of genetic mutation (which explains how new characteristics may arise). Besides natural selection and sexual selection (the choice of mates by individuals) chance may play a large part in deciding which genes become characteristic of a population, a phenomenon called "genetic drift". It is now also clear that evolutionary change does not always occur at a constant rate, but that the process can have long periods of relative stability interspersed with periods of rapid change.

excretion

The removal of the waste products of metabolism from the cells of living organisms. In plants and simple animals, waste products are removed by diffusion, but in higher animals they are removed by specialized organs. In mammals, for example, carbon dioxide and water are removed via the **lungs**, and nitrogenous compounds and water via the **liver**, **kidneys** and rest of the urinary system.

exocrine gland
Any gland that discharges secretions, usually through a tube or a duct, onto a surface. Examples include sweat glands, which release sweat onto the skin, and digestive glands, which release digestive juices onto the walls of the intestine. *See* **endocrine gland**.

exocytosis
The way in which material (often waste) passes out of a cell when an internal vesicle fuses with the cell membrane and then voids its contents.

extinction
The complete disappearance of a species. In the past, extinctions are believed to have occurred because species were unable to adapt quickly enough to a naturally changing environment. Today, most extinctions are due to human activity. Some species, such as the dodo of Mauritius, the moas of New Zealand and the passenger pigeon of North America, were exterminated by hunting. Others became extinct when their habitat was destroyed, or when they were preyed upon by alien predators, such as cats, that were introduced by humans.

CONNECTIONS

DIETS GALORE **84**
FUSSY FEEDERS **96**
GROWTH AND REPRODUCTION **116**

eye
The organ of vision. In the human eye, the light is focused by the combined action of the curved cornea, the internal fluids and the lens. It is a roughly spherical structure contained in a bony socket. Light enters it through the cornea, and passes through the circular opening (pupil) in the iris (the colored part of the eye). The ciliary muscles act on the lens (the rounded transparent structure behind the iris) to change its shape, so that images of objects at different distances can be focused on the retina. This is at the back of the eye and is packed with light-sensitive cells (rods and cones), connected to the brain by the optic nerve. In insects, the **compound eye** is made up of many separate facets (ommatidia). Insects and some other arthropods, such as predatory copepods, also have simpler eyes with corneal lenses backed by a light-sensitive retina. Some invertebrates have even simpler pigment cups with no lenses. Among mollusks, cephalopods have complex eyes similar to those of vertebrates, but they focus by changing the position of the lens rather than its shape.

family
See **classification**.

fat
Also called **lipids**, fats are compounds that contain fatty acids and glycerol. Most fats are triglycerides (lipids containing three fatty acid molecules linked to a molecule of glycerol), which are normally solid at body temperatures. Fats are essential constituents of food, with a calorific value twice that of carbohydrates. In many animals, excess carbohydrates and proteins are converted into fats for storage. Mammals and other vertebrates store fats in specialized connective tissues (adipose tissue or "fat"), which not only act as energy reserves but also insulate the body and cushion its organs. *See* **glycerol**.

fatty acid
Any of a number of organic compounds consisting of a hydrocarbon chain (a chain of carbon atoms each of which is attached to hydrogen atoms), up to 24 carbon atoms long, with a carboxyl group at one end. Fatty acids form the components of **lipids**.

EYE

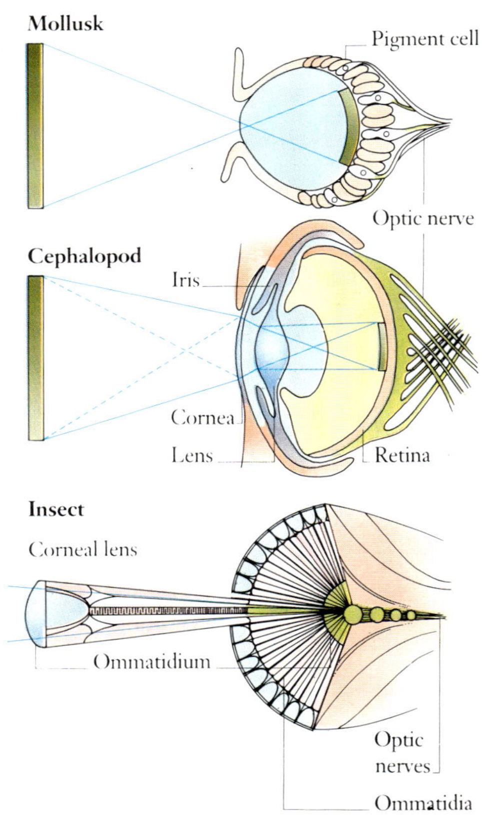

FERTILIZATION

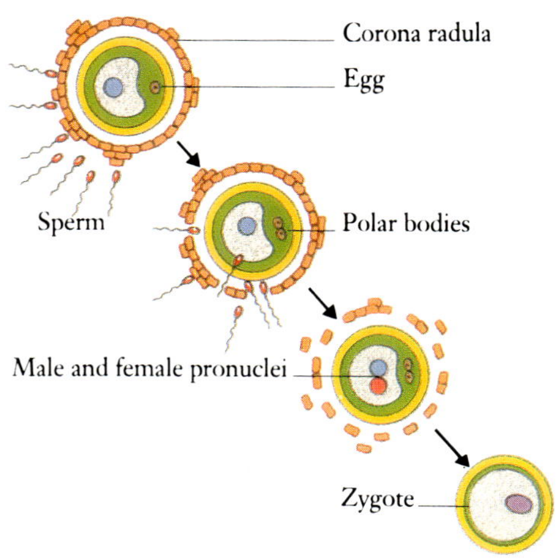

feather
A rigid outgrowth of the outer layer of the skin of birds, made of **keratin**. Feathers provide insulation and facilitate flight. There are several types, including long quill feathers on the wings and tail, fluffy down feathers for retaining body heat, and contour feathers covering the body.

feces
Waste material that is expelled from the alimentary canal through the anus or cloaca. It largely consists of the undigested food residue that remains after the digestion and absorption of nutrients and water has occurred, together with dead cells and bacteria shed from the lining of the intestines, and bile pigments. The elimination of feces from the body is called egestion.

fertilization
The union of two **gametes** to produce a **zygote**, which combines the genetic material contributed by each parent, in sexual reproduction. In self-fertilization the male and female gametes come from the same plant; in cross-fertilization they come from different plants. Self-fertilization occurs in some hermaphroditic animals. Fertilization can be internal (as in birds and mammals) or external (as in fishes and amphibians).

CONNECTIONS

GROWTH AND REPRODUCTION **116**
PATTERNS OF GROWTH **118**
ANIMAL REPRODUCTION **122**
FROM EGG TO EMBRYO **124**

fetus
The unborn young of a vertebrate, from the time it develops organ systems until the time of its birth. Before this stage of development the young is called an embryo.

fibrin
An insoluble blood protein used in **clotting**. When an injury occurs fibrin is deposited around the wound in the form of a mesh, which dries and hardens, so that bleeding stops. Fibrin is developed in the blood from a soluble protein, fibrinogen, which is converted into fibrin by the enzyme thrombin.

filter-feeder
An aquatic animal that feeds by straining tiny food particles from the water surrounding it. Some remain fixed and draw the water through themselves (*see* **ciliate**), whereas others move through the water, filtering as they go.

fin
Organs that chiefly provide locomotion in aquatic vertebrates. Most fish have dorsal and ventral fins for balance, pectoral and pelvic fins for steering, and a caudal (tail) fin for propulsion.

fish
An aquatic vertebrate that uses gills for obtaining oxygen from fresh or sea water. There are three main groups: bony fish of the class Osteichthyes (including goldfish, cod and tuna), which have bony scales; cartilaginous fish with scales made of dentine covered by enamel, which belong to the class Chondrichthyes (sharks and rays); and the jawless fish of the subphylum Agnatha (hagfish and lampreys), which have no jaws or paired appendages. Fish breathe by means of internal gills. Most lay eggs, but a few species of bony fish protect their eggs in nests or brood them in their mouths. Some fish are internally fertilized and retain eggs until hatching inside the body, then give birth to live young.

There are about 20,000 living species of bony fish. The skeleton is of bone, movement is controlled by mobile fins, and the body is usually covered with scales. The gills are covered by a single flap. Most bony fish have a swim bladder.

Most cartilaginous species are ray-finned fish (the fins are supported by rays of bone) but a few, including lungfish and coelacanths, have fleshy fins. There are fewer than 600 species of sharks and rays. The skeleton is of cartilage, the mouth is generally behind the snout, the nose is large and sensitive, and there is a series of gill slits behind the head. Sharks and rays may lay eggs in leathery pouches ("mermaid's purses") or bear live young.

There are only about 70 species of lampreys and hagfish. Jawless fish have no true backbone, but a **notochord**. Lampreys are parasitic on other fish for part of their life cycle. They attach themselves to the other fish by a suckerlike rasping mouth. Hagfish are entirely marine, and very slimy; they feed on carrion and injured fish.

flagellate
Any single-celled organism that moves by beating a long, whiplike flagellum (*see also* **ciliate**). Flagellates belong to the phylum Zoomastigina of the kingdom Protoctista.

flagellum
Any microscopic whiplike structure at the surface of a cell. Flagella are used for locomotion by certain single-celled organisms and by the sperm cells of higher animals. Unlike cilia, flagella usually occur singly or in pairs, although they have a similar internal structure (except the flagella of bacteria, which work in a different way). They are also longer and have a more complex whiplike action that propels cells through fluids (as in euglena) or moves fluids past cells (as in the flagellate cells of sponges). *See* **cilia**.

fly
Any of more than 90,000 species of insect of the order Diptera. A fly has a single pair of wings, antennae, and **compound eyes**; the hind wings have become modified into knob-like projections (halteres) used to maintain equilibrium in flight. The mouthparts project from the head as a proboscis used for sucking fluids, modified in some species, such as mosquitoes, to pierce a victim's skin and suck blood. Disks at the ends of hairs on their feet secrete a fluid enabling them to walk up walls and across ceilings. Flies undergo **metamorphosis**; their larvae (maggots) are without true legs and the pupae are rarely enclosed in a cocoon.

food chain
The sequence of steps by which energy is transferred between plants and animals. Plants trap light energy and convert it into the chemical energy of organic compounds. The plants are then eaten by animals, which in turn are eaten by other animals, so that the energy is passed from one organism to another. At each stage, energy is lost as heat, undigested food (droppings or feces) or energy of movement. Food chains are often complex and branching, with each species eating and being eaten by a number of other species. Several food chains may be combined to form a food web.

gamete
The **haploid** sex cells of the male (sperm) and female (ovum or egg). Haploid cells have only one copy of each **chromosome**. The sperm and egg fuse during **fertilization** to produce the **diploid** zygote, which has two copies of each chromosome and develops into a new organism.

gene
The basic unit of inheritance that controls a characteristic of an organism. A gene can be considered as a length of **DNA** with a very specific sequence of bases which form part of the organism's genetic code, and which codes for a single polypeptide chain. *See* **DNA**.

genetic code
A code, embodied in **DNA**, which carries the instructions for a **cell** to synthesize proteins. It specifies the order in which **amino acids** are assembled to form particular proteins, including **enzymes**.

CONNECTIONS

CHEMISTRY OF LIFE **62**
BUILDING BLOCKS OF LIFE **64**
CHEMICAL CONTROL **74**
GROWTH AND REPRODUCTION **116**
ANIMAL REPRODUCTION **122**

genetics
The study of inheritance and of the units of inheritance (genes). The founder of genetics was the Austrian biologist Gregor Mendel, whose experiments with plants, such as peas, showed that inheritance takes place by means of discrete "particles", which later came to be called genes. Prior to Mendel's investigations, it had been assumed that the characteristics of the two parents were

FOOD CHAIN

blended during inheritance, but Mendel showed that the genes remain intact, though their combinations change. Since Mendel, the science of genetics has advanced greatly, first through breeding experiments and light-microscope observations of genes (classical genetics) and later by means of biochemical and electron-microscope studies (molecular genetics).

genus
A group of species with many characteristics in common. Thus all doglike species (including dogs, wolves and jackals) belong to the genus *Canis*. Species of the same genus are thought to be descended from a common ancestor species. Related genera are grouped into families. *See* **classification**.

gestation
See **pregnancy**.

gut
See **alimentary canal**.

haploid
A type of cells having only one copy of each **chromosome**, as seen in **gametes** in sexual reproduction. *See also* **alternation of generations fertilization meiosis**, **diploid**, and **sexual reproduction**.

heart
A specialized muscular organ that rhythmically contracts to pump **blood** around the body of an animal with a circulatory system (*see* **circulation**). Annelid worms and some other invertebrates have a number of simple "hearts" consisting of thickened sections of main blood vessels that pulse regularly. Vertebrates have a single heart. A fish heart has two chambers which will eventually develop in the thin-walled atrium that expands to receive blood and the thick-walled ventricle that pumps it out. Amphibians and most reptiles have two atria and one ventricle; birds and mammals have two atria and two ventricles, which support a double circulation (into the lungs, and around the remainder of the body). The beating of the heart is controlled by the **autonomic nervous system** and an internal control center or pacemaker, the sinoatrial node.

HEART

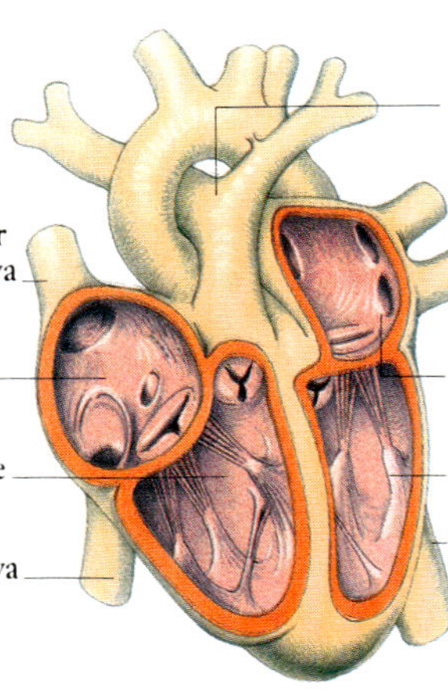

heat pit
An organ that is sensitive to infrared radiation (heat), used by some snakes in order to locate their warm-blooded prey in the dark.

hemoglobin
A respiratory pigment containing iron, used by all vertebrates and some invertebrates for oxygen transport. In vertebrates it occurs in **red blood cells** (erythrocytes), giving them their color. In the lungs or gills where the concentration of oxygen is high, oxygen attaches to hemoglobin to form oxyhemoglobin. The oxygen is later released in the body tissues where it is at a low concentration, and the deoxygenated blood returned to the lungs or gills.

herbivore
Any animal that feeds on green plants or algae (or photosynthetic single-celled organisms) or their products, including seeds, fruit and nectar. Herbivores have specially developed teeth and digestive systems to help them deal with tough plant fibers. For example, mammals that rely on cellulose as a major part of their diet (such as cows and sheep) generally possess millions of specialized bacteria and protozoans in their intestines to digest the cellulose. Herbivores form a vital link in the food chain between plants and carnivores.

CONNECTIONS

DIETS GALORE **84**
PLANT-EATERS **86**
FUSSY FEEDERS **96**

hermaphrodite
Any organism that has both male and female reproductive organs. This is a common condition in plants and in some invertebrates, such as earthworms.

hibernation
A state of greatly reduced metabolism and suspended bodily activity in which some animals (bats, hedgehogs and some species of bear) pass the winter months as a means of surviving food scarcity and cold weather.

homeothermic
See **warm-blooded animal**.

hormone
A chemical secretion produced by the **endocrine glands** which helps to affect control of body functions. The main mammalian glands are the thyroid, parathyroid, pituitary, adrenal, pancreas, uterus, ovary and testis. Hormones are enzymes that bring about changes in the functions of various organs according to the body's requirements. The pituitary gland, at the base of the brain, is a center for overall coordination of hormone secretion. *See* **adrenaline estrogen progesterone** and **thyroxine**.

CONNECTIONS

CHEMISTRY OF LIFE **62**
CHEMICAL CONTROL **74**
PATTERNS OF GROWTH **118**
ANIMAL REPRODUCTION **122**

hydrofoil
An object, such as the flippers of certain aquatic animals, whose curved shape makes water move farther (and therefore at lower pressure) over the upper surface than over the lower one as it travels through the water. The lower pressure results in an upward force (lift).

immune system
The body's system of defenses against disease. The main components of the immune system are **antibodies** (chemicals which recognize foreign substances or antigens, and either destroy them or help other cells to recognize and destroy them), and antitoxins (body chemicals which neutralize toxins produced by invading organisms). Both antibodies and antitoxins are produced by specialized white blood cells (leukocytes). By storing specific antibodies, the body can raise its resistance to future infection from the same antigen. The basis of the immune system is a complex system for distinguishing between foreign cells and the cells of the host organism, using recognition molecules embedded in the cell membranes. It is this feature of the immune system which leads to the rejection of organ and tissue transplants.

incisor
A sharp tooth at the front of the mammalian mouth. Incisors are mainly used for cutting. Rodents, such as rats and squirrels, have large, continually growing incisors, adapted for gnawing. An elephant's tusks are greatly enlarged incisors.

insect
Any **arthropod** of the class Insecta. An insect's body is divided into head, thorax and abdomen. The head bears a pair of feelers or antennae and a set of mouthparts, and attached to the thorax are three pairs of legs and sometimes two pairs of wings. The skeleton is external and is composed of chitin. In the female, there is very commonly an egg-laying instrument (ovipositor) and many insects have a pair of tail feelers (cerci). Most insects breathe by means of tracheae (a system of air tubes) which open to the exterior by a pair of spiracles. Reproduction is by diverse means. Most of the lower orders of insects pass through a direct or incomplete **metamorphosis**. The young closely resemble the parents and are known as **nymphs**. The higher groups of insects undergo indirect or complete metamorphosis. They hatch at an earlier stage of growth than nymphs and are termed **larvae**. This is followed by the pupal stage, during which the larval organs and tissues are transformed into those of the adult (imago). Before pupating, the insect protects itself in a "hard case". When an insect is about to emerge from the **pupa** it undergoes its final molt. Insects are divided into two subclasses, apterygotes (wingless insects, four orders) and pterygotes (winged insects, 25 orders).

intestine
The digestive tract from the stomach outlet to the anus or cloaca in vertebrates. The human intestine can be divided into the small and the large intestine. The small intestine is a relatively narrow tube (up to 6 m long) that consists of the duodenum, jejunum and ileum, and is the main area for digestion and the absorption of nutrients. The large intestine is slightly larger in diameter (up to 1.5 m long) and includes the cecum, colon and rectum, and is the main area for the reabsorption of water and vitamins prior to excretion of the feces. Both are muscular tubes with an inner lining of many villi and microvilli that secretes alkaline digestive juice; a submucous coat containing fine blood vessels and nerves; a muscular coat; and a serous coat covering all, supported by a strong peritoneum, which carries the blood and lymph vessels and the nerves. The contents are passed along slowly by **peristalsis**. The term intestine is also applied to the lower digestive tract of invertebrates.

invertebrate
Any animal without a **backbone**. The invertebrates comprise over 95 percent of the known animal species, and include sponges, coelenterates, flatworms, nematodes, annelid worms, arthropods, mollusks, echinoderms and primitive aquatic chordates, such as sea squirts and lancelets.

involuntary action
Any behavior not under conscious control, such as the contractions of the intestines during peristalsis or the secretion of adrenaline by the adrenal glands. Breathing and urination reflexes are involuntary, although both can be controlled to some extent. These processes are part of the **autonomic nervous system**.

ion
An atom or molecule that has lost or gained one or more electrons and thereby acquired a positive or negative charge. Soluble salts dissociate into ions when they dissolve in water.

iris
The colored opaque muscular diaphragm that controls the size of the pupil in the vertebrate **eye**. It contains radial muscle that increases the pupil diameter and circular muscle that constricts the pupil diameter. Both types of muscle respond involuntarily to light intensity.

JELLYFISH

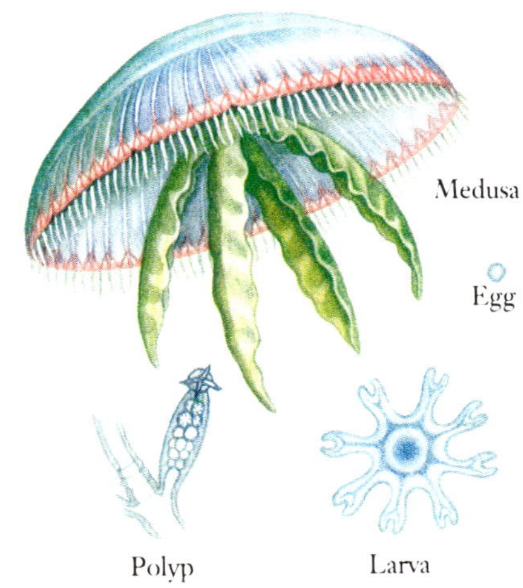

Jacobson's organ
An organ located in the roof of the mouth of certain vertebrates, such as some snakes and lizards, that is connected with the sense of smell. The animal flicks out its tongue, picking up olfactory substances in the air, which are then detected by the organ.

jaw
One of two bony structures that form the framework of the mouth in all vertebrates except lampreys and hagfishes (the Agnatha or jawless vertebrates). The upper jawbone (maxilla) is fused to the skull, and the lower jawbone (mandible) is hinged at each side to the bones of the temple by ligaments.

jellyfish
Any marine invertebrate of the class Scyphozoa (true jellyfish) of the phylum Cnidaria (**coelenterates**). About 200 species

INSECT

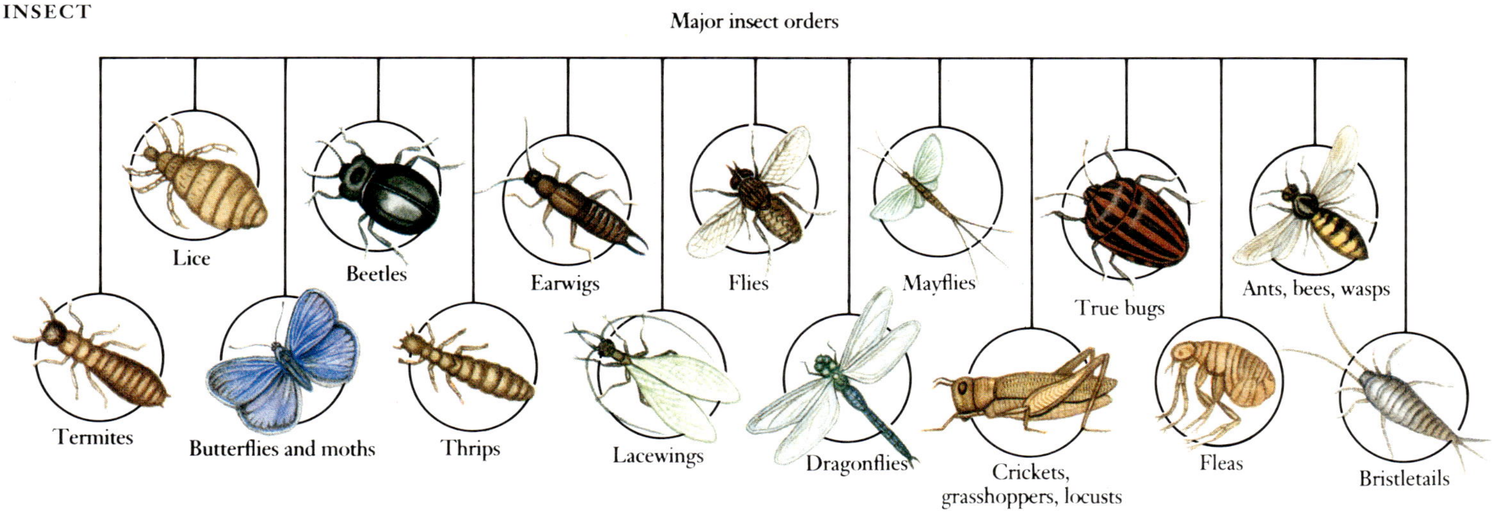

are known. Jellyfish have an umbrella-shaped body composed of a translucent gelatinous substance, with a fringe of stinging tentacles. Most adult jellyfish move freely, but during parts of their life cycle many are polyplike and attached to a substrate. The medusae of hydroids are often called jellyfish, but they differ from true jellyfish in that their sexual organs are not inside the gastric cavity.

jet propulsion
A form of movement produced using special muscles to force a jet of water out of an animal's body, thus propelling it in the opposite direction. In its simplest form, jet propulsion is used by jellyfish and medusae. Cephalopods such as octopuses and squid can move swiftly by squirting water out though a siphon situated just behind the head. This funnel can be angled in almost any direction. Scallops jet propel by rapidly snapping shut their valves (shells) to eject water from the body cavity, and lobsters flex their curled-under abdomens against their bodies.

CONNECTIONS

SHELLS AND SPINES **52**
JOINTED LEGS **54**
MOVING THROUGH WATER **114**

joint
Any point of movement or articulation in an animal with a skeleton. In vertebrates, a joint is the point where two **bones** meet. Some joints allow no motion (the sutures of the skull), others allow a very small motion (the sacroiliac joints in the lower back), but most allow a relatively free motion. Of these, some allow a gliding motion (one vertebra of the spine on another), some have a hinge action (as in the elbow and knee) and others allow motion in all directions (hip and shoulder joints) by means of a ball-and-socket arrangement. The ends of the bones at a moving joint are covered with **cartilage** for greater elasticity and smoothness, and enclosed in an envelope of tough white fibrous tissue lined with a membrane that secretes a lubricating and cushioning fluid (synovial fluid). The joint is further strengthened by tough bands of tissue called ligaments, which hold the bones together.

In invertebrates with an exoskeleton, the joints are places where the exoskeleton is replaced by a more flexible outer covering, the arthrodial membrane, which allows the limb (or other body part) to bend at that point. The muscles operating the joint are attached to the inside of the exoskeleton. *See also* **muscle** and **spine**.

keratin
Any of a group of strong, fibrous, elastic sulfur-based **proteins** found in the outer skin layer (epidermis) of vertebrates and also in hair, nails, hooves, feathers and horns in animals such as cows and sheep. Keratin is a major component of silk.

kidney
The main organ responsible for water regulation, excretion of waste products, and maintaining the dissolved substances in the blood in vertebrates. In mammals there are a pair of kidneys situated on the rear wall of the abdomen. Each kidney consists of a number of long tubules; the outer parts filter the aqueous components of blood and the inner parts selectively reabsorb vital salts, leaving waste products in the remaining fluid (urine), which is passed along the ureter to the bladder.

kingdom
The primary division of living organisms in biological classification. Only two kingdoms were originally recognized: animals and plants. The predominantly accepted modern system recognizes five kingdoms: Animalia (all multicellular organisms that, during development from the zygote, form a hollow ball of cells called a blastula); Plantae (multicellular organisms containing pigments such as chlorophyll enclosed in membrane-bound organelles, which develop from embryos that are nourished by special sterile tissue); Fungi (organisms that lack walls separating the cells of the vegetative [non-reproductive] body); Monera (all **prokaryotes** including bacteria and blue-green algae or cyanobacteria); and Protoctista (organisms that do not belong to any of the other four kingdoms, including protozoans, algae, diatoms, slime molds, molds, rusts and mildews and other **eukaryotic** microbes). *See* **classification**.

KIDNEY

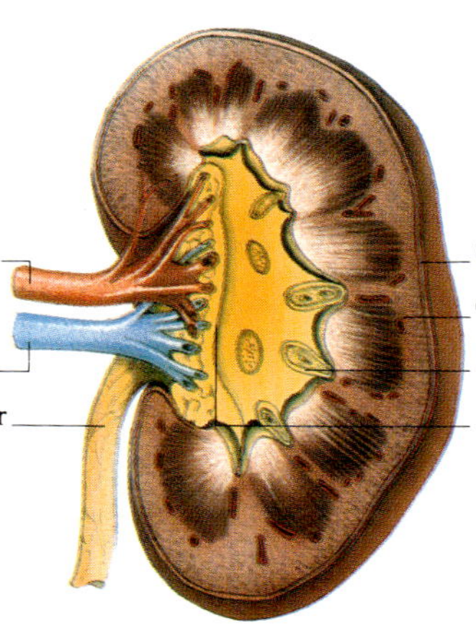

lactation
The secretion of **milk** from the **mammary glands** of **mammals**. In late pregnancy, the cells lining the lobules inside the mammary glands begin extracting substances from the blood to produce milk. The supply of milk starts shortly after birth with the production of colostrum, a clear fluid consisting largely of water, protein, antibodies and vitamins. The production of milk continues as long as the infant continues to suckle. The formation of milk is stimulated by the hormone prolactin. Before birth it is inhibited by high levels of progesterone. The continued production of milk also requires the hormone estrogen. Milk is ejected from the nipple of the mammary gland in a reflex response to the sucking action of the young.

lacteal
Small blind-ended lymph vessel in the villi in the intestines of vertebrates. It collects emulsified fats (from digestion) and passes them to the **lymph system**. *See* **villus**.

lancelet
A kind of fishlike marine animal belonging to the chordate subphylum Cephalochordata. There are fewer than 20 species. Lancelets are thought to be very similar to the ancestors of the vertebrates. They have no skull, brain, eyes, heart, vertebral column or paired limbs, but their almost transparent bodies do contain a **notochord** which extends into the head; a post-anal tail; a dorsal hollow nerve cord; and a number of gill slits (all features of chordates). Lancelets live in the sediments on the sea bed in shallow water, where they filter food particles from the water with their gill bars. They can swim for short distances.

larva
The juvenile stage between hatching and adulthood in those species of animals in which the young have a different appearance (often including their physical structure) and way of life from the adults. Examples include tadpoles (frogs) and caterpillars (butterflies and moths). Larvae are typical of the invertebrates, some of which (such as shrimps) have two or more distinct larval stages. Among vertebrates, a larval stage is experienced only by amphibians and some species of fish. *See* **metamorphosis**.

CONNECTIONS

CHEMISTRY OF LIFE **62**
BREAKDOWN SPECIALISTS **94**
LIVING OFF OTHERS **98**
INSECT SOCIETIES **140**

LATERAL LINE SYSTEM

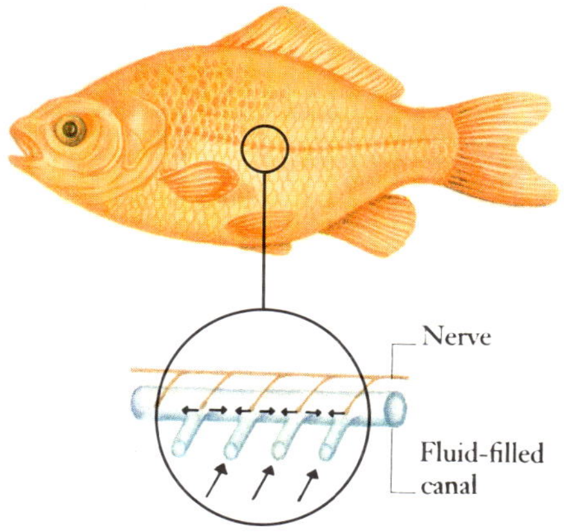

lateral line system
A sensory system found in fish and various larval amphibians involved in the detection of external movements or vibrations of the water. It consists of a line of interconnected pores on each side of the body that divide into a system of canals across the head. Hair cells line the canals and project into the fluid-filled space. These hairlike projections are embedded in a cupula, which is displaced by any movement of the surrounding water. The movements of the cupula are then detected by specialized nerve endings.

leukocyte
See **white blood cell**.

life cycle
The complete sequence of developmental stages through which members of a given species pass. Most vertebrates have a simple life cycle consisting of fertilization of sex cells or gametes, a period of development as an embryo, a period of juvenile growth after hatching or birth, an adulthood including sexual reproduction and finally death. Invertebrate life cycles are generally more complex and may involve major changes of appearance (**metamorphosis**) and completely different styles of life.

ligament
The strong flexible connective tissue, made of the **protein** collagen, that joins bone to bone at movable joints. Ligaments prevent bone dislocation (under normal circumstances) but permit flexing of joints.

lipid
Any of a large number of esters of **fatty acids**, commonly formed by the reaction (condensation) of a fatty acid with glycerol. They are soluble in alcohol but not in water. Lipids are the chief constituents of plant and animal waxes, fats and oils. They play a number of important roles in energy (food) storage, protection, waterproofing and membrane structure and function.

CONNECTIONS

CHEMISTRY OF LIFE **62**
BUILDING BLOCKS OF LIFE **64**
PROCESSING FOOD **66**

liver
A large, lobed organ situated in the abdomen of vertebrates that plays an essential role in many regulatory and storage functions. The liver receives the products of **digestion**, converts glucose to glycogen (a long-chain carbohydrate used for storage), and breaks down **fats**. It removes excess amino acids from the blood, converting them to urea, which is excreted by the **kidneys**. The liver also synthesizes vitamins, produces bile and blood-clotting factors, and removes damaged red cells and toxins from the blood. With its many heat-releasing metabolic reactions the liver is the body's main source of heat, which is distributed by the bloodstream. In invertebrates, the liver is the main digestive gland.

lung
A respiratory organ for gas exchange in air-breathing vertebrates, including lungfish. It is essentially a sheet of thin, moist membrane folded so as to offer the largest surface area for a given space. Most four-legged vertebrates have a pair of lungs in the thorax. The lung tissue, consisting of numerous air sacs and blood vessels, is very light and spongy, and functions by bringing inhaled air into close contact with the blood so that oxygen can pass into the organism and waste carbon dioxide can be passed out. The lung is supplied with air through the bronchus. In mammals and reptiles the membranes of the lungs take the form of numerous sacs (alveoli) that are connected to the bronchus via bronchioles, and help to increase the surface area of the membrane for gas exchange. The efficiency of lungs is enhanced by breathing movements (the lungs themselves do not contain any muscular tissue), by the thinness and moistness of their surfaces, and by a constant supply of circulating blood. Lungs are also found in some slugs and snails (as a modified part of the mantle) and in some fishes (lungfish and early fossil fishes).

luteinizing hormone
A **hormone** produced by the pituitary gland. In males, it stimulates the testes to produce androgens (male sex hormones). In females, it works together with follicle-stimulating hormone to initiate production of egg cells by the ovary. If fertilization of the egg cell occurs, it plays a part in maintaining pregnancy by controlling levels of the hormones **estrogen** and **progesterone** in the body.

lymph
The colorless liquid in the lymph system of vertebrates that resembles blood plasma.

lymphocyte
A type of leukocyte (white blood cell) with a large, DNA-rich nucleus. Lymphocytes produce **antibodies** for combating disease.

lymph system
A network of vessels by which lymph is collected from and returned to the blood supply. Lymph is drained from the tissues by lymph capillaries, which empty into larger lymph vessels (lymphatics) leading to lymph nodes. These process the lymphocytes produced by the bone marrow and filter out harmful substances and bacteria. The lymph system returns the filtered tissue fluid and some large newly synthesized proteins to the bloodstream via the large veins in the neck (the caudal vein near the tail in fish). Lymph

LUNG

KEYWORDS

vessels also transport fats from the digestive tract to the blood. Lymph flows slowly, massaged by the pressure of nearby muscles. In fish, amphibians, reptiles and birds it is also pumped by muscular lymph hearts. Valves prevent backflow in large vessels.

mammal
Any member of the vertebrate class Mammalia, which contains some 4250 species. Mammals are characterized by mammary glands in the female; these are used for suckling the young. Other features of mammals are hair (very reduced in some species, such as whales); a middle ear formed of three small bones (ossicles); a lower jaw consisting of two bones only; seven vertebrae in the neck; and no nucleus in the red blood cells. Mammals are warm-blooded. They are divided into three groups: **1** placental mammals, where the young develop inside the uterus, receiving nourishment from the blood of the mother via the placenta; **2** marsupials, where the young are born at an early stage of development and develop further in a pouch on the mother's body; and **3** monotremes, where the young hatch from an egg outside the mother's body and are then nourished with milk. The monotremes are the least evolved and have been largely displaced by more sophisticated marsupials and placentals, so there are only a few surviving species (platypus and echidnas or spiny anteaters).

mammary gland
The gland in female mammals that produces **milk**, derived from epithelial cells underlying the skin and active only after the birth of young. In all but monotremes (egg-laying mammals), the mammary glands terminate in teats (nipples) which aid infant suckling. The number of glands and their position vary between species, from two in humans to four in cows and 19 in some opossums.

mandible
One of a pair of horny mouthparts of insects, centipedes, millipedes and crustaceans that lie in front of the weaker maxillae. The lower jaw of a vertebrate and the two parts of a bird's beak are also known as mandibles.

CONNECTIONS

DIETS GALORE **84**
PLANT-EATERS **86**
UNFUSSY FEEDERS **92**

mantle
The skin covering the dorsal surface of the body of **mollusks** and brachiopods which extends into lateral flaps to protect the gills. In species that have a shell, it is the outer part of the mantle that secretes the shell. In cephalopods its the muscles of the mantle that power jet propulsion. The part of the barnacle carapace that secretes the shell is also called the mantle.

marsupial
A mammal in which the female has a pouch (marsupium) in which she carries her young (born tiny and immature) for a considerable time after birth. Examples are kangaroos, wombats, koalas, bandicoots and opossums.

maxilla
One of a pair of horny mouthparts of insects, centipedes, millipedes and crustaceans that lie behind the stronger mandibles. In insects, the second pair are fused together to form the **labium**. The large upper jawbones of vertebrates are also known as maxillae.

medulla
The general term for the central part of an organ. In the mammalian **kidney**, the medulla lies beneath the outer cortex and is responsible for the reabsorption of water from the fluid that passes through the kidney. In the vertebrate brain, the medulla is the posterior region responsible for the coordination of basic activities, such as breathing and temperature control.

medusa
The free-swimming phase in the life cycle of a cnidarian (coelenterate) showing **alternation of generations**, such as a hydroid.

meiosis
A process of **cell division** in which the number of chromosomes in the cell is halved. It occurs only in **eukaryotic** cells and is part of a life cycle that involves sexual reproduction because it allows the genes of two parents to be combined without the total number of **chromosomes** increasing. In sexually reproducing diploid animals, meiosis occurs during formation of the **gametes**, so that they are haploid. When the gametes unite during fertilization, the diploid condition is restored. *See* **alternation of generations** and **mitosis**.

melanin
Any of a group of polymers derived from the **amino acid** tyrosine that produces pigmentation in the eyes, skin, hair, feathers, and scales of many vertebrates. In humans, melanins help protect the skin against ultraviolet radiation from sunlight. Both genetic and environmental factors determine the amount of melanin in the skin.

MEMBRANE

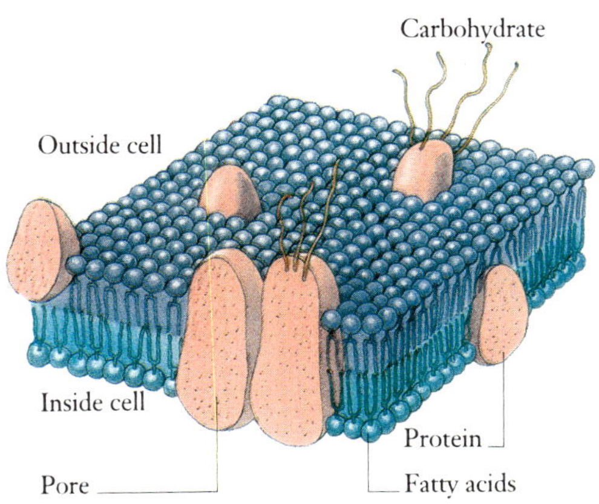

membrane
A continuous layer that encloses a cell or organelles within a cell, organs or other structures. Membranes consist of polar **lipids** and **proteins**, the lipids forming a double layer with protein molecules suspended within it. Certain small molecules can pass through the cell membrane, but most must enter or leave the cell via pores in the membrane made up of special proteins. The Golgi apparatus within the cell is thought to produce certain membranes. Enzymes may also be attached to the cell membrane at specific positions, often alongside other enzymes involved in the same process. Thus membranes help to make cellular processes more efficient.

metabolic pathway
A sequence of enzyme-controlled biochemical reactions that occur during metabolism, involving the formation or destruction of various compounds with consumption or production of energy.

metabolism
The chemical processes occurring in the **cells** of living organisms, involving building up (anabolism) and breaking down (catabolism) of substances (metabolites). For example, during **digestion**, animals partly break down complex organic substances, ingested as food, and use them to synthesize new substances in their own bodies.

CONNECTIONS

CHEMISTRY OF LIFE **62**
BUILDING BLOCKS OF LIFE **64**
PROCESSING FOOD **66**
CHEMICAL CONTROL **74**
CONTROLLING HEAT AND WATER **78**
HIDDEN SENSES **138**

METAMORPHOSIS

metamorphosis

A substantial change in form and structure that some animals undergo during development from the larva to the adult. The term is usually used to describe rapid rather than gradual changes. Metamorphosis occurs in many invertebrates, most amphibians and some fish. For example, adult frogs are produced by metamorphosis from tadpoles, and butterflies are produced from caterpillars.

metazoan

A member of the animal kingdom possessing two or more tissue layers. The subphylum Parazoa, which includes sponges, has special flagellate cells called collar cells and does not have tissues organized into organs; Eumetazoa or "true metazoans" have well-defined organs, usually have nervous coordination between cells and no collar cells.

microorganism

Any living organism invisible to the naked eye but visible under a microscope. Microorganisms include viruses and single-celled organisms such as bacteria, protozoa, yeasts and some algae. The term has no taxonomic significance in biology. The study of microorganisms is known as microbiology.

microvillus

One of a number of small fingerlike projections of cytoplasm on the surface of certain cells, such as the cells of the villi in the small intestine. They are covered with the **cell membrane**. Their purpose is to increase the surface area of the cell.

migration

The movement, either seasonal or as part of a single life cycle, of certain animals, chiefly birds, fish, mammals, marine turtles and a few invertebrates, to distant breeding or feeding grounds. The precise methods by which animals navigate and know where to go are still obscure. Birds have much sharper eyesight than humans, but in long-distance flights appear to navigate by the Sun and stars, possibly in combination with a "reading" of the Earth's magnetic field through an inbuilt "magnetic compass", which is a tiny mass of tissue between the eye and brain in birds. Similar cells occur in honeybees and in certain bacteria. Most striking, however, is the migration of young birds that have never flown a route before and are unaccompanied by adults. It is postulated that they may inherit as part of their genetic code an overall "sky chart" of their journey that is triggered into use when they become aware of how the local sky pattern, above the place in which they hatch, fits into it. For some birds, infrasound is thought to play a part, indicating the presence of waves on the shore or of wind rising over mountains. In fish, such as eels and salmon, vision plays a lesser role, but currents and changes in the chemical composition and temperature of the sea in particular locations may play a part, for example in enabling salmon to return to the precise river in which they were spawned.

CONNECTIONS

MOVING THROUGH THE AIR **112**
HIDDEN SENSES **138**

milk

The secretion of the **mammary glands** of female mammals, with which they suckle their young (during lactation). Over 85 percent is water, the remainder comprising protein, fat, lactose, calcium, phosphorus, iron, and vitamins. Milk composition varies among species, depending on the nutritional requirements of the young. Human milk contains less protein and more lactose (a kind of sugar) than that of cows.

milk tooth

The first of two sets of teeth in mammals (also known as deciduous teeth). These teeth are smaller than the final set of adult teeth, more uniform in shape and fewer in number (because there are no deciduous molars).

millipede

Any **arthropod** of the class Diplopoda, of which there are about 8000 species. It has a segmented body, each segment usually bearing two pairs of legs, and the distinct head bears a pair of short clubbed antennae. Millipedes live in damp, dark places, feeding mainly on rotting vegetation. Certain orders have silk glands.

mite

A tiny **arachnid** of the subclass Acari. Some mites are free-living scavengers or predators. Others are parasitic, such as the itch mite *Sarcoptes scabiei*, which burrows in human skin, and the red mite *Dermanyssus gallinae*, which sucks blood from poultry and other birds.

mitochondrion

One of the membrane-enclosed organelles within eukaryotic cells (*see* **eukaryote**), containing enzymes responsible for energy production during aerobic respiration. These rodlike or spherical bodies are thought to be derived from free-living bacteria that, at a very early stage in the history of life, invaded larger cells and took up a symbiotic way of life inside. Each still contains its own small loop of DNA called mitochondrial DNA and its own ribosomes; new mitochondria arise by the division of existing ones. The enzymes for electron transport and ATP synthesis are arranged on stalked particles on the inner membrane of the mitochondrion, which has many folds, called cristae, to increase the surface area for reaction. Other important respiration reactions take place in the fluid matrix which fills the remainder of the mitochondrion.

MITOCHONDRION

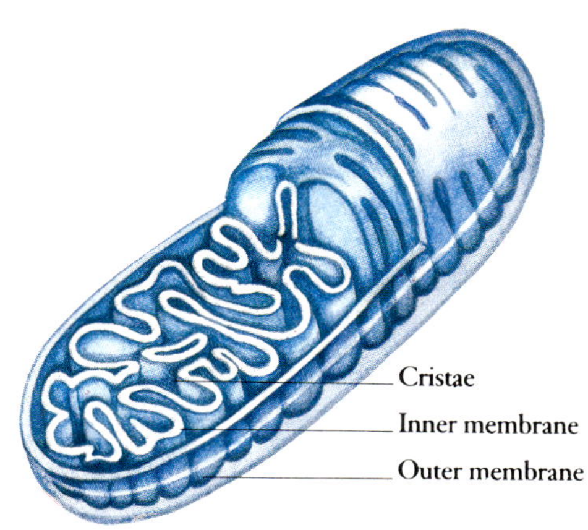

mitosis
The process of **cell division** by which normal body cells (as opposed to those that produce the sex cells) multiply, and which is also used in asexual reproduction. The genetic material of eukaryotic cells is carried on a number of chromosomes. To control their movements during cell division so that both new cells get an identical complement of chromosomes, a system of microtubules known as the spindle organizes the chromosomes into position in the middle of the cell before they replicate. The spindle then controls the movement of the daughter chromosomes as the cell divides. *See* **meiosis**, **eukaryote**, **microtubule**, **chromosome**, **asexual reproduction**.

molar
One of the large teeth found at the back of the mammalian mouth. The jaw and muscles allow a massive force to be applied to molars. In herbivores the molars are flat with sharp ridges of enamel and are used for grinding. Carnivores have sharp powerful molars (carnassials), adapted for cutting meat.

mollusk
Any invertebrate of the phylum Mollusca (about 110,000 species), with an unsegmented body divided into a head and a muscular foot and a visceral mass (containing the main organs). Mollusks are cold-blooded, soft and limbless. There is no internal skeleton, but many species have a hard shell covering the body. Most mollusks are marine animals, but some inhabit fresh water, and a few live on land. The group includes mussels, oysters, snails, slugs, octopus and squid. Some species are carnivorous, some herbivorous. Some are filter-feeders. Reproduction is by means of eggs, which in many species hatch into planktonic larvae. Many species are **hermaphrodite**. Every mollusk has a fold of skin, the mantle, which covers the whole body or the back only, and secretes the calcareous substance that forms the shell. The lower (ventral) surface forms the foot.

molting
The periodic shedding of the hair or fur of mammals, the feathers of birds or the skin of reptiles. In mammals and birds, molting is usually seasonal and is triggered by changes of daylength. The term is also applied to the shedding of the exoskeleton of arthropods, but this is more correctly called **ecdysis**.

monogamy
A sexual pairing between animals in which each partner has only one mate; some monogamous animals mate for life. *See also* **polygamy**.

monotreme
Any member of the order Monotremata, the only living egg-laying mammals, found in Australasia. The order contains only three living species, the platypus and two species of echidnas.

motor neuron
Any **nerve** cell (neuron) that transmits nerve impulses from the central nervous system to an effector organ to produce a physiological response, such as a muscle contraction.

mucus
A lubricating protective fluid, secreted by mucous membranes in many different parts of the body. In the gut, mucus smooths the passage of food and keeps potentially damaging digestive enzymes away from the gut lining. In the lungs, it traps airborne particles so that they can be expelled through the movement of cilia. Mucus also helps to keep surfaces moist for diffusion of gases. Many marine and freshwater invertebrates have a coating of mucus that lubricates their passage through the water.

muscle
Contractile tissue in animals that produces locomotion and maintains the movement of body substances. Muscle is made of long cells that can contract to between one-half and one-third of their relaxed length. There are three kinds of muscle: striated, smooth and cardiac. Striated muscles are activated by motor neurons under voluntary control; their ends are usually attached via tendons to bones. Striated muscle tissue consists of cells with many nuclei and cross-striations in the cytoplasm, and it usually occurs in bundles. Involuntary or smooth muscles are controlled by motor neurons of the **autonomic nervous system**, and are located in the gut, blood vessels, iris and various ducts. In smooth muscle tissue the cells usually form simple tubes or sheets. Cardiac muscle occurs only in the heart and is also controlled by the autonomic nervous system. Cardiac muscle consists of cross-striated fibers.

CONNECTIONS

SOFT-BODIED ANIMALS **50**
BUILDING BLOCKS OF LIFE **64**
AIR PUMPS **72**
FAST AND SLOW SPEEDS **104**
BUILT FOR MOVEMENT **106**
WALKING, RUNNING, JUMPING **108**

muscle fibers
The elongated cells that form the bundles of striated **muscles**, and which consists of fine threads (myofibrils) which contain the contractile proteins myosin, actin, and tropomyosin.

mutation
A change in the genes of an organism which is produced by an alteration in its **DNA**. Mutations result from mistakes during replication or copying of DNA molecules during cell division. Common mutations include the omission or insertion of a base (one of the chemical subunits of DNA), known as point mutations. Larger-scale mutations include removal of a whole segment of DNA or its inversion within the DNA strand.

mutualism
Another name for **symbiosis**.

myelin sheath
An insulating layer that surrounds **nerve** cells in vertebrate animals and which acts to speed up the passage of nerve impulses. Myelin is made up of fats and proteins and the sheath is formed from up to a hundred layers of myelin, laid down by special cells, the Schwann cells.

myoglobin
A globular protein, closely related to hemoglobin and located in vertebrate **muscle**. Oxygen binds to myoglobin and is released only when the hemoglobin can no longer supply adequate oxygen to muscle cells.

myosin
A contractile protein which is the most abundant elements of myofibrils (*see* **muscle fibers**).

natural selection
The process whereby gene frequencies in a population change through certain individuals producing more descendants than others because they are better able to survive and reproduce in their environment. The accumulated effect of natural selection is to produce favorable **adaptations**. The process is slow, relying on random variation in the genes of an organism being produced by mutation and on the genetic recombination of sexual reproduction. It is recognized as the main process driving **evolution**.

nematocyst
A specialized type of stinging cell found on the tentacles of cnidarians (**coelenterates**).

nematode
Any unsegmented worm of the phylum Nematoda. Nematodes are pointed at both ends, with a tough, smooth outer skin. They include many free-living predators found in

soil and water, including the sea, but a large number are parasites, such as the roundworms and pinworms that live in humans. Nematodes differ from flatworms in that they have two openings to the digestive tract (a mouth and an anus).

nephridium
The excretory organ in many invertebrate animals, consisting of a tube that leads from the central body cavity to the skin surface.

nerve
A collection of axons (nerve fibers) leading to or from the central nervous system; also describes any bundle of nerve fibers.

CONNECTIONS

BUILDING BLOCKS OF LIFE **64**
NERVOUS CONTROL **76**
RECOVERY AND REPAIR **80**
FAST AND SLOW SPEEDS **104**

nervous system
The system of interconnected nerve cells of most invertebrates and all vertebrates. It is composed of the central and autonomic nervous systems. It may be a simple nerve net (as in jellyfishes) or a complex nervous system, with a central nervous system comprising **brain** and **spinal cord**, and a peripheral nervous system connecting up with sensory organs, muscles and glands.

neurohormone
A chemical secreted by **nerve** cells and carried by the blood to target cells. The function of the neurohormone is to act as a messenger, for example the neurohormone ADH (antidiuretic hormone) is secreted by the hypothalamus, stored in the pituitary gland, then released into the bloodstream and carried to the kidney, where it promotes water reabsorption in the kidney tubules.

neuron
An elongated cell forming part of the nervous system that transmits information rapidly between different parts of the body. When neurons are collected together in significant numbers (as in the **brain**), they not only transfer information but also process it. The unit of information is the nerve impulse, a traveling wave of chemical and electrical changes affecting the membrane of the nerve cell. The impulse involves sequential changes in the permeability of the neuron membrane to sodium and potassium ions, which result in electrical signals called **action potentials**. Impulses are received by the cell body and passed, as a pulse of electric

NOTOCHORD

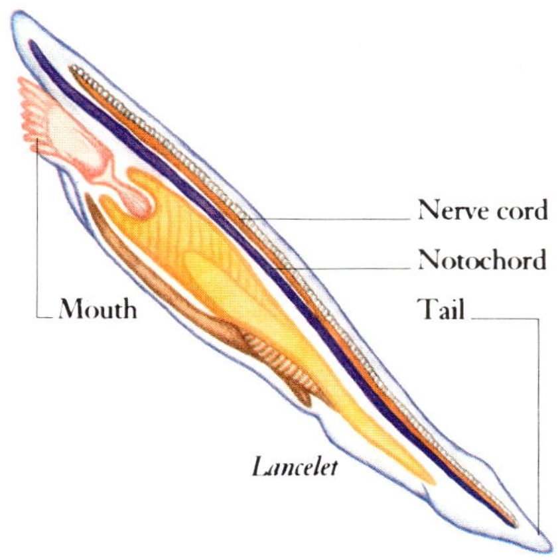

charge, along a long extension, called the axon. The axon terminates at the **synapse**, a specialized area closely linked to the next cell (which may be another nerve cell or a specialized effector cell such as a muscle). On reaching the synapse, the impulse releases a chemical called a **neurotransmitter**, which diffuses across to the neighboring cell and there stimulates another impulse or the action of the effector cell.

neurotransmitter
A chemical that passes nerve impulses between cells of the nervous system across a synapse, or between nerve cells and muscle cells (at a neuromuscular junction).

night vision
The ability to see under low-intensity light. Night vision uses the rod cells present on the **retina** of the eye. These cells are more sensitive to light of low intensity than the cone cells, but are insensitive to color. They are, however, capable of seeing in greater detail, and are also sensitive to movements. Many nocturnal vertebrates, such as cats and owls, have a reflective layer (the tapetum) at the back of the retina, which reflects light back through the retina so that it has a better chance of being absorbed. This layer glows yellow or orange when a torch is shone on the eyes. *See* **color vision**.

nipple
See **mammary gland**.

nocturnal
Activity associated with the hours of darkness. Compare **diurnal**.

notochord
The stiff but flexible rod of cartilage that lies between the gut and the nerve cord of all chordates that go through the embryonic and larval stage, including the vertebrates. It forms the supporting structure of the adult lancelet, but in vertebrates it is replaced by the vertebral column (spine) during embryonic development.

nuclear envelope
The double membrane surrounding the nucleus of a **eukaryote** cell.

nucleic acid
A complex organic acid vital to life and consisting of a long chain of nucleotides. The two types, known as **DNA** (deoxyribonucleic acid) and RNA (ribonucleic acid), form the basis of heredity. The nucleotides are made up of a sugar (deoxyribose or ribose), a phosphate group, and one of four purine or pyrimidine bases. The order of the bases along the nucleic acid strand contains the **genetic code**.

nucleus
The central, membrane-enclosed part of a eukaryotic cell (*see* **eukaryote**), containing the **chromosomes** and acting as the control center of the cell.

nutrient
Any material taken in by a living organism that allows it to grow and replace lost or damaged tissue, and provides energy for the metabolic functions. Nutrients may be mineral substances (in plants) or organic nutritious substance found in the food of animals. *See also* **vitamin**.

NUTRIENT

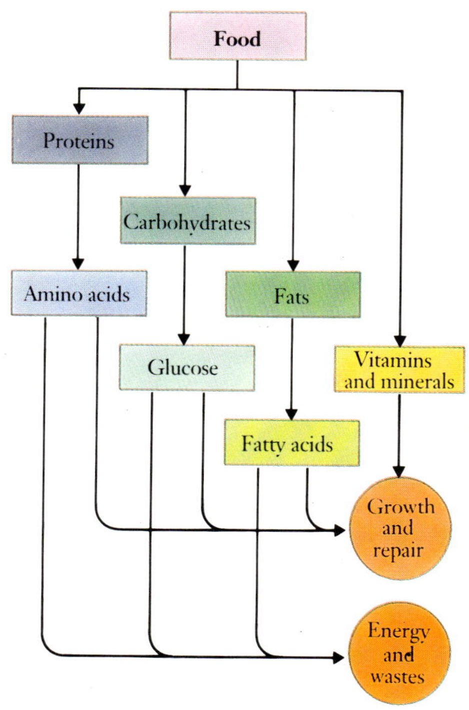

KEYWORDS

nutrition
The means by which an organism obtains the chemicals it needs to live, grow and reproduce. In animals it involves the ingestion of food, its digestion and absorption. This food comes directly or indirectly from plant matter, so all animals ultimately depend on plants for their nutrition. *See also* **protein** and **vitamin**.

nymph
The immature form of insects that do not have a pupal stage, such as grasshoppers and dragonflies. Nymphs generally resemble the adult (unlike larvae), but do not have fully formed reproductive organs or wings.

olfactory
Having to do with the sense of smell.

omnivore
Any animal that feeds on both plant and animal material. Omnivores have digestive adaptations intermediate between those of herbivores and carnivores, with relatively unspecialized digestive systems and microorganisms in the intestines that can digest a variety of foodstuffs.

open circulation
A circulatory system in which the blood moves freely through the body spaces for most of its circulation. Blood from the arteries bathes the major tissues before diffusing back to the open ends of veins. There are no capillaries. Open circulatory systems are commonly found in **arthropods**. The blood that circulates through an open circulatory system is often called hemolymph.

operculum
Describes the gill cover of bony fish, or the calcareous lid that closes the shell of some gastropods and barnacles. The gill cover can be raised or lowered by means of muscles, and assists in drawing water across the gills.

optic nerve
The large nerve passing from the **eye** to the **brain**, carrying visual information. In mammals, it may contain up to a million nerve fibers, connecting the sensory cells of the retina to the optical centers in the brain. The optic nerve develops as an outgrowth of the brain in the **embryo** stage of development.

order
A group of related families. For instance, the horse, the rhinoceros and the tapir families are grouped in the order Perissodactyla, the odd-toed ungulates, because they all have either one or three toes on each foot. *See* **classification**.

organ
A distinct part of a living organism that has a specialized function or set of functions, such as the liver and brain in animals. An organ contains many different types of **tissues**.

organelle
A specialized structure in a living **cell**. Organelles include chloroplasts, mitochondria, lysosomes, ribosomes and a nucleus.

osmoregulation
The process whereby the water content of living organisms is maintained at a constant level. If the balance is disrupted, the concentration of salts will be too high or too low, and vital functions, such as nerve conduction, will be adversely affected. In mammals, loss of water by evaporation is counteracted by increased intake and by mechanisms in the **kidneys** that enhance the rate of water absorption before urine production.

CONNECTIONS

ONE-CELLED WONDERS **58**
DISPOSAL OF WASTE **68**
AIR PUMPS **72**
CONTROLLING HEAT AND WATER **78**
HIDDEN SENSES **138**

osmosis
The **diffusion** of a solvent through a selectively permeable membrane, thus separating solutions of different concentrations. Osmosis is a special case of diffusion: the solvent is moving from an area where it is in high concentration to an area where it is in lower concentration, until the two concentrations are equal. Many **cell membranes** behave as selectively permeable membranes and osmosis is a vital mechanism in the transport of fluids in living organisms.

ossicles
The small bones in the middle **ear** of vertebrates that connect the tympanum (ear drum) with the inner ear. There are three ossicles in mammals, the malleus (hammer), incus (anvil), and stapes (stirrup). Ossicle also describes the plates in the skin of many echinoderms.

ovary
The reproductive organ in female animals that generates the ova (eggs). In humans, the ovaries are two whitish rounded bodies located in the abdomen near the ends of the fallopian tubes. The ovaries of female animals secrete the steroid hormones (estrogen and progesterone) responsible for the secondary sexual characteristics of the female.

oviduct
The tube along which eggs (ova) pass from the ovaries to other parts of the reproductive system or out of the body. In mammals, it is also known as the fallopian tube.

ovipary
A method of reproduction in which the fertilized eggs are laid or spawned by the mother and hatch outside of her body.

ovivipary
A method of reproduction in which the fertilized eggs develop and hatch in the oviduct of the mother.

oxytocin
A **hormone** produced by the posterior **pituitary gland** in mammals that stimulates the uterus in late pregnancy to initiate and sustain labor. After birth, it stimulates the uterine muscles to contract, reducing bleeding at the site where the placenta was attached. It also stimulates the ejection of milk in lactating females.

pain
The sense that gives awareness of harmful effects on or in the body. The sensation may be triggered by a number of different stimuli such as trauma, inflammation and heat. It is thought that pain is transmitted by specialized **neurons** and involves a **neurotransmitter** known as "substance P", which is found in certain areas of the **spinal cord**. Pain also involves psychological components controlled by higher centers of the brain. Substances that control pain are known as analgesics.

palp
A jointed sensory structure found in many invertebrates, usually near the mouthparts. Examples are the olfactory parts of the second **maxillae** found in some insects and crustaceans.

pancreas
An accessory gland of the digestive system (*see* **digestion**), located close to the duodenum. When stimulated by the hormone secretin, it secretes enzymes into the duodenum that digest carbohydrates, proteins and fats. It contains groups of cells called the islets of Langerhans, which secrete the hormones insulin and glucagon that regulate the blood sugar level.

parasite
Any organism that lives on (ectoparasite) or in (endoparasite) another organism (the "host") and depends on it for nutrition. Some parasites cause relatively little damage

to the host, whereas others cause characteristic diseases. Some parasites can survive and reproduce only as parasites; others can also live as saprotrophs, that is, by absorbing dead organic matter.

parasympathetic nervous system
Part of the **autonomic nervous system** whose actions tend to antagonize those of the sympathetic nervous system. Its nerve endings release the neurotransmitter **acetylcholine**. The parasympathetic system tends to slow down the activity of smooth muscles and glands, but promotes digestion.

parthenogenesis
A form of **asexual reproduction** in which the egg develops without any genetic contribution from a male. Parthenogenesis is the normal means of reproduction in a few animals (including water fleas, flatworms). Some sexually reproducing species, such as aphids, show parthenogenesis at some stage in their life cycle. Male bees, wasps and ants are produced by parthenogenesis from unfertilized eggs.

pecking order
A system of hierarchy in social groupings of mammals and birds in which there is a linear order of precedence for access to food and mates. Gregarious birds such as chickens form pecking orders where bird A is dominant to birds B, C, and D; bird B is dominant to birds C and D; and so on.

pectoral girdle
Also called shoulder girdle, the bones and cartilaginous structures of vertebrates to which the muscles used to move the forelimbs (arms or pectoral fins) are attached. In mammals it consists of two scapulae (shoulder blades) attached to the backbone and two clavicles (collar bones) attached to the sternum (breastbone).

pedipalp
The second pair of jointed appendages immediately in front of the mouthparts of **arachnids**. These sensory appendages may also be used for walking, seizing and killing prey, defense, digging and manipulating food into the mouth. In male spiders spoon-shaped pedipalps are used to transfer sperm to the female.

pelvic girdle
Also called the pelvis, the bones and cartilaginous structures of vertebrates to which the muscles used to move the hindlimbs (legs or pelvic fins) are attached. In mammals it consists of two halves, each made up of three fused bones: the ilium, ischium and pubis.

PERISTALSIS

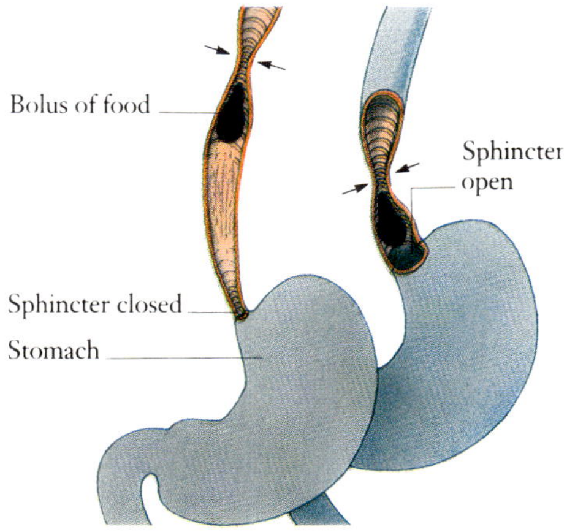

penis
Male organ used to transfer sperm to the female reproductive tract for internal **fertilization**. In mammals, the penis is made erect by vessels that fill with blood, and in most mammals (but not humans) it is stiffened by a bone. The vertebrate penis also contains the urethra, through which urine leaves the body. A kind of penis is also found in insects, flatworms, gastropod mollusks, some reptiles and a few species of birds.

peristalsis
The wavelike contractions produced by the contraction of smooth muscle, that pass along tubular organs, such as the **intestines**. The same term describes the wavelike motion of earthworms and other invertebrates, in which part of the body contracts as another part elongates, during movement. Peristaltic movements are the result of alternate contraction and relaxation of circular and longitudinal muscle.

pH
A logarithmic scale numbered from 0 to 14 for expressing acidity or alkalinity. A pH of 7.0 indicates neutrality, below 7 is acid, and above 7 is alkaline.

phagocyte
A cell that engulfs external solid material, often as part of a defense against invading microorganisms. The action is termed phagocytosis (*see* **pinocytosis**).

pharynx
The cavity in vertebrates at the back of the mouth which serves for the passage of both food and respiratory gases. Its walls are made of muscle strengthened with a fibrous layer and lined with a mucous membrane. The nostrils lead backward into the pharynx, which continues downward to the tops of the esophagus and trachea. In terrestrial vertebrates, Eustachian tubes enter the pharynx from the middle ear cavities.

pheromone
A chemical signal (such as an odor) that is emitted by one animal and which has a specific behavioral or physiological effect on other members of the same species. Pheromones are used by many animal species to attract mates.

CONNECTIONS

TASTE AND SMELL **136**
INSECT SOCIETIES **140**
MAMMAL SOCIETIES **142**

photosynthesis
The process by which green plants trap light energy and use it to drive a series of chemical reactions, leading to the formation of carbohydrates. For photosynthesis to occur, the plant must possess chlorophyll and must have a supply of carbon dioxide and water. The chemical reactions of photosynthesis occur in two stages. During the light reaction sunlight is used to split water (H_2O) into oxygen (O_2), protons (hydrogen ions, H^+), and electrons, and oxygen is given off as a by-product. In the dark reaction, for which sunlight is not required, the protons and electrons are used to convert carbon dioxide (CO_2) into carbohydrates ($(CH_2O)_n$). Photosynthesis depends on the ability of chlorophyll to capture the energy of sunlight and to use it to split water molecules into their constituent components. Other pigments, such as carotenoids, are also involved in capturing light energy and passing it on to chlorophyll. *See also* **food chain**.

phylum
In the classification of living things, a major subdivision of a kingdom, comprising a number of classes. *See* **classification**.

phytoplankton
The plant component of **plankton**.

pigment
A substance that imparts color (for example to skin, hair, blood, and so on).

pincer
One of a pair or pairs of jointed grasping appendages on crabs, lobsters and a number of other arthropods.

pinocytosis
The action by which a cell engulfs a droplet of liquid. *See also* **phagocyte**.

pituitary gland
A major **endocrine gland** of vertebrates, located in the center of the brain and linked directly to the hypothalamus by blood vessels. The anterior lobe secretes **hormones**, some of which control the activities of other glands (thyroid, gonads and adrenal cortex). Others are direct-acting hormones affecting milk secretion and controlling growth. The posterior lobe stores antidiuretic hormone (ADH), produced by the hypothalamus and used to control body water balance; the posterior lobe also secretes oxytocin, which stimulates the uterus to contract when females give birth.

CONNECTIONS
CHEMISTRY OF LIFE 62
CHEMICAL CONTROL 74
NERVOUS CONTROL 76

placenta
The organ that attaches a developing embryo to the **uterus** in placental mammals. It is composed of both maternal and embryonic tissue, and links the blood supply of the embryo to the blood supply of the mother, allowing the exchange of oxygen, nutrients and waste products. The two blood systems are separated by thin membranes, with nutrients and other materials diffusing across from one system to the other. The placenta also produces the **hormones** that maintain and regulate pregnancy.

plankton
The collective term for small, often microscopic, forms of life that live in the upper layers of fresh and salt water, and are an important source of food for larger animals. The algae make up the phytoplankton, while nonphotosynthetic protoctists (protozoans) and tiny animals (often larvae) constitute the zooplankton.

plasma
The liquid part of **blood**.

platelet
A tiny membrane-bound cell fragment in the **blood**, which buds off from large cells in the red bone marrow and helps the blood to clot. Also known as thrombocyte. *See* **clotting**.

poikilothermic
See **cold-blooded animal**.

polygamy
Pairings between animals in which one (usually the male) mates with several females. *See also* **monogamy**.

POLYMORPHISM

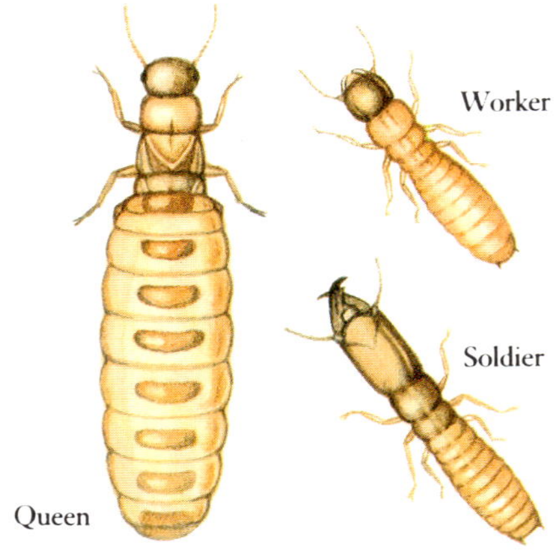

Termites

polymorphism
The coexistence of several distinctly different forms in a group of plants or animals of one species. Examples include the different blood groups in humans, different color forms in some butterflies, and snail shell size, length, shape, color and stripiness, and the differences between male and females of many species.

polyp
The sedentary phase in the life cycle of certain cnidarians (**coelenterates**), the other life form being the free-swimming **medusa**. A polyp is a cup-shaped individual with a single body opening, the mouth, surrounded by stinging tentacles. *See also* **alternation of generations**.

population
A group of animals or plants of one species, living in a certain area and able to interbreed.

pregnancy
Also called gestation, the period during which a human embryo grows within the womb. It begins at fertilization and ends at birth. Human pregnancy lasts 40 weeks.

primate
An order of placental mammals that includes monkeys, apes and humans (together called anthropoids), as well as lemurs, bushbabies, lorises and tarsiers (together called prosimians). Primates have large, complex brains, unspecialized teeth, forward-looking eyes, gripping hands and feet, opposable thumbs, and big toes. They tend to have nails rather than claws, with gripping pads on the ends of the digits, all adaptations to a tree-dwelling, climbing mode of life. Primates produce few young, which need a long period of parental care before reaching maturity.

proboscis
The elongated mouthparts of certain invertebrates, such as the nectar-sucking mouthparts of butterflies.

progesterone
A steroid **hormone** that occurs in vertebrates and prepares the inner lining of the uterus for implantation of a fertilized egg cell. In mammals, it regulates the estrus cycle and pregnancy. Progesterone is secreted by the corpus luteum (the ruptured Graafian follicle of a discharged ovum). It also stimulates the development of the **mammary glands** during pregnancy.

prokaryote
Any unicellular organism whose cells lack membrane-enclosed **organelles**. Prokaryotes include the bacteria and cyanobacteria (blue-green algae). Prokaryote **DNA** is not arranged in chromosomes but forms a coiled structure called a nucleoid. Prokaryote ribosomes are smaller than those of **eukaryotes**.

protein
A complex substance composed of joined amino acids and essential to all living organisms. As enzymes, proteins regulate metabolism. Structural proteins such as keratin and collagen make up the skin, claws, bones, tendons and ligaments; muscle proteins such as myosin produce movement; hemoglobin transports oxygen; and membrane proteins regulate the movement of substances into and out of cells.

CONNECTIONS
CHEMISTRY OF LIFE 62
BUILDING BLOCKS OF LIFE 64
PROCESSING FOOD 66
BUILT FOR MOVEMENT 106

protoctist
Any member of the kingdom Protoctista, which includes the protozoans, algae, diatoms, slime molds, molds, rusts and mildews and other eukaryotic microbes.

protozoan
Any of a group of single-celled organisms without rigid cell walls. Some, such as amebas, ingest other cells, but most are saprotrophs (feeding on nonliving matter) or parasites. All require a fluid environment, and include ciliates, flagellates, dinoflagellates, radiolarians, foraminiferans and sporozoans such as the malaria parasite. Most protozoans reproduce by **binary fission**, although some forms undergo a form of **sexual reproduction** called conjugation.

pseudopod
A "false foot" found in some single-celled animals and in some cells of other organisms (such as human white blood cells). It is an extension of the cell's protoplasm that expands and contracts, propelling the cell forward. Some organisms may also feed by engulfing a food source with a pseudopod.

puberty
The stage in human development when a person becomes sexually mature. It may occur from the age of 10 upward. The sexual organs take on their adult form and pubic hair grows. In girls, menstruation begins, and the breasts develop; in boys, the voice becomes deeper, and facial hair develops.

pupa
The non-feeding, largely immobile stage of some insect life cycles, in which larval tissues are broken down, and adult tissues and structures are formed. In many insects, the appendages (legs, antennae and wings) are visible outside the pupal case; in butterflies and moths, the pupa is called a chrysalis, and is encased in a hardened secretion, with the appendages developing inside the case.

pupil
The central aperture in the iris of the **eye** which allows light to enter the eye.

radial symmetry
The type of symmetry of an organism in which its structures radiate out from a central axis point such that one half of the organism's body will resemble the other half if a cross-section is made through any diameter. The body is usually cylindrical or round. Radial symmetry occurs in **cnidarians** (coelenterates) and **echinoderms**.

red blood cell
Also called erythrocyte, the commonest type of blood cell, responsible for transporting oxygen around the body. Red blood cells contain **hemoglobin**, which combines with oxygen from the lungs to form oxyhemoglobin. When transported to the tissues, these cells then release the bound oxygen. Mammalian erythrocytes are disk-shaped with a depression in the center and no nucleus, and are manufactured in the bone marrow. Those of other vertebrates are oval and nucleated.

reflex action
A very rapid automatic response to a particular stimulus – such as withdrawing the hand from a source of pain – which is controlled by the **nervous system**. A reflex action involves only a few **nerve** cells, consisting of a receptor linked to a sensory neuron, which connects via a **synapse** with a motor neuron (the effector) in the spinal cord or brain (a circuit known as a reflex arc). It is much more rapid a reaction than the more complex responses produced by the many processing nerve cells of the brain.

REPRODUCTION, ASEXUAL

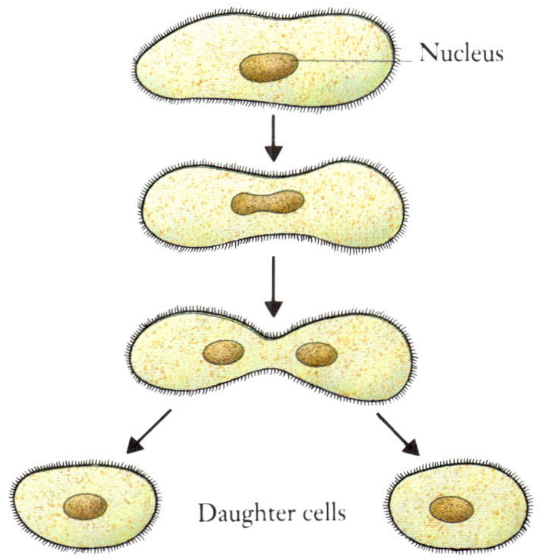

regeneration
The regrowth of a new organ or tissue after the loss or removal of the original. It is common in plants, where a new individual can be produced from a "cutting" of the original. In animals, regeneration of major structures is limited to simple organisms, such as flatworms, corals, spiders and **echinoderms**. In vertebrates, regeneration is limited to the repair of tissue in wound healing and the regrowth of peripheral nerves following damage. An exception is certain lizards, which can regrow their tails.

regurgitation
The act of bringing back digested or partially digested food to the mouth. Regurgitation is a form of feeding that is common in birds and a number of other vertebrates, in which the regurgitated food is used to feed the offspring. *See* **ruminant**.

REPRODUCTION, SEXUAL

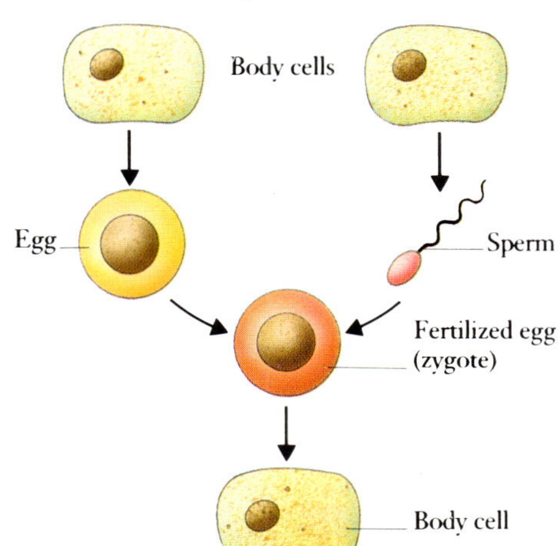

reproduction
The process by which a living organism produces other organisms (its offspring) genetically and physiologically similar to itself. Reproduction may take the form of **asexual reproduction** and **sexual reproduction**. In the latter, specialized organs are required which make up the reproductive system.

CONNECTIONS

PATTERNS OF GROWTH **118**
GETTING TOGETHER **120**
ANIMAL REPRODUCTION **122**
EGG TO EMBRYO **124**

reptile
Any member of the vertebrate class Reptilia, which contains over 6500 species. Reptiles are cold-blooded, and their skin is dry and covered in scales. They have uniform teeth and breathe by means of lungs. Unlike amphibians, reptiles have hard-shelled, yolk-filled eggs containing internal membranes (amniote eggs). These are laid on land and fully formed young hatch from them. Some female snakes and lizards retain their eggs and give birth to live young. Reptiles include the tortoises and turtles, alligators and crocodiles, lizards, snakes, worm lizards (amphisbenids) and the lizard-like tuatara.

respiration
The biochemical process whereby food molecules are broken down (oxidized) to release energy in the form of **adenosine triphosphate (ATP)**. In all higher organisms, respiration occurs in the **mitochondria** of the **cells**. In the first stage (glycolysis) glucose is broken down to pyruvate. This is a form of anaerobic respiration: it does not require oxygen. In the second stage (the Krebs cycle), the pyruvate is further broken down to produce carbon dioxide and water. This is the main energy-producing stage and requires oxygen. Glycolysis and the Krebs cycle are common to all organisms that respirate aerobically. Respiration is different from breathing – drawing of air in and out.

CONNECTIONS

CHEMISTRY OF LIFE **62**
BUILDING BLOCKS OF LIFE **64**
AIR PUMPS **72**
LIVING OFF OTHERS **98**

retina
The light-sensitive area at the back of the **eye**. In vertebrates it is connected to the brain by the **optic nerve**. The retina has several layers and in humans contains over a million rods and cones, sensory cells capable of converting light into nerve impulses that pass along the optic nerve to the brain.

rib
One of the long, usually curved bones that extend laterally from the spine in vertebrates. Most fish and many reptiles have ribs along most of the spine, but in mammals they occur only in the chest area. In humans, there are 12 pairs of ribs. The rib cage, a barrel-shaped cavity formed by the ribs that occurs in many vertebrates, encloses and protects the lungs and heart. Its movement is also important in breathing.

ribosome
A particle within a cell that acts as the site of protein synthesis. Ribosomes are located on the endoplasmic reticulum and are free in the cytoplasm of eukaryotic cells (*see* **eukaryote**), and are made of proteins and a special type of **RNA**, ribosomal RNA. They receive messenger RNA (copied from the DNA) and amino acids, and "translate" the messenger RNA by using its chemically coded instructions to link amino acids in a specific order and thus make a strand of a particular protein. A ribosome measures about 10 nanometers. *See also* **nucleic acid**.

rod
One kind of light-sensitive cell in the **retina** of the eyes of vertebrates (the other kind is a **cone**). Rods respond to low levels of illumination and are concerned mainly with peripheral vision and black and white, unlike cones which provide **color vision**.

rumen
The first part of the four-chambered stomach of a **ruminant**, in which food is stored temporarily before being regurgitated and chewed as cud.

ruminant
A hoofed mammal (suborder Ruminantia), such as cattle, deer, goats and sheep, that chews the cud. Ruminanta have a four-chambered stomach (*see* **rumen**) containing microorganisms that can break down cellulose, the chief component of their food.

rut
A period of sexual excitement and reproductive activity that occurs in certain ruminants (notably deer) and corresponds to periods of **estrus** in the female of the species.

saliva
The secretion from the salivary glands that aids the swallowing and **digestion** of food in the mouth. It contains water, mucus for lubrication, and various enzymes. In humans and herbivorous mammals saliva contains the enzyme amylase, which converts starch to sugar. The saliva of many insects contains other digestive enzymes, and that of blood-sucking insects such as mosquitoes also contains anticoagulants, which halt blood clotting.

scales
Any of a number of small bony or horny plates that form the body covering of reptiles and fish. The wings of some insects, such as butterflies and moths, are covered with small scales which are modified cuticular hairs. Some single-celled protoctists (algae and flagellates) are covered in calcareous scales.

scavenger
Any animal that lives off the dead remains of other animals or plants.

CONNECTIONS

DIETS GALORE **84**
FLESH-EATERS **88**
BREAKDOWN SPECIALISTS **94**

scorpion
Any **arachnid** of the order Scorpiones. Common in the tropics and subtropics, scorpions have large pincers, a squat eight-legged body, and long upcurved abdomens ending in poisonous stings.

sea squirt
A small marine animal belonging to the class Ascidiacea; a type of tunicate. Most sea squirts remain anchored to a rock, filtering food particles from water that flows through their sac-like body.

sebaceous gland
A small **exocrine gland** in the mammalian skin. Its duct opens into the hair follicle, through which it secretes fatty sebum.

sebum
The fatty, mildly antiseptic secretion from the **sebaceous glands** that acts as a skin lubricant and helps to waterproof the skin and hair to prevent desiccation.

segmentation
The division of an animal's body, apart from the head, into a number of compartments each of which contains the same organs. Segmentation is most clearly seen in annelid worms (such as earthworms), in which the muscles, nerve cells, and blood vessels are repeated in each segment.

semicircular canal
One of three looped tubes positioned at right angles to each other that form part of the labyrinth in the inner **ear** of most vertebrates. They are filled with fluid that flows in response to movement and thus detects changes in the position of the head. At the base of each canal is a swollen chamber, the ampulla, which contains a gelatinous plate (cupula) attached to the sensory hairs of a sensory cell. Movement of the fluid move the cupula, which pulls on the hairs, triggering nervous impulses which travel to the brain. *See* **balance**.

sensor
A receptor cell or group of such cells that react to a particular stimulus, such as light or the presence of certain chemicals.

sensory neuron
Any neuron that carries nerve impulses from a sensory receptor to the central nervous system. *See* **nerve**.

septum
A dividing wall such as the septa between the nostrils and those that separate the different chambers of the heart.

sex
The quality of being male or female and the ability to produce two types of **gametes** – sperm in the male and eggs in the female. Whether an organism is male or female may be determined by genetic factors, environmental factors (temperature or the availability of food), or if an egg has been fertilized or not. Hermaphrodites have both male and female reproductive organs.

SEGMENTATION

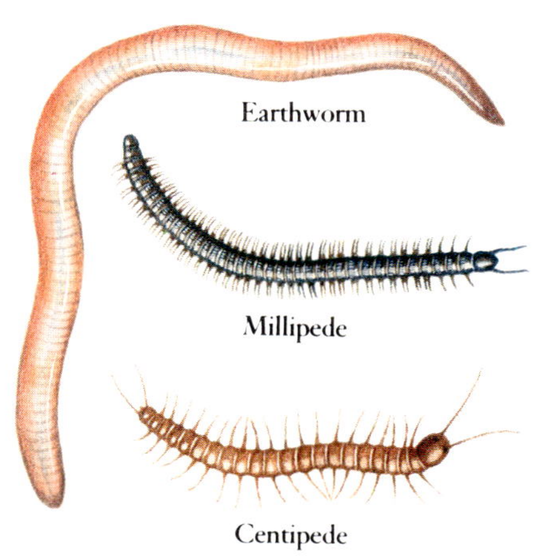

SHELL

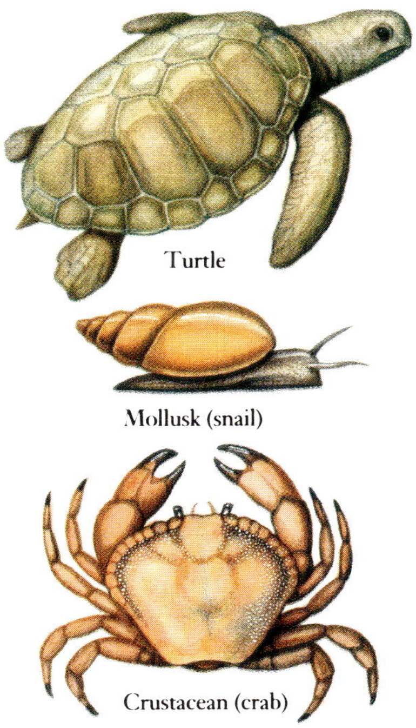

sexual reproduction
The reproductive process in organisms that involves the union (**fertilization**) of **gametes** (sex cells such as sperm and ova) of opposite sex to produce a zygote (fertilized egg) from which a new organism develops. The gametes are usually produced by two separate organisms, although in a number of **hermaphrodites** self-fertilization is also found. *See also* **asexual reproduction** and **parthenogenesis**.

shell
Any protective outer covering, such as the hard covering on crustaceans and mollusks or the outer surface of a bird's egg.

shivering
A mechanism of **thermoregulation** in mammals in which involuntary muscle contraction produces more heat in the body by raising the metabolic rate.

shoulder girdle
See **pectoral girdle**.

single circulation
A circulatory system in which blood passes through the heart once during each complete circuit. Many fishes have single circulatory systems. *See* **circulation**.

siphon
Any of a number of tubular organs used to inhale or expel water, especially in mollusks, sponges and sea squirts. *See* **jet propulsion**.

skin
The outer layer of the body of a vertebrate. It is composed of two layers: an upper layer known as the epidermis (containing **keratin** and cells that produce **melanin**) and a lower layer known as the dermis, together with a complex blood supply and nervous system. The skin protects the body from water loss, disease organisms and mechanical injury, and acts as a sensory organ by detecting pain, pressure and temperature. The skin may be specialized in several ways, such as fur, feathers and scales. In warm-blooded animals, the skin also plays an important role in **thermoregulation**.

small intestine
See **intestine**.

smell
The sense (also known as olfaction) that responds to molecules of chemicals in air or water and is used to detect food and communicate (*see* **pheromone**). Olfactory organs (such as the nose) detect the molecules through the triggering of specific receptors, which transmit the information to the brain along the olfactory nerve.

social insect
An insect that exhibits social behavior, and lives harmoniously in groups with established hierarchies. Examples include bees, wasps, ants and termites. An individual's status and relationship with others depends mainly on its biological form or caste – whether it is a worker, soldier or reproductive. Caste may be determined genetically or influenced by factors such as nutrition during development.

CONNECTIONS

CHANGING SHAPE **128**
INSECT SOCIETIES **140**

sodium pump
The means by which sodium ions are transported out of a **neuron** across a cell membrane. The process is a form of **active transport** and thus requires energy in the form of ATP. It regulates the concentration of sodium ions on each side of the neuron membrane so as to maintain the resting potential of the neuron.

solenocytes
Also known as flame cells. Cup-shaped cells found in a number of multicellular invertebrates, such as flatworms, which draw waste fluids into their cavity by the beating of **cilia** then expel it to the exterior.

spawning
The act of depositing large numbers of eggs (spawn) in water, as seen in fishes, frogs, mollusks and crustaceans.

speciation
The development of a new type of species from an existing species. It occurs when different populations diverge so much from the parent populations that interbreeding can no longer take place between them.

species
See **classification**.

sperm
The mature **gamete** of male animals which is produced in the testes. It consists of a head section which contains the chromosomes and is used for penetrating the egg; a middle, energy-producing section containing many mitochondria; and a tail section (flagellum) which propels the sperm to fertilize the egg.

spermatophore
A packet of sperm which the males of some animals (for instance annelid worms, newts, octopuses, squid) deposit within the females to achieve internal fertilization.

sphincter
A circular muscle that surrounds an organ's opening, allowing it to be opened or closed. For example, the pyloric sphincter controls the flow of food out of the stomach.

spinal cord
The part of the central **nervous system** in vertebrates behind the brain and enclosed in the vertebral column (spine). It is made up of a central hollow core of grey matter (consisting mainly of nerve cell bodies, synapses and dendrites) surrounded by an outer layer of white matter (consisting mainly of nerve axons enclosed in white myelin sheaths). The central cavity contains cerebrospinal fluid, similar in composition to lymph, which bathes the central nervous system.

CONNECTIONS

ANIMALS WITH BACKBONES **56**
ANIMAL MOVEMENT **102**
BUILT FOR MOVEMENT **106**
MOVING THROUGH WATER **114**

spine
Also known as the vertebral column or backbone, a flexible bony column situated along the long axis of **vertebrates** and which provides the main skeletal support. In most mammals it is made up of a series of 26 small

bones called **vertebrae**, separated by a series of cartilaginous disks. It also contains and provides protection for the **spinal cord**.

spiracles
Any of a series of external openings along the side of the body of an insect or arachnid through which oxygen enters the body and carbon dioxide is expelled. The small pair of openings that mark the remains of the first gill slit on the heads of cartilaginous fishes (rays and sharks) are also known as spiracles as are the external openings of the internal gill chamber in amphibian tadpoles and the external nasal opening of cetaceans (whales, dolphins and porpoises).

sponge
Any member of the animal phylum Porifera. Any of the fresh water or marine invertebrates of the phylum Porifera. Sponges have hollow bodies formed from a loose agglomeration of cells between which there is relatively little nervous coordination. The body is supported by an internal skeleton of protein, silica or calcium carbonate. Sponges live permanently attached to rocks or other surfaces. Sponges are filter-feeders. They draw water into their bodies through pores in the body wall using the beating flagella of very characteristic collar cells. The water leaves through a single large exhalant pore. Sponges have only two layers of cells. Some of the cells are amebalike and can move around the sponge. In some species, if the sponge is fragmented and passed through a sieve, the component cells can reassemble into a sponge. For this reason, it has been debated whether sponges are true multicellular animals or colonies of single cells of various types. The former view prevails.

suspension feeding
An important method by which many aquatic and marine animals collect suspended food particles such as plankton from water by sieving, straining or trapping on sticky mucus. Suspension feeders are sedentary animals which either extend appendages into existing water currents or actively waft water past or through their bodies. They include some annelid worms, sponges, plumose anemones, hydroids, sea fans and sea pens, sea mats and featherstars.

sweat
The fluid secreted onto the surface of the **skin** by the sweat glands. The evaporation of sweat cools the skin surface in hairless animals and thus helps to reduce excess body heat. Sweat contains salt (which is depleted by sweating) and small amounts of urea. *See also* **thermoregulation**.

SYNAPSE

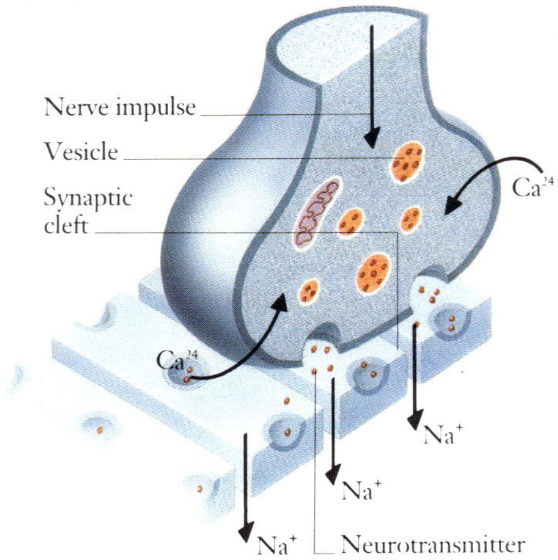

sweat gland
A gland within the epidermis (outer skin) of mammals that produces sweat. Sweat glands are more numerous and widespread in humans and other primates but more restricted in most mammals, especially furry mammals.

swim bladder
A thin-walled air sac between the gut and spine in bony fish. Changes in the air pressure within the swim bladder, produced by air entering the bladder from the gut or surrounding capillaries, help the fish to maintain buoyancy at different water depths.

symbiosis
A close relationship (sometimes called mutualism) between two different species in which both partners benefit from the association. In obligatory symbiosis, the two partners cannot exist without the relationship.

symmetry
The orderly repetition of parts in an organism; in particular, the correspondence of body parts, in terms of relative position, size, and shape, on the opposite sides of an imaginary dividing line or around a central axis. Certain animals, such as an ameba, lack symmetry, although the vast majority of other animals show a definite pattern of symmetry: for example, a left and right arm and leg. *See also* **radial symmetry** and **bilateral symmetry**.

sympathetic nervous system
One of two parts of the **autonomic nervous system** (outside voluntary control). It responds to the body's needs during increased activity and in emergencies, as in the "fight or flight" response. Its nerve endings release the **neurotransmitters** noradrenaline or adrenaline. The actions of the sympathetic nervous system tend to oppose those of the parasympathetic nervous system. For example, the sympathetic nervous system increases the heart rate and decreases salivary gland secretion, whereas the parasympathetic nervous system , which controls regular body functions, has the opposite effect.

CONNECTIONS

CIRCULATION **70**
NERVOUS CONTROL **76**
BUILT FOR MOVEMENT **106**

synapse
The junction between two **nerve** cells or between a nerve cell and a muscle (a neuromuscular junction) across which a nerve impulse is transmitted. The cell membranes are separated by a very small gap (the synaptic cleft). The nerve impulse causes the release of calcium ions, which stimulate vesicles containing a **neurotransmitter** to move to the membrane bordering the synaptic cleft. The neurotransmitter is released into the cleft, and diffuses across to receptor sites on the membrane of the second cell. This triggers the dendrites of the second cell to propagate an impulse along its length; this action may either excite or inhibit further impulses in the second cell. To prevent continued transmission of the impulse, the neurotransmitter is immediately broken down by an **enzyme**.

tapetum
A light-reflecting layer in the eyes of nocturnal vertebrates such as cats and owls. It reflects light onto the retina, improving night vision and causing the animal's eyes to shine in the dark.

taste
The sense that detects some of the chemical constituents of food. The human tongue can distinguish four basic tastes: sweet, salt, bitter or sour. The sense of taste is strongly influenced by smell.

taste bud
A sense organ specialized for the detection of **taste**. In land-living animals the taste buds are concentrated on the upper surface of the tongue.

taxonomy
See **classification**.

tears
A watery substance secreted from the tear (lacrimal) glands in the upper nose of most higher vertebrates. Tears wash the eyes and keep them free from dust.

teeth
The set of hard, strong structures on the jaws and in or around the mouth and pharynx of vertebrates, used to bite and chew food and for aggression and defense. Vertebrate teeth evolved from bony outgrowths of the skin. They usually comprise an enamel coat (made mainly of hardened calcium phosphate deposits), dentine (a thick bony layer), and an inner pulp cavity containing nerves and blood vessels. There are some exceptions: lampreys have simple horny teeth, and amphibian tadpoles have horny jaws. The teeth of fish and amphibians have no roots, but are anchored to the bones by **connective tissue**. The teeth of mammals, snakes and lizards have roots which are cemented in place. Except in mammals, the teeth are usually continually replaced as they wear down – new ones move forward from the inside of the jaw. The teeth of fish and mammals come in a wide variety of shapes and sizes, specialized for different diets.

tendon
A thick cord or sheet of tissue that attaches a **muscle** to a **bone**. Tendons are largely composed of collagen and are relatively inelastic, ensuring transfer of the force exerted by muscle contraction to the part of the body that is to be moved.

tentacle
A slender, elongated flexible organ found in some invertebrates, and around the mouths and chins of certain fish. Tentacles may be used for grasping prey, filter-feeding, locomotion, defense, or as sense organs.

territory
A defined area from which an animal or group of animals excludes other members of the same species. Outside of the territory other animals are not threatened. Animals may hold territories to provide nesting areas, to ensure a constant food supply for themselves or their families, to display to the opposite sex and/or monopolize potential mates. Territorial behavior such as establishing, marking and defending a territory occurs in many different species and may differ within a species depending on the availability of resources.

CONNECTIONS

GETTING TOGETHER **120**
MAMMAL SOCIETIES **142**

testes
The reproductive organs that produce **sperm** in male animals. In vertebrates there are two testes, which also produce steroid **hormones** (mainly testosterone). In most animals the testes are located within the body; however, in mammals they descend from the body during development to hang outside the abdomen in the scrotal sac.

TEETH

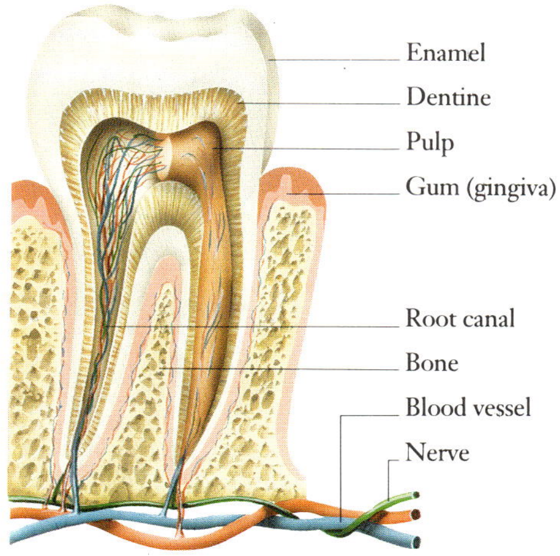

testosterone
The reproductive hormone secreted by the **testes** and to a lesser extent by the adrenal cortex. In human males it promotes the development of male secondary sex characteristics, such as the growth of facial hair and the deepening of the voice.

thermoregulation
The general mechanism by which an organism controls its body temperature. In **cold-blooded animals** the body temperature depends upon the temperature of the surroundings. Such an animal can control its temperature only by behavioral means, such as moving into the shade in hot weather, or basking on sun-warmed rocks in cool weather or sheltering underground in cold weather. **Warm-blooded animals** (mammals and birds) have specific internal mechanisms for maintaining their body temperature within narrow limits, often considerably higher than that of their surroundings.

CONNECTIONS

CIRCULATION **70**
NERVOUS CONTROL **76**
CONTROLLING HEAT AND WATER **78**
HIDDEN SENSES **138**

thorax
In vertebrates, the part of the body containing the lungs and heart, and protected by the rib cage. It is separated from the abdomen by the muscular diaphragm. In insects the thorax bears the legs and wings. In crustaceans and spiders the thorax is fused with the head to form the cephalothorax.

thrombin
The enzyme that catalyzes the conversion of soluble fibrinogen to insoluble fibrin during blood **clotting**.

thyroid gland
An **endocrine gland** of vertebrates situated in the neck at the front of the trachea. It secretes a number of important iodine-containing **hormones** (thyroxine and triiodothyronine) which act as regulators of the body's metabolic rate and control physical growth and development, and calcitonin, which decreases blood calcium level by promoting the deposition of calcium and phosphate in bone. The activity of the thyroid is controlled by the enzyme thyrotrophin, secreted by the anterior pituitary gland.

thyroxine
The principal hormone secreted by the thyroid gland. *See* **thyroid gland**.

tissue
A group of cells of similar structure which are organized to carry out a particular function. There are many different types of tissue. Examples are nerve and muscle tissues and the sheet-like epithelia lining the intestines in animals. Different kinds of tissues may be grouped together to form an organ.

tongue
A muscular organ in vertebrates, usually attached to the floor of the mouth. It plays an important role in directing food during chewing and swallowing. In land-living vertebrates the upper surface of the tongue may be covered with **taste buds**. In some advanced vertebrates the tongue is used to produce sounds. Thus humans use it as an important element in producing speech.

touch
The sensation produced by stimulation of specialized nerve endings in the skin. Some respond to light pressure, some to heavy pressure. Some animals have special organs of touch that protrude from the surface of the animal's skin; these include whiskers (**vibrassae**) and antennae.

toxin
Any chemical that can cause damage to the body, particularly those produced by living organisms. For example, bacteria produce numerous toxins. An endotoxin is released when the cell dies and disintegrates. An exotoxin is secreted into the surrounding

medium by the bacterial cell. Toxins are broken down by the action of enzymes, mainly those of the liver. Antitoxins counteract the effect of the toxin molecules.

trachea
The tube that forms the main airway in air-breathing animals. In land-living vertebrates it is a strong flexible tube (also known as the windpipe) strengthened by incomplete rings of cartilage that runs from the larynx to the upper chest, where it divides to form the two bronchi. Insects have a branching network of tubes called tracheae that conduct air from the spiracles in the body surface to all of the body tissues. The finest of these branches of the tracheae are called tracheoles.

tube foot
Any of the small, mobile tubular structures found on echinoderms (such as starfish) which are used for movement or grasping. Tube feet are extended and retracted by hydrostatic pressure as fluid is admitted from the water vascular system. Their movement is controlled by muscles. Some tube feet may end in suckers.

tubeworm
Any tube-dwelling worm, but especially annelid worms which secrete tubes of calcium carbonate (such as serpulid worms and featherduster worms) or construct cylinders of sand grains glued together with mucus (such as sandmason worms). These worms extend a crown of feathery tentacles into the water to filter-feed, but can retract them rapidly into the tube for protection.

ungulate
The general name given to any hoofed mammal. Ungulates are further divided into odd-toed ungulates (order Perissodactyla): (horses, tapirs, rhinos) and even-toed ungulates (order Artiodactyla): pigs, camels, cows, deer, antelope), along with subungulates such as elephants.

urea
The waste product formed when proteins are broken down in the **liver**. The **amino acids** are broken down to ammonia and carbon dioxide (the process of deamination), which are then combined to form urea ($CO(NH_2)_2$). Urea is a soluble compound and is excreted in the urine.

urine
The watery fluid formed by the excretory organs of animals for the removal of metabolic waste. It is produced in the **kidneys** and stored in the bladder before being excreted through the urethra or cloaca. In addition to water, the major constituents of urine are ammonia, uric acid, urea, creatine, inorganic ions, amino acids and purines. The precise composition varies greatly according to the species, its diet and its environment.

uterus
The sac-like organ in female mammals in which the **embryo** develops. It is located between the bladder and the rectum, with the fallopian tubes above and the vagina below. It has a thick muscular outer wall which, by contracting, forces the fully developed **fetus** through the vagina to the outside at the end of **pregnancy**. The uterus increases greatly in size during pregnancy. In lower vertebrates and invertebrates, uterus describes the lower part of the female reproductive tract.

vacuole
A membrane-bound fluid-filled cavity within a **cell** that may be used to store or digest food, store harmful waste or, in certain protozoans such as ameba, to regulate the water content and osmotic potential of the cell.

vagina
The elastic muscular tube in female animals leading from the **uterus** to the outside. Sperm are deposited in the vagina during copulation and the fully developed fetus is born through it at the end of pregnancy. The lining of the vagina produces mucus which prevents friction and traps and destroys bacteria.

variation
The difference between individuals of the same species, caused by environmental and/or hereditary (genetic) factors. Some examples of variation can be seen in coloring, size, behavior, and biochemistry.

CONNECTIONS
LIFE'S GREAT VARIETY **48**
FINDING FOOD **82**
GROWTH AND REPRODUCTION **116**
ANIMAL REPRODUCTION **122**
CHANGING SHAPE **128**

vasoconstriction
A reduction in the internal diameter of blood vessels, especially arterioles or **capillaries**. Vasoconstriction of arterioles results in an increase in **blood pressure**.

vasodilation
An increase in the internal diameter of blood vessels, especially arterioles or **capillaries**. Vasodilation of arterioles results in a decrease in **blood pressure**.

vein
A vessel that carries **blood** from the body to the heart. Veins have thin walls and a relatively large internal diameter. Veins always carry deoxygenated blood, with the exception of the pulmonary veins, which carry newly oxygenated blood from the lungs. The term is more loosely used for any system of channels which strengthens a living tissue or which provides nutrients to them, such as leaf veins in plants and wing veins in insects.

venom
Any toxic secretion produced by animals either for killing or paralyzing prey or as a defense mechanism. Venomous species are found in many animal groups, but few are dangerous to humans. Exceptions include certain snakes, scorpions, spiders, social insects and jellyfishes. The effects of venoms on the prey include violent inflammations, widespread hemorrhage and irritative effects on the nervous system.

CONNECTIONS
FLESH-EATERS **88**
HUNTING TECHNIQUES **90**

ventilation
The method by which air or water carrying oxygen is brought into contact with respiratory surfaces inside an animal so as to enable gas exchange. *See* **breathing**.

ventral
Relating to the lower surface of an animal: in a four-legged vertebrate, the surface nearest the ground. *See also* **dorsal**.

vertebral disk
Any of the cartilaginous disks that separate the vertebrae (individual bones) in the backbone (**spine**).

vertebrate
Any animal of the subphylum Vertebrata in the phylum Chordata. All vertebrates possess a backbone (vertebral column, or spine). There are more than 41,000 species of vertebrates, divided into seven classes: Agnatha (jawless fishes), Chondrichthyes (cartilaginous fishes), Osteichthyes (bony fishes), Amphibia, Reptilia, Aves (birds) and Mammalia. In vertebrates the more flexible vertebral column has replaced the **notochord**, permitting greater freedom of movement, the control of which required the evolution of more developed sense organs and a larger brain. The **brain** of all vertebrates is enclosed in a skeletal case, the cranium or skull. *See* **spine**.

villus
Any numerous small fingerlike outgrowths from the lining of the small **intestine** which serve to increase its surface area for the absorption of **nutrients**.

virus
A microscopic infectious particle consisting of a core of nucleic acid (DNA or RNA) enclosed in a protein coat. Viruses are not made up of cells and are capable of independent metabolism and reproduction only within a living cell. They program the host cell to synthesize replicas of themselves, disrupting the host's own DNA and cellular function. Viruses cause many diseases such as AIDS, influenza and rabies in animals.

vitamin
Any of a number of chemically unrelated nutrient compounds essential for normal body function and growth. Most act as coenzymes (small molecules that help enzymes to function properly). Deficiency of a vitamin normally leads to a metabolic disorder or "deficiency disease" which can be corrected by sufficient intake of the vitamin. For instance, scurvy is a deficiency disease which results from the lack of vitamin C in the diet. Vitamins are generally classed as water-soluble (vitamins B and C) or fat-soluble (vitamins A, D, E and K).

CONNECTIONS
CHEMISTRY OF LIFE **62**
BUILDING BLOCKS OF LIFE **64**
PROCESSING FOOD **66**

vivipary
A method of reproduction in which the developing embryo obtains its nourishment directly from the mother via a **placenta** or

VIRUS

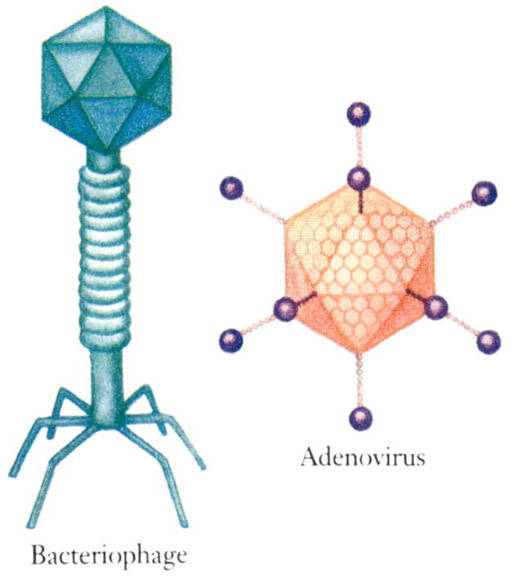

other means, before being born live. It occurs in some insects and other arthropods, certain fish, amphibians and reptiles, and the majority of mammals. Marsupials are not viviparous: the mother nourishes the embryo within the body in the early stages of development, but the tiny immature creature is then transferred to the mother's external pouch and fed on milk while developing sufficiently to leave the pouch.

warm-blooded animal
An animal whose body temperature is internally regulated. Birds and mammals are the only warm-blooded animals; all others are cold-blooded. Warm-blooded animals (also called endothermic or homeothermic) use the energy generated by body metabolism to keep their body temperature within narrow limits, usually independent of the surrounding environment.

warning coloration
The use of bright and conspicuous coloring by an animal that advertises to a possible predator that the animal is unpalatable. For example, many stinging bees and wasps and venomous snakes have distinctive markings of black with red or yellow stripes.

wax
Semisolid or solid lipid derivatives secreted by plants or animals that have a protective function. *See* **sebum**.

whiskers
Stiff sensory hairs (also known as vibrassae) that are found on the faces of many mammals and as short bristlelike hairs around the beak in birds.

white blood cell
(or leukocyte). Unpigmented cells found in the **blood** and bone marrow that are part of the body's defenses and give immunity against disease. There are several different types of white blood cell. Some (phagocytes and macrophages) engulf invading microorganisms, others kill infected cells, whereas lymphocytes produce more specific immune responses. Leukemia is a cancer involving excessive production of white blood cells.

windpipe
See **trachea**.

womb
See **uterus**.

yolk
The store of nutrients in an egg for use by the developing **embryo**. In animals, the yolk sac contains little or no yolk.

zooplankton
The nonphotosynthesizing eukaryotes in the **plankton** (mainly protozoans and the larvae of various invertebrates and fish). *See* **eukaryote**.

VERTEBRATE

1

THE Great Variety

MORE THAN 1.5 MILLION different kinds of plants, animals and other types of living creatures on the Earth today have been identified, and perhaps another 10 million are still to be discovered. One square kilometer of rainforest may contain several hundred species of birds and many thousands of species of butterflies, beetles and other insects, as well as reptiles, amphibians, mammals and soil organisms. Among the great variety of life on Earth is the blue whale, 33.5 meters long and weighing more than 200 tonnes, and giant squids over 17 meters across. At the other end of the scale are tiny worms and other microscopic animals too small to see without the aid of a microscope. There are tortoises that live for more than 150 years, and clams that live for more than two centuries. Animals are to be found in almost every corner of the Earth, from the mountain peaks to dark caves and sunless ocean deeps, from the hottest deserts to the coldest icefields.

Despite the diversity of animal life, all animals have certain features in common. All must take in oxygen and eliminate carbon dioxide gas; feed; remove body wastes; find mates and reproduce. All animals are mobile in some way, even if it is only to move tentacles or mouthparts while feeding. They have many different vital functions, and many body plans adapted to carry them out.

A featherstar clings to a sea fan, waving its arms to filter food particles from the water washing over a coral reef in Papua New Guinea. The sea fan itself is a kind of coral. It owes its bright colors to algae living in intimate association with its tissues. Coral reefs are some of the richest habitats on Earth: they support about 25 percent of all the species found in the oceans, including some 125,000 kinds of animals, from tiny crustaceans to great sharks and octopuses.

SOFT-BODIED ANIMALS

THE earliest animals were one-celled creatures that lived in water, from which they obtained nutrients, and with which they removed wastes produced by their bodies. Because they were small, they did not need a complex body organization to perform these functions. Later, larger bodies with many cells evolved, enabling animals to take in larger quantities of food, move faster and farther, and colonize new areas.

The simplest multicellular animals are known as cnidarians – hydroids, jellyfish, sea anemones and corals. They have simple two-layered bodies with groups of cells (tissues) that are specialized for digestion, movement, coordination, reproduction and so on.

KEYWORDS

ANNELID WORM
CELL
CNIDARIAN
CORAL
DIFFUSION
INVERTEBRATE
JELLYFISH
PERISTALSIS
SEGMENTATION

The next major advance in body structure was the development of a three-layered body, as in platyhelminthes – flatworms, flukes and tapeworms. Between the body wall and the saclike intestine is a cavity, the coelom, in which lie various special structures, called organs, each with a specific function.

Flatworms have sense organs concentrated at a distinct head end and arranged in pairs. This enables them to detect the direction of stimuli. Chemical-sensing cells line pits or grooves at the head end, and probably give a sense of taste, to help the flatworm find food. There are two concentrations of nerve tissues at the head end, the cerebral ganglia. If they are damaged, the animal has problems in feeding, moving and breeding. The intestine, being enclosed, makes digestion more efficient. Most food is taken in by cells lining the intestine and digested inside them.

As animal bodies became larger, proper circulation systems became essential for distributing nutrients and removing waste. Annelid worms, which include earthworms and leeches, represent the next level of organization. In these, a special fluid containing dissolved nutrients and gases – blood – is pumped by multiple hearts through a series of vessels. Because of the worm's long, thin shape, it can still get enough oxygen by diffusion through its body wall; it does not need special structures for oxygen transport.

The annelid worm has hard mouthparts for cutting food, and a more digestive complex system than a flatworm's for processing it. An earthworm feeds by taking in mouthfuls of soil, then extracting organic material from it. The intestine is separated from the rest of the body by a body cavity, so it is free to move and contract independently of the body wall. Waves of muscular action, a process called peristalsis, push the food along the intestine. Most of the digestion is done by digestive juices in the intestine. The earthworm's intestine opens to the outside at the rear end through a special opening, leaving the mouth free simply to take in food.

An earthworm's body is divided into segments, which show as a series of rings on the outside. This is a way of building a large body without increasing complexity. Each segment has its own blood vessels, nerve ganglia, muscles and excretory organs. The segments are filled with fluid, which forms a semi-rigid structure against which the worm's muscles can push to enable it to move.

The annelid worm's movements are much more powerful that those of the flatworm. Earthworms can tunnel through soil, and marine annelids can swim and burrow in sediments.

■ Beautiful but dangerous, a jellyfish RIGHT traps small water creatures on its trailing tentacles. Jellyfish swim by jet propulsion as they contract their bells. Sensory cells in notches around the edge of the jellyfish bell detect changes in light intensity and in food (chemicals) in the water, and the movements of special hard particles (statoliths) provide information about the jellyfish's position in the water and its direction of swimming. Batteries of stinging cells on the tentacles and mouth lobes inject barbed, poison-tipped threads into their prey – and their enemies.

A flatworm BELOW RIGHT is capable of more powerful, finely tuned movements than jellyfish. Bands of cilia help it to glide over solid surfaces, aided by mucus secretions to reduce friction. Some flatworms also swim by undulating their bodies. The muscular pharynx can be protruded to capture prey, and is strong enough to break it into smaller pieces.

■ Jellyfish RIGHT and hydras BELOW are cnidarians and have similar bodies. The walls of their bodies have two layers, separated by a jellylike substance, the mesoglea. A single opening allows the entrance of food and the exit of waste material. Prey trapped by stinging cells is moved by the tentacles to the mouth; in the jellyfish, prey is also swept along grooves in the mouth lobes by beating cilia. The hollow body is lined with beating flagella which move fluid containing food and oxygen around the body. Contractions of the jellyfish bell and movements of the hydra tentacles are achieved by the opposing actions of longitudinal and circular bands of muscle cells, coordinated by a simple network of nerve cells.

▶ Flatworms have a three-layered body with individual organs. Branches of the intestine distribute food around the body. A series of flame cells linked to the intestine extract waste and pass it into excretory tubes for discharge through excretory pores. Concentrations (ganglia) of nerve cells at the head end serve the eyespots and other sensory areas.

▶ Earthworms have a separate mouth and anus. The pouchlike crop is used for storing food. The gizzard has muscular walls for grinding food, aided by small stones swallowed by the worm. Waste is extracted by organs called nephridia. The fluid in the body segments forms a semi-rigid structure against which the worm's muscles push as it moves. Blood is pumped by a series of hearts through the blood vessels.

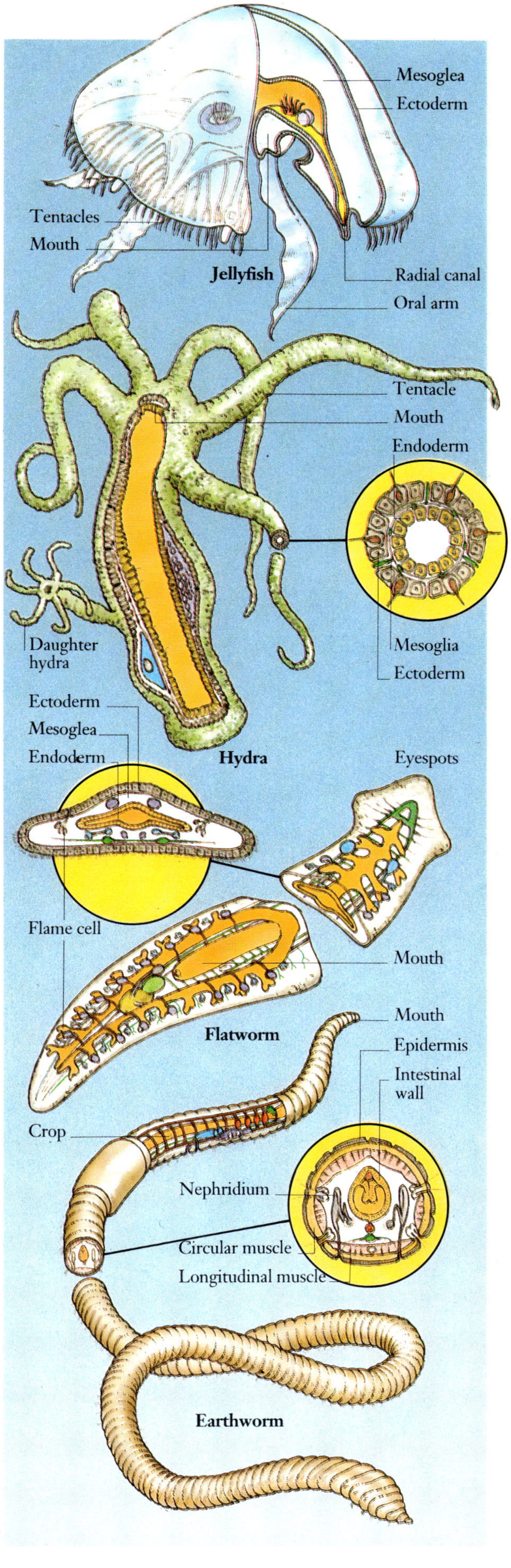

SHELLS AND SPINES

MOLLUSKS and echinoderms have a single fluid-filled body cavity with complex organs for breathing, processing food and getting rid of waste. Early in their evolution, these two groups of animals developed hard protective shells. The shell greatly reduces the area across which oxygen can diffuse into the body, so a circulatory system is needed to transport The mollusk's body is filled with blood, which carries oxygen, food, carbon dioxide and other waste materials. A muscular heart pumps the blood through vessels into the body cavity, and it returns through veins. Most mollusks have gills for absorbing oxygen from water and releasing waste carbon dioxide into it. Fine blood vessels run through the gills, bringing carbon dioxide for removal and picking up oxygen. The gills lie protected in the mantle cavity, which lies between the body organs and the shell. The mantle, a thin layer of tissue, is secreted by the shell and protects the internal organs.

KEYWORDS

BIVALVE
CEPHALOPOD
ECHINODERM
JET PROPULSION
MANTLE
TUBE FOOT

In bivalves – mollusks such as scallops, clams and mussels – the gills act as strainers, filtering food from the water. Most other mollusks have a special structure called a radula for breaking down their food. The mollusk's digestive system includes a pharynx, stomach and intestine. The muscular pharynx helps food pass to the stomach, which is supplied with digestive juice by large digestive glands. Plant-eating mollusks have a long intestine, because plant material is not easy to digest, and a cecum – a pouch linked to the intestine which contains bacteria to break down tough plant fibers. Waste material passes into the blood and is removed by the kidneys before leaving the body through small pores in the body wall. The most advanced mollusks, the cephalopods, have highly sophisticated eyes to track their quarry, a complex nervous system, and (for mollusks) a large brain.

In most echinoderms – the group including starfish, sea urchins and sea cucumbers – the body parts are arranged in fives, or multiples of five, an arrangement not found anywhere else in the animal kingdom. The shell of an echinoderm is not its outer layer; rather, it acts as a skeleton.

Echinoderms have a circulatory system of water-filled canals operated by water pressure. Muscle contractions extend the tube feet, which in some species end in powerful suckers strong enough to pull apart the shells of mussels.

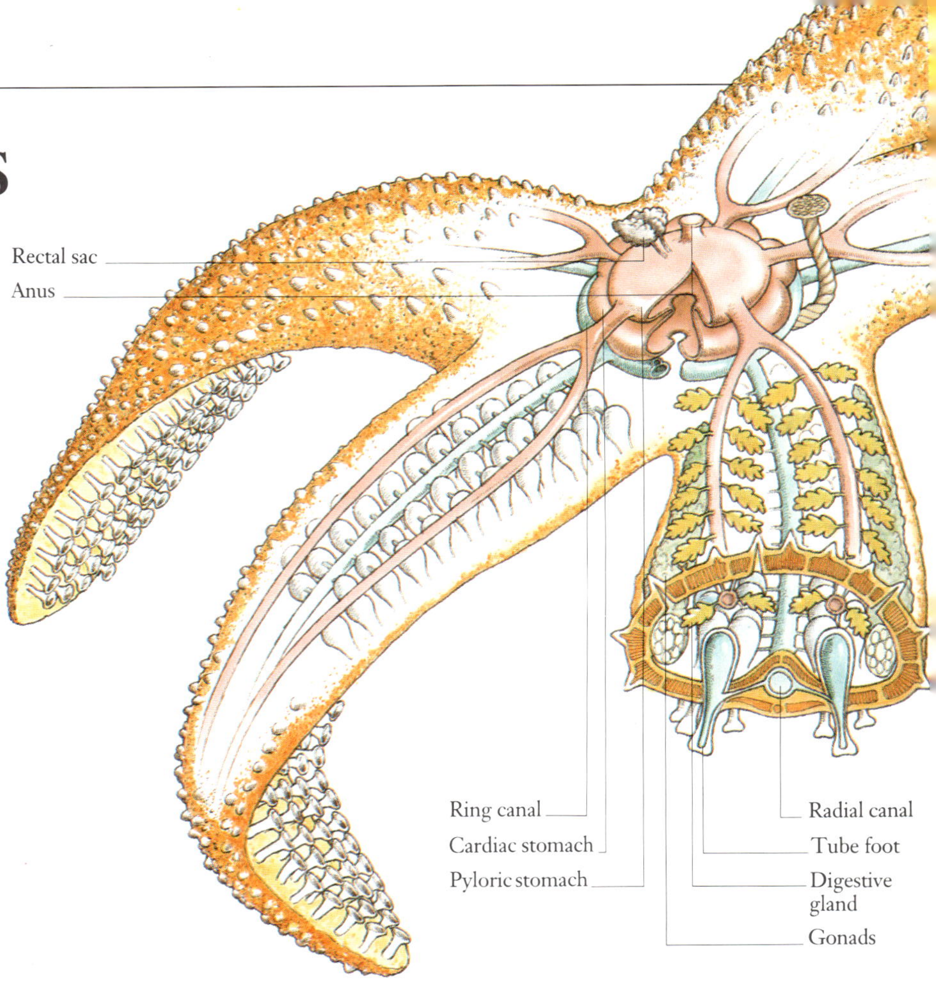

■ The most common mollusk groups are the gastropods, bivalves, chitons (coat-of-mail shells), cephalopods (octopus, cuttlefish and squid) and nautiluses. Cephalopods travel by jet propulsion, pumping water out of the mantle cavity through a special funnel. Gastropods, chitons and bivalves use a large muscular foot for locomotion and burrowing.

Gastropods and chitons have a radula, a tiny tongue with small teeth, which is used to rasp at plants or prey. Bivalves such as scallops, mussels and clams are filter-feeders. They draw in water through a siphon and pass it over their gills, where food particles are strained through tiny pores. The water leaves the mantle cavity through another siphon.

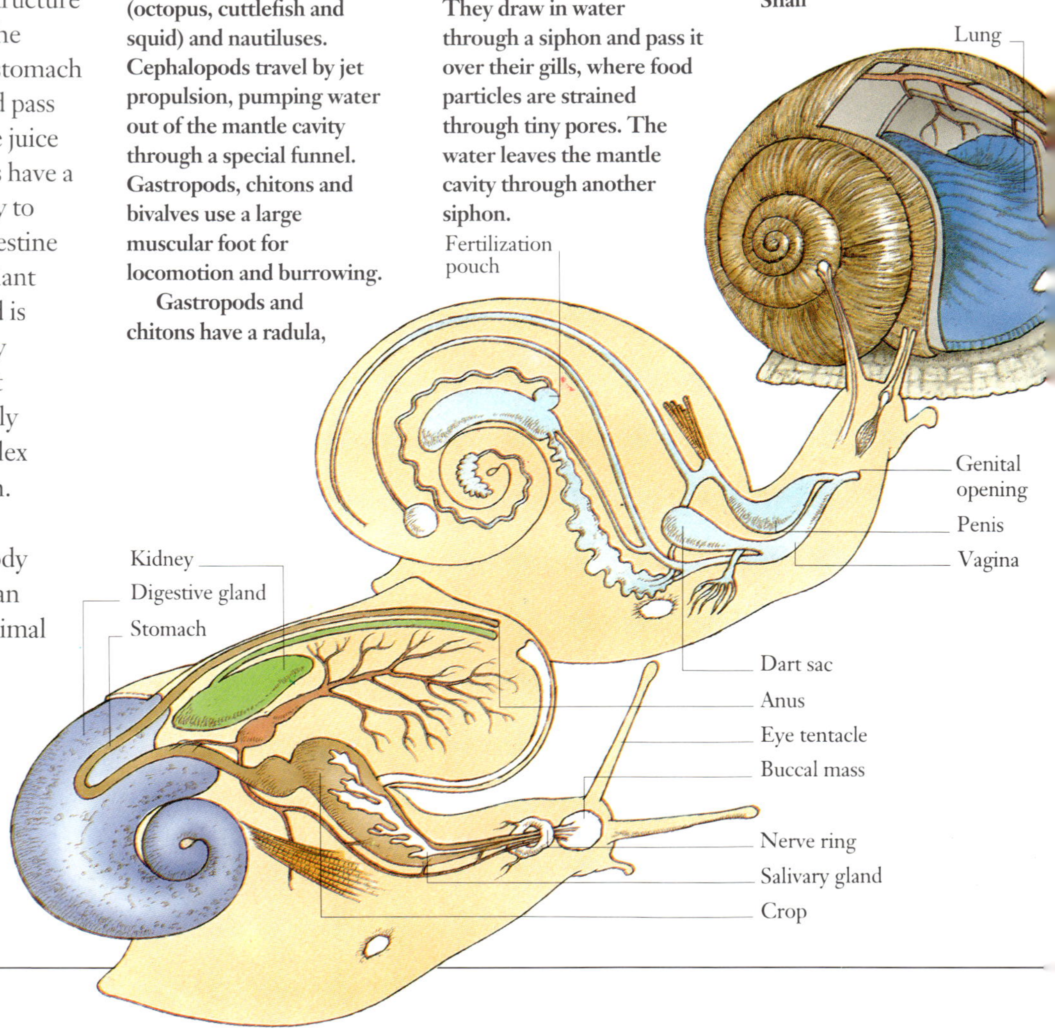

■ Starfish FAR LEFT and sea urchins LEFT and BELOW have a unique vascular system operated by water pressure, used to transport dissolved gases, food and waste products. The water-filled canals also fill tiny tube feet used for movement and gripping. On starfish and sea urchins, pincerlike pedicellariae are used for grooming, or produce venom for defense. Sea urchins also have movable spines.

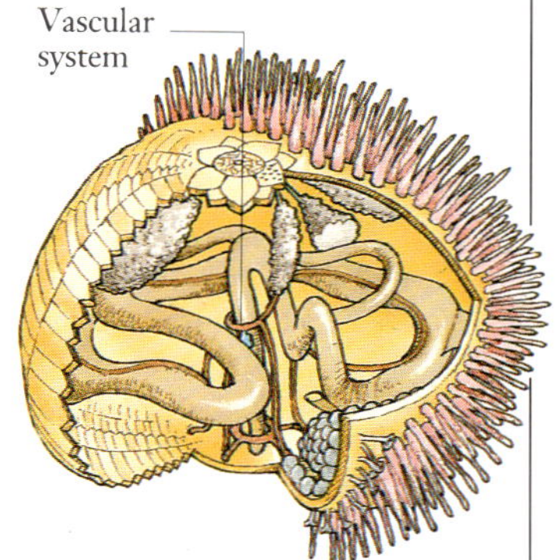

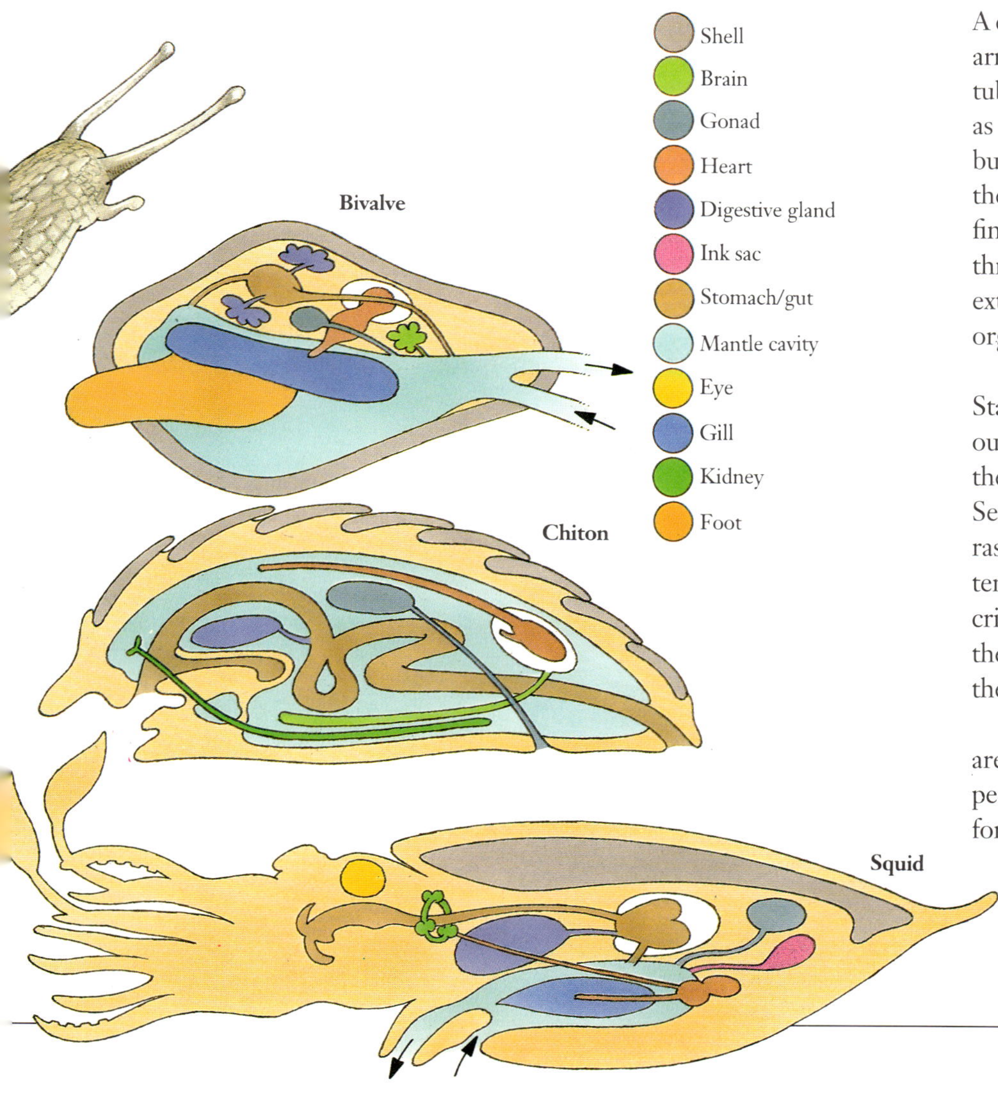

A central nerve ring coordinates the movements of the arms, and smaller fibers control movements of the tube feet. At the tips of the arms, modified tube feet act as eyespots. There are no other obvious sense organs, but echinoderms are sensitive to chemicals dissolved in the water. Gas exchange takes place through small fingerlike skin gills, or tabulae, which protrude through spaces between the shell plates, and to a lesser extent through the tube feet. There are no special organs for excretion.

The mouth varies with the mode of feeding. Starfish feed externally by turning the stomach inside out through the mouth to envelope the prey, digesting the soft parts and sucking in the digested material. Sea urchins have a group of hard plate-like teeth for rasping at corals and algae. Many sea cucumbers have tentacles for sifting detritus, and feather stars and crinoids feed by filtering food from the water around them, using sheets of sticky mucus that stream over their arms.

On the outer surface of starfish and echinoderms are many small movable structures. There are many pedicellariae – small pincers on stalks. Some are used for grooming, while others carry venom sacs and are used for defense. Sea urchins also have movable spines as well as external structures. In sea cucumbers, the tube feet around the mouth take the form of tentacles, and are used in feeding.

Jointed Legs

THERE are some 750,000 known species of insects, and perhaps several million more species that are as yet undiscovered. Insects can be said to be the most successful animals on Earth in terms of their survival and numbers. They occupy almost every habitat where life can be found, from polar ice sheets to the driest, hottest deserts and the smallest rain puddles. Only in the oceans are there almost no insects. There, their place is taken by their close relatives, the crustaceans.

KEYWORDS

ARACHNID
ARTHROPOD
CHITIN
CRUSTACEAN
CUTICLE
INSECT
MOLTING
SEGMENTATION
SKELETON

Crustaceans, insects, and arachnids (spiders and scorpions) all belong to the animal phylum Arthropoda, or "joint-legged animals". Their bodies are covered in a hard, light shell made of chitin (a carbohydrate). Their limbs, antennae and other appendages are made up of many small segments linked at flexible joints. In the insects, these segments are fused together to form three main sections – the head, thorax and abdomen. In arachnids and crustaceans there are only two sections: the cephalothorax (head and thorax) and the opisthosoma or abdomen.

The rigid external skeleton provides a firm base for muscles. For its weight, the tubular structure of arthropod skeletons is far stronger than the solid structure of a vertebrate's internal bones. Arthropods can walk, run, jump, swim and fly. Their tough chitin exterior provides protection not only against their enemies, but also against the weather, especially the drying effect of sun and wind. Many arthropods are so small that they can live in places that few other animals can reach.

In order to grow, arthropods have to shed their shells – molt – from time to time, exposing their soft bodies to danger from predators. The shell also limits the size to which they can grow. The largest arthropod, the giant spider crab, with a leg span up to 5.79 meters, lives in the ocean, where the water supports its bulk.The largest land arthropod, a longhorn beetle from South America, is only 20 centimeters long.

In some ways, arthropods resemble annelid worms. Many body structures, such as the tracheae they use for breathing, branches of the blood vessels and of the nervous system, are repeated in each segment, and the pairs of limbs are each attached to a single segment. But they have well-developed and complex organs like those of mollusks – a digestive system in which different sections play different roles; one heart and a blood transport system that discharges the blood into the body cavity, or hemocoel; a brain and nervous system; and sense organs that include eyes, antennae for touch and taste, and sensory hairs and bristles.

The exoskeleton restricts the amount of oxygen that can be taken in by diffusion. Insects have a series of breathing tubules, the tracheae, that open to the outside through tiny pores. Many arachnids have book lungs – highly folded layers of the body wall with a large surface area for diffusion. Crustaceans breathe through gills on the body segments.

Arthropods feed on almost any kind of organic material. Grasshoppers, caterpillars and wasps have hard saw-edged mouthparts for chewing tough vegetation and fruit. Aphids and other bugs have piercing stylets for penetrating plant stems and sucking out the sap. Crabs and lobsters can tackle shellfish with their pincers and tough mouthparts; and many shrimps, barnacles and other small water creatures filter-feed using rows of bristles as sieves. There are aerial hunters such as dragonflies; predators that lie in wait like praying mantids; and trappers like web-spinning spiders. Many other arthropods, especially insects and crustaceans, have become parasites, living in or on other animals.

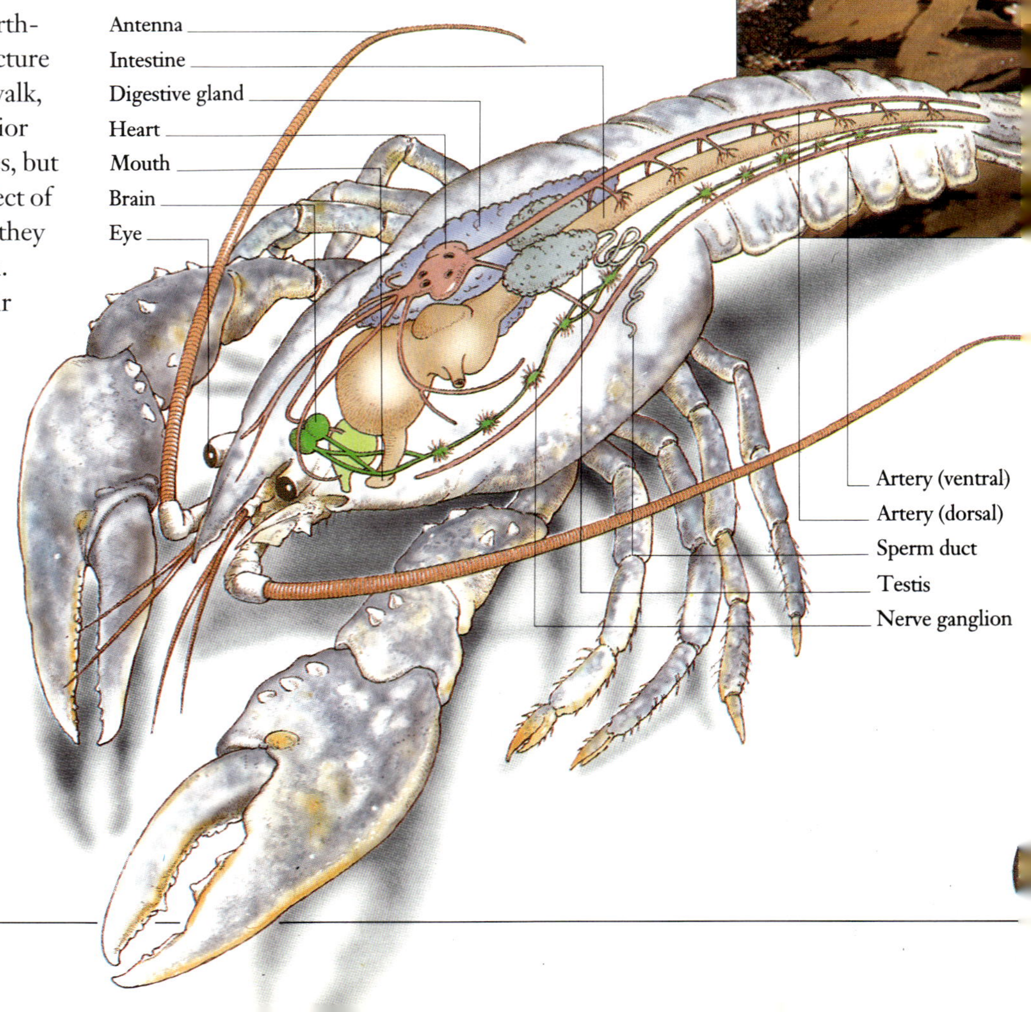

■ The crustaceans include crabs, lobsters FAR LEFT, shrimps and prawns, barnacles, copepods, water fleas, woodlice and pillbugs. Most crustaceans have very strong shells reinforced with calcium salts. Whereas insects have only one pair of antennae (feelers), crustaceans have two pairs, which are branched, and their limbs are often branched, too.

The arachnids include spiders TOP and BELOW LEFT, scorpions, ticks and mites. They have simple eyes (spiders often have more than one pair) and four pairs of walking legs. In spiders the body divides into two main sections – the prosoma and opisthosoma. There are no antennae, but the pedipalps act as feelers. Spiders feed by secreting or injecting digestive juices onto or into their prey, then sucking up the liquid food that results.

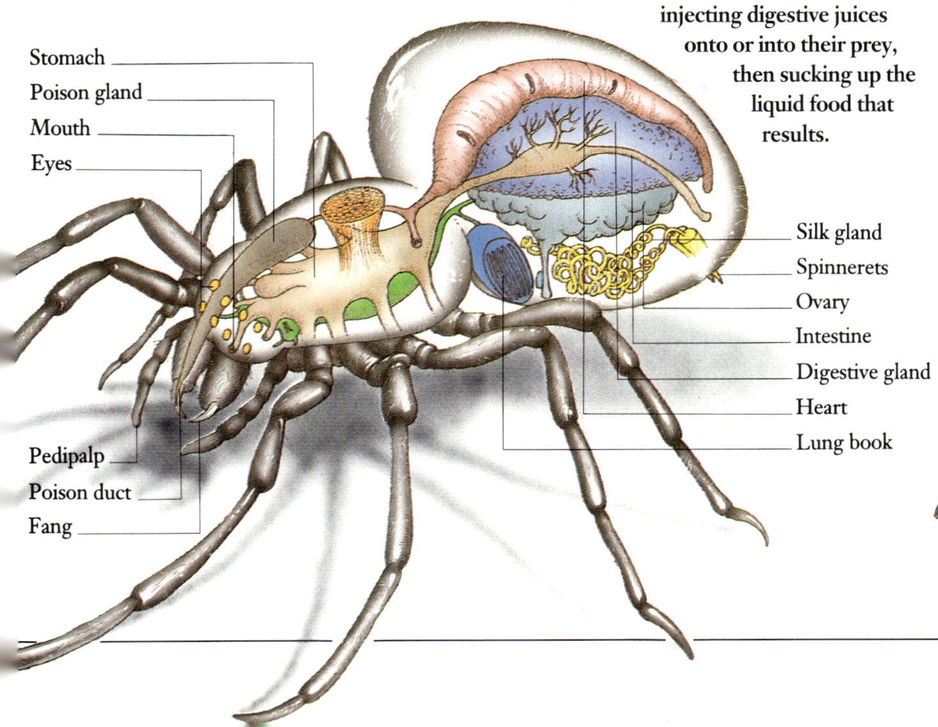

Insect Bodies

Insects range in size from beetles only 0.1 millimeter long to tropical moths with a wingspan of 30 centimeters. The nearly one million species are distinct from other arthropods. The insect body is divided into the head, thorax and abdomen. The head has one pair of antennae; two large compound eyes (in the adult); and sometimes one or more simple eyes. There are usually three pairs of legs, and up to two pairs of wings, attached to the thorax, which is made up of three segments. The abdomen is divided into further segments with the digestive, excretory and reproductive organs. Males and females are often strikingly dissimilar.

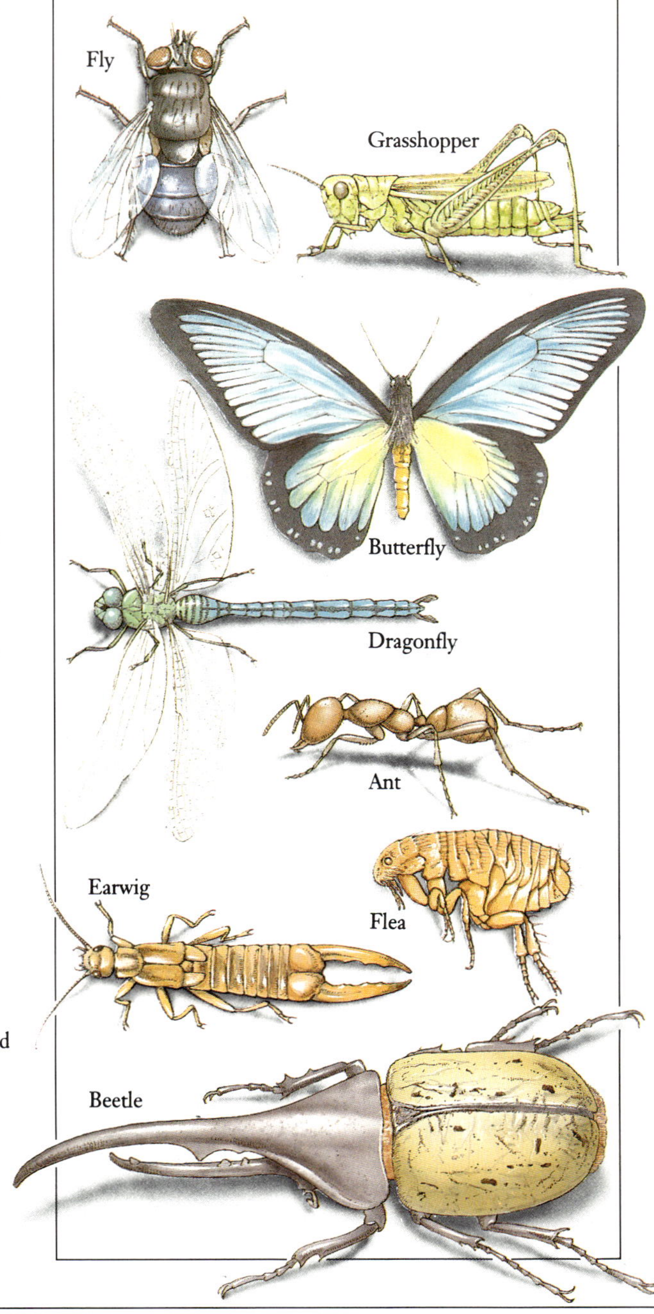

Animals with Backbones

Some of the most numerous animals are the vertebrates. The oceans are teeming with fish, whales and dolphins. Frogs, newts and salamanders thrive in wet places on land; reptiles are equally at home in deserts and steamy jungles. Mammals dominate land habitats, and birds the air.

All these animals are vertebrates: their bodies are supported by an internal skeleton with a jointed backbone, usually made of bone. Bone is a strong material capable of holding up considerable body weight: an African elephant weighs some 5.7 tonnes. The brain case or skull encloses the delicate tissues of the brain, and the rib cage protects most of the internal organs. Deposits of fat also help protect the vital organs.

KEYWORDS

BINOCULAR VISION
BONE
CHORDATE
ENDOSKELETON
LATERAL LINE SYSTEM
NOTOCHORD
SKIN
SPINE
VERTEBRATE

Like the limb segments of arthropods, the bones of vertebrates act as levers that pivot around a series of joints. Vertebrate ball-and-socket joints such as the shoulder and hip joints allow a much wider range of movement.

Vertebrate body plans have been adapted for swimming, diving, crawling, burrowing, walking, running, jumping, climbing, gliding and flying. This range of locomotion calls for sophisticated sense organs. Vertebrate eyes are the most highly developed in the animal kingdom. They are so large that they occupy distinctive hollows, or orbits, in the skull. Many vertebrates have binocular vision, which allows them to judge speed and distance. Hearing and smell are also highly developed in some mammals: sound and scnet are important forms of communication. Fish and some amphibians have a lateral line system which is sensitive to vibrations in the water caused by the movements of nearby objects or other animals. Interpreting so many sensory signals and coordinating responses and movements calls for a large, specialized brain and a complex nervous system.

Because the vertebrate skeleton is internal, the outer body covering is important for protection against physical injury and against the elements. The skin is a complex, self-renewing covering that contains many sensory cells for detecting touch, pressure, heat and pain. Outgrowths of the skin form the most distinctive features of the different groups of vertebrates. The scales of fish help to waterproof them, and also improve their streamlining. Amphibians have moist skins through which they absorb oxygen. Reptiles have tough scales which prevent the skin from drying out. Birds have feathers to provide warmth, streamlining and a strong, light surface for pushing against the air during flight. Mammals have hair for warmth. Hair and feathers are often colored for display or camouflage, and can be further waterproofed by coating in oily secretions.

Vertebrates belong to a larger group of animals, the phylum Chordata or chordates. This group includes sea squirts and lancelets (small, fishlike animals that live on seabeds). All animals in the phylum Chordata are distinguished by a flexible, segmented supporting rod, the notochord, which runs along the animal's back. This is still easy to see in the lancelet, and in the tadpoles of sea squirts. In vertebrates it is represented by the backbone.

Another chordate feature is a dorsal nerve cord lying above the notochord. In vertebrates this spinal cord is enclosed within the vertebrae and disks. The third feature of chordates is the presence of gill slits along the sides of the gill chamber behind the mouth. Whereas these are obvious in fish and in amphibian tadpoles, they are still present in the early embryos of all other vertebrates.

■ Mammals represent the pinnacle of vertebrate evolution. Their limbs are positioned under the body rather than at the side, for faster and more efficient movement. Animals such as the lion BELOW, which travel long distances, have part of the foot raised off the ground to reduce friction. Ridges on the skull provide attachment points for powerful jaw muscles.

The frog skeleton RIGHT is adapted for jumping. The powerful hind limbs provide thrust, while fusion of bones in the forelimbs and spine helps resist the impact of landing.

Fish FAR RIGHT are supported by the water, but they need a strong, flexible skeleton against which muscle blocks can pull to provide propulsion.

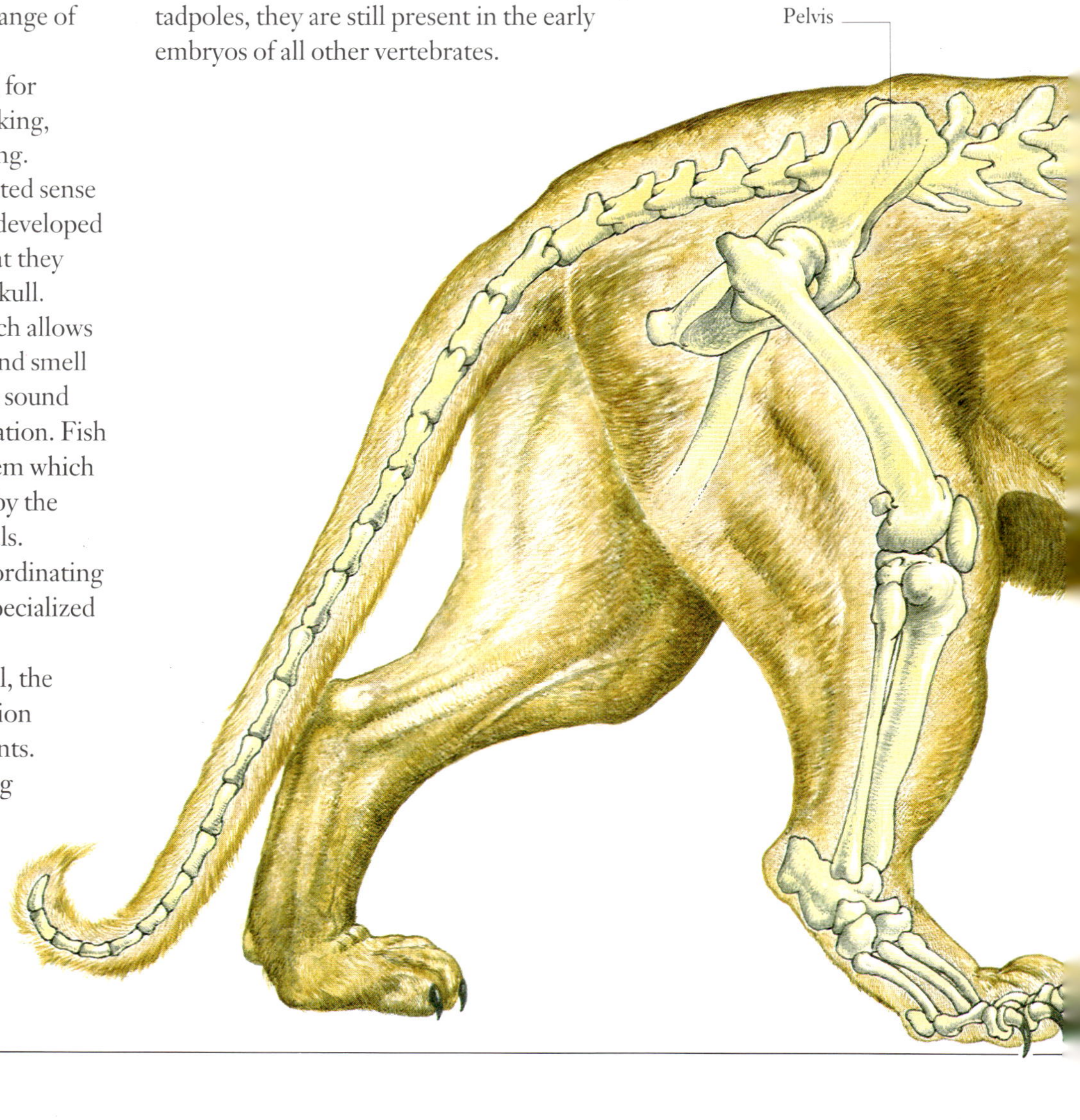

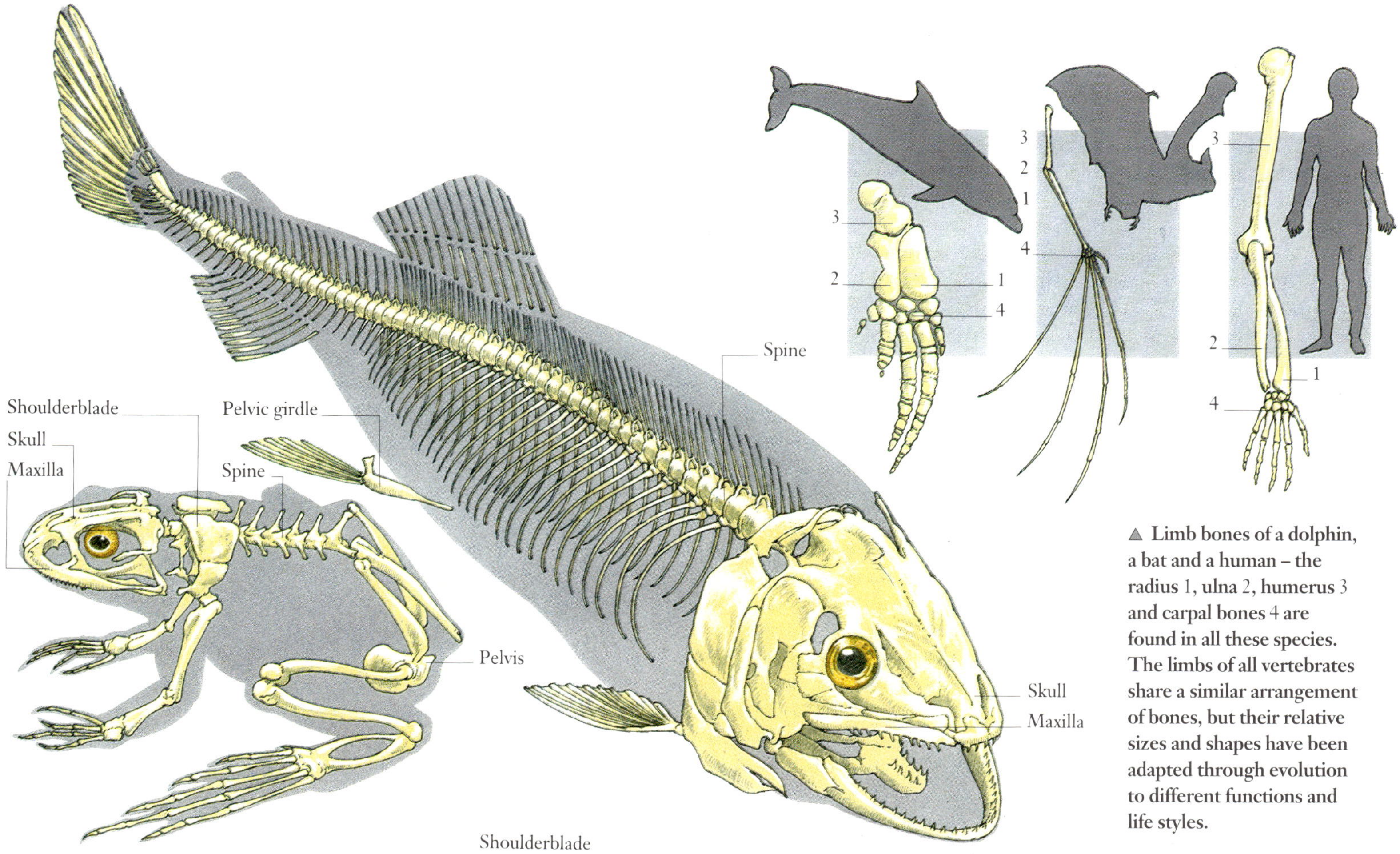

▲ Limb bones of a dolphin, a bat and a human – the radius 1, ulna 2, humerus 3 and carpal bones 4 are found in all these species. The limbs of all vertebrates share a similar arrangement of bones, but their relative sizes and shapes have been adapted through evolution to different functions and life styles.

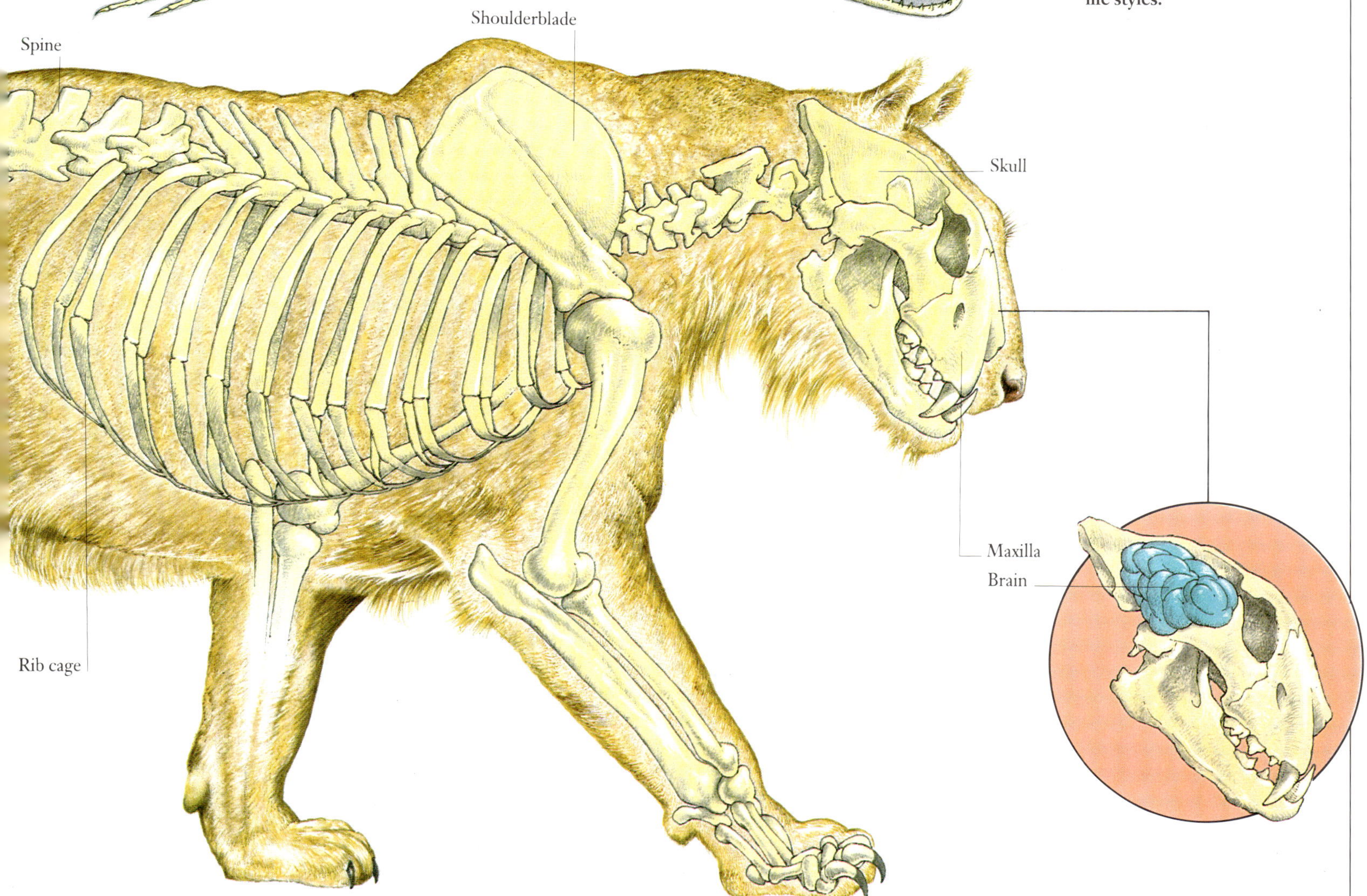

One-Celled Wonders

There are more than 30,000 known animal species that consist of single cells, and there may be even more one-celled species that have not yet been discovered. Most are so small that they can be seen only with a microscope. Yet single-celled creatures are found in even more habitats than more "advanced" multicellular animals. On the coldest snowfields of the world's highest mountains and most remote polar deserts, the snow may turn pink because of the presence of millions of tiny single-celled algae, which contain reddish pigments to protect them against the Sun's intense radiation. Tropical seas become luminescent because of other single-celled creatures in the surface waters, and the stomach of a cow contains millions of single-celled creatures that help to break down plant material. Malaria, one of the worst killer diseases of humans, is caused by the single-celled parasite *Plasmodium vivax*.

ALGAE
AMEBA
CELL
CILIATE
CONTRACTILE VACUOLE
MITOCHONDRION
ORGANELLE
PROTOZOAN
VACUOLE

One-celled animals – which are sometimes called protozoans – may appear to be simple compared with more complex animals, but they function like multicellular animals in miniature. Whereas multi-cellular bodies have different organs performing functions such as respiration, excretion and digestion, the cells of protozoans are divided into specialized compartments, called organelles, each with its own environment and set of biochemical reactions. Some organelles are free to move around the cell, carrying food and waste products.

These multifunctional cells are much more complex than those of multicellular animals. Because of this difference, one-celled animals used to be classified in a separate kingdom, the Protozoa. Today they are classified as belonging to a new kingdom, the Protoctista, which includes algae.

Like all animal cells, protozoans contain organelles such as mitochondria, in which substances are broken down to release energy, and a nucleus, which encloses the genetic material and controls protein synthesis. Many protozoans regulate their water content by means of special vacuoles – organelles full of liquid. The contractile vacuoles collect excess water and transport it to the cell surface, where they release it.

▶ **A single droplet of pond water may contain thousands of microscopic creatures. This living microcosm is every bit as complex as a rainforest. Tiny algae called diatoms and desmids trap the Sun's rays and use their energy to power the synthesis of organic materials, the basis of the food chain.**

▼ **The cell of Paramecium, a protozoan, is divided into different compartments or organelles, each with a particular job to do. Paramecium belongs to a group of protozoans called the ciliates, which swim by means of rows of tiny beating hairs, or cilia. These are coordinated to beat in succession to propel the animal along. Because of the way cilia are arranged, Paramecium twists as it swims. It feeds on particles of organic material in the water, drawing them into its gullet. Species of Paramecium are common in ponds and ditches.**

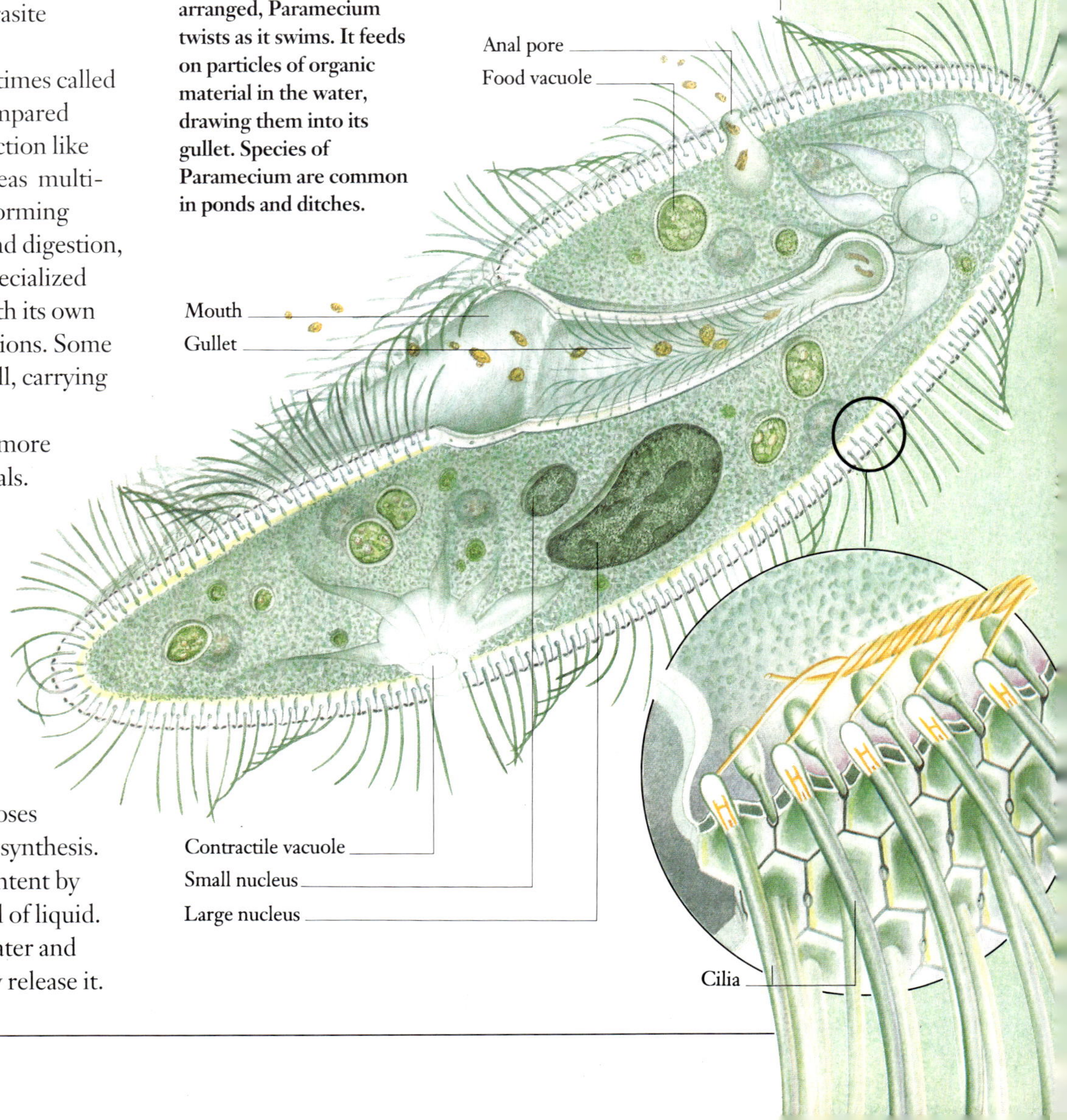

◀ Flask-shaped vorticellids and stentors, like paramecia, are ciliates. They are fixed to the substrate, while the dinoflagellates and paramecia are free-swimming. Diatoms are among the most abundant one-celled creatures in water. Their glassy shells and colorful pigments trap light energy to form the basis of aquatic and marine food chains. Dinoflagellates may also use photosynthesis, but some species take in animal food, and others are parasites.

▶ Strikingly beautiful radiolarians are floating traps for smaller creatures. Sticky mucus streams along the delicate glassy spines, trapping other microscopic creatures drifting in the water. Symbiotic algae give the radiolarians their bright color.

Food particles taken into the cell are surrounded by a membrane to form a food vacuole. Enzymes are secreted into the food vacuole to digest the food; the membrane prevents them digesting the other cell contents. The undigested remains collect in the food vacuole, and may eventually be released to the outside. Some protozoans have eyespots, light-sensitive areas of the cell which seem to control the direction of movement. Paramecia have devices that can eject thin barbed threads, perhaps for defense or to anchor themselves while feeding.

Protozoans can crawl and swim in several different ways. Flagellates have long whiplike hairs which wriggle to propel the animal through the water, whereas ciliates use lines of tiny beating hairs to row themselves along. Amebae and their relatives seem to flow along, putting out long tentacle-like processes, then drawing the rest of the cell forward by means of tiny contracting strands of protein.

Protozoans feed in many different ways. Ciliates such as paramecia have gullets lined with beating cilia that waft food particles toward the mouth, whereas stentors and vorticellids are trumpet-shaped cells with beating cilia around the rim that create a vortex of water, sucking in food. The radiolarians and foraminiferans have long spines which support trailing threads and nets of sticky mucus to trap food particles and small water creatures such as copepods. Amebae put out lobes of cytoplasm to surround food particles and engulf them. The surface waters of ponds, ditches, lakes and oceans, and the thin films of water around soil particles, are as full of living creatures eating, being eaten, dying and being decomposed as are the African savannas or the tropical jungles.

2

LIFE *Processes*

THE EXISTENCE of animal life depends upon the interactions of chemicals, the conversion of energy into different forms, and lightning-speed communication between parts of the body. Animals' bodies have special compartments or organs in which life processes are carried out. For example, the highly folded membranes of the mitochondrion, the energy source of every animal cell, provide a large surface area on which reacting chemicals can be arranged for energy-releasing reactions. Elastic lungs expand and contract to suck air into the body and allow it to diffuse in solution into surrounding blood vessels.

Because different processes are carried out in different parts of the body, chemicals need to be transported from one place to another, and signals must pass around the body to coordinate all its activities. In very small animals, the process of diffusion transports chemicals around the organism, and chemical signals can reach their targets fast enough. Larger animals need more elaborate systems for transport and communication because of the greater distances between cells and organs. All these processes and their supporting body structures need to be adapted to the animal's particular lifestyle and habitat – whether it breathes air or water, moves fast or slowly, eats meat or plants, or lives in a hot or cold climate.

The spectacular plunge of a kingfisher calls for chemical and physical reactions of great complexity. The limbs must be coordinated to achieve the high-speed dive, and information from the eyes must be interpreted and signals sent to the muscles to ensure that the dive is accurate enough for the prey to be seized. Oxygen must be pumped faster to the muscles to provide energy, and to the brain while it processes information as the bird nears its target. At the same time, the bird's cells must be supplied with oxygen and food, and their waste removed, so that the chemical reactions proceed as fast as possible.

Chemistry of Life

LIFE depends on energy transformations carried out in a controlled way in a multitude of tiny steps, each releasing a small quantity of energy that can be trapped and used for other purposes. Animals use many different kinds of energy. They build their body structures using chemical energy; break down food to release heat energy; and use mechanical energy for movement or lifting weight. Electrical energy conducts nerve signals around the body, and light energy is used to sense the world outside. The transformations that take place within an organism's body are collectively called metabolism. They rely upon the kinetic energy of molecules, which allows them to move around.

KEYWORDS

ADENOSINE TRIPHOSPHATE (ATP)
CHEMICAL REACTION
ENZYME
FOOD CHAIN
METABOLISM
PHOTOSYNTHESIS
PROTEIN
RESPIRATION

The basis of life is the trapping of the Sun's rays – light energy – by plants and its transformation into the chemical energy of the compounds that make up the plant's body. Carbon dioxide from the atmosphere and water from the soil, together with various minerals, are combined in plants into a vast array of organic (carbon-containing) compounds. This is the process of photosynthesis. Plants are then eaten by animals, who break down these compounds or rearrange their components to produce different compounds needed to build and repair their own bodies. These animals in turn provide energy and food for predators.

The breaking down of food and storage compounds involves the use of oxygen. This combines with the final breakdown products, releasing carbon dioxide and water (the same components that were used by the plants to make the compounds in the first place). This process is called respiration.

Energy can be transferred between compounds in the form of bonds, or links, between atoms. A small compound called ATP (adenosine triphosphate), which contains two high-energy phosphate bonds (bonds that link phosphate groups to adenosine), is used to carry energy around the cell. For long-distance transport between cells and other parts of the body, sugars are used. As sugars are broken down during respiration, the energy released is used to add a phosphate group to an ADP (adenosine diphosphate) molecule to form ATP. The ATP travels to sites at which energy is needed, then breaks down to ADP, releasing energy.

More than 99 percent of a cell's weight is due to compounds made up of just six elements – carbon, hydrogen, nitrogen, oxygen, phosphorus and sulfur. About 70 percent is water, the medium in which most of the cell's chemical reactions take place. Most of the remaining compounds contain carbon. There are about a thousand kinds of small organic molecules in a single cell. Some play important roles in chemical reactions, whereas others are the building blocks from which much larger "macromolecules" are made.

There are four main groups of small organic molecules – sugars, fatty acids, amino acids and nucleotides. Sugars are used mainly as sources of energy, but they are also present in the genetic material of the cell. Sugars attached to the membranes of cells are important for recognizing other molecules, such as hormones, and other cells, including invading bacteria. Long strings of sugars make up compact, insoluble storage compounds such as starch and glycogen. Fats are important foods, containing even more energy

▶ The rate at which metabolic reactions proceed is intimately related to an animal's lifestyle. The sloth lives a lazy life, moving very slowly and sleeping for long periods. Its slow metabolic rate means that it has a low demand for energy and hence for food. This allows it to subsist on a diet of tough leaves which contain relatively few nutrients, a food for which there is little competition in the South American rainforest.

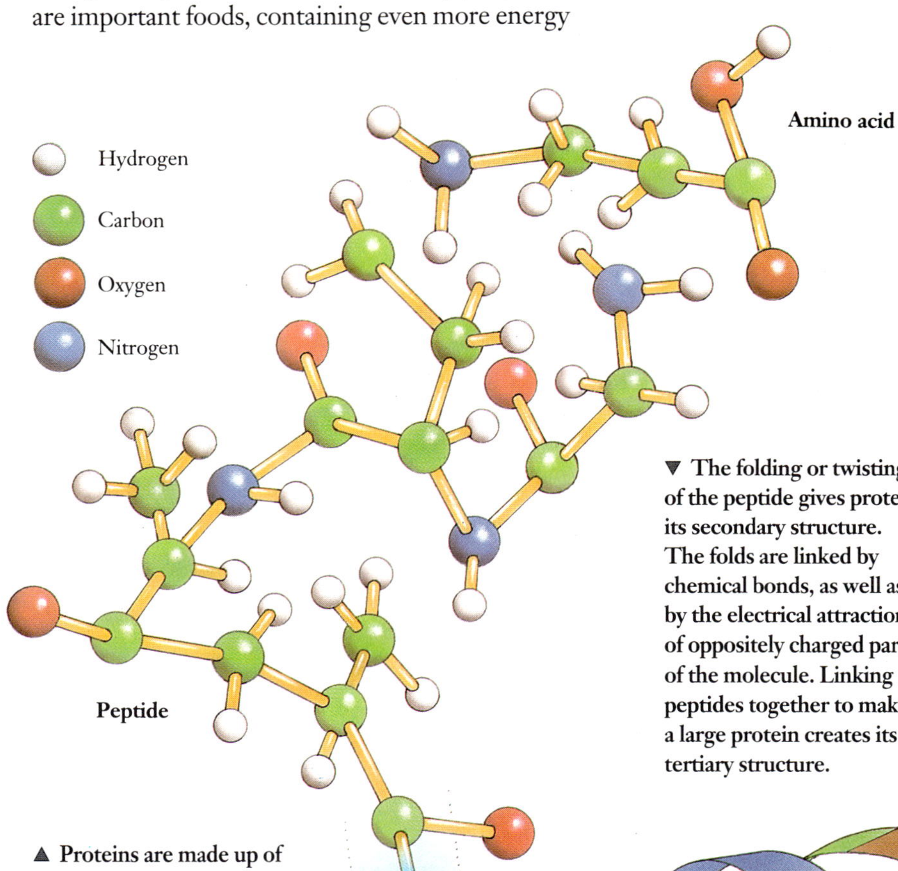

▲ Proteins are made up of long strings of small subunits called amino acids. The particular sequence of amino acids forms a kind of code which determines the shape and properties of the protein molecule, and sets limits on how it can be twisted and folded. This is known as its primary structure.

▼ The folding or twisting of the peptide gives protein its secondary structure. The folds are linked by chemical bonds, as well as by the electrical attraction of oppositely charged parts of the molecule. Linking peptides together to make a large protein creates its tertiary structure.

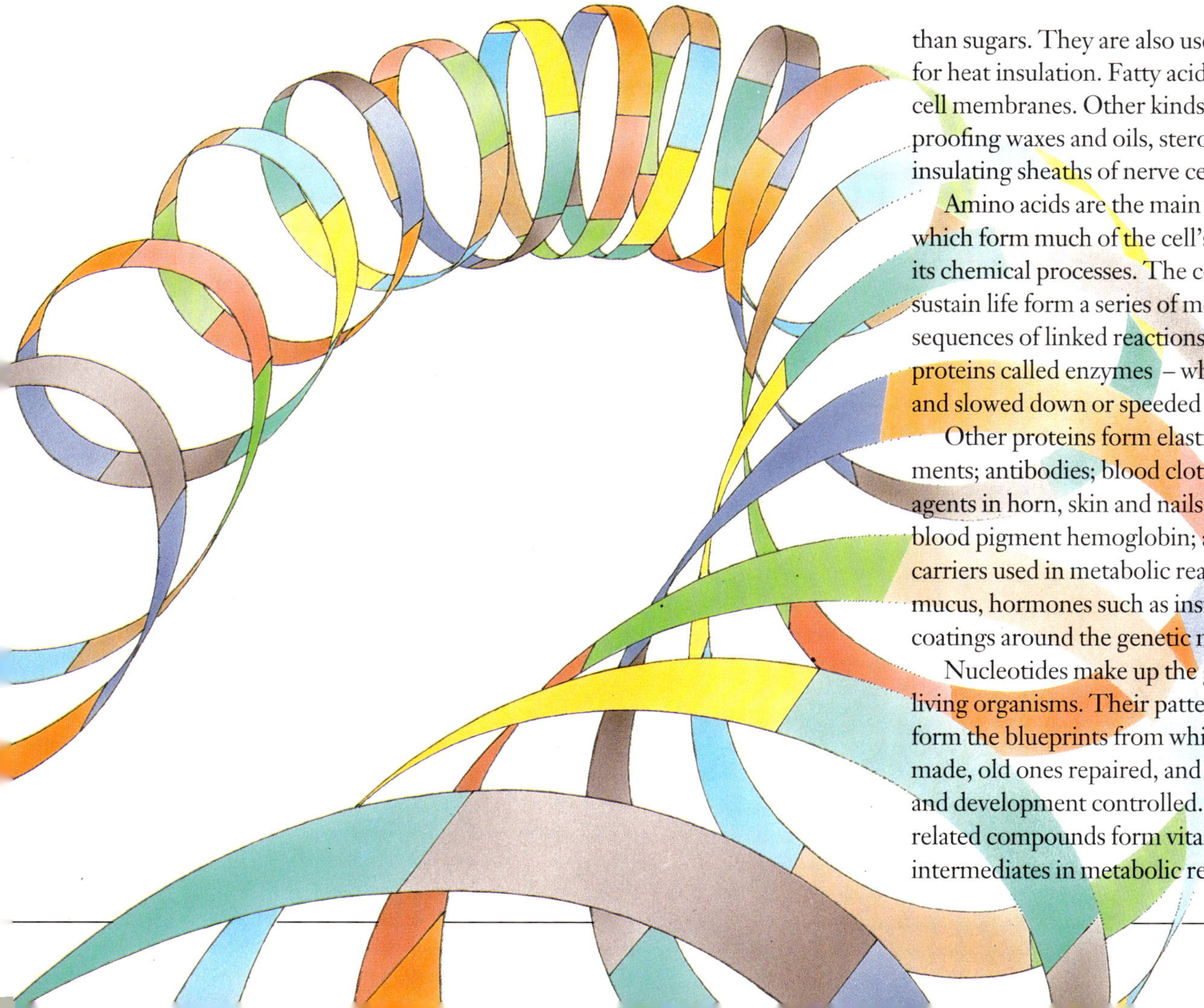

than sugars. They are also used for energy storage and for heat insulation. Fatty acids form the major part of cell membranes. Other kinds of fats include water-proofing waxes and oils, steroid hormones and the insulating sheaths of nerve cells.

Amino acids are the main components of proteins, which form much of the cell's structure and control its chemical processes. The complex reactions that sustain life form a series of metabolic pathways – sequences of linked reactions controlled by special proteins called enzymes – which can be switched on and slowed down or speeded up as needed.

Other proteins form elastic muscle fibers and ligaments; antibodies; blood clotting agents; hardening agents in horn, skin and nails; the oxygen-carrying blood pigment hemoglobin; a range of electron carriers used in metabolic reactions; lubricating mucus, hormones such as insulin, and protective coatings around the genetic material in the nucleus.

Nucleotides make up the genetic material of all living organisms. Their patterns of repeating units form the blueprints from which new organisms are made, old ones repaired, and bodily processes, growth and development controlled. Other nucleotides and related compounds form vital energy carriers and intermediates in metabolic reactions.

Building Blocks of Life

DESPITE the huge variety of animal forms, the bodies of all animals are made up of very similar units, called cells. Some animals are just a single cell, whereas large animals such as humans may contain 10 trillion cells, of about 200 different types, all acting together as a single animal. Not only do cells have to carry out particular duties such as secreting digestive juices or carrying oxygen, but they also have to keep in contact with each other so that their activities do not interfere with those of other cells in the body.

KEYWORDS

CELL
CYTOPLASM
DNA
ENDOPLASMIC RETICULUM
EUKARYOTE
MITOCHONDRION
ORGANELLE
VACUOLE

There are four main groups of cell types in the bodies of larger animals. Epithelial cells form sheet-like layers over the internal and external surface of the body; connective cells make supporting materials such as bones and tendons; muscle cells are responsible for movement; and nerve cells form an important internal signaling system. Cells are grouped into tissues, such as sheetlike epithelia or fat-rich adipose tissue (body fat). Different kinds of tissues, in turn, are arranged together to form organs such as the heart, lungs and stomach.

A few animal cells can be seen with the naked eye, but most are only 10–20 micrometers in diameter, and can be seen only with the aid of a microscope. In order to see the detailed structure of a cell, an electron microscope may be used. This can resolve details one thousand times smaller than those seen with the light microscope.

Under a microscope, a cell looks like a small baglike structure surrounded by a double membrane, the cell membrane, and containing a jelly-like substance, the protoplasm. A cell is so small that substances can easily travel through it by diffusion. Internal membranes divide up the interior of the cell into separate regions, called organelles, which keep the many chemical reactions in the cell from interfering with each other. Protein-lined pores in the membrane allow certain water-soluble materials to pass through but exclude others. Because membranes can control which substances pass through them, each organelle has its own special environment. The enzymes (proteins) that promote cell reactions are extremely sensitive to their surroundings. Different organelles specialize in different series of reactions, and provide the best possible environment for these to take place. The most prominent organelle is usually the nucleus. It contains the hereditary blueprint of the species, and controls the activities of the cell and its replication. The mitochondrion is the powerhouse of the cell, where respiration takes place, while the rough endoplasmic reticulum bears chains of ribosomes, which are involved in protein synthesis.

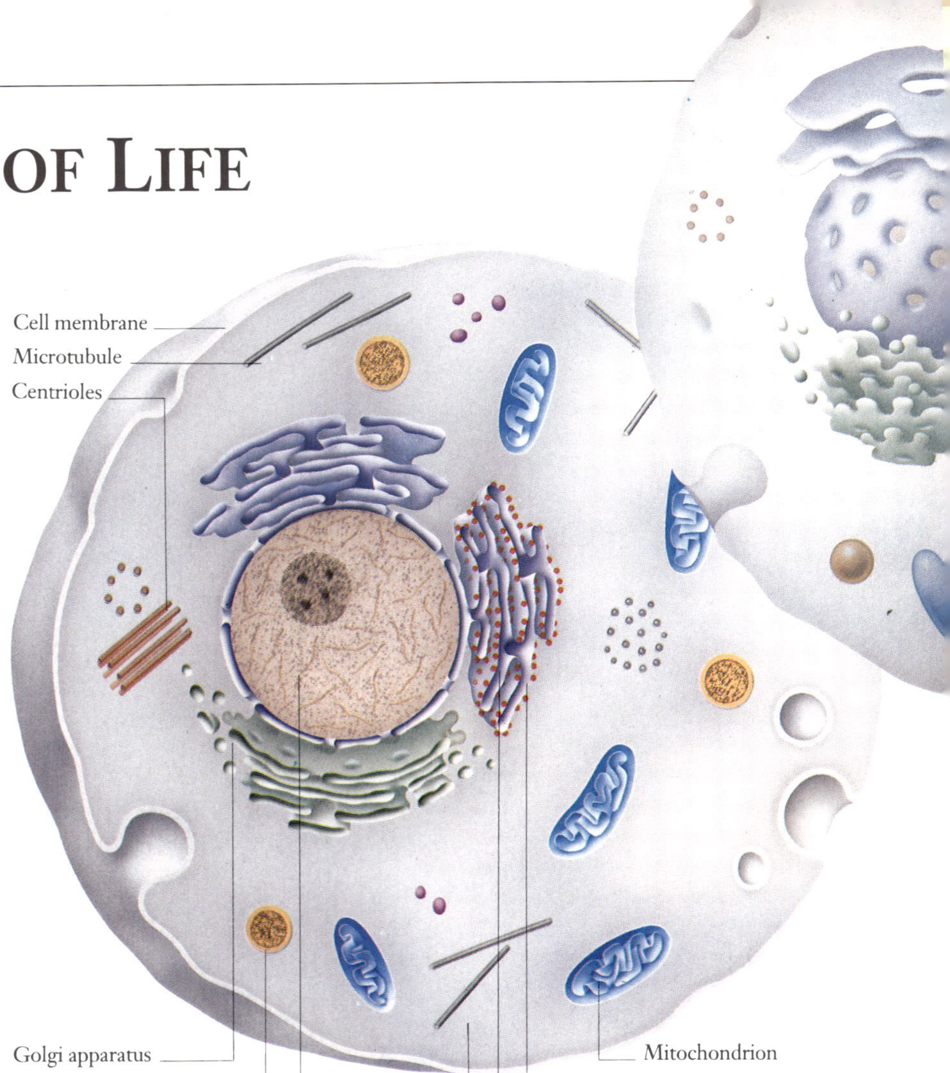

▲ The nucleus controls the cell's activities. Mitochondria provide energy by respiration. Protein synthesis occurs on the ribosomes. Many substances are made in the Golgi apparatus and in the endoplasmic reticulum.

Materials pass in and out through the cell membrane. Worn-out organelles are destroyed in the lysosomes. The centrioles organize the spindle apparatus of microtubules which helps control cell division.

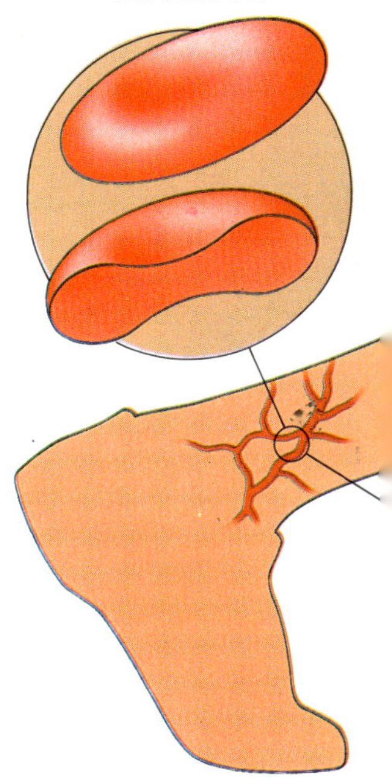

The jelly-like material between all the organelles is called the cytosol. Together with the organelles, it forms the cytoplasm. Scattered throughout the cytosol are long tubular protein filaments called microtubules, which can expand, contract and move around the cell. They provide a kind of cell skeleton, and are particularly numerous where new organelles or membranes are being built. They appear to play a role in organizing cell components into larger structures, but it is not known exactly how this function is performed. The various organelles depend upon the type of cell and its task.

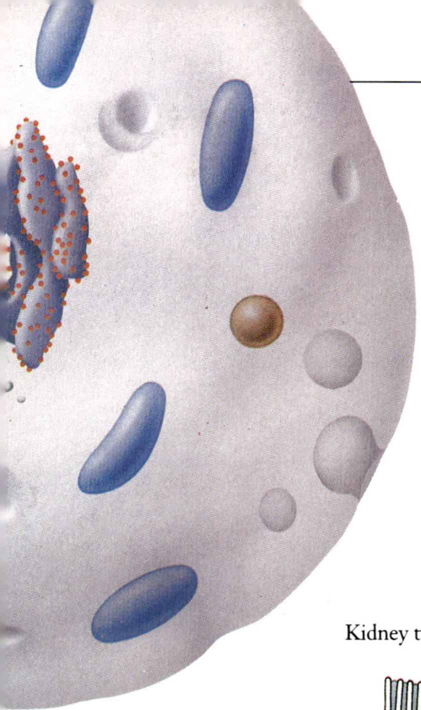

▼ The numbers and types of organelles in cells vary according to the type of cell and its role in the body. Red blood cells have no nuclei. This gives them their concave shape, increasing the surface area for oxygen uptake. Sperm cells have a tail for swimming and are packed with mitochondria to provide energy. Osteocytes control the secretion of bone, and have fine processes to keep in contact with each other. Cells of the kidney tubule and intestine have fringes of microvilli to increase the surface area for absorption. Goblet cells in the stomach have many Golgi bodies for secreting mucus and digestive enzymes. Sensory cells in the ear have fine hairlike cilia, which detect movements of the ear fluids. Rod cells in the retina of the eye detect changes in light intensity.

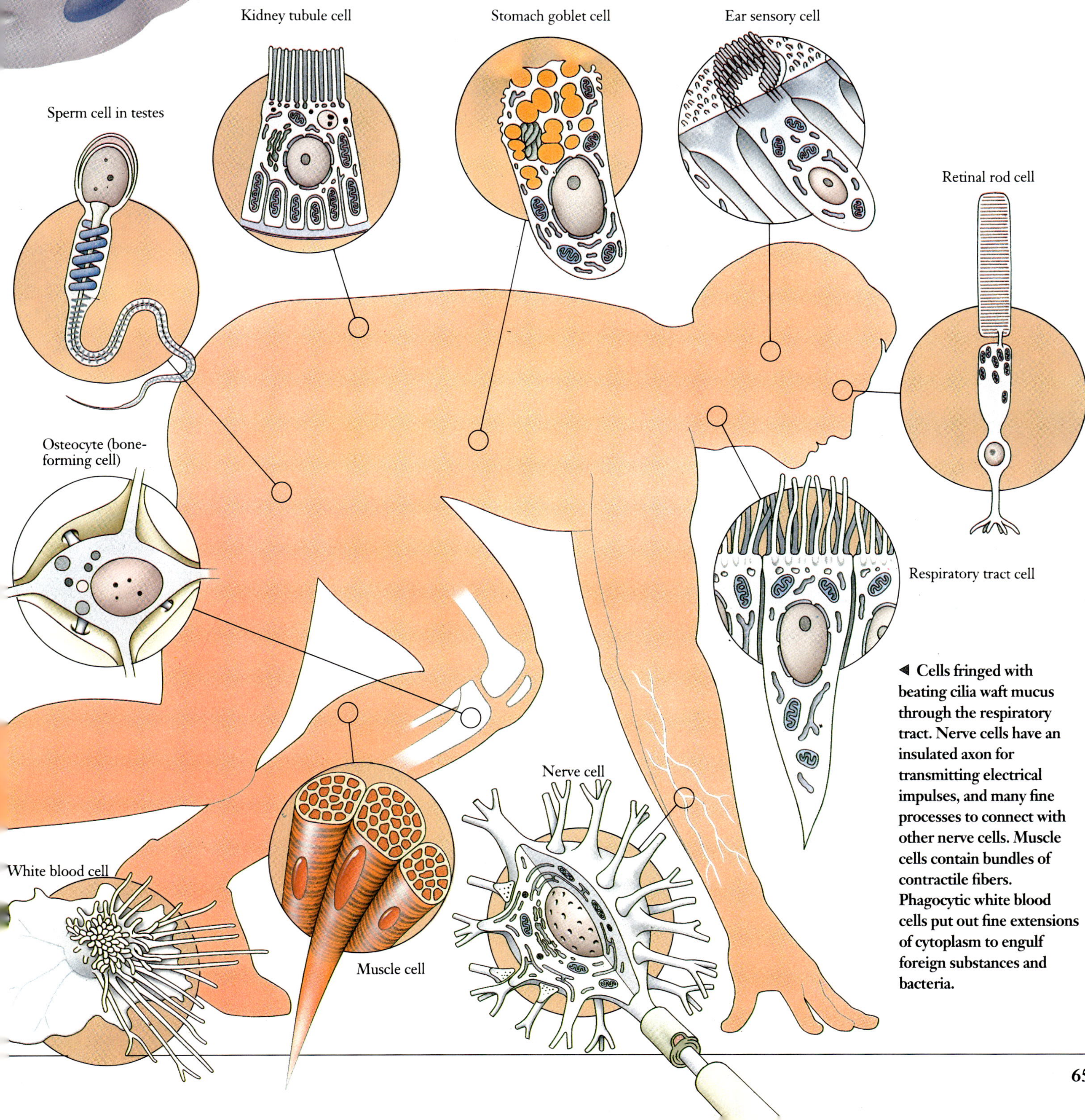

◀ Cells fringed with beating cilia waft mucus through the respiratory tract. Nerve cells have an insulated axon for transmitting electrical impulses, and many fine processes to connect with other nerve cells. Muscle cells contain bundles of contractile fibers. Phagocytic white blood cells put out fine extensions of cytoplasm to engulf foreign substances and bacteria.

PROCESSING FOOD

THE life of every animal is sustained by the continual input of food. Food molecules are broken down to yield energy and smaller molecules, which in turn can be combined with other substances to build the components of the animal's body.

The ways in which food is taken in, broken down and absorbed vary according to an animal's diet and body plan. A few animals, such as spiders and flies, partly digest their food before they take it in: they secrete digestive enzymes onto the food and suck up the soluble products of digestion. But most animals ingest complex food substances made up of large, insoluble organic molecules. These molecules are then broken down in the process of digestion. The end products are small, simple molecules that can diffuse in solution and be absorbed by the body. Undigested food materials are eliminated from the body.

KEYWORDS

ABSORPTION
ASSIMILATION
DIGESTION
ENZYME
EXCRETION
INTESTINE
LYMPH SYSTEM
PERISTALSIS
VACUOLE

Very simple animals, such as an ameba, may take in simple food by diffusion through their body surfaces. Larger particles are surrounded by footlike extensions of the outer cell membrane, then enclosed in a membrane-bound sac called a food vacuole. Enzymes are secreted into the vacuole to break down the food into smaller molecules that diffuse or are transported into the cytoplasm. By carrying out digestion inside a vacuole, the cell ensures that the enzymes do not

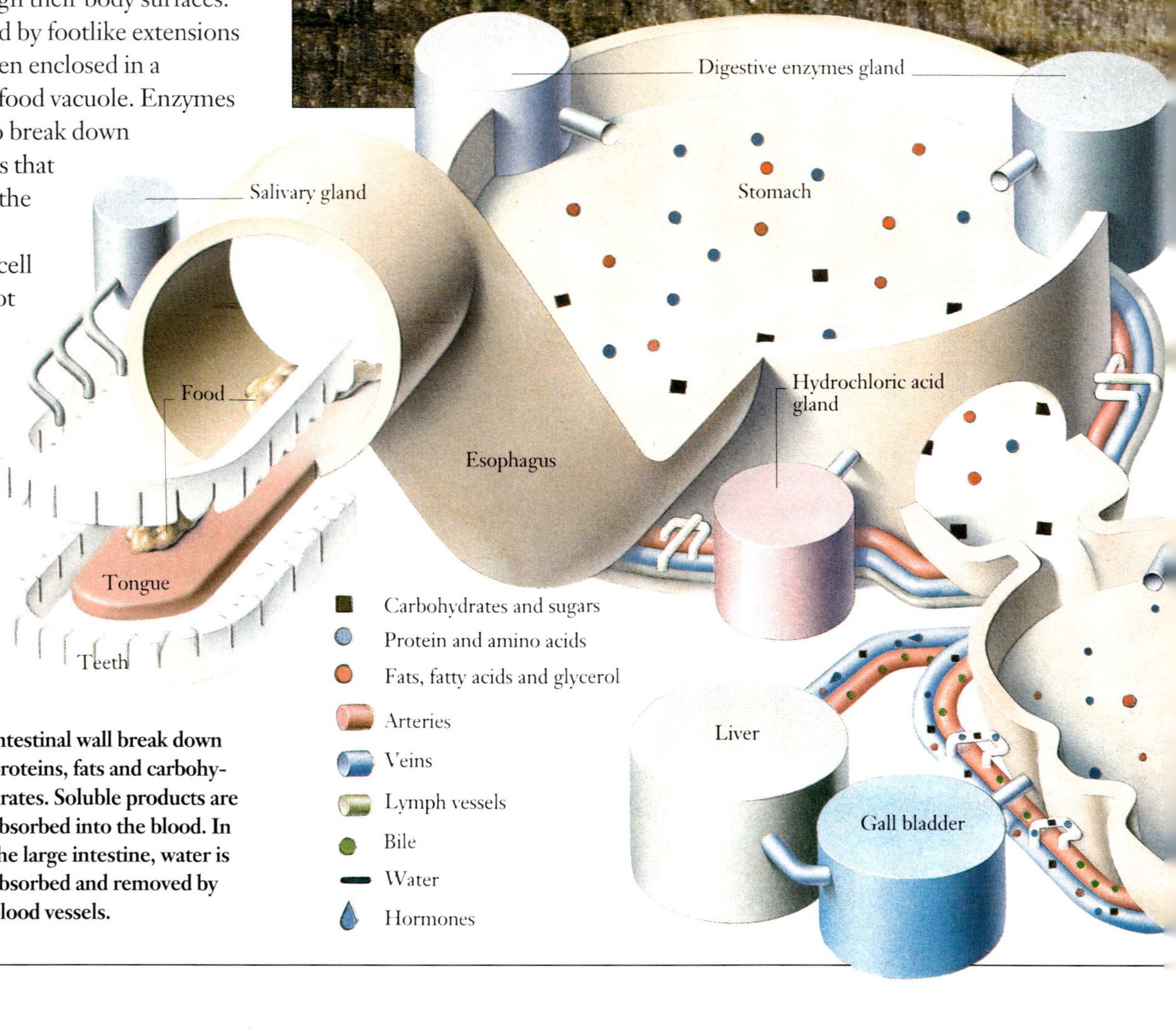

▶ **In the human digestive system, food is broken down in the mouth. Hydrochloric acid in the stomach destroys bacteria and acidifies the food so that gastric enzymes can begin breaking down proteins. The food passes into the duodenum and the small intestine; convoluted walls lined with villi increase the surface area for digestion and absorption. Salts from the pancreas neutralize the acid, and bile from the liver is released from the gall bladder, separating fats into small droplets. Enzymes from the pancreas and the intestinal wall break down proteins, fats and carbohydrates. Soluble products are absorbed into the blood. In the large intestine, water is absorbed and removed by blood vessels.**

break down useful substances in the rest of the cell.

Larger animals also need to ensure that the enzymes of their digestive systems stay separate from the rest of the body. They have a long tube called the intestine or gut, through which food passes and is acted upon by digestive enzymes. Different parts of the intestine may be specialized for particular types of digestion, forming stomachs, glands, pouches for housing symbiotic bacteria, and various types of intestines. Some animals, such as earthworms and some birds, have a strong muscular section of the intestine called a gizzard, in which they store small stones. The action of the gizzard causes the stones to grind food. Plant cells are difficult to digest, and herbivores (plant-eating animals) usually have longer intestines than carnivores (meat-eating animals). Many herbivores have pouches of the intestine, such as the cecum or appendix, which contain bacteria to help break down plant material. Deer, antelope and cattle – the ruminants – have a series of stomachs in which digestion takes place.

Digested food is taken into the blood vessels that line the intestine. Some small molecules pass across the intestinal wall by diffusion; others are pumped out. They pass into the blood and, in some vertebrates, the lymph system, which carry them to individual cells. The intake of digested food and its incorporation into body compounds is called assimilation.

Digestion, absorption and assimilation are controlled by hormones and the nerves. Sensory cells inform the brain of food in the digestive tract, and hormones stimulate the secretion of digestive enzymes and other substances. The muscle waves of peristalsis are coordinated by nerves in the intestine wall. Surplus food is stored, usually as the carbohydrate glycogen in the muscles and other parts of the body, or as fat globules in fatty tissues. The storage of food and the breakdown of storage compounds to release nutrients are controlled by hormones, which respond to changes in the composition of the blood.

▲ After a good meal, the vulture's crop is swollen and clearly visible. The crop is a swelling of the esophagus, which is used to store food that the bird has swallowed whole, so the stomach is not overloaded.

◀ Many termites feed on wood, one of the toughest diets known. Inside the termite's digestive system, an army of 100 different kinds of protozoans and bacteria breaks down the wood fibers into substances that can be absorbed as nutrients.

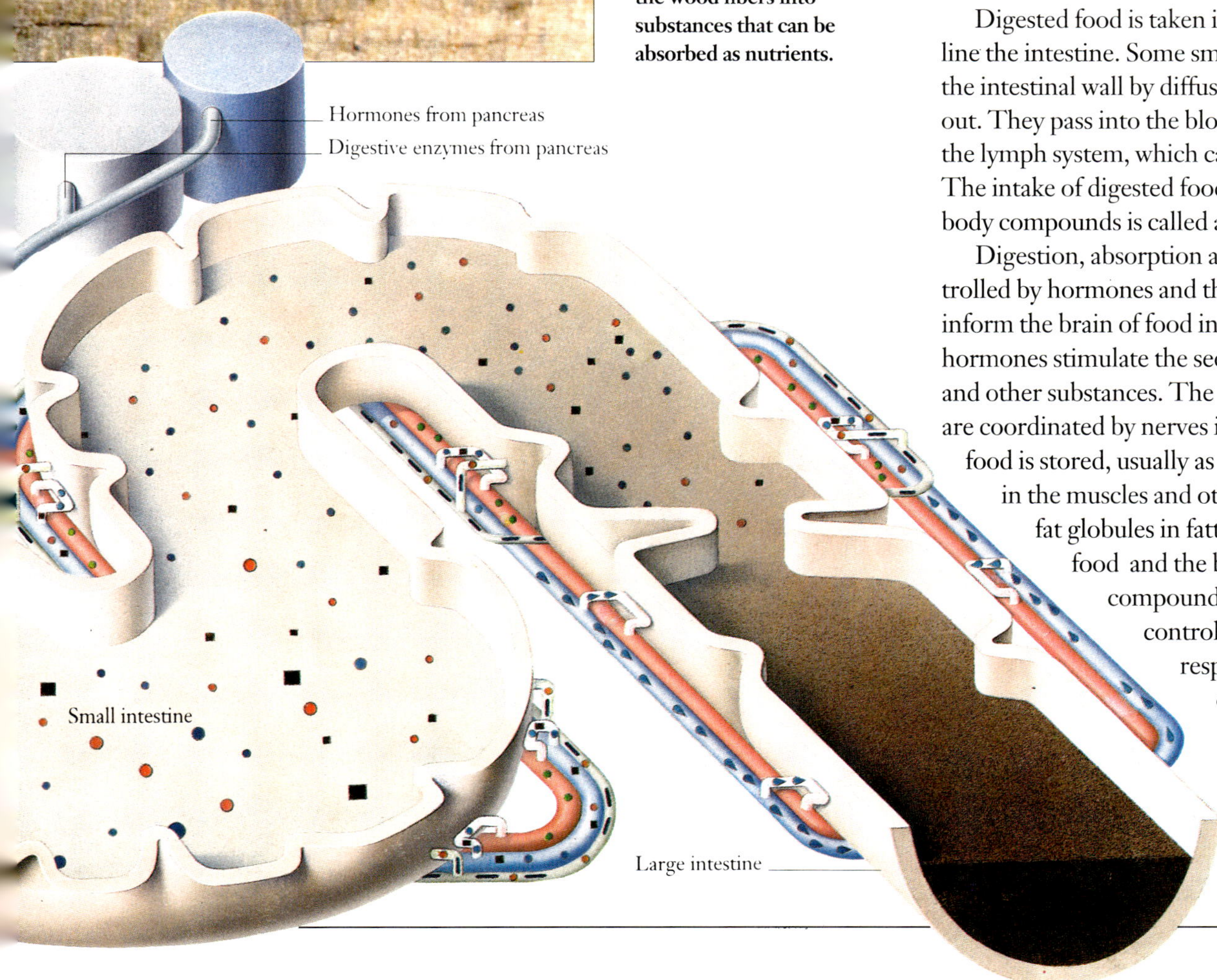

WASTE DISPOSAL

THE hundreds of chemical reactions involved in metabolism produce some substances that are not needed by the body. Some of these may interfere with other cell reactions, or they may even be poisonous. Animals have evolved special ways of getting rid of their bodies' waste products. These methods are known as the processes of excretion.

There are many different kinds of waste products. Unwanted carbohydrates are usually built up into large, inert (not chemically reactive), insoluble molecules such as glycogen for storage, or converted to fats and stored in fatty tissue. Proteins, however, may be very toxic, and they cannot be stored. Instead, they must be converted into a less toxic form for transport out of the body. Proteins are broken down into their basic units (amino acids), which are carried to the liver to be made less toxic. In the liver they are further degraded by the process of deamination to release ammonia and carbon dioxide.

KEYWORDS

CONTRACTILE VACUOLE
KIDNEY
METABOLISM
OSMOREGULATION
OSMOSIS
UREA

But ammonia itself is highly poisonous. It is also very soluble, and in fish and aquatic animals it readily passes in solution into the surrounding water. Marine fish cannot afford to excrete ammonia, because this involves losing a lot of water. Instead, some excrete a substance called trimethylamine oxide and others excrete urea, produced in the liver by combining ammonia with carbon dioxide.

Urea is soluble but less poisonous than ammonia, and requires less water for excretion. This is the form in which mammals, including humans, excrete ammonia. But excreting urea still requires significant amounts of water, and animals such as reptiles, which live in dry habitats, and birds that fly and cannot carry much weight, convert ammonia into crystals of a whitish solid called uric acid. Arthropods are small animals with a large surface-area-to-volume ratio; on land they face the problem of preventing water loss by evaporation, so they, too, excrete uric acid. Uric acid is also a convenient, compact form in which to store waste products inside bird eggs.

There are other waste products to be eliminated. The destruction of worn-out red blood cells in the liver produces broken-down pigments, which are stored in the gall bladder, then released into the intestine and expelled with the feces. The process of respiration produces carbon dioxide, which diffuses from the cells into the blood, and then is carried into the lungs or gills to be expelled. Most unwanted

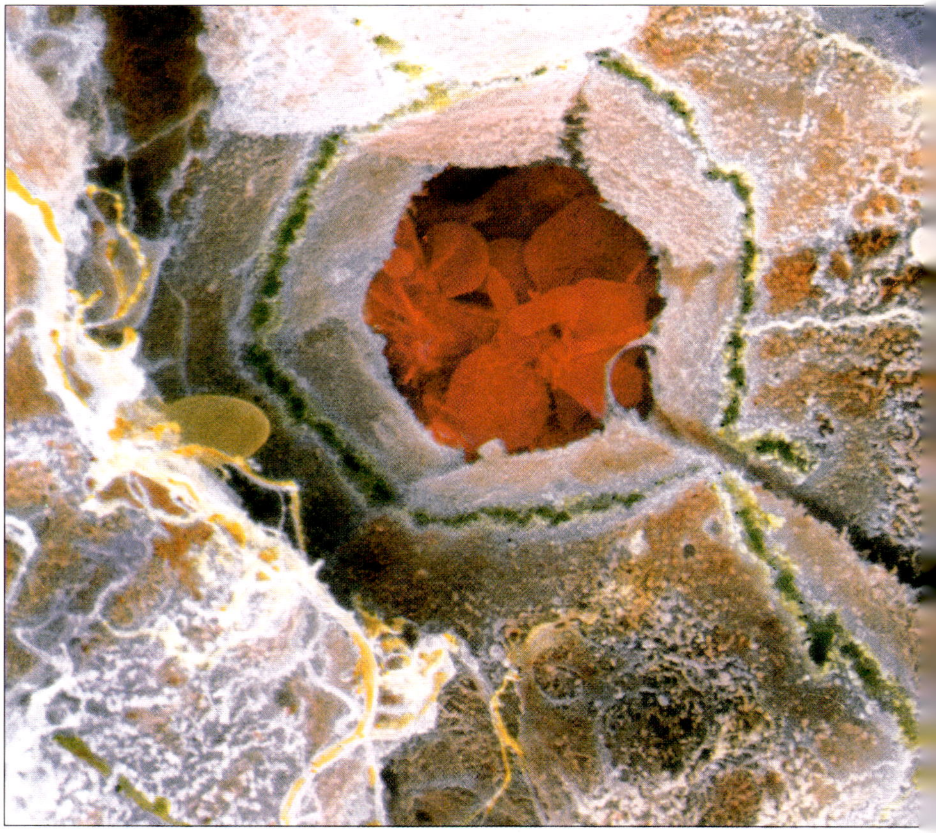

▶ European cormorants sit amid their droppings. Birds excrete solid waste that requires little water for its formation; water in the waste would weigh down the bird in flight.

◀ Cape cormorants gather on Sinclair Island, off the Namibian coast, to breed. The rocks are covered in a thick layer of guano – the excrement of the birds. Guano is rich in nitrates and phosphates. In many parts of the world it is collected for use as fertilizer, often in huge quantities: the Pacific island of Nauru exports some two million tonnes of guano annually.

materials such as hormones, toxins produced by invading bacteria, toxic substances from plant food, drugs and alcohol are broken down and made safe in the liver. The breakdown products pass into the bloodstream and are transported to the kidneys to be separated out and excreted.

The body fluids and cells of animals contain many dissolved materials. Animal cells are bordered by membranes which are only partly permeable. The concentrated cell solutions draw water in by the process of osmosis. This may alter the concentration of the cell solution and upset the reactions going on there. It may even cause the cell to burst. Too much water may cause problems outside the cells, too. If there is too much water in the blood, its volume is increased, and the heart has to pump harder to push it around the body.

Disposing of excess water is a particular problem for animals that live in fresh water. Animals that live in the sea face just the opposite problem: water tends to move by osmosis from their bodies into the surrounding salt water, which is more concentrated than the fluids in their bodies. The control of water content is called osmoregulation. Because many waste products are excreted in a soluble form, it is not surprising that the excretory organs of animals fulfill a dual role: they excrete waste substances, and they also control the water and salt content of the blood and other body fluids.

In very small animals, waste products can simply diffuse out of the body through the cell walls. Water content is regulated by contractile vacuoles, which collect excess water, then move to the cell membrane and discharge the water to the outside. Small multicellular animals such as hydras get rid of most of their waste products through the mouth. Larger animals extract wastes from their body fluids and pass them through a separate excretory organ, where water and salt content are adjusted before the waste products are expelled.

◀ Liver cells are well supplied with blood, bringing toxic substances to be rendered harmless before being transported to the kidneys for excretion.

▶ Newly digested food is absorbed into the dense network of blood vessels that surrounds the intestines. From here the various food materials travel in the blood to the liver. Here, excess sugars are stored as the insoluble carbohydrate glycogen, or glycogen is converted to sugar to boost the blood sugar level, according to the needs of the body. Other food substances are converted into useful substances such as vitamins or, if present in excess, converted into inactive storage compounds that will not interfere with the body's metabolism. Here, too, worn-out red blood cells are broken down, and their degraded pigments pass into the intestines to be eliminated. The liver also breaks down toxins such as alcohol and drugs into products that are removed by the kidneys. Amino acids, produced by the digestion of proteins, may be converted by the liver to other proteins or detoxified by the process of deamination. This produces ammonia, which is combined with carbon dioxide to form urea. This is carried by the blood system to the kidneys, where it is removed from the blood and incorporated into the urine, to be excreted from the body with waste water.

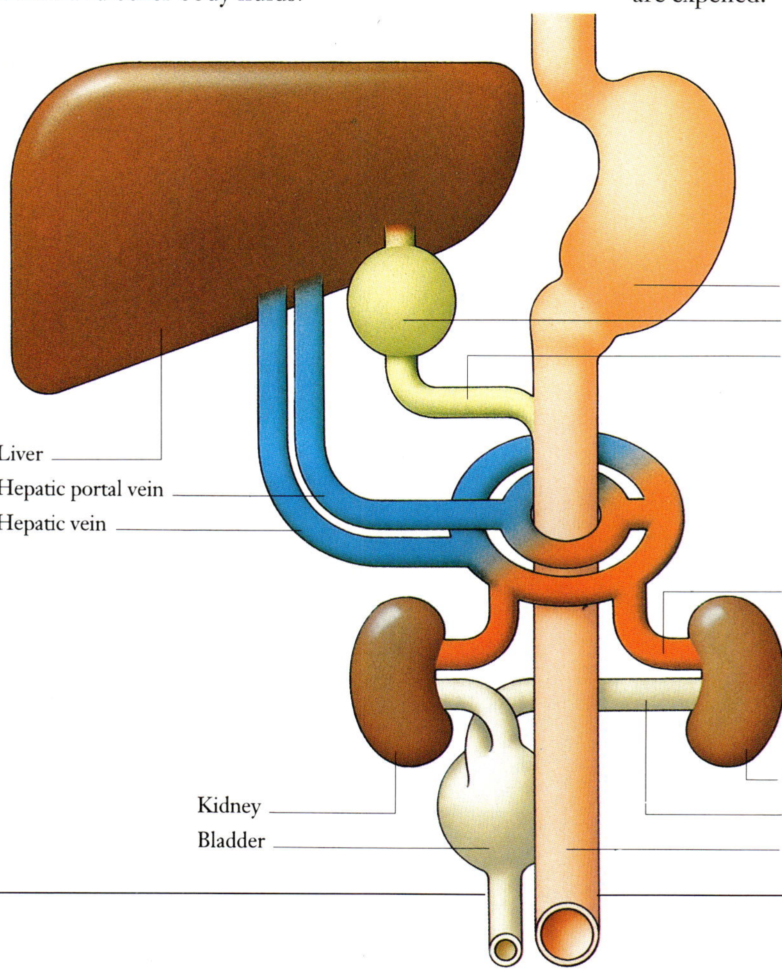

CIRCULATION

CIRCULATORY systems probably appeared very early in the evolution of life. Even in the earliest living cells, the chemicals required for the processes of life had to be transported from one part of the cell to another. The simple process of diffusion is fast enough to carry dissolved substances across individual cells, but it is too slow for many of the internal transport needs in multicellular animals. Another disadvantage of diffusion is that there is a considerable risk that diffusing chemicals will be destroyed by interaction with other chemicals on the way. Cells use membranes to separate transported materials from the rest of the cell. Some of these materials move in vesicles, whose movement is thought to involve microtubules of elastic proteins that can contract and relax. Other chemicals move through flattened sacs of membranes such as the endoplasmic reticulum and Golgi apparatus.

KEYWORDS

BLOOD PRESSURE
CAPILLARY
CILIA
CIRCULATION
DIFFUSION
ENDOPLASMIC RETICULUM
HEART
LYMPH
OPEN CIRCULATION
OSMOSIS
PLASMA

The transport systems of larger animals have much in common with the cell's internal transport system. Instead of membranes, there are tubes formed from connective tissues and muscle fibers. Blood and other body fluids circulate around the body and transport nutrients, waste products, oxygen, hormones and antibodies to and from individual cells, or into and out of an animal's body.

The simplest circulatory systems involve tiny beating hairs called cilia and flagella. Whiplike flagella or rows of cilia waft water containing food and oxygen into the bodies of sponges and many protozoans, and across the sieve-like gills of mussels. In mammals, cilia are used to move mucus from the nose, throat and lungs into the stomach, where trapped particles of foreign matter can be rendered harmless. Cilia also waft the egg down the oviducts towards the uterus, and help to move the fluid along the kidney tubules.

Air is drawn into the bodies of many land-dwelling animals and expelled again by muscular sucking and pumping actions. The main pump for blood circulation in many animals is the heart, but in some invertebrates the major blood vessels are just as

▼ Many invertebrates, such as earthworms and arthropods (including lobsters), have "open" circulation systems, in which the blood is pumped throughout the body at fairly low pressure. The blood is able to enter the body cavity from the ends of the blood vessels. Oxygenated and deoxygenated blood cannot be kept separate in this "open" system, so oxygen transport is always relatively inefficient.

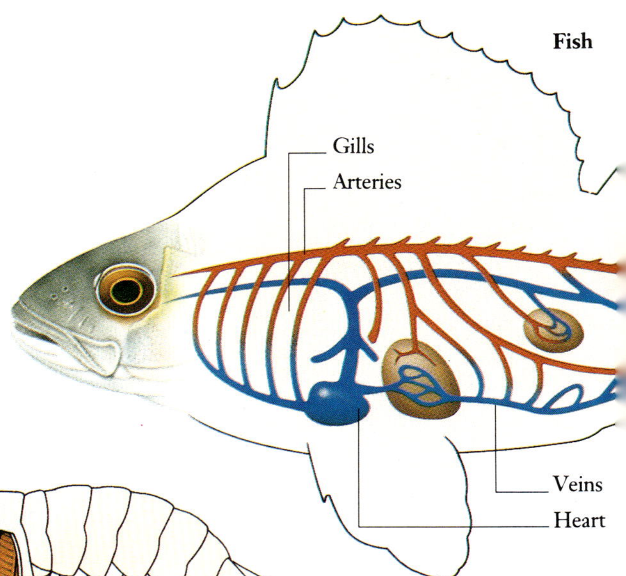

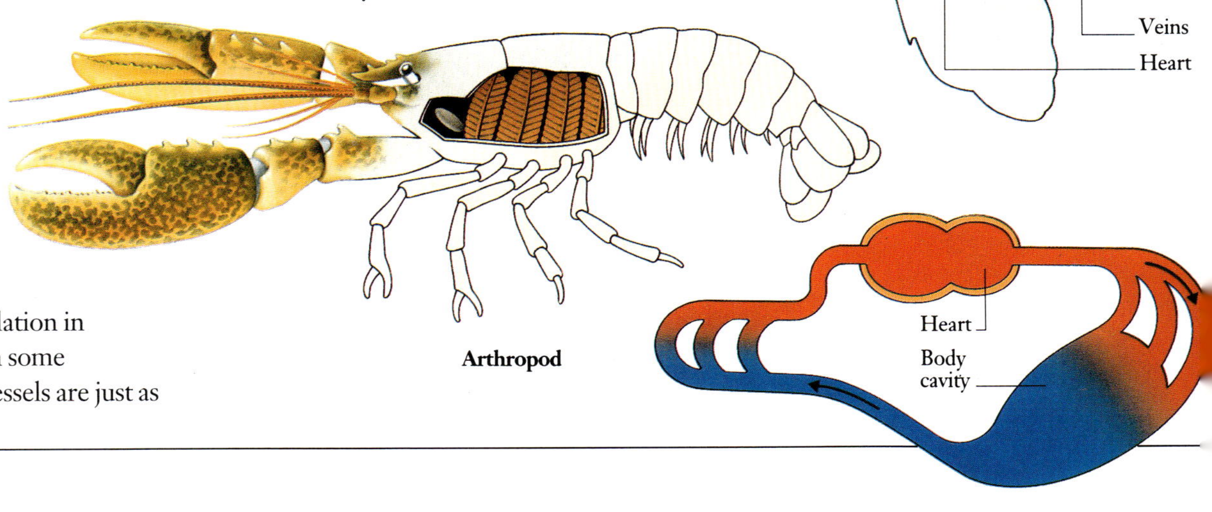

◀ The large ears of a jackrabbit show a network of fine blood vessels. Heat is readily lost from the vessels across the thin ears, helping to cool the animal in the heat of the desert.

▼ In a single circulation system, as in a fish, the heart pumps the blood directly to the lungs or gills, and from there oxygenated blood travels to the rest of the body. This restricts the pressure at which blood can be pumped: the respiratory organs are delicate.

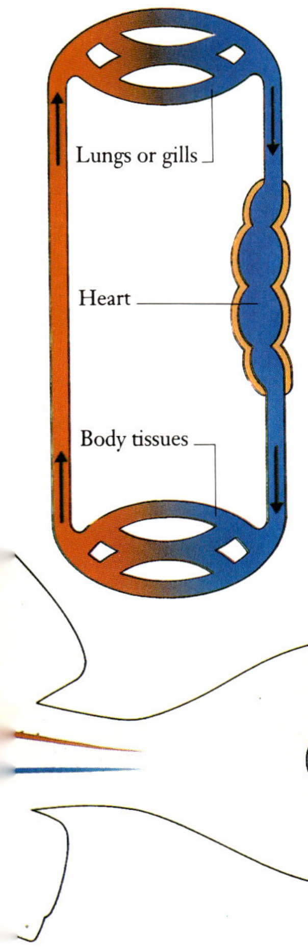

important. In many invertebrates, such as earthworms and arthropods, a heart or series of hearts pump the blood through vessels that run the length of the body. The blood then leaks out of the end of the vessels into the body cavity, where it bathes the cells. The pumping action of the hearts sucks blood back into the front end of the vessels. Such an "open" circulation tends to operate at low pressure.

Larger animals need a more powerful circulatory system. Their blood is pumped under high pressure through a series of narrow vessels from which it cannot escape. Substances needed by the cells diffuse out through the thin vessel walls of the capillary networks that supply the tissues, while waste products diffuse in the opposite direction. However, the high pressure causes part of the blood fluid to leak out through the thin capillary walls. This fluid is collected by another system of vessels, the lymphatic system, and returned to the main circulation at a point of low pressure. Only 3 to 5 percent of the capillaries are open at any time in this "closed" circulation, permitting fine control of the blood supply to the tissues.

There are other advantages of closed circulation. It allows high-pressure filtration of the blood in the kidneys, an efficient way of removing waste products. For species that rely on blood to transport oxygen, the slowness of open circulation limits the metabolic rate, and with it the activity of the animal. Insects have overcome this by having a separate circulatory system for respiratory gases.

In mammals and birds, high-speed, high-pressure circulation is essential for moving heat around the body to maintain an almost constant internal temperature. Certain animals, especially marine animals that spend a lot of time in cold water, have special arrangements of capillaries in which the arterioles (branched tips of arteries) and venules (fine tips of veins) run parallel to each other, so that heat and gases can be exchanged between them, reducing heat loss. These capillary complexes are found in the flippers of marine mammals and the feet of seabirds.

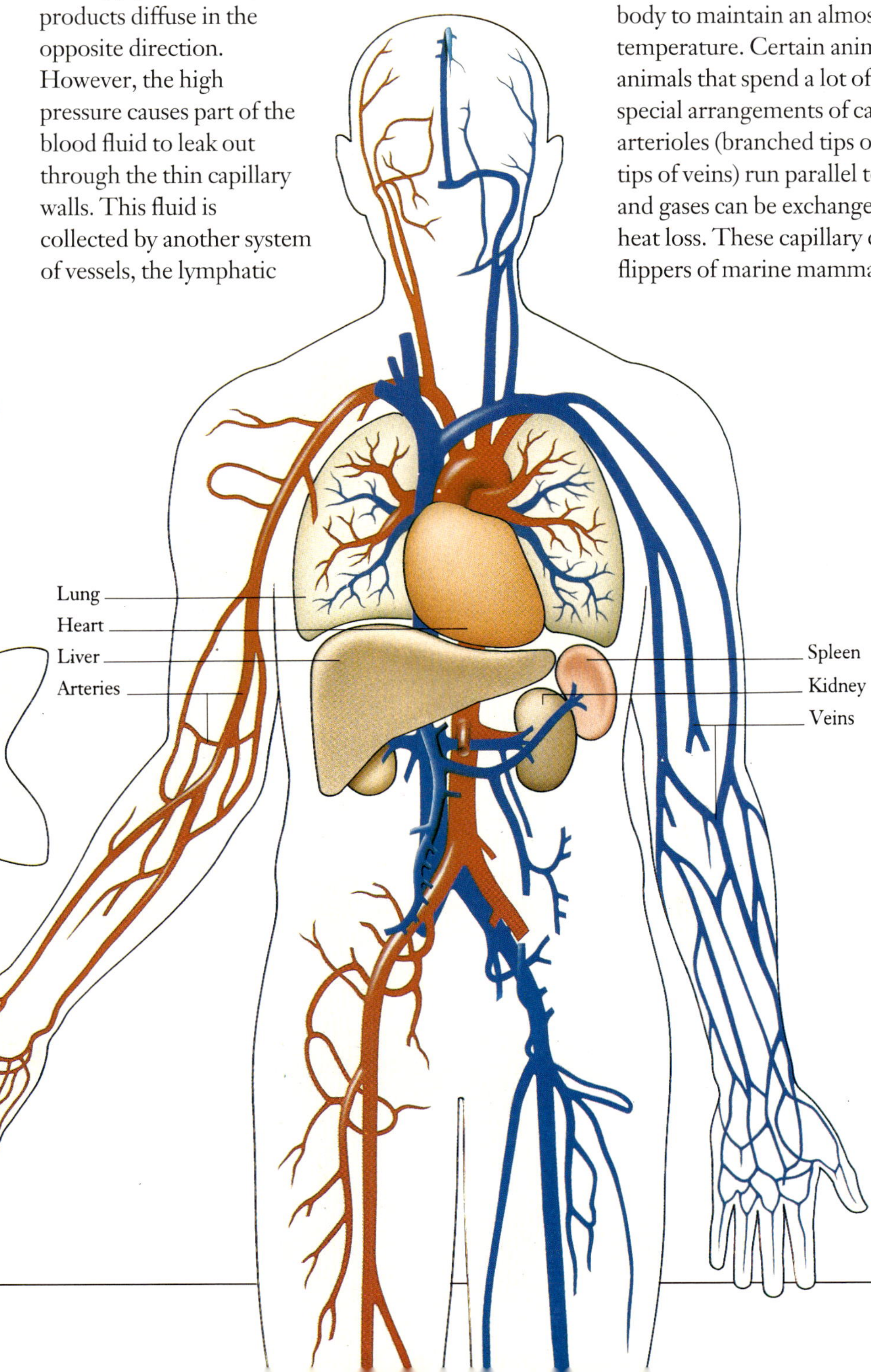

◀ In double circulation (as found in humans), the heart first pumps blood to the lungs, then pumps oxygenated blood to the body at higher pressure. The hearts of animals with double circulations are either three- or four-chambered, so that oxygenated blood from the lungs and deoxygenated blood from the body can be kept separate.

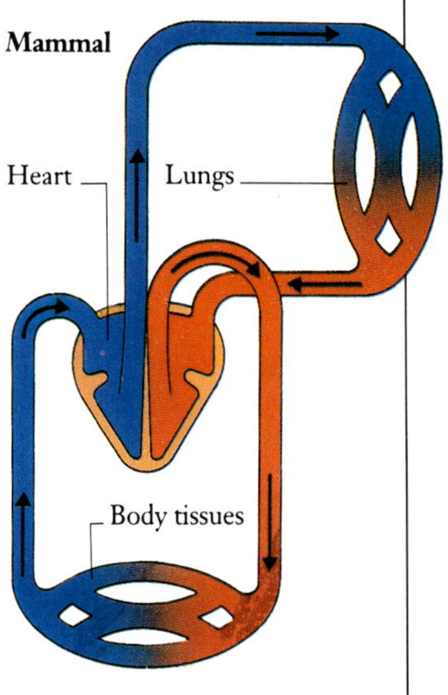

AIR PUMPS

THE average human body contains some 30 billion red blood cells, of which 2–10 million are being continuously destroyed and replaced every second. This huge quantity and rate of turnover is a measure of the importance of red blood cells, which carry oxygen from the lungs to the tissues.

Animals obtain most of their energy from the process of respiration,which uses up oxygen and releases carbon dioxide. Many animals exchange oxygen and carbon dioxide with air or water by means of lungs or gills. The fingerlike processes of the gills and the branching tubes and air sacs of lungs provide a large surface area for diffusion. The surface area of human lungs may be as much as 100 square meters; the rest of the body surface covers only 2 square meters.

KEYWORDS

ALVEOLUS
BOOK LUNG
BREATHING
BRONCHUS
CARBON DIOXIDE
HEMOGLOBIN
LUNG
RESPIRATION
TRACHEA

Gills and lungs are covered in a thin layer of cells less than 5 micrometers thick, and networks of fine capillaries pass close to this surface. Capillaries also exchange gases in the tissues, and can be opened or closed according to local oxygen demand. During periods of strenuous physical activity, ten times more muscle capillaries may be open than when at rest.

In most animals, the blood contains a respiratory pigment, which greatly increases its ability to take in oxygen. Such pigments are protein molecules, often combined with metal ions such as iron or copper, which have a high affinity for oxygen. Without the pigment hemoglobin, human blood could carry only 0.3 percent by volume of oxygen, but with hemoglobin it can carry 20 percent oxygen.

Hemoglobin has the special property of taking in oxygen when it is present in high concentrations (as in the lungs) and releasing it rapidly in areas of low oxygen concentration (the tissues). Another pigment, myoglobin, is used in the muscles to store oxygen, releasing it only at very low oxygen levels. Seals and other diving mammals, which must go for a relatively long time without breathing, have particularly large amounts of myoglobin.

There are various methods of ventilation – moving oxygen-containing air or water into and out of the body. Fish use pumping actions of the floor of the mouth, combined with rhythmic opening and closing of the operculum (gill flap) that covers the gill slits, to send a stream of water over the gills. A frog draws air through its nose into the mouth cavity, then closes valves in its nostrils and raises the floor of the mouth to force air into the lungs. To breathe out, the frog closes the trachea with a valve, then raises the floor of the mouth.

Most reptiles and mammals move their ribs forward and upward to increase the volume of the thorax (upper body). This reduces pressure inside the thorax, causing air to move into the lungs. In mammals, this process is enhanced by contracting a muscular diaphragm that completely seals off the thoracic cavity. Birds have air sacs connected to their lungs which are squeezed by movements of the breast bone and ribs.

Ventilation is coordinated by the respiratory center in the brain. One set of nerves stimulates breathing out, another set breathing in. Stretch receptors in the bronchioles (in the lungs) tell the brain which set of nerves to activate. Highly developed control of breathing also allows humans to whistle, sing and talk.

In all animals, the rate and depth of breathing is altered in response to signals from sensors in the blood vessels and brain that detect changes in the oxygen and carbon dioxide concentration and the acidity of the blood. Receptors trigger coughing if they are irritated by mucus, dust or other foreign particles.

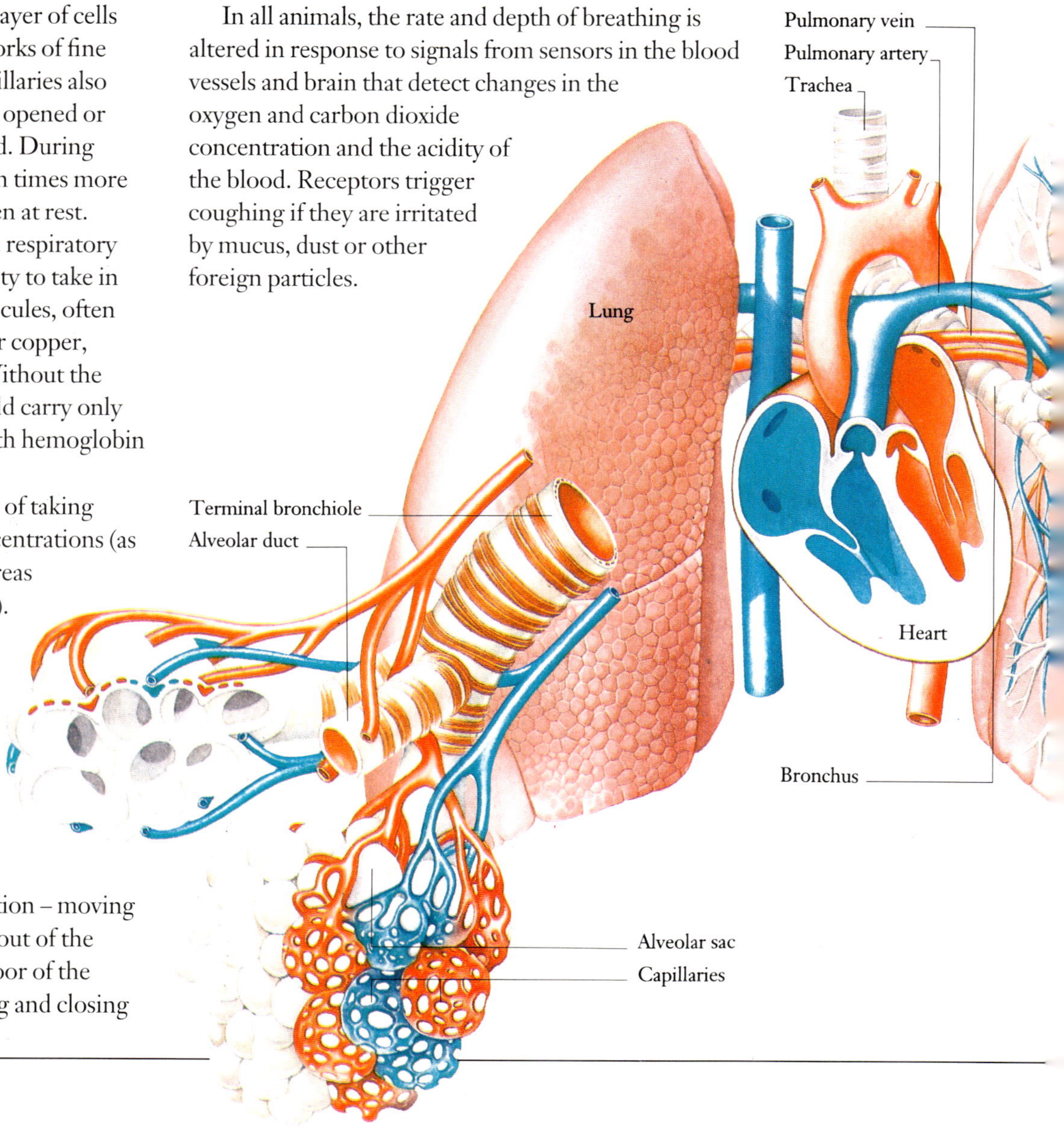

▼ In the human ventilation system, branching bronchi and bronchioles, with the saclike alveoli, provide a large, moist surface for gas exchange. A network of capillaries surrounds each alveolus. Rings of cartilage in the trachea and bronchi, and muscles in the bronchioles, keep the airways open. The surfaces of the lungs are coated in a surfactant fluid which prevents them sticking together and collapsing. The lungs are surrounded by the pleural membrane. This produces the oily pleural fluid, which reduces friction between the lungs and the wall of the chest during breathing.

▼ Whales and dolphins come to the surface from time to time to breathe out a spout of water vapor and air, and gulp in fresh air through a blowhole on the top of their heads. Powerful muscles close the hole while they are diving.

◀ The axolotl is a salamander that retains its juvenile external gills when it reaches adulthood. Water is slowed down as it passes through the tuft of gills, allowing more time for gaseous exchange to take place.

▲ In insects, a series of finely-branching tubules carry oxygen to the tissues. The tubules open to the outside through spiracles, which in this caterpillar are surrounded by colored spots on each segment.

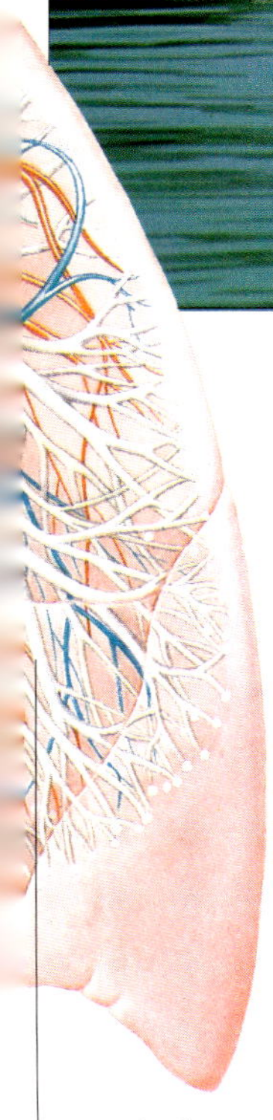

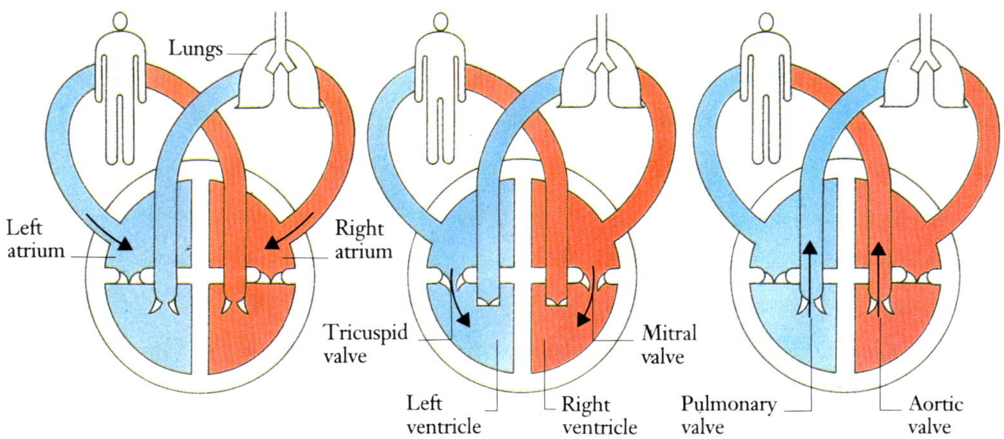

1 Deoxygenated blood from body and oxygenated blood from lungs enter atria

2 Tricuspid and mitral valves open; blood flows into ventricles

3 Pulmonary and aortic valves open, forcing blood to the lungs and body

◀ The "double circulation" of birds and mammals allows blood to be pumped efficiently to the body at pressures too great for the lungs to withstand. This helps to maintain body heat and supply oxygen rapidly to the tissues, permitting more active metabolism. Oxygenated blood from the lungs is pumped to the body, while deoxygenated blood from the body is sent to the lungs.

Chemical Control

In order to survive, an animal must respond to a wide variety of stimuli. It must recognize external signals, such as danger or the overtures of a potential mate, and seasonal changes that tell it when to migrate or hibernate. It also needs to respond to internal signals – indicating that it is running short of food or water, or that its blood pressure is too high or too low.

Responses to all these stimuli require an internal communication system. There are two main kinds of internal signals: nerve impulses and chemical messages. Nerve impulses lead to quick reactions; chemical messages are slower, but they have more long-lasting effects. In very simple animals, chemicals move throughout the bofy by diffusing from cell to cell. In more complex animals, certain parts of the body have become specialized for specific functions, and require long-distance communication between their cells. Control chemicals that are produced in one part of the body and act on another are called hormones.

KEYWORDS

ADRENAL GLAND
ENDOCRINE GLAND
ESTROGEN
EXOCRINE GLAND
HORMONE
NEUROHORMONE
PITUITARY GLAND
TESTOSTERONE
THYROID GLAND

In animals with a circulatory system, most hormones are secreted directly into the bloodstream by clusters of secretory cells called endocrine glands. Examples of these secreting cells are the pituitary gland in the brain, the thyroid gland in the neck and the adrenal glands on the kidney. The specific effects of hormones depend on their recognition by receptors on the membranes of the target cells.

Both the nervous system and hormone-producing glands are controlled by the brain.There are two master glands in the brain of vertebrates – the hypothalamus and the pituitary gland. The hypothalamus is the vital link between the nervous and hormonal control systems. It collects information from the rest of the brain and from sensors in the blood vessels that pass through it. The hypothalamus is linked directly to the pituitary gland by blood vessels, through which it sends hormones that cause the pituitary gland to release or stop releasing other hormones into the bloodstream. There is also some fine-tuning of responses by nerves and chemicals acting locally in parts of the body.

Some glands – such as the hypothalamus and pituitary glands, the parathyroids, the adrenal medulla and parts of the pancreas – produce water-soluble hormones (peptides or amino acids). These are carried to their target cells by special proteins. They may

▼ The hormones epinephrine and norepinephrine (also called adrenaline and noradrenaline), controlled by the adrenal gland, stimulate animals' bodies for combat, promoting heightened awareness and faster reactions. Blood is diverted to the muscles and lungs from the digestive system, to supply oxygen for respiration. Nervous control may evoke these reactions rapidly, but hormones allow the response to be maintained over a longer period.

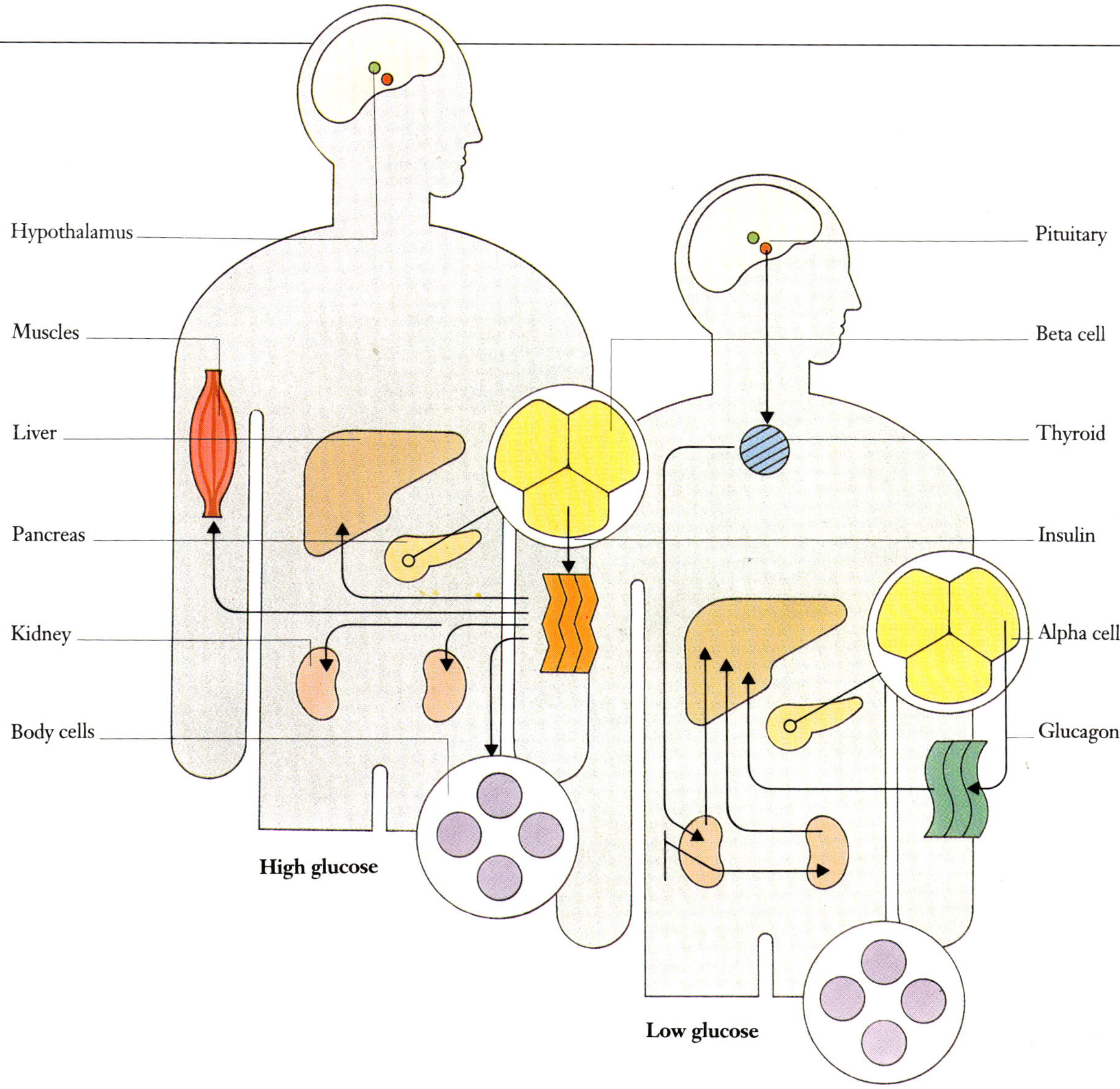

stimulate the cell or shut down its activity. Some hormones, such as insulin and epinephrine (also called adrenaline), act directly on cell membranes.

Glands such as the thyroid, adrenal cortex, testicles and ovaries produce fat-soluble steroid-based hormones, which pass into the cell and switch certain genes on or off. This produces effects such as the growth of the reproductive organs in puberty, accompanied by the growth of facial hair and the deepening of the voice in human males.

The secretion of hormones may be triggered by changes in certain chemicals in the blood, by the presence of other hormones, or by nervous signals. In situations of anxiety or danger, signals from the autonomic nervous system stimulate the release of the hormones epinephrine (adrenaline) and norepinephrine (noradrenaline). These hormones prepare the body for rapid reaction to the threat – called the "fight or flight" response. The heart beats rapidly to pump more blood to the muscles, and blood pressure increases. A rise in blood sugar causes the pancreas to secrete the hormone insulin, which influences a number of biochemical processes to lower the blood sugar level. The liver swiftly converts stored food from the tissues to supply extra energy.

▲ One method of controlling hormone action is feedback control, as in the control of blood sugar levels. The primary control occurs in the pancreas, in a group of glands called the islets of Langerhans. When the pancreas detects too much glucose, the beta cells produce insulin, stimulating the body to use or store glucose. If the glucose level falls too low, insulin production is reduced and the alpha cells secrete the hormone glucagon, stimulating the liver to convert glycogen to glucose. If the liver has too little glycogen, the hypothalamus promotes the conversion of amino acids and glycerol to glucose in the liver.

NERVOUS CONTROL

THE human nervous system can send messages at speeds of up to 120 meters per second, with a control center that directs the activities of hundreds of millions of signal paths. The vast coordinating center is the brain. Not only is it capable of receiving information from the sense cells and organs and producing responses, but it can also compare this information with stored experiences (memory) to produce a calculated response and learn new ways of interpreting the information.

KEYWORDS

ACETYLCHOLINE
ACTION POTENTIAL
NERVOUS SYSTEM
NEURON
PARASYMPATHETIC NERVOUS SYSTEM
SYMPATHETIC NERVOUS SYSTEM
SYNAPSE

Within a cell, distances are very small, so electrical signals can be effective. For signaling over longer distances, electrical impulses must be insulated from their surroundings to travel fast enough. This happens when impulses are conducted along the fibers of nerve cells.

Two or more nerve cells, or neurons, are linked together to form a pathway. Chemicals are secreted across the minute gaps between neurons, called synapses, to start off a new nerve impulse in the next neuron. This system allows for control and direction of the signaling, and for coordination of the activities of large numbers of neurons. For instance, the impulse may not be transmitted to the second neuron unless a series of impulses arrives at the synapse, or it may be inhibited by signals arriving at the second neuron from other neurons.

During the course of evolution, the numbers of neurons and the ways in which they link up have become larger and more complex, reflecting the increasing organization of animal bodies. Individual nerve fibers were grouped into bundles of fibers, usually protected by a tough sheath.The cell bodies of adjacent fibers came to lie next to each other, forming a ganglion, so the rest of the nerve takes up less space. Complex collections of intermediate neurons developed as coordinating and control centers, the largest being the brain. The head is in front as the animal moves, so it is this end that is usually the first part to experience new stimuli. Sense organs such as eyes, ears and chemical sensors became concentrated here, only a short distance from the brain, so the animal could respond quickly.

In some animals, such as arthropods, other coordination centers are quite important. Ganglia in the thorax control movement, since the limbs (and wings) are attached there. In more advanced animals, the brain has become even more dominant. In vertebrates, the brain and spinal cord are the main coordinating centers, and together they are called the central nervous system (CNS). From the CNS two sets of nerves spread out to the rest of the body. The somatic or voluntary nervous system leads to the skeletal muscles, and is chiefly responsible for reflex or automatic responses. The voluntary nervous system is also responsible for the deliberate movements of different parts of the body, but although the direction and speed of movements such as walking may be under conscious control, they usually involve reflex responses to information from stretch sensors in the muscles, balance organs, and so on. The involuntary or autonomic nervous system is not normally under conscious control. It maintains the heart beat, blood pressure, breathing, movement of food along the intestines, excretion and temperature control.

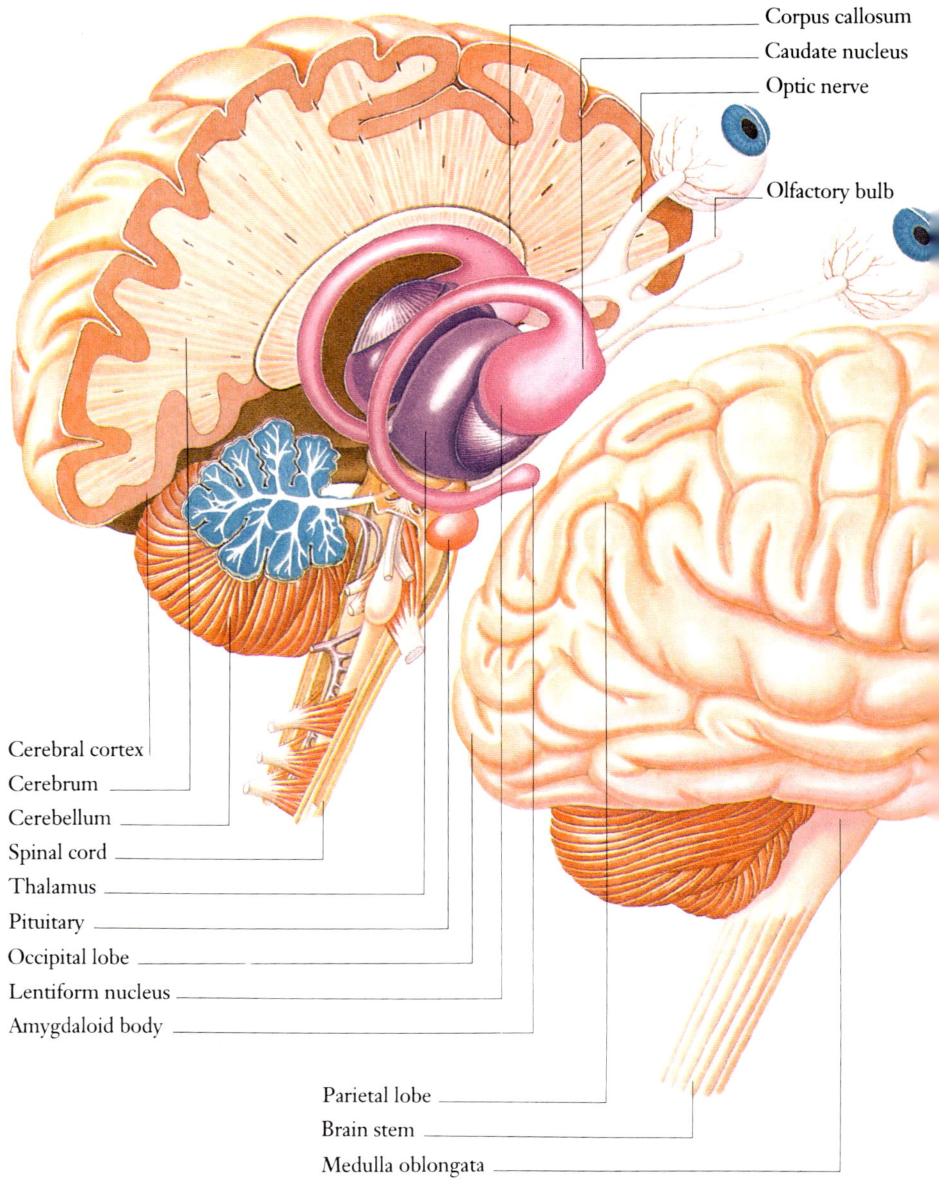

▲ The human brain is different from most other vertebrate brains in the great development of the cerebral cortex – the outer 3mm of the cerebral hemispheres, where most sensory information is processed. Incoming information is interpreted according to the point on the cortex at which it arrives. Association areas interpret the incoming signals in relation to previous experience in memory, and effector areas initiate movements of a particular part of the body.

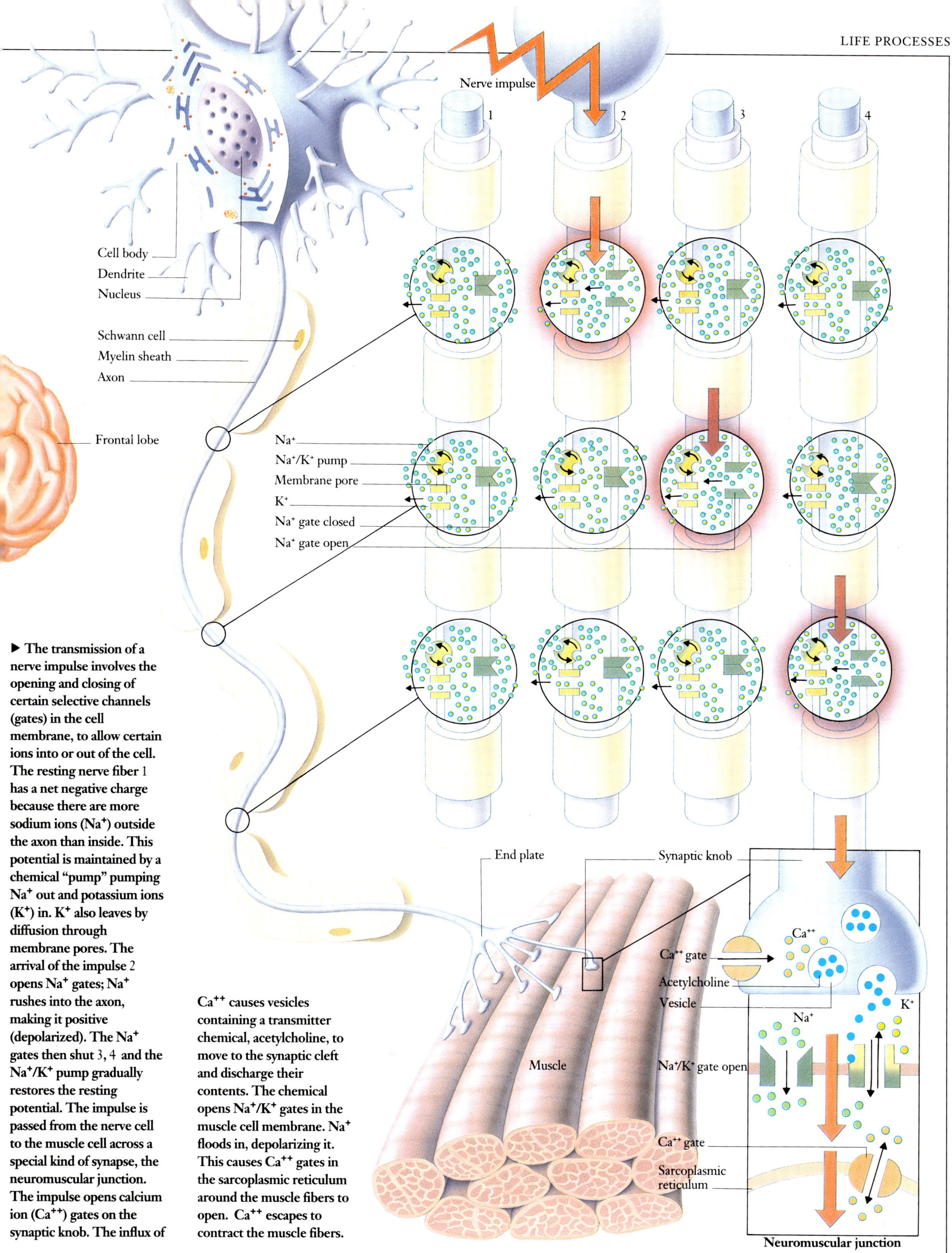

▶ **The transmission of a nerve impulse involves the opening and closing of certain selective channels (gates) in the cell membrane, to allow certain ions into or out of the cell. The resting nerve fiber** 1 **has a net negative charge because there are more sodium ions (Na^+) outside the axon than inside. This potential is maintained by a chemical "pump" pumping Na^+ out and potassium ions (K^+) in. K^+ also leaves by diffusion through membrane pores. The arrival of the impulse** 2 **opens Na^+ gates; Na^+ rushes into the axon, making it positive (depolarized). The Na^+ gates then shut** 3, 4 **and the Na^+/K^+ pump gradually restores the resting potential. The impulse is passed from the nerve cell to the muscle cell across a special kind of synapse, the neuromuscular junction. The impulse opens calcium ion (Ca^{++}) gates on the synaptic knob. The influx of Ca^{++} causes vesicles containing a transmitter chemical, acetylcholine, to move to the synaptic cleft and discharge their contents. The chemical opens Na^+/K^+ gates in the muscle cell membrane. Na^+ floods in, depolarizing it. This causes Ca^{++} gates in the sarcoplasmic reticulum around the muscle fibers to open. Ca^{++} escapes to contract the muscle fibers.**

Controlling Heat and Water

The highly efficient metabolism of birds and mammals is the result of a nearly constant body temperature. Such animals are called endotherms (endotherm means inner heat). Their temperature is usually in the range 35–44°C; the human body normally maintains a temperature of 37°C. Endotherms control their internal temperature (thermoregulate) by controlling the loss of metabolic heat. A temperature control center in the brain is linked by nerves to sensory cells which detect temperature changes, particularly in the skin, where most heat exchange takes place.

KEYWORDS

ANTIDIURETIC HORMONE (ADH)
ECTOTHERMIC
ENDOTHERMIC
HIBERNATION
METABOLISM
OSMOREGULATION
SWEAT GLAND
THERMOREGULATION

Many animals control their temperature by simply moving into or out of the sun, or by burrowing underground, where the temperature changes are much smaller. Where large temperature changes are a regular occurrence, animals may enter a resting state in which metabolism is greatly slowed and body temperature falls, thus reducing heat loss to the environment. Hibernation, for example, is used by some animals to survive cold winter weather with its accompanying shortage of food.

All animals have their own central heating systems: the millions of metabolic reactions produce heat, especially in the liver. In higher animals this heat is transported around the body by the blood circulation. This heat output increases during periods of muscle activity (including shivering). Heat can be absorbed from or lost to the environment if the animal's surroundings are at a different temperature.

Feathers and hair help birds and mammals to control heat exchange by trapping a layer of air next to the skin. Air is a poor conductor of heat, so it keeps in body heat. If the hair or feathers are raised, this air layer becomes thicker, with an even greater insulating effect. (Humans have very little hair, but in cold weather the hairs stand up, producing goose pimples.) Hairs also keep out heat from the environment and reduce water loss from the skin, which would have a cooling effect. A camel without fur would lose 50 percent more water from its skin.

Much heat is lost from the blood in capillaries running close to the surface of the skin. In hot weather, nerve signals cause the capillaries to contract, so less blood is warmed up, and vice versa. Control of cooling by evaporation is also important. Some mammals sweat, losing water by evaporation. In hot weather, humans can produce a liter of sweat an hour, and strenuous exercise at high temperatures can lead to losses of 30 liters a day. A great deal of salt is lost at the same time. Dogs have few sweat glands, since sweating is not very effective through thick fur. Instead, they pant, cooling the blood passing through the tongue and mouth. Rabbits lick their fur.

Cooling by evaporation is costly in terms of salt and water loss. A reduction in salt content of the blood means it draws in less water by osmosis, so becoming thicker and harder to pump. This causes a rise in blood pressure. Too high a blood volume, however, also causes an increase in blood pressure. Water loss is controlled in the kidney by hormones produced in response to information from osmotic sensors in the blood vessels of the hypothalamus. If the blood is short of water, antidiuretic hormone is secreted, so more water is reabsorbed and a more concentrated urine is produced. The kidneys may also show structural adaptations to conserve water: desert animals usually have a very long kidney tubule to allow for more reabsorption of water.

Animals that live in water must also have special arrangements for regulating water and salt loss. Freshwater animals tend to absorb water by osmosis due to the concentration of salts in their tissues, which is higher than that in the surrounding water. They produce large amounts of very dilute urine. Marine animals have the opposite problem: as they take in more water, they also take in the salt it contains. The salts must be excreted across the gills or through special glands such as the tear glands of sea turtles. Some fish solve this by retaining urea in the blood.

▲ Elephant ears contain small blood vessels close to the surface, so heat is easily lost to the surrounding air. By flapping their ears elephants keep the air moving, maintaining the temperature gradient (for heat loss).

◀ The dormouse hibernates throughout the winter. It drops its metabolic rate, and to some extent its body temperature, so it loses less heat to its surroundings. Its fur and tail help insulate it from the cold.

◀ All animals are affected by the temperature of their surroundings. The cat is absorbing heat from the rays of the Sun, and by direct conduction from warmer objects such as the wall. In cooler surroundings, the cat loses some of its body heat by the same processes – that is, by conduction and radiation.

▲ The emperor penguin incubates its egg in the icy Antarctic winter. Its feet and flippers have a special arrangement of blood vessels: cold blood from the extremities is warmed by the blood flowing into them.

◀ A kangaroo licks its forearms. The saliva soon evaporates, cooling blood vessels under the skin. In order to leave the moist surface and escape into the air, the water molecules absorb heat energy from the skin.

RECOVERY AND REPAIR

THE bodies of animals have a large surface area exposed to the outside world, through which bacteria, viruses, fungal infections and poisons can invade. Blinking, wax in the ears, tears, mucus and stomach acid are all examples of the variety of natural defense systems employed by animal bodies.

The skin is the major physical barrier against disease and injury in vertebrates. Its surface is covered in fatty secretions and other substances that inhibit the growth of bacteria. When the skin is torn, clotting prevents the loss of large amounts of blood, and is followed by the regrowth of tissue. A scar may form, marking the spot; the wound is then healed, though it lacks the sensory cells present in the original uninjured tissue.

KEYWORDS

ANTIBODY
ANTIGEN
CLOTTING
IMMUNE SYSTEM
LYMPHOCYTE
LYMPH SYSTEM
PAIN
REGENERATION
SKIN

A similar process takes place when internal injury occurs in blood vessels and lungs. The linings of the respiratory tract, digestive and excretory systems are continuously worn down by abrasion and renewed by cell division. They do not usually form scars unless badly damaged. Liver cells can also divide to replace damaged ones nearby. The repair of more specialized tissues is not always so easy. Nerve cells in the central nervous system do not seem capable of repair. Mature brain cells cannot be replaced, although the brain sometimes compensates for the loss by diverting the function of those cells to other areas in the brain.

Bones are repaired by cells called osteoblasts, which form a tough bridge between the broken edges and gradually reshape them. Other cells called osteoclasts remove splinters of bone, and white blood cells clear away damaged tissues. All these repair processes appear to be under the control of chemicals.

Damage to entire organs or limbs can often be repaired in simple animals such as flatworms. Starfish, spiders and crabs can also grow replacement legs at the next molt, although these may not be the same size as the original ones.

Just are important as physical repairs are the body's chemical defenses, including the immune system. The basis of this system is the white blood cells, called leukocytes. Of the five kinds of leukocytes, the large white blood cells (macrophages) and smaller white blood cells (neutrophils) are particularly important. They are able to recognize particular invading organisms (pathogens) and their toxic secretions and attack them. They may engulf and digest foreign

■ **The immune system is based upon recognition between defending and invading cells. Defending cells attack invaders directly or produce antibodies (chemicals) that recognize and attach to one specific type of invader or toxin. This begins as soon as foreign organisms invade.**

Wound formation

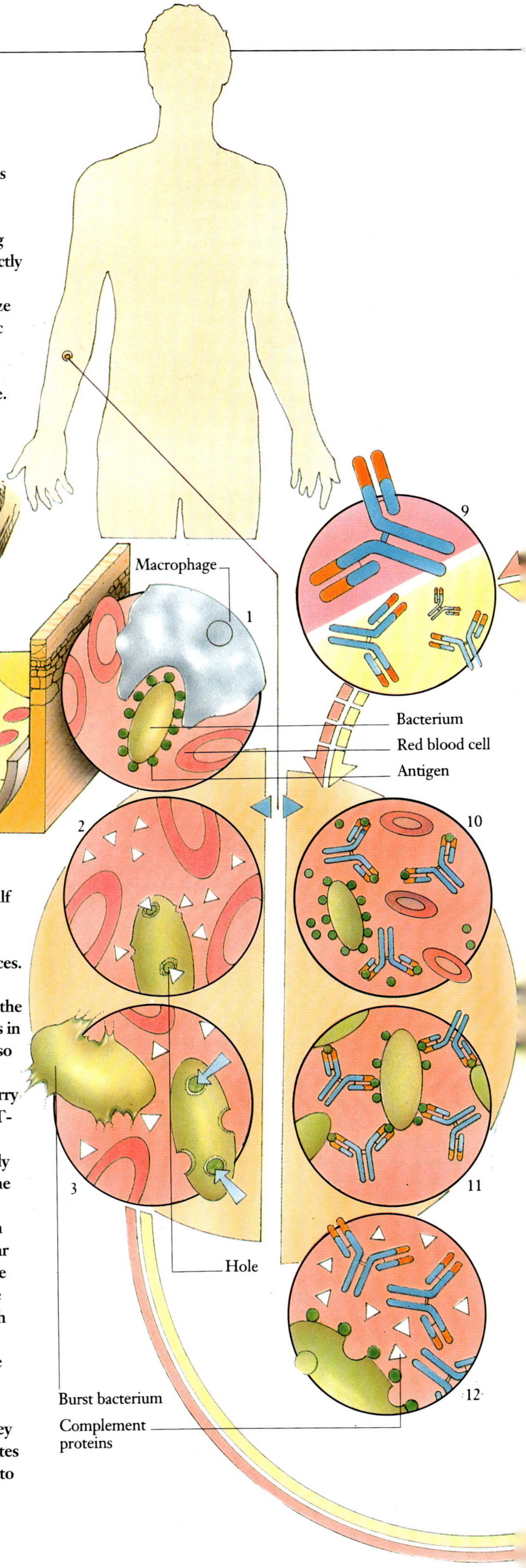

■ **Macrophages (white blood cells) start to engulf bacteria 1 bearing recognizable chemicals (antigens) on their surfaces. They also activate complement proteins in the blood. These make holes in the bacterial cell walls 2 so they take up liquid and burst 3. Macrophages carry the bacteria 4 to helper T-cells 5, which stimulate certain B-cells to multiply 6. Some B-cells stay in the lymph nodes as memory cells 7, ready to deal with future invasions of similar antigens. Others produce antibodies specific to the invading antigen 8, which are transported by the lymph and blood 9 to the infected wound 10. The antibodies bind with the antigens in a lock-and-key manner 11. This stimulates the complement system to destroy the bacteria 12.**

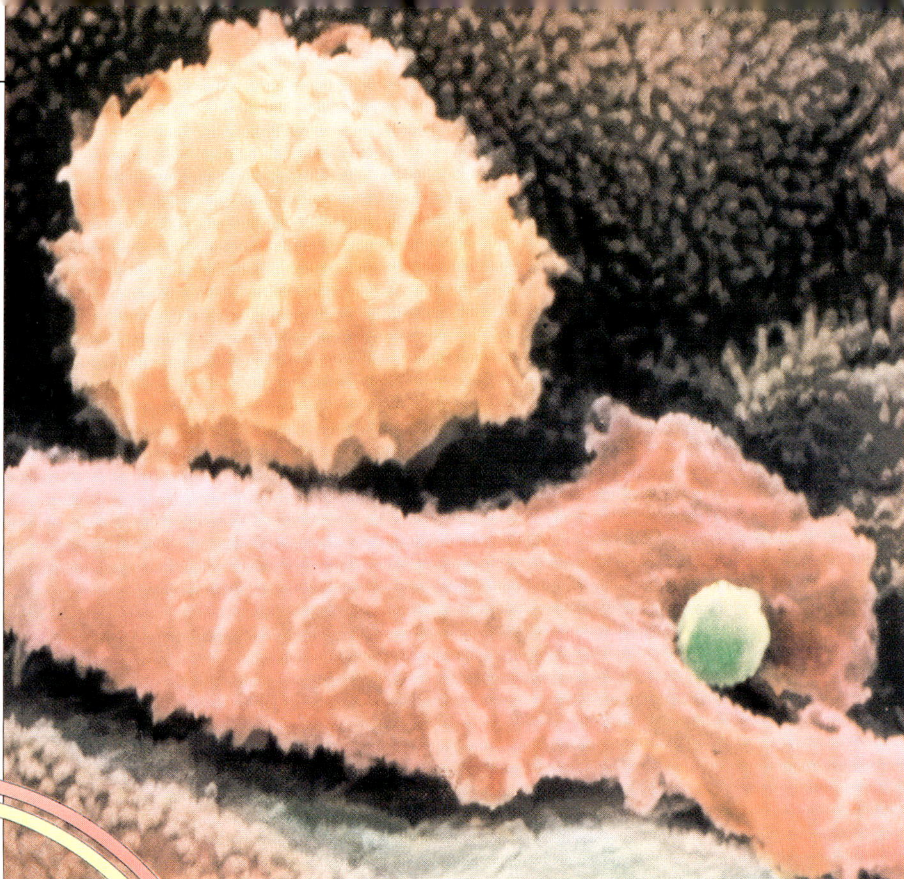

▲ **Macrophages are large white blood cells. The macrophage at the top is its usual shape, but the lower one has elongated itself, ready to engulf the small round particle on the right.**

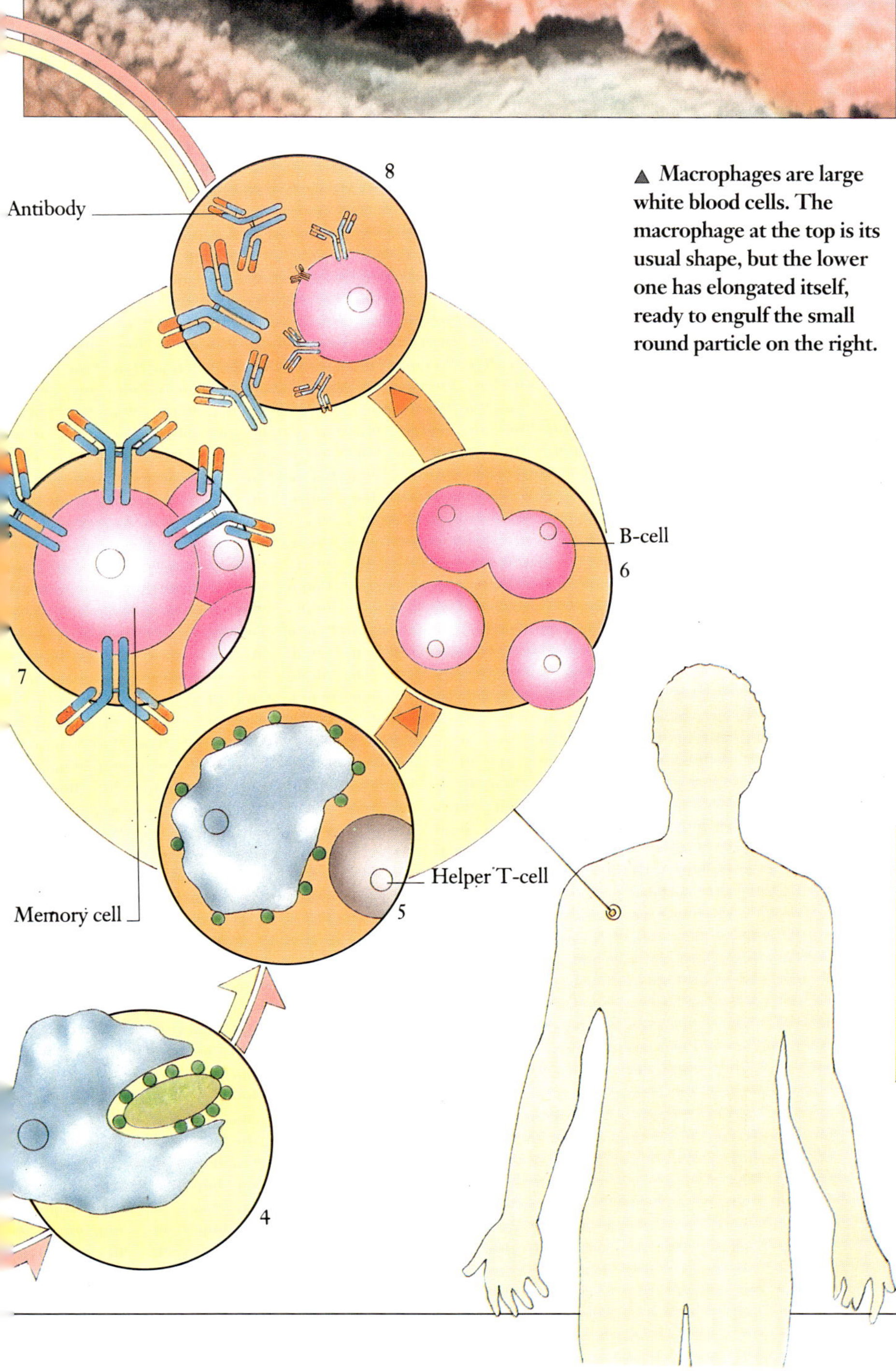

particles, or they may produce chemicals to neutralize them. Genetic programming allows these defensive cells to distinguish between foreign cells and normal body cells; for example, when a human receives a blood transfusion, the blood used for the transfusion must match the person's blood type, or the "foreign" blood cells will be rejected by the person's body. Proteins in the blood may attach to the white blood cells and help them to recognize chemicals on the coats of bacteria. Neutrophils also destroy the remains of dead tissue cells after injury or infection.

The main defenses against pathogens are specialized white blood cells called T-cells and B-cells, which have a complex recognition system that helps them to fight disease. T-cells are produced in bone marrow and pass through the thymus gland in order to work. B-cells are produced in all the main lymph centers such as the bone marrow, spleen, tonsils, intestinal lining, appendix and lymph nodes. The immune response is controlled by some 20-30 messenger chemicals called lymphokinins, which travel in the lymphatic system. This is a system of vessels through which blood plasma that has bathed the body tissues is returned to the blood. At intervals are special pockets – lymph nodes – containing high concentrations of defensive white blood cells.

▼ **Wound healing. Damaged tissue cells and blood platelets release the chemical thromboplastin, setting off a chain reaction involving blood proteins. Prothrombin is converted into thrombin, an enzyme, which changes fibrinogen into long chains of fibrin to form a network over the wound. This network traps platelets and blood cells to form a protective scab. Skin cells divide and migrate over the wound, eventually forming new tissue. Fibroblast cells stimulate regeneration of underlying tissues and blood vessels.**

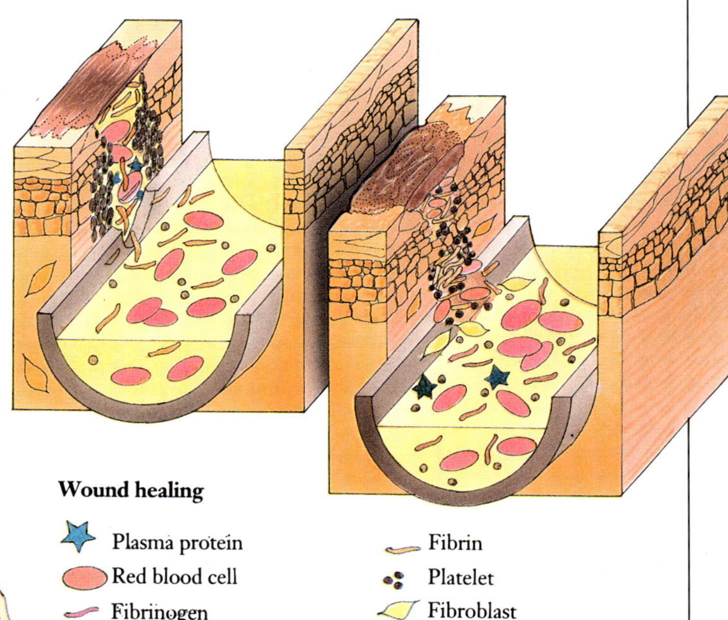

3

FINDING *Food*

NATURE IS remarkably economical. From the tiniest algae and protozoans to the bulk of an elephant or a giant redwood tree, nothing survives forever, and most of it is recycled: almost every plant or animal eventually becomes food for something else. This cycle of feeding is called the food chain. It begins with the energy of sunlight, which is trapped by plants and algae and passed on to the animals that eat them. These animals are sapped by parasites or killed and eaten by other animals. Their carcasses attract large scavengers such as vultures and hyenas, which themselves die and leave remains that attract more scavengers and decomposers. Beetles, worms and a host of small organisms break down the remains further until they become food for bacteria and fungi. At the far end of the chain, nutrients pass back into the soil and the cycle begins once more.

An animal's diet affects its entire body plan. The great variety of food available in Nature demands a dazzling array of adaptations for finding food, capturing and killing prey, eating and digesting it. The reverse is also true – an animal's choice of food is limited by its size, shape, strength and speed; and especially by the size and strength of its mouthparts. Much of the diversity of life on our planet today has evolved in response to the need to eat and to avoid being eaten.

A grasshopper tucks into a fragrant meal of flowers. Plant material is tough and fibrous, and plant-eaters need strong mouthparts with good cutting edges and some means of breaking up the plant fibers. The grasshopper's mandibles are made of a hard material called chitin, and have serrated edges for cutting. Taste sensors on various parts of the grasshopper's body, especially on its antennae, tell it whether a leaf or flower is suitable to eat. Its large compound eyes give it good all-around vision: it can detect the nearby movements of potential predators while it feeds.

DIETS GALORE

HUNGER is necessary for the survival of animals, and the diversity of living creatures is matched by the diversity of their diets. Animals consume all kinds of organic materials, from flowers to flesh, bark, wood and even dung. According to their diets, animals may be classified into plant-eaters (herbivores), flesh-eaters (carnivores) and plant-and-flesh-eaters (omnivores). There are also carrion-eaters, which feed on dead animals; decomposers, which feed on the remains of dead plants and animals; and parasites, which feed in or on other living creatures.

KEYWORDS

FILTER FEEDER
FOOD CHAIN
HERBIVORE
OMNIVORE
PARASITE
SCAVENGER

In the sea, it is not so easy to distinguish between herbivores and carnivores. Droppings and dead remains tend to disintegrate into small particles called detritus. These, together with living microscopic organisms – both plant and animal – are filtered out of the water by suspension-feeding animals or gathered from the seabed by detritus feeders.

An animal's diet and its body structure are closely linked. Cutting and chewing mouthparts are needed to tackle tough, fibrous plant material, and a long intestine to digest it. Predators need claws and sharp mouthparts to capture and kill their prey. Animals that filter food from the water have internal or external sieves, while detritus feeders (which feed on dead organic material at the bottom of lakes, rivers and oceans) often have long tentacles covered in sticky mucus to which particles of food adhere.

Some animals eat a wide range of food which may vary in availability with the seasons. Seagulls are quite capable of catching fish, but also feed on carrion and crabs along the shore, and on anything they can find in garbage dumps. Other animals are highly specialized. The snail kite of the Florida Everglades in the United States feeds only on the apple snail, while the Australian koala eats only the leaves of a few species of eucalyptus trees.

Each kind of diet – general and specialized – has advantages and disadvantages. An animal with a varied diet may be able to adapt well to environmental changes: many animals have invaded farms and towns to exploit new food sources. But these animals are always in competition with other species for part of their diet. Those with specialized diets, on the other hand, may use sources of food not sought by other animals. The sloth's slow lifestyle consumes relatively little energy; as a result, it can survive on a diet of nutrient-poor leaves that are unsuitable for more

■ **The vampire bat ABOVE feeds on the blood of mammals, often while they are asleep. Its teeth are so sharp that its victim may not feel the bite until afterwards. The bat injects an anticoagulant into the victim's blood to prevent it from clotting while the bat drinks its fill.**

The red meat diet of carnivores such as lions RIGHT provides more energy than a vegetable diet, but this energy is quickly expended in the strenuous hunt for food. The lion's prey is mobile and must be pursued and caught, and often dragged to cover following the kill. Most of the hunting for the pride is done by the females, who must also provide food for their cubs until they are strong enough to fend for themselves. Lionesses conserve energy by hunting together and sharing the kill. One or two lionesses lie in wait while the others stampede the prey in their direction.

◀ The koala's lazy lifestyle serves a purpose. By moving slowly, the koala uses very little energy, allowing it to survive on a diet of tough eucalyptus leaves – for which there is little competition with other animals.

▼ The acorn woodpecker drills holes in a tree to store its nuts. Food stores help many birds and rodents survive the scarcity of food in winter. Nuts and seeds may also be buried underground or carried back to nests and burrows.

active forest animals. But the giant panda of China, which feeds mainly on bamboo, depends on forests, which may be cut down, or depleted when the bamboos die back after rare periods of flowering. Because of its slow lifestyle and the need to eat large quantities of not very nutritious leaves every day, the panda finds it difficult to travel far in search of new food sources. Such specialists have been the main losers in the face of habitat destruction and pollution by humans.

An animal's diet may change drastically during its lifetime. Young birds in the nest, unable to digest the seeds normally eaten by their parents, are fed insects to provide the proteins and other nutrients necessary for growth. The breeding season of birds is usually timed to coincide with peak insect populations. Butterfly caterpillars eat leaves, but adult butterflies lead an active aerial life and have specialized mouthparts for feeding on high-energy nectar.

Animals' diets also play an important role in nature. Bees and hummingbirds feed on high-energy nectar, and in turn they pollinate the flowers that supply them. Jays, woodpeckers and squirrels, which store acorns for eating later, help to distribute the seeds of the oak. Predators such as wolves and lions catch their food mainly among old, weak and sick animals, thereby improving the overall health of the prey population.

PLANT-EATERS

PLANTS are an abundant source of food for animals, but many of them are also rather tough and indigestible. Their leaves and stems contain many fibers, made mainly of a carbohydrate called cellulose which many animals find difficult to digest. Plant-eaters need mouthparts capable of cutting and chewing the tough plant material into smaller pieces and making it more easily digestible.

Many different animal groups have evolved mouthparts capable of cutting up plant material. Slugs and snails have a tongue-like structure, called a radula, armed with rows of tiny recurved teeth. As the teeth wear down, they are replaced by new sets.

Insects also have hard cutting mouthparts, made of an extremely hard substance called chitin. One pair of mouthparts guides the leaf or stem into position; the saw-edged mandibles cut off pieces, which are transported into the mouth by a third pair of mouthparts. Insects' success at tackling tough plant fibers is well illustrated by the vast swarms of locusts that sweep across the tropics, stripping off the vegetation.

Most vertebrates have bony jaws lined with teeth. Herbivorous mammals usually have a series of large, flat, ridged molars and premolars at the back of the mouth for grinding and chewing; they also have sharp incisors at the front for nibbling the plants, but lack the prominent sharp-pointed canine teeth which carnivores use for shearing flesh. Tortoises and turtles have no true teeth, but their mandibles are quite capable of cutting through leaves and stems – and even through human fingers.

Birds, too, have beaks instead of jaws. Bird bills may be ridged and grooved for gripping seeds, heavy and pointed for hammering open nuts, or specially shaped to deal with particular plant foods. An example is the crossbill, whose crossed mandibles are used to hook seeds from conifer cones.

KEYWORDS

CHITIN
DIASTEMA
HERBIVORE
INCISOR
MANDIBLE
MAXILLA
MOLAR
REGURGITATION
RUMINANT

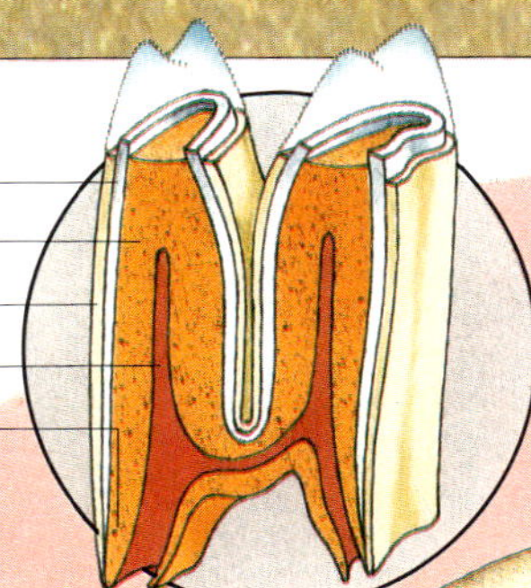

■ Teeth RIGHT consist of a core of bone-like dentine wrapped in a tough case of enamel. The pulp cavity contains blood vessels and nerves. BELOW The sharp canine teeth of a rat are a contrast with the blunter incisors and molars of a deer and a horse.

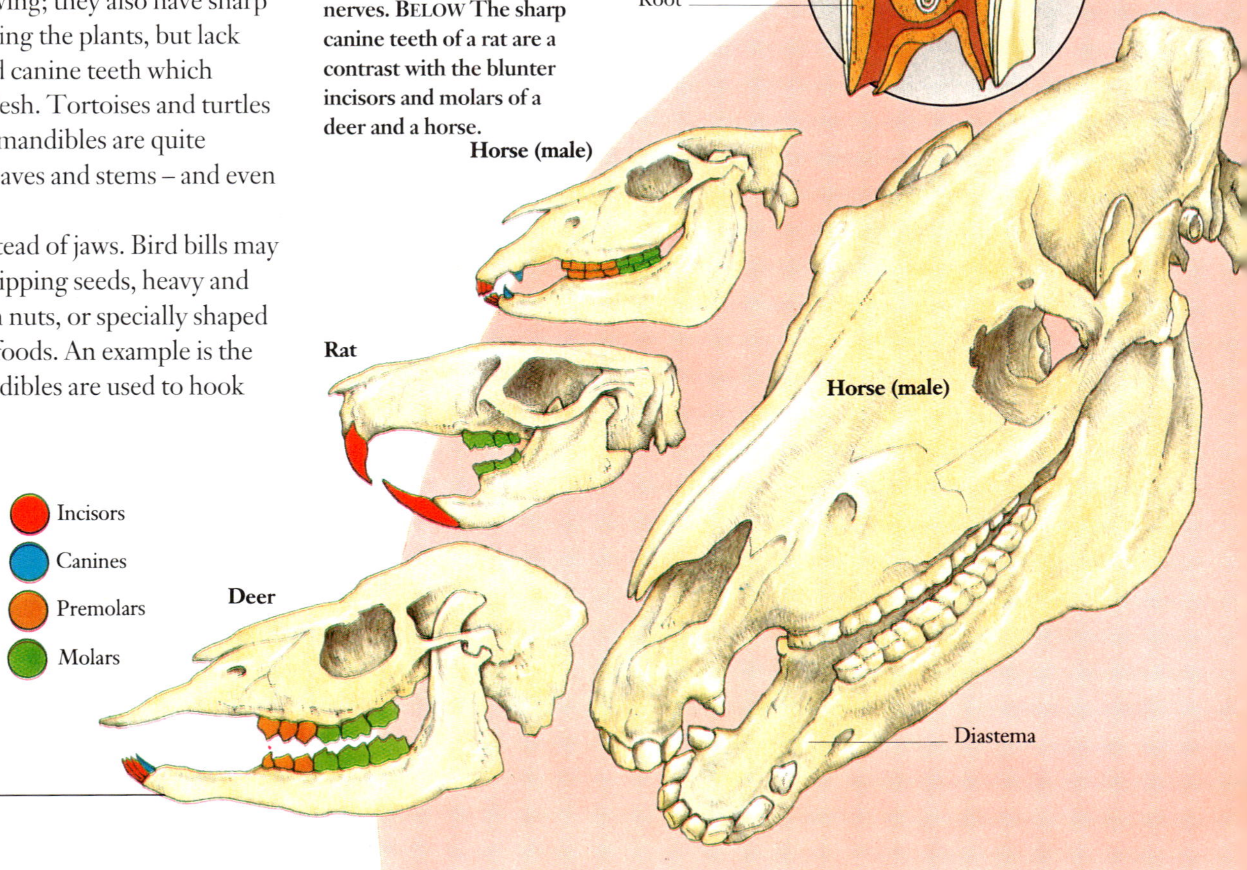

▶ Plant-eating hoofed mammals typically have a gap (diastema) between the front and back teeth for the tongue to mix the food with saliva before swallowing. Ruminants tend to have shorter jaws and small, if any, upper front teeth.

◀ **The sharp front teeth of rodents chisel through tough nuts. Many rodents hoard nuts and seeds underground as a precaution against shortage.**

■ **Grazers BELOW have consumed much of the world's grasslands. Their specialized diets reduce competition for food. Plant-eaters exploit every level of vegetation FAR LEFT, from high branches to the seeds on the ground.**

Many rodents – mice, rats and squirrels – can tackle particularly hard foods such as nuts. They have very long chisel-shaped incisors (front teeth). These are so strong that beavers use theirs for cutting down whole trees. Rodents and many grazing herbivores, such as sheep and horses, have a large toothless gap between the incisors and molars, called the diastema. This allows room for the tongue to manipulate the food.

Although mammals' teeth are covered in hard enamel, vegetation is such a tough diet that even this durable surface is eventually worn away. To compensate for this wear and tear – and allow the animal to continue to eat – the teeth of most herbivores continue growing throughout their lifespan. An exception is the elephant, which has only six huge pairs of molars in its long lifetime. Only one set of molars is in operation at any one time. New molars develop at the back of the jaw and move forward as the old ones wear down. When the sixth set has worn down – usually when the animal is about 60 years of age – the elephant may die of starvation.

Many herbivores have bacteria in their guts which help to break down the cellulose cell walls of plants. These bacteria are often housed in special pouches of the intestine, such as the cecum or appendix. Deer, antelope and cattle – the ruminants – have a series of special stomachs in which bacterial digestion of cellulose takes place. Partly digested food is regurgitated and rechewed later.

Many different sizes and shapes of herbivores have arisen to take advantage of particular food sources or to eliminate competition. Giraffes can reach branches high above the heads of other animals. Gerenuks (long-limbed antelopes) reach slightly lower branches by standing on their hind legs. Below them browse smaller animals, such as dikdiks (a smaller antelope), which feed on low branches and shrubs, and finally grazers, which eat the grass and herbs.

Among grazers, different grazers favor different plants. On the African plains, mixed herds of antelopes, zebra and wildebeest coexist and migrate together. The zebras move on to new pastures first, trampling the vegetation so that the smaller grazers can reach the lower-growing species.

◀ **The crossbill 1 extracts seeds from conifer cones; the hawfinch 2 can crack seeds and nuts; warblers 3 have finer bills to probe for insects. Ducks' bills 4 are serrated for straining.**

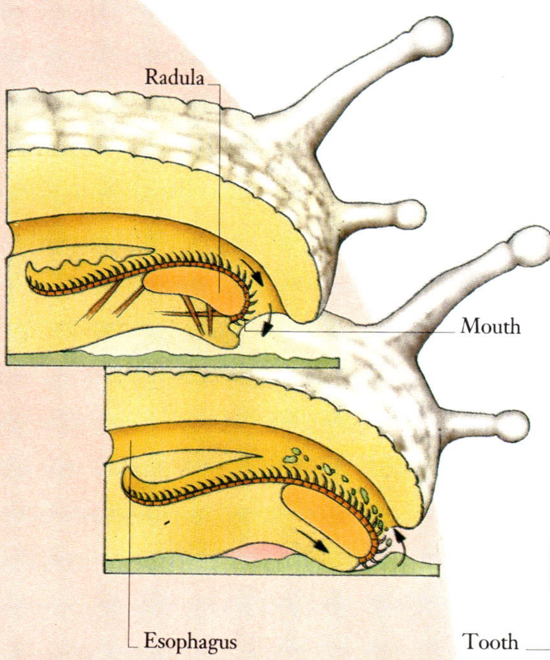

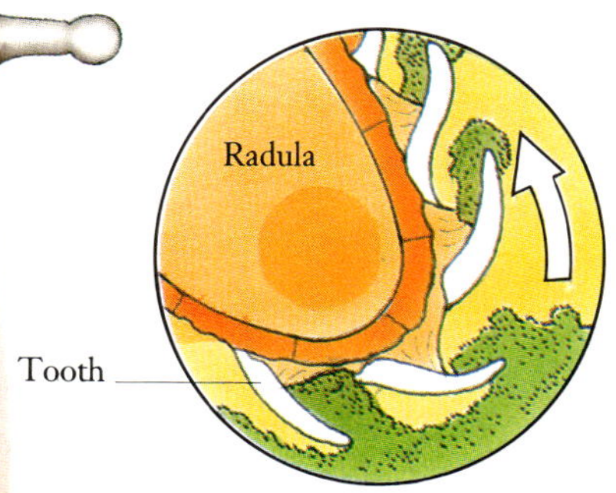

◀ **Snails, slugs and other mollusks use a toothed file called a radula to rasp at vegetation (and, in some species, at prey). The strip of tissue, armed with rows of small sharp teeth, is pulled back and forth over a supportive strut.**

FLESH-EATERS

CARNIVORES – flesh-eating hunters – are some of the most powerful animals. All hunters need to be able to capture and kill their prey, as well as to eat and digest it. Most vertebrate predators use teeth or claws to kill their prey. Some, like hunting dogs, simply tear at the softer parts of their quarry until it either bleeds to death or dies of shock. Others deliver a carefully aimed bite which brings a swift death: lions and other members of the cat family sink their teeth in the prey's throat, so it quickly dies of suffocation.

KEYWORDS

CANINE
CARNASSIAL TEETH
INCISOR
JAW
MOLAR
OMNIVORE

Strength is also an asset to the hunter. Crocodiles and thresher sharks may stun their prey with a swipe of their powerful tails, while mantis shrimps knock out their victims with a blow from their large claws. Dolphins and sperm whales are thought to emit very loud sounds that stun or perhaps even kill fish and other prey, or at least make them easier to catch. Electric eels deliver electric shocks of up to 550 volts. Constrictor snakes, such as boas, use a slower, quieter method of killing. They coil themselves around the prey, then slowly tighten the coils, until the animal dies of suffocation.

Other predators, less physically powerful than their prey, may use poison to paralyze or kill them. There are many devices for delivering poison. Sea anemones, corals and jellyfish have batteries of stinging cells on their tentacles, which inject barbed poison-tipped threads into anything that they touch. Venomous insects often have poison-producing glands at the base of biting mouthparts or stingers. The fangs of snakes and spiders also inject venom, sometimes strong enough to kill a human.

The shape and size of the mouth is important in a predator. Many swallow their prey whole, including anteaters, frogs and chameleons, which use their tongues to capture an insect and flick it into the mouth. Gulper eels and swallowers have huge, baglike mouths that may occupy up to 25 percent of their bodies. These fish live in the deep ocean, where prey are few and far between and large quarry cannot be refused in the expectation of something smaller passing by. Fishing birds such as kingfishers often toss their prey into the air so that they can swallow it headfirst. Snakes in particular can swallow very large prey – also headfirst so that the limbs fold down and the scales or feathers lie flat. A snake's skin stretches very easily, and its body has no breast bone, so it can expand to accommodate large meals. For other

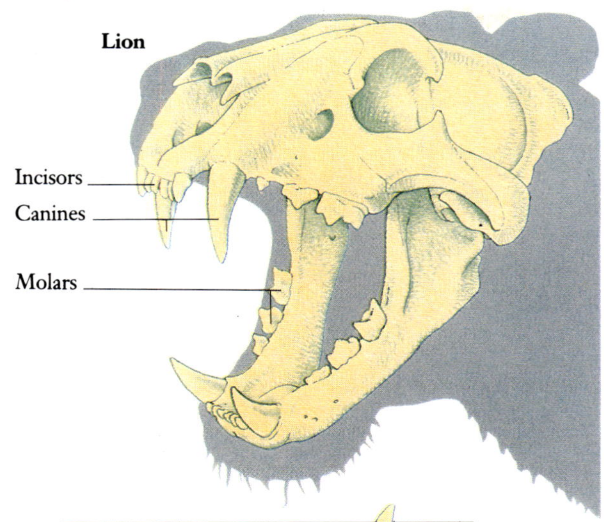

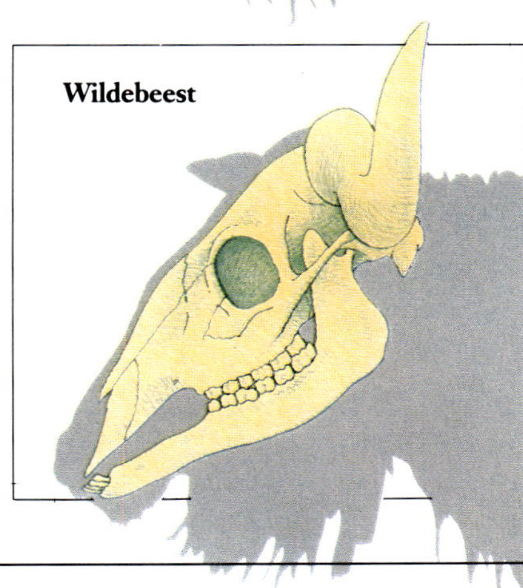

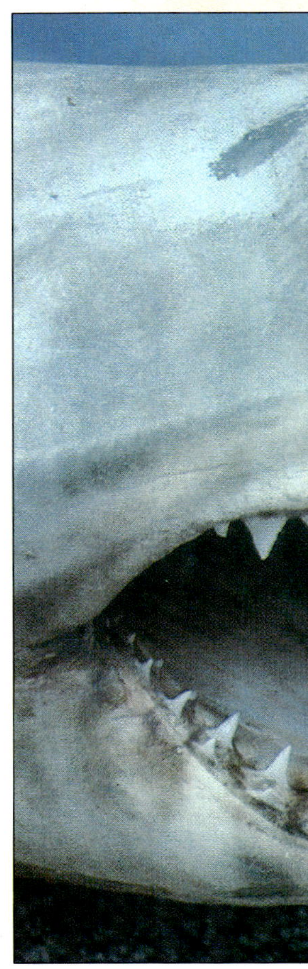

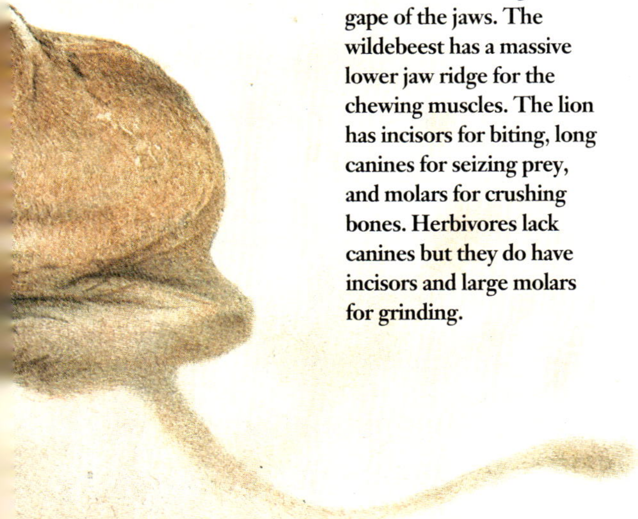

■ **Master killer – a lioness LEFT pounces on a wildebeest, slashing with her claws. Ridges on the top of the lion's skull BELOW LEFT anchor the muscles controlling the gape of the jaws. The wildebeest has a massive lower jaw ridge for the chewing muscles. The lion has incisors for biting, long canines for seizing prey, and molars for crushing bones. Herbivores lack canines but they do have incisors and large molars for grinding.**

animals, a few quick snaps of the jaw may help to flatten the meal or break it into smaller pieces before swallowing.

Teeth are used both for killing prey and for tearing the flesh. Sharks and piranhas have rows of sharp, pointed teeth. Insects have no teeth as such, but rely on hard biting and cutting mouthparts. Sea urchins, which feed on animals such as corals and sponges with hard skeletons, have an arrangement of five platelike rasping teeth. The teeth of parrotfish, which have a similar diet, are fused together to form a horny beak which is used as a scraper. Another deep-sea fish, the viperfish, has many needle-like teeth that curve backward to prevent prey escaping from the mouth.

Birds' bills are adapted to deal with a whole variety of prey, from rabbits to other birds, eggs, fish and insects. Thrushes hammer snails against stones to smash their shells;. Bearded vultures sometimes drop tortoises on to rocks from a great height to smash them, and Egyptian vultures may throw stones at bird eggs to break them open. Sea otters lie on their backs in the water, balancing their prey on their stomachs while they strike it with a stone they have brought up from the seabed ; more sophisticated tools are used by chimpanzees, which cut and fray sticks and poke them into termite nests to extract the insects.

◀ **Sharks have needle-sharp pointed teeth that curve backward to keep their food from falling out of their huge mouths. The shark eats by tearing off chunks of its prey's flesh and swallowing them whole.**

▲ **Rattlesnakes have huge fangs that fold out of the way when not in use. Poison trickles down a groove in the fangs to be injected into the victim. Many snakes have a hinge at the back of the jaw to widen the gap.**

▲ **Birds' bills come in different shapes that accommodate their feeding habits and reflect the diets of different species. The hooked bill of an eagle 1 can rip open carcasses. The oyster-catcher 2 feeds in shallow water by prising open bivalves with its long, pointed bill. The kookaburra's robust bill 3 is used to catch lizards and snakes. The gaping bill of the nightjar 4 is a moving trap for flying insects. The puffin 5 can hold more than 20 small fish in its serrated bill.**

Hunting Techniques

Cheetahs – swift, silent and deadly – are usually solitary hunters. There would be no advantage in having hunting companions; they would probably get in each other's way. Many other animal hunters work alone and chase down their prey at high speeds, including roadrunners and the peregrine falcon, whose sky dives can reach speeds of 350 miles per hour.

The chase is not the only way a solitary hunter can operate. Birds such as bee-eaters and flycatchers simply wait for a suitable insect to pass, then dart out and catch it. Lizards and jumping spiders do likewise. Foxes and cats, too, pounce on mice in long grass. Tree snakes hang motionless from branches, like rigid vines, as they wait for birds to pass by. The archerfish spits well-aimed streams of water droplets at insects on overhanging branches to knock them into the water.

KEYWORDS

BINOCULAR VISION
CAMOUFLAGE
FOOD CHAIN
INCISORS
VENOM

Many hunters wait for the prey to come to them. Praying mantises, chameleons, frogs and toads all wait almost motionless for long periods until unwary animals come within reach of their long arms or their long, sticky tongues. Successful ambush usually involves camouflage, which is used by a variety of hunters from chameleons and mantises to octopuses and flatfish, which can also change color to keep in tune with their background. Other hunters stalk their prey, adopting special body poses to make themselves less conspicuous. Polar bears stalk seals on the sea ice where there is no cover at all. Crocodiles lurk just below the surface of lakes and rivers, with only their bulging eyes and nostrils showing, edging closer and closer to the shore when the prey come to drink.

A lure helps to draw the prey to the predator. Anglerfish have lures which are modified spines of the first dorsal fin. The lure dangles in front of the angler's mouth and wiggles like a worm, attracting the attention of small fish. Once a fish is within reach, the angler suddenly opens its huge mouth, and the prey is sucked in with the inrushing water. Deep-sea anglerfish use luminous lures that glow in the dark. The snapping turtle has a fleshy pink wormlike lure in the floor of its mouth, and young copperhead snakes have a sulfur yellow tip to their tail which they wave to entice frogs within striking distance.

There are also more elaborate traps. Spider silk is used to construct a whole range of traps, from orb webs that catch flying insects to funnel webs for unwary insects, and silken trap-lines which tell the trapdoor spider when to pounce. The net-casting

spider makes a small rectangular sheet web which it dangles from its legs just above the ground, ready to throw over any insect that passes beneath. The antlion larva makes a funnel-shaped depression in the sand and waits for passing insects to fall in, bombarding them with sand to help them fall. There are floating traps, too: the trailing tentacles of jellyfish, armed with barbed threads for stinging.

Hunting in a pack is a more efficient method of catching relatively large prey. Sharks and piranhas gather in large numbers in a "feeding frenzy", attracted by the scent of blood. Vast hordes of army ants can overrun and kill animals many times their own size. The horns and speed of antelopes and wildebeest are no match for the packs of hunting dogs and hyenas that roam the African savannas.

There are other advantages of group hunting. Such hunters can combine the chase with the ambush: some members of the pack drive the prey toward others lying in wait. Lionesses and wolf packs often do this. Hunting dogs may simply run down prey as a group, or some members may work the herd of antelope or zebra into a state of panic while others head off an individual animal. Lions hunt in smaller groups than hunting dogs and hyenas, but they are larger and more powerful predators. Within a group, some animals may be sharper at spotting prey, while others are faster at chasing it. A pack can take advantage of a range of skills unlikely to be found in a single animal.

Killer whales hunt in packs of up to 60 animals. They often encircle their prey – usually seals or smaller whales or dolphins – or drive them into shallow water dead-ends along the coast. White pelicans use a similar method. Six to ten birds swim in a horseshoe formation to trap shoals of fish, scooping up mouthfuls in unison.

■ A crocodile's eyes and nostrils lie on small bumps on the top of its head LEFT, so it can lurk unseen in the water. It ambushes its prey, edging closer and closer as animals come to the water's edge to drink BELOW. A quick lunge forward, a slash from the powerful tail, and the prey is caught.

■ A group of humpback whales ABOVE LEFT feeding on krill in the Arctic. The whales dive deep, then rise to the surface, blowing streams of bubbles to form a bubble "net" that herds the krill into the center. The whales then rise through the net with their mouths open, gulping in the krill.

A jumping spider LEFT about to pounce on its prey. The fields of vision of two large eyes at the front of the head overlap, allowing the spider to judge speed and distance. The other eyes detect the approach of prey – or of predators.

UNFUSSY FEEDERS

NOT all animals can be classified into plant-eaters or flesh-eaters. Many animals, including humans, eat both plant and animal material. A lot of small filter-feeders – animals that strain food from water currents – trap anything of the right size that comes along, even dead organic material.

Large blue whales and tiny sea squirts are both filter-feeders: they sieve food from the water around them. The blue whale has no teeth. Instead, huge plates of baleen, or whalebone, hang down from its upper jaw. The plates are fringed with bristles. The whale gulps in mouthfuls of water, then forces the water back out through the baleen plate. Shrimps and other water creatures are left behind on the bristle fringes and licked up. This method of feeding is so successful that the largest species of whales live entirely on a diet of small crustaceans.

KEYWORDS

BALEEN
DETRITUS FEEDER
FILTER-FEEDER
OMNIVORE
SUSPENSION FEEDING

There are many kinds of filters and filter-feeders. The flamingo's filter works in much the same way as the whale's. Herring and many ocean fish feed in a quite different way. Their filters are their gills, which are extended into many tiny fingerlike filaments, called gill-rakers, to form a sieve. The herring swim along with their mouths open, so the water rushes past the sieve. The great basking shark, up to 9 meters long, also feeds like this, its huge mouth gaping open as it cruises the surface waters. It can filter 2 million liters of sea water an hour.

Sea squirts, mussels and many other bivalves remain stationary, but use tiny beating hairs called cilia to waft water into their bodies past internal filters.

▶ Bears are opportunists in their choice of food: they eat whatever is plentiful, such as salmon in a river RIGHT. This protein-rich food is readily found when the fish swim upriver to spwan. Fishing does not come naturally to bears, however, and they are content to nibble on berries, as this black bear FAR RIGHT is doing. They may also raid garbage dumps near towns.

▼ Flamingoes and barnacles feed in the same way – by straining food from the water. The barnacle sweeps its feathery legs through the water, trapping food particles on rows of bristles. The flamingo takes in mouthfuls of water, then uses its tongue to squeeze out the water through the serrated edges of the bill. It then licks up the food particles trapped on the inside of its bill.

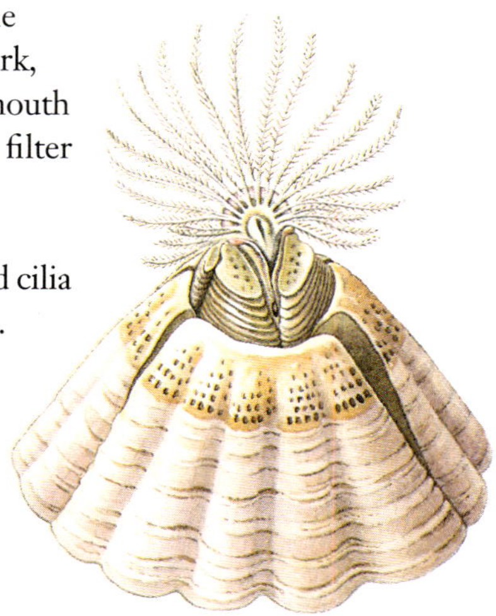

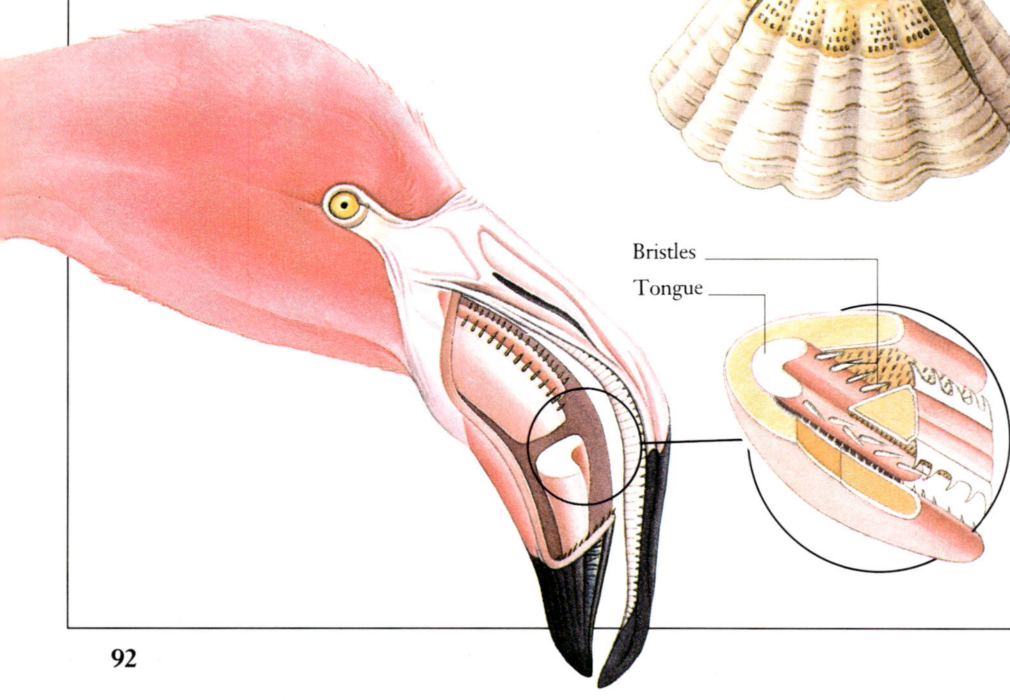

Mussels, for example, use their gills as filters. Like sea squirts and sponges, they have separate tubelike siphons for letting water in and out, so that the food-bearing stream is not contaminated by wastes leaving the body. Many one-celled animals use cilia both for drawing water into their bodies and as a filter. Some small crustaceans, such as shrimps, trap food particles on bristles on their legs, which act as external filters. Among the most spectacular filter feeders are the tubeworms, especially the feather duster worms, which trap food on the bristles of their colorful feathery tentacles.

A wide range of filter feeders use sticky mucus as a food trap. The arms of featherstars, for instance, are covered in a coat of mucus, which is wafted by cilia along special grooves to the mouth.

Animals that sieve food particles from the water are often called suspension feeders, because they trap particles in suspension in the water. Such food is common in the oceans, which are full of floating particles of detritus – dead organic material and one-celled organisms. Animals that feed on detritus that sinks to the ocean floor are called detritivores. They include sea cucumbers and many kinds of worms, some with sticky tentacles, tongues or mucus nets.

Some land animals actually choose to eat a mixture of plant and animal food. They are opportunists, taking whatever happens to be abundant at the time. Gulls have learned to forage on human garbage dumps, as have bears. Raccoons often scavenge around towns and cities, where there is plenty of waste food. Animals with mixed diets are called omnivores.

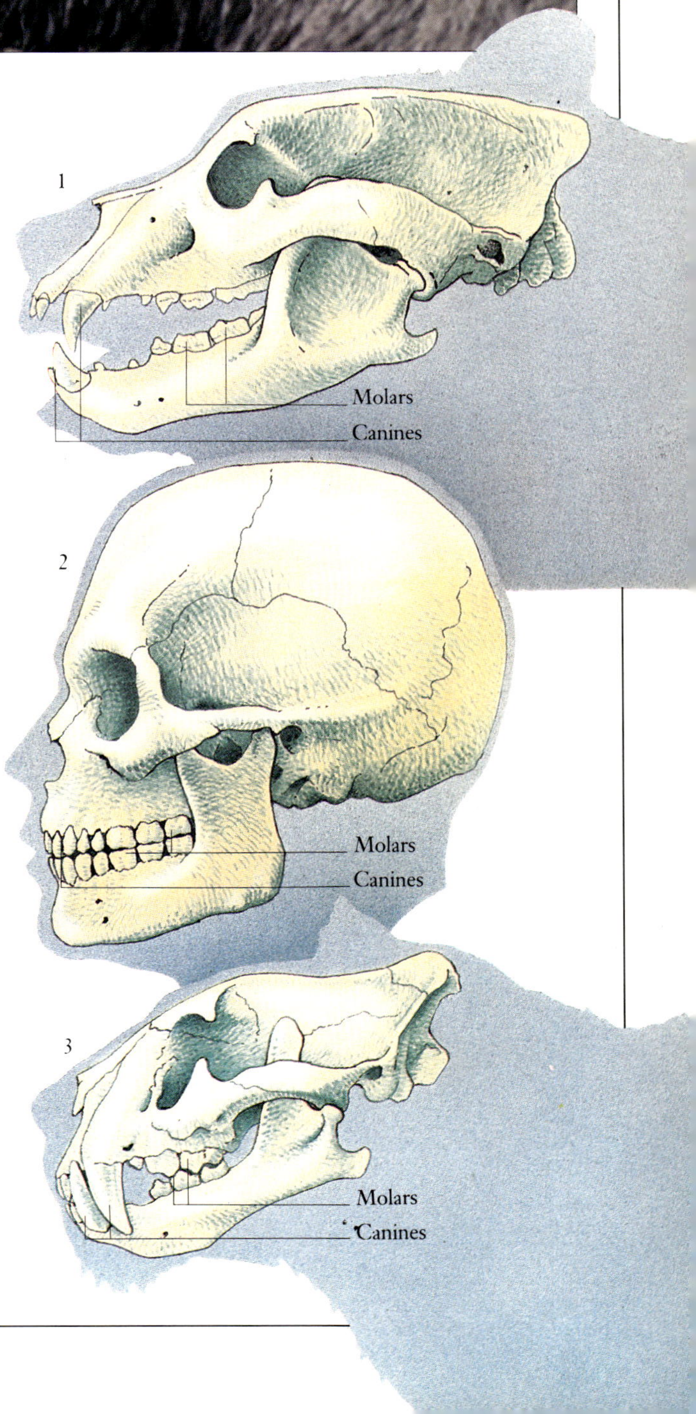

▶ **The skulls of omnivores such as bears 1 and humans 2 are intermediate in form between those of carnivores such as lions 3 and herbivores. The lower jaw is quite pronounced, reflecting the need to chew tough plant fibers. All omnivores have canine teeth, but these are not as large and strong as those of carnivores. The molars have a flattened shape for grinding, but they also have pronounced cusps to help crush flesh.**

BREAKDOWN SPECIALISTS

WITHOUT decomposers – animals that feed on dead organic material, both plant and animal – the Earth would soon become cluttered up with dead creatures, plants would run out of nutrients and food chains would collapse. About 90 percent of all plant material is not eaten at all – while it is living, that is. Dead plant material, including fallen branches, leaves and flowers, is broken down by various animals and microorganisms until the nutrients trapped in it are released into the soil, to be taken in again by growing plants. A similar process happens to animal remains, droppings and various excretions, both on land and in the sea. This is called decomposition, and the organisms responsible are decomposers.

KEYWORDS

BACTERIA
DECOMPOSER
DETRITUS FEEDER
ENZYME
LARVAE
SCAVENGER

Decomposition involves a huge variety of animals. Some of them are decomposition specialists, while others supplement an all-meat or all-plant diet with dead organic material which requires less effort to collect. Large scavenging decomposers such as hyenas, raccoons, vultures and seagulls start the breakdown of carcasses into smaller pieces which can be tackled by smaller and smaller decomposers – ultimately fungi and bacteria.

The dog family plays an important role in scavenging. Jackals and foxes attack the outer parts of a carcass, but hyenas are strong enough to break it apart to reach the internal organs. They have powerful jaws and massive teeth that can crush bone and slice through flesh and muscle. A pack of 25 hyenas can reduce the bodies of three adult zebras and a foal to bare bones in half an hour.

Vultures, with their long wings, can soar high above the grasslands searching for carcasses. As they glide down, the wind whistling through their feathers attracts other vultures. They in turn attract other scavengers such as hyenas and lions. There are several different kinds of vultures. Some species eat only soft meat; others eat tougher parts, down to the tendons and ligaments or even bone. The lammergeier vulture smashes its way into bones by dropping them onto rocks from a great height.

After a carcass has been opened up by large scavengers, a host of smaller creatures moves in. Fly, midge and beetle larvae (maggots) feed on the soft parts, the larvae of tinaeid moths and hide beetles feed on skin, while tendons and ligaments are attacked by termites. Blowfly larvae have been known to reduce the dead body of a mouse to bare bones in less than

▶ Scavengers arrive to begin the breakdown of a zebra carcass. Vultures are often first on the scene. Their sharp beaks are ideal for pulling at flesh. This white-backed vulture has very few feathers on its head and neck, so it can easily clean itself after delving into the carcass. The massive jaws and teeth of the hyenas can even slice up bones, which are later found in their droppings in powdered form.

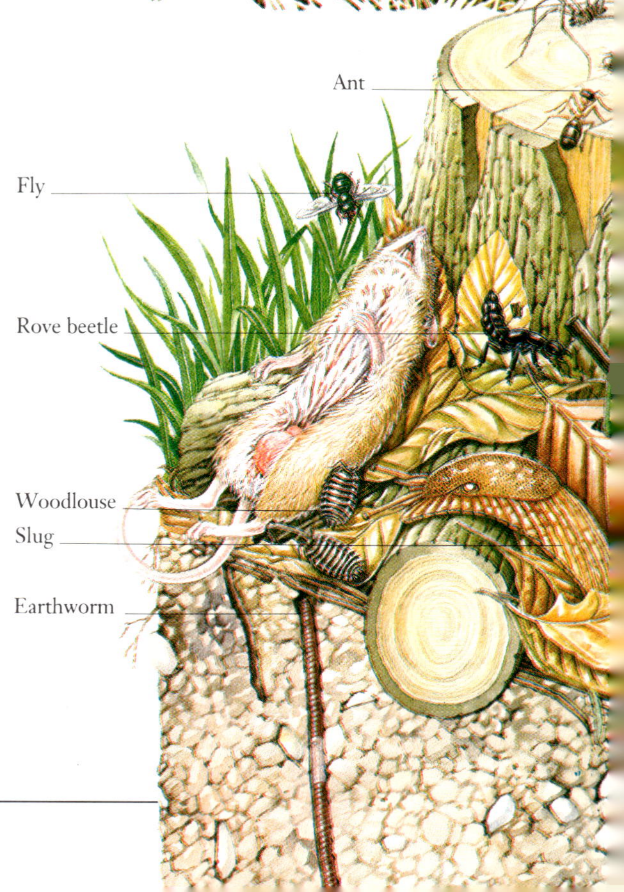

▶ Snails, slugs and millipedes feed on leaf litter. Tiny fungal threads penetrate dead wood and leaves. Flies lay their eggs in corpses, which are food for their maggots. Earthworms and ants drag leaves underground where they rot faster. Their droppings are eaten by bacteria, protozoans and microscopic nematode worms. Woodlice and rove beetles scavenge on dead plant and animal remains and droppings. Predators such as centipedes and spiders feed on these decomposers.

two weeks. Even bones are eventually broken down. Droppings are also food for other animals. Dung flies and dung beetles feed on dung and also lay their eggs in it, so that their larvae, too, can feed on it.

Plant material can be even harder to break down than animal carcasses. The fibers are particularly tough and indigestible, and there are no rewards to be gained by large animals breaking open logs and large fallen branches. Bark- and wood-boring beetles and fungi work jointly to strip off the bark and penetrate the heartwood. The beetles carry in spores of fungi and bacteria from other trees they have visited. As the fungi soften the wood, it is attacked by other animals including woodpeckers, woodlice, craneflies and millipedes. In warmer climates, the master wood-destroyers are termites. Like many other wood-borers, termites digest the cellulose of plant fibers by means of symbiotic microorganisms in special pouches in their intestines.

Plant litter on the ground is attacked by a similar assemblage of small decomposers: a single gram of soil may contain up to 4 billion bacteria. Earthworms are the main animals that break up the litter to let other decomposers in.

Quite different animals are at work in the sea. Along the shoreline seagulls, crabs, and sandhoppers scavenge among the seaweed and debris washed up by the tide. Crustaceans are important decomposers at all depths. In the wet environment of the ocean, bacteria soon get to work, too, and few corpses reach the deep sea floor intact. Wave action helps to break up the organic material, forming millions of tiny particles that are taken in by filter-feeders and suspension feeders. Many are devoured by plankton animals in the surface waters, but some escape to drift slowly downward, forming a rain of debris called "marine snow". This settles on the sea bed as detritus, providing food for scavengers such as sea cucumbers, gray mullet and a host of marine worms. Hagfish and yet more crustaceans and worms soon move in on the few large corpses that reach the deep sea floor, detecting them in the darkness by touch and smell.

▲ The Dor beetle is a burying beetle. It burrows under dung until it falls into the soil, then lays its eggs in the dung, which will later feed the larvae.

◀ Springtails and mites are some of the commonest small decomposers. Their flattened bodies enable them to creep along cracks. Mites, which are members of the class Arachnida, also act as parasites on many vertebrates.

▲ Crabs are important scavengers at all depths in the oceans and along the seashore. They begin the process of decomposition by tearing open carcasses with their strong claws, allowing smaller scavengers and decomposers to enter.

Fussy Feeders

SOME of the rarest animals on the planet are fussy feeders. Their highly specialized diets have often proved to be their undoing in the rapidly changing modern world. But, when their environment does not change faster than they can adapt, fussy feeders are able to take advantage of food that other animals cannot deal with. This means that they have little competition for food, and they can afford to use more of their energy for growth and reproduction.

KEYWORDS

ADAPTATION
CLAW
DIGESTION
EVOLUTION
EXTINCTION

Any food found in a crevice or shell is difficult to extract. The ayeaye of Madagascar (a nocturnal lemur) has one extra long finger for fishing insects out of cracks in bark. The rewards are worth it; the striped possum of Australia has evolved an identical extra digit for the same purpose. The Hawaiian akiapolaau bird has a long curved upper bill and a short stout sharp-tipped lower bill. It uses its lower bill to scrape away bark and its upper bill to fish out the insects. Coral reefs have many nooks and crannies that require special equipment for plundering. Butterflyfish and pipefish with long narrow snouts probe the hollows for small invertebrates, and scaleworms, flatworms and ribbonlike eels slide right inside crevices on their hunting forays.

A diet of ants and termites is best tackled by powerful claws to break open the nests; a narrow, tough-skinned snout to push inside, undeterred by bites and stings; and a long sticky tongue to pick up the prey. The anteater does not need to see its quarry; it just tears a hole in the nest and inserts its tongue, which is coated with sticky saliva to trap the ants. Anteaters, the African aardvark, the pangolins of Africa and Asia and the spiny anteaters of Australia and New Guinea all have similar snouts, tongues and large curving claws. This is an example of convergent evolution, in which animals with a similar lifestyle have independently evolved similar adaptations, even though they live in different parts of the world.

Not all fussy feeders have restricted diets. Nectar- and sap-feeders feed on a wide variety of plant species, and blood-sucking flies and mosquitoes find many victims. A liquid diet avoids the need for biting, chewing and grinding, and nutrients are already in solution for easier digestion. Plants offer liquid food in the form of sap and nectar. Nectar just needs to be sucked or lapped up. The mouthparts of butterflies and moths can be extended to form a long strawlike sucking tube which can reach deep into flowers to the

▼ The panda feeds on only a few species of bamboo, which flower and die out every 40 to 100 years. The panda must then find a new species. An adult panda needs to eat about 20 kg of fresh bamboo leaves every day – it has little time to search for food.

▶ Hummingbirds are adapted to feed on nectar. The long, rolled tongue is extended by means of a stiffening rod. The two halves of the tongue roll inward to form a tube, which fills with nectar by capillarity, perhaps aided by sucking.

▼ Hawaiian honeycreepers have evolved different beaks for different diets: insects 1, insects and nectar 2 and seeds 3 .

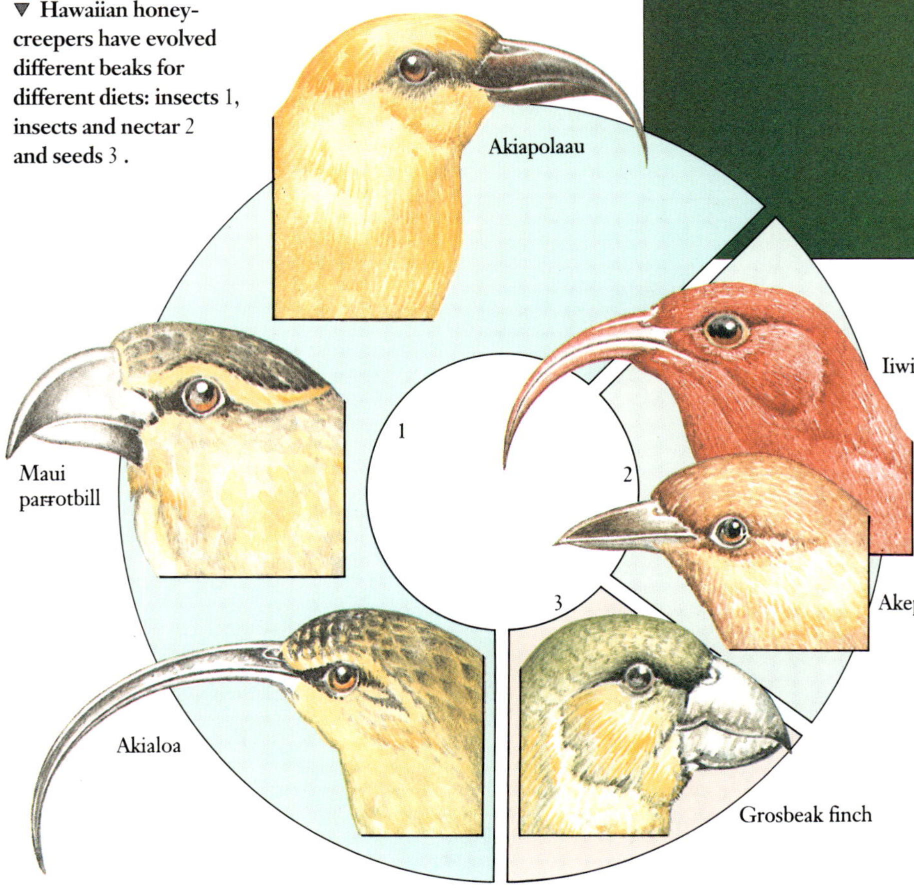

nectar. Nectar-feeding bats and birds such as honey-eaters have specially adapted tongues, which often have a bush of fine hairs at the tips to mop up the liquid. Many of these nectar-feeders cling to the petals or stand on the flowers while they sip, but moths and hummingbirds hover in front as they feed. This uses up a lot of energy, but nectar provides so much energy that the effort is worthwhile. Hummingbirds are the masters of hovering, and they feed on a wide range of flowers.

In order to feed on sap, an animal must first pierce the plant stem. Aphids have piercing mouthparts called stylets, which also contain a tube into which the liquid can flow. The sap in a plant stem is under so much pressure that once it is tapped it is literally pumped into the insect. The sap in tree trunks is even more inaccessible, but sapsuckers (a group of woodpeckers) manage to reach it, and marmosets can scrape away the bark with their teeth to lick up the sap.

Bloodsucking poses similar problems to sapsucking. The mosquito and the tsetse fly also have piercing stylets, while the vampire bat has such sharp teeth that it can lap blood from sleeping victims without waking them. Bloodsuckers inject an anticoagulant into their victim's blood to prevent it clotting while they feed.

Some insects and spiders generate their own liquid food. They dribble digestive juices on to the food, then suck up the soluble products of digestion. Shriveled flies left in spider webs have been sucked dry of their soft parts. This external digestion is most commonly used by small animals that feed on flesh or dead meat, which would be tough to bite off and chew. Starfish have a unique form of feeding: they turn their stomachs inside out to envelope their prey, then take in the liquid digested food.

▶ Insect mouthparts are adapted for different diets. In the mosquito the mandibles and maxillae form piercing stylets, supported by the labium. Anticoagulant is injected through the hypopharynx and blood is sucked up through the labrum. The housefly's labium forms a wide, many-channeled proboscis. It secretes saliva through it from the hypopharynx and sucks the liquefied food through the labrum. The butterfly's maxillae lock together to form a sucking tube for nectar.

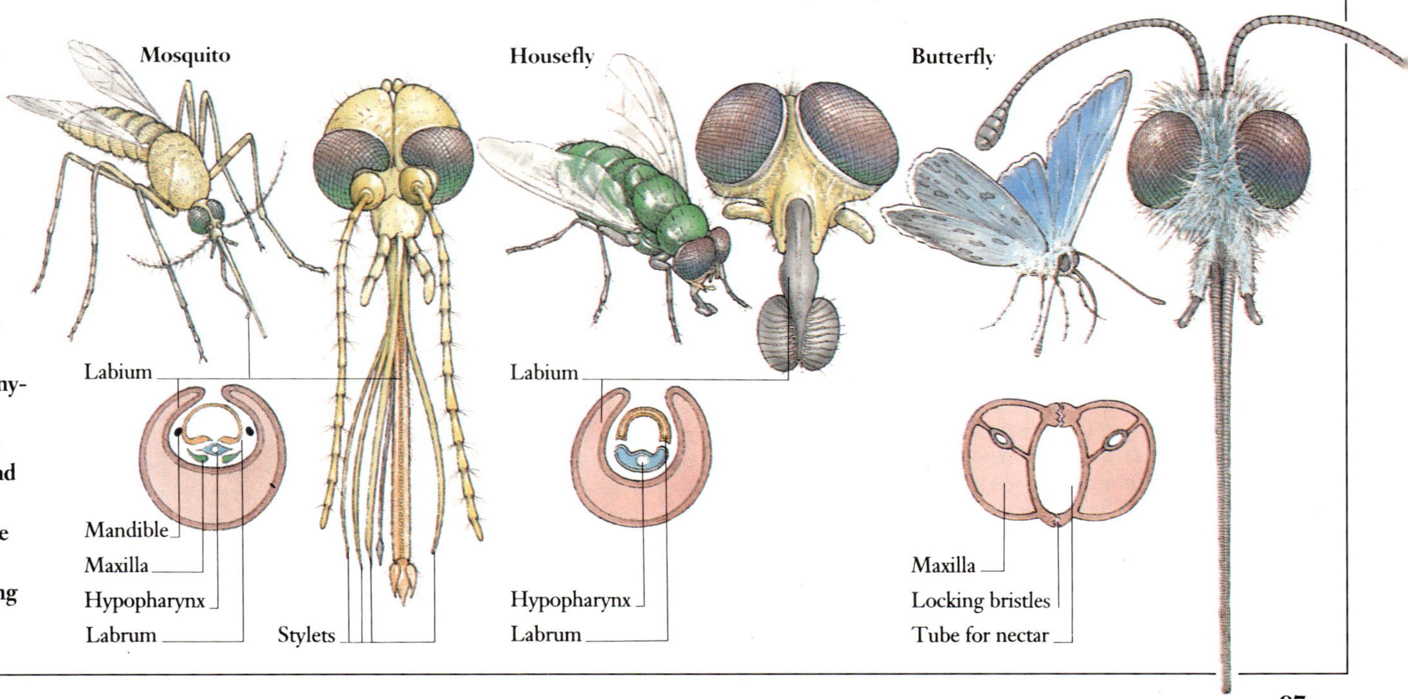

Living Off Others

Parasites are creatures that use another living animal or plant (their "host") as a source of food for themselves or their young. The host suffers as a result. This saves a lot of energy and sometimes may even avoid the need for certain digestive organs. However, the parasite is also dependent upon the presence of the host species, and is often too highly specialized to lead an independent life.

External parasites (ectoparasites) live on the surface of their hosts – in the skin, fur, hair or scales. Most ectoparasites are arthropods – insects, arachnids (mites and ticks) or crustaceans. Many bugs feed on the lifeblood of plants – their sap. Fleas, lice, ticks and mites are common parasites of mammals. They have hooked claws or special mouthparts or suckers for clinging to their host, and their bodies are often flattened to avoid being brushed off. Some of these parasites feed on the skin itself, or just below it, while others suck blood. Often their mouthparts are so sharp that the victim feels nothing until immune responses to injected saliva or anticoagulants (chemicals which prevent blood clotting) produce an itching sensation.

KEYWORDS

ADAPTATION
ARTHROPOD
ECTOPARASITE
ENDOPARASITE
PARASITE
VARIATION

Many ectoparasites attach only temporarily to their hosts. Leeches and bed bugs feed until they can hold no more blood, then drop off and hide while they process the food. Ectoparasites have highly specialized senses to find their hosts. Fleas may detect the presence of host mammals by their body heat, or by carbon dioxide given off while breathing. The flea's powerful back legs enable it to leap great distances onto other animals. Other parasites, such as parasitic barnacles, are more permanent lodgers.

A single parasite may appear to do little harm, but if an animal carries a high load of parasites, it will use a lot of energy in repairing the damage or processing the extra food.

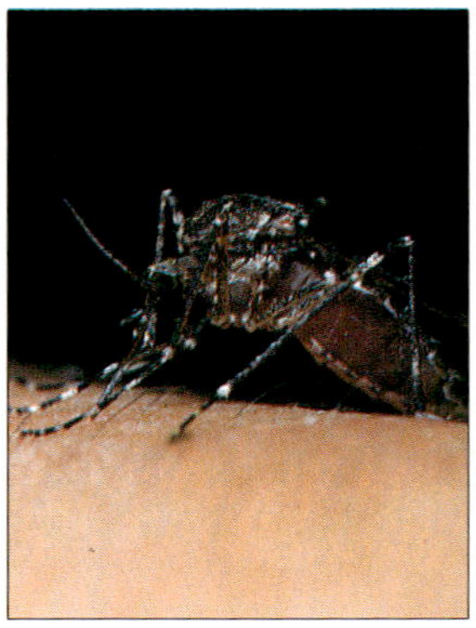

▲ **Female mosquitoes feed on the blood of other animals to gain nutrients for egg production. They can pass on disease from infected hosts.**

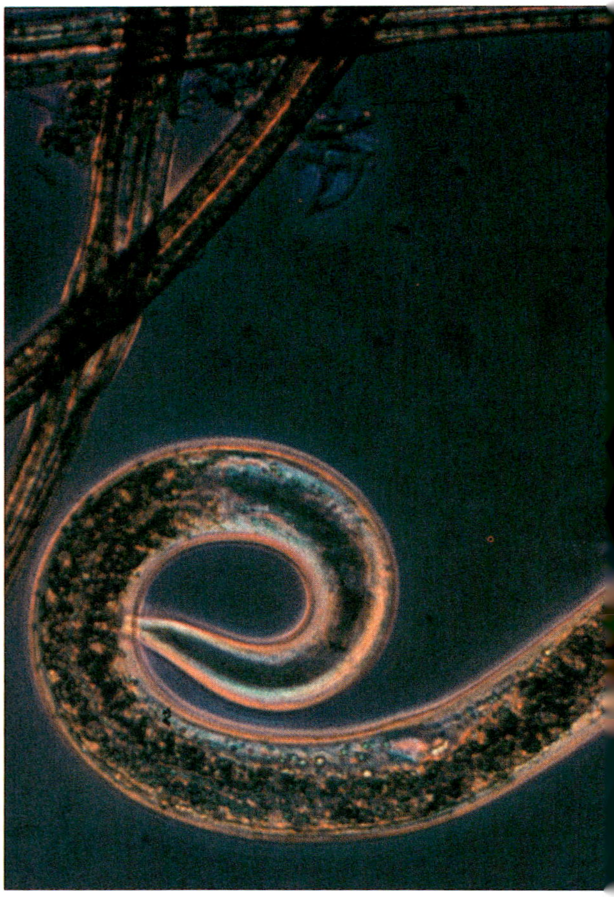

▶ **Many of the thousands of species of threadworms (nematode worms) are parasites. They damage crops and livestock, and cause disease in humans. Some habitats contain 3 million threadworms per square meter.**

▶ **A river lamprey sucks the blood of a living trout. Many adult lampreys are parasites on other fish: they are the only parasitic verbetrates. The suckerlike mouth has horny teeth, which rasp at the flesh of the victim.**

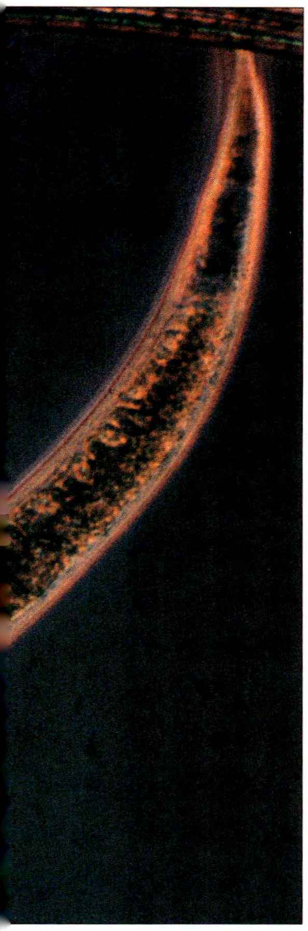

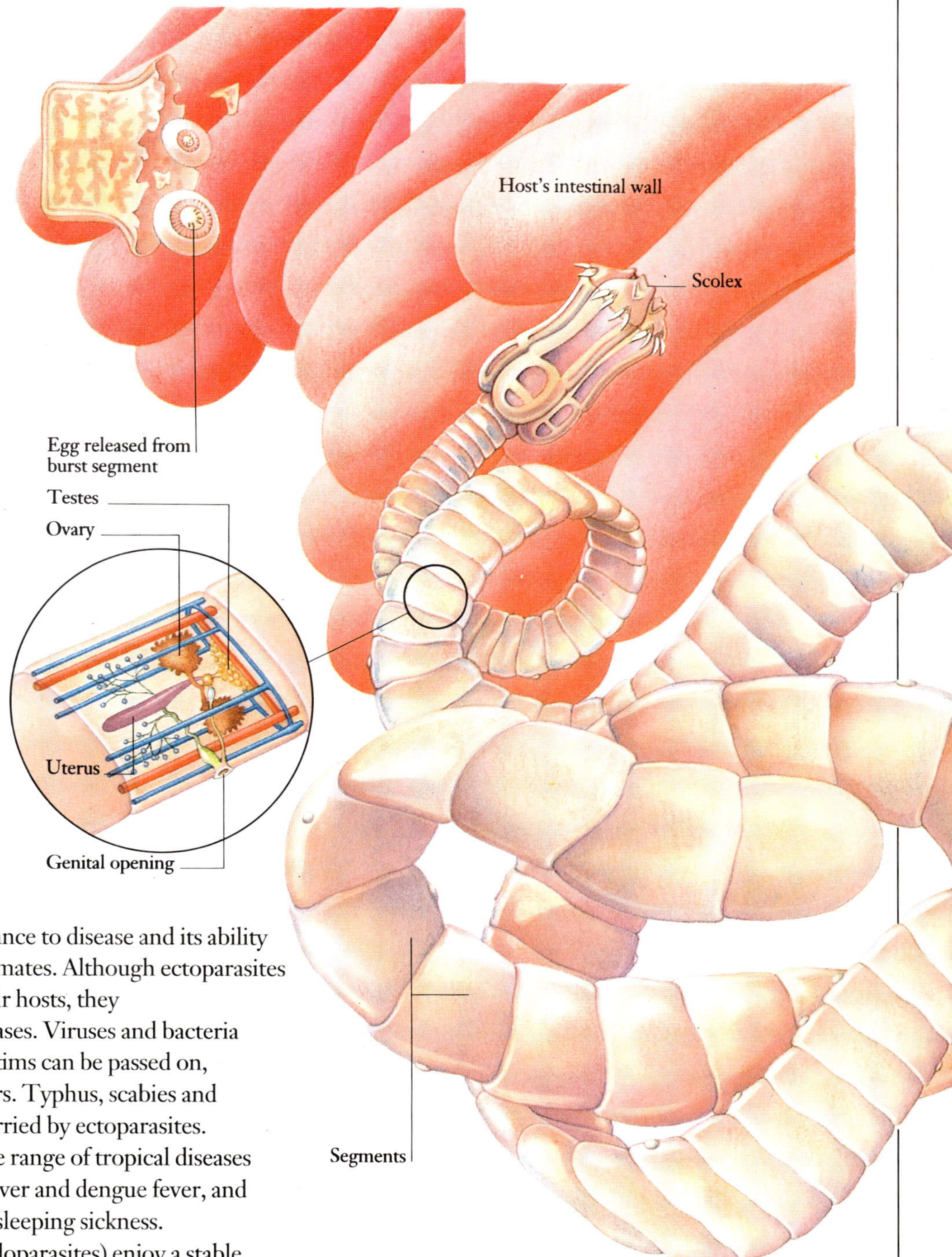

▷ The tapeworm's long, flat body absorbs dissolved nutrients, already digested by the host, all over its large surface. It needs no digestive or sense organs. Special enzymes and a mucus coating enable it to resist the host's digestive enzymes. Hooks and suckers on its head (scolex) prevent it being swept out of the intestine. The tapeworm's metabolism is adapted to cope with the low oxygen levels in the intestine. Its body segments each contain the basic organs for digestion, excretion and reproduction, and can "mate" with each other to produce fertile eggs. Segments full of ripe eggs break off and are passed out with the host's feces, to be picked up by pigs foraging on the infected ground. Human tapeworms can grow up to 18.3m (60 ft) long.

This may lower its resistance to disease and its ability to compete for food and mates. Although ectoparasites seldom prove fatal to their hosts, they can carry dangerous diseases. Viruses and bacteria picked up from other victims can be passed on, especially by bloodsuckers. Typhus, scabies and bubonic plague are all carried by ectoparasites. Mosquitoes carry a whole range of tropical diseases such as malaria, yellow fever and dengue fever, and tsetse flies are bearers of sleeping sickness.

Internal parasites (endoparasites) enjoy a stable, warm, moist environment, and often have the added benefit of ready-digested food in the form of blood or intestinal contents. Many have lost their digestive organs in the course of evolution, and are able to devote much of their energy to reproduction. As well as sapping the host's energy, some parasites, such as those causing malaria and yellow fever, also produce toxins that cause unpleasant symptoms or even death.

The commonest groups of internal parasites are flukes, tapeworms and other kinds of worms , and microscopic protozoans and bacteria. These parasites are usually highly specific, living in only one particular species of host. Many have a complex life cycle, sometimes requiring two or more host animals in succession. The common tapeworm that infests human intestines passes one stage of its life cycle in the pig. Humans pick up the parasite by eating contaminated pork or through contact with pig droppings.

Some internal parasites can dramatically change the host's metabolism. Filaria worms cause elephantiasis – the gross growth of tissues in parts of the body affected by the worms. A parasitic barnacle, *Sacculina*, lives in the bodies of crabs. An adult *Sacculina* has few organs, consisting of a branching mass of cells controlled by a nerve ganglion. It branches into every part of the crab's body absorbing nutrients. The crab's sexual organs cease to function and it can no longer molt its skin to grow. Male crabs turn into females and develop more fat, improving the parasite's food supply.

LIVING TOGETHER

LIVING with animals of another species – without harming the host, as a parasite does – provides many animals with opportunities to obtain food without exerting much effort. Cattle egrets are often found around cattle and antelopes – sometimes riding on their backs – waiting to snatch insects flushed out of the grass by the advancing grazers. Other opportunists hitch a ride to new food sources. Mites and pseudo-scorpions cling to the legs of flies and grasshoppers. Barnacles and a host of small invertebrates ride permanently on whales, dolphins and sea turtles.

KEYWORDS

ADAPTATION
COMMENSALISM
MUTUALISM
PARASITE
SYMBIOSIS

Many animals are wasteful feeders. Scraps crumble from their food or fall from claws and mouthparts, easy pickings for any animals within reach. Pilotfish swim behind sharks to feed on their leftovers or to pick off skin parasites. They need to be agile to avoid being eaten by the shark. Sharksuckers actually travel on the shark itself, attached by their dorsal fin, which is modified into a powerful sucker. They can detach themselves to scavenge pieces of food dropped by the shark.

The parasitic sea anemone is often found on the backs of hermit crabs. The crabs may actively solicit the anemones, tickling them to persuade them to climb on the shell. The crab gains protection from the anemone's tentacles while the anemone is carried to new feeding grounds, and has the added bonus of scavenging the crab's scraps.

Such an arrangement, which is of mutual benefit to both partners, is called "symbiosis". The most important symbiosis, however, is probably that of animals with cellulose-digesting microorganisms in their stomachs or intestines which break down plant fibers. Without this arrangement, sheep, cattle and the great grazing herds of antelopes of the African savannas would not exist.

One of the most common kinds of symbiosis is cleaning – one partner feeds on the external parasites and infected wound tissues of the other. Cleaner shrimps are easily noticed with their striking white stripes and violet spots. Their swaying bodies and waving antennae attract the attention of passing fish. The fish stop and present damaged areas and parasites to the shrimps for cleaning. A fish may even let the shrimp inspect its mouth and gill cavity and cut into its skin to remove parasites. Similarly, species of fish called cleanerfish dance on a coral reef to attract other fish to come to them for cleaning. A pair of cleanerfish can clean more than 200 other fish in an hour.

The social behavior of ants makes them ideal partners in symbiosis, because they are programmed for sharing with other animals (beginning with their own species). Ants solicit liquid food from other ants by stroking them with their antennae. Long ago, ants discovered that if they stroked aphids, the aphids would produce droplets of honeydew, the sugary liquid they excrete. Many species of ants now herd aphids, some of which have become dependent on the ants: they will not defecate unless stroked, and they have lost their normal defenses against predators.

Symbiotic relationships may occur between animals and plants as well as between animals. Many plants, especially in the tropics, have hollow stems in which live colonies of ants. Certain acacias have hollow thorns instead. The plants often produce special nectaries at the base of leaves, or even round food bodies on the leaves, which the ants feed on. In return, the ants defend the plants from herbivorous insects and even from larger animals. Some of these ant colonies actually supplement the plant's nitrogen supply with their droppings and excretions.

Hydras, corals and clams all have algae living in their tissues. Oxygen produced by the photosynthesis of the algae is used by the animal for respiration, while carbon dioxide produced by the animal's respiration is used in the algae's photosynthesis. The algae's need for light restricts the hosts to shallow water.

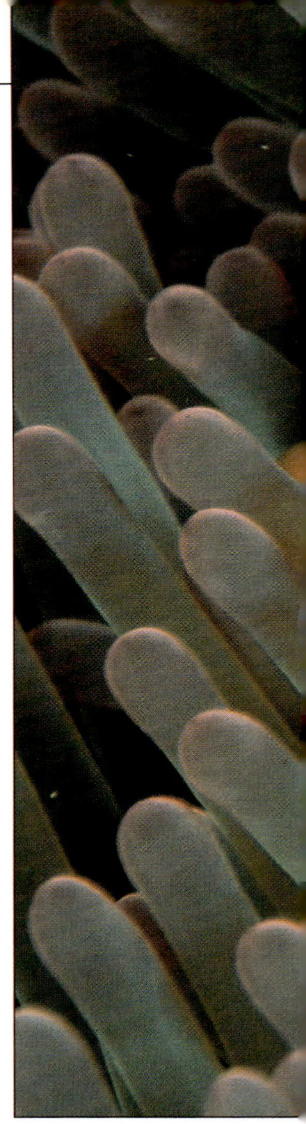

▼ Oxpeckers are a common sight in the tropics, where they are found around large herds. In spite of their name, they feed not only on the external parasites of oxen, but also on those found on other grazing mammals and cattle, such as antelope.

■ Larvae of the Genoveva azure butterfly being "milked" in an ant nest LEFT. Honeyguides BELOW guide humans or honey badgers to bees' nests and feed on the wax.

▲ Clownfish live among the tentacles of sea anemones and feed on scraps dropped by the anemone. Coated in the anemone's mucus, they are protected from stinging.

4

ANIMAL *Movement*

All animals can move. Even animals such as corals and barnacles, which cannot move from place to place, can move parts of their bodies to capture food from the water. For most animals, movement is essential for finding food and escaping from danger. Special sequences of movement may be used to attract mates, warn off rivals or threaten attackers.

Movement has played a vital role in evolution, too, enabling animals to colonize new places and enhancing the opportunities for maintaining genetic variation by bringing together animals from different locations or dispersing the young over a wide area. Some animals travel long distances on migration to avoid seasons of low food availability and harsh weather.

Land, water and air present different challenges for animal movement. Air and water offer resistance to moving objects. Water provides considerable support, but on land there is friction with the ground. Supportive skeletons and a reduction of the area of the body in contact with the ground can improve the efficiency of walking and running. In the treetops, special skills are called for: the ability to judge speed and distance, and to grip trunks and branches. The great diversity of animal forms illustrates the ways in which different body plans have become adapted for a variety of movement.

A gemsbok travels long distances across the southern African plains in search of sparse grazing. Its small hooves reduce the area of the foot in contact with the ground, so reducing friction. At times, all four feet may be off the ground, a great saving in energy. As the animal speeds up, balance becomes less of a problem, because it does not remain long in any one position. This means that the animal can afford to swing its hind legs well forward, providing a powerful thrust against the ground. The gemsbok's long legs enable it to run fast – its main defense against predators.

MUSCLE-POWERED MOVEMENT

ALL animal movement, from the wriggling of the smallest cell to the pouncing of a tiger, is achieved by changing the shape of chains of protein molecules which pull on different parts of the body or cell. In individual cells, long chains of molecules of the protein tubulin form microtubules, some of which are attached to the cell membrane and other structures in the cell. In a muscle, long chains (filaments) of molecules of the proteins actin and myosin are bound together into bundles called myofibrils. The myofibrils contract as the actin and myosin filaments slide past each other. The myofibrils are grouped into larger bundles – muscle fibers – which in turn are bound together to form the muscle itself.

KEYWORDS

ACTIN
ADENOSINE TRIPHOSPHATE (ATP)
JOINT
MUSCLE
MYOSIN
NERVOUS SYSTEM
PROTEIN
TENDON

There are several different types of muscle. Skeletal muscles are attached to rigid parts of the body, such as bones or the hard shell (exoskeleton) of insects and other arthropods, and are involved in movement. Rigid sections of the skeleton act as levers and are linked by joints at which movement is possible. The active, energy-requiring process in movement is the contraction of a muscle, which moves one section of the skeleton relative to another section. To reverse the movement, another muscle working in the opposite direction contracts, while the first muscle relaxes. Pairs of opposing muscles are called antagonistic muscles.

In soft-bodied animals the muscles are not arranged in pairs, but bands of muscle perform work in opposite directions. Worms and similar animals have longitudinal muscle fibers running down the length of their bodies and circular muscles running around their circumference. When the longitudinal muscles contract, the animal becomes short and round; contraction of the circular muscles makes its body long and thin. These muscles pull against the fluid in the worm's segments.

A different kind of movement occurs in flatworms and snails, where waves of muscle contraction ripple along the animal's flat lower surface, which is in contact with the ground on which it moves. These muscles push against small bumps on the ground to propel the animal forward.

How does a muscle contract? By studying the structure of muscles using a high magnification electron microscope, scientists have discovered how muscles contract. Thin strands, or filaments, of the proteins myosin and actin are arranged in a distinctive pattern. When a muscle contracts, these filaments slide across each other by means of a "ratchet mechanism". Little hook-like heads on the myosin filaments reach forward and hook on to the actin filaments, pulling them forward. Then the heads detach themselves, ready to pull on the next section of the actin filament. During rapid muscle contraction, this cycle may happen five times a second.

The energy needed for this cycle is supplied by the molecule ATP (adenosine triphosphate), which is produced by the process of respiration. During contraction, the chemical energy in the ATP molecule is converted to the mechanical energy used to slide the actin filament past the myosin filament. This process is extremely efficient: 50 to 70 percent of the chemical energy is converted to mechanical energy, compared with only 10 to 20 percent of the energy from the gasoline burned in a car engine.

Protein microtubules are also responsible for the movements of protozoans, such as ameba, as well as for the beating of cilia and flagella and the lashing of the tails of sperm. Cilia and flagella contain rings of protein microtubules. Like the actin and myosin filaments of muscles, these microtubules also slide past each other by a ratchet mechanism powered by adenosine triphosphate.

Skeletal muscles are controlled by the nervous system. Some movements, such as jerking away from a hot stove, are automatic; others, such as picking up a particular object, are voluntary. Motor nerves send signals to all the fibrils in a muscle so that they all contract at the same time.

■ A flea ABOVE can jump over 130 times its own height, using a special catapult mechanism in its hind legs. Weight for weight, fleas are the best jumpers in the animal kingdom – far superior to the kangaroo, which is more commonly associated with jumping.

The kangaroo's long feet BELOW make very effective levers for hopping. When the foot is bent, energy is stored in the tendons at the back of the heel as they stretch. When the ankle straightens, this energy is released, bouncing the kangaroo forward. Up to 40 percent of the energy of the hop comes from the tendons. The long tail is used as a counter-balance for hopping, and as a prop when at rest.

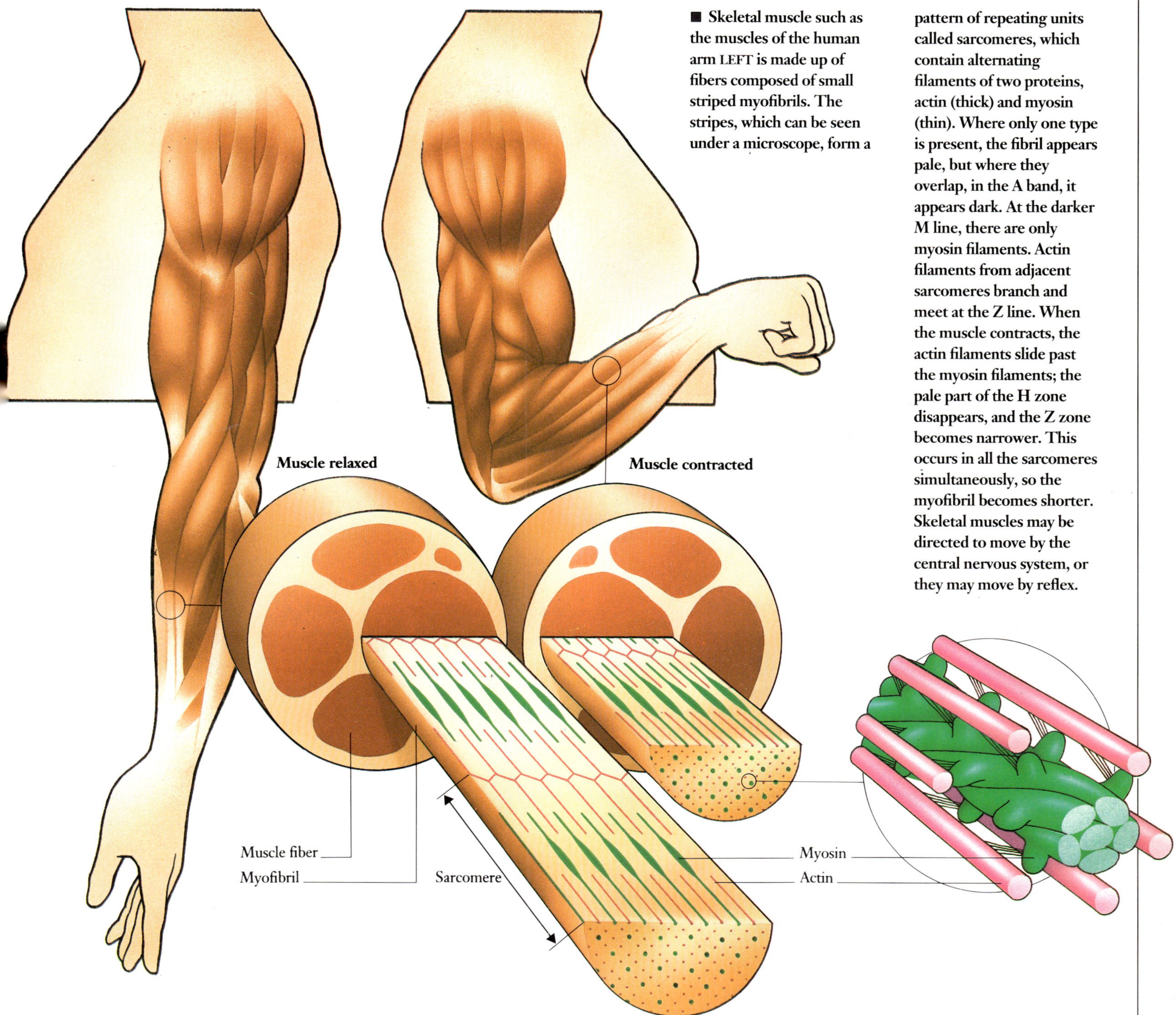

■ Skeletal muscle such as the muscles of the human arm LEFT is made up of fibers composed of small striped myofibrils. The stripes, which can be seen under a microscope, form a pattern of repeating units called sarcomeres, which contain alternating filaments of two proteins, actin (thick) and myosin (thin). Where only one type is present, the fibril appears pale, but where they overlap, in the A band, it appears dark. At the darker M line, there are only myosin filaments. Actin filaments from adjacent sarcomeres branch and meet at the Z line. When the muscle contracts, the actin filaments slide past the myosin filaments; the pale part of the H zone disappears, and the Z zone becomes narrower. This occurs in all the sarcomeres simultaneously, so the myofibril becomes shorter. Skeletal muscles may be directed to move by the central nervous system, or they may move by reflex.

BUILT FOR MOVEMENT

ANIMALS move one part of the body relative to another part by means of muscles attached to various body structures – bones, shells, skin, scales and so on. The force exerted by the muscles is transmitted to other parts of the body through the skeleton.

There are three main types of animal skeleton. Humans and other vertebrates have an internal skeleton consisting of cartilage or bones linked together at joints. Insects and other arthropods have an external skeleton in the form of a carapace or "shell" that surrounds the animal. The muscles are attached to pegs on the inside of the carapace. Like the vertebrate skeleton, the arthropod skeleton consists of many sections joined together at flexible joints. Soft-bodied animals use a hydrostatic skeleton – the muscles press against a fluid-filled compartment. In many mollusks this is the blood-filled body cavity. In annelid worms, such as the earthworm, concentric layers of muscle fibers in the body wall press against the fluid-filled body segments. Echinoderms have a system of fluid-filled canals that penetrates all parts of the body.

KEYWORDS

BONE
ENDOSKELETON
JOINT
MUSCLE
LIGAMENT
TENDON

In addition to providing anchor points for the muscles, the skeleton of an arthropod or vertebrate also acts as a system of levers which pivot at the joints, minimizing the muscle effort needed to make each movement. In walking or jumping, the limbs are pushed back and down against the ground. This thrusts the body up and forward.

The vertebrate skeleton is extremely versatile. In different species it is adapted for walking, running, jumping, flying and swimming, and for a wide range of other activities such as feeding from high branches, digging and burrowing, and fighting. Vertebrates evolved in the sea, where water provides considerable support. Marine mammals are among the largest in the world. To carry such weight on land, without the support of the water, would impose too much strain on the skeleton and muscles.

On land the body must be lifted clear of the ground, otherwise friction slows down movement. In the basic four-footed body plan, the skeleton acts like a double cantilever bridge – a girder carried on two pairs of legs. In some vertebrates, the weight is not evenly distributed between the four limbs. Humans are an obvious example. The elephant, with its heavy head and tusks, bears most of its weight on its forelegs, as does the giraffe. The huge hind legs of the kangaroo are the main weight-bearing limbs. In mammals that have returned to the sea in the course of evolution, such as seals and whales, the limbs have been greatly reduced, or converted into flat paddles, and the body is once again streamlined.

To support an animal and generate thrust during movement, the limbs must be strongly attached to the spine but also free to move in relation to it. The earliest land mammals had developed shoulder girdles and pelvic girdles – a series of supporting bones and joints linking the limbs to the spine. The shoulder girdle is usually formed by the shoulder blades and two small bones called the clavicles (collar-bones), which curve down to the breastbone. In many vertebrates the bones of the pelvic girdle have become fused to form a rigid structure, the pelvis. Most vertebrates also have tails. In some species, the tail is used as a counterbalance while moving, or as a prop when resting. In others, it may be used like an extra hand for gripping branches, or as a device for signaling to other animals.

Different kinds of movement are associated with differences in the proportions of the major bones. For example, the smaller the area of foot in contact with the ground, the less friction there is. Fast-moving animals tend to walk on their toes rather than on the flat of the foot. They have small feet, often with fused toes or hooves. Jumping animals such as kangaroos and hares have hind limbs that are much larger than

▶ Arthropods such as scorpions have a hard external skeleton (exoskeleton). Thinner areas of the exoskeleton act as joints: pairs of opposing muscles are attached inside these joints to pegs on the skeleton.

▶ The wolf of northern North America is both powerful and graceful as it moves through the snow. Like other members of the dog family, it has relatively long legs that make it well adapted for running, which it does on its toes. Although the wolf can move quickly, it has stamina rather than sudden bursts of speed – contrasted with big hunting cats such as cheetahs – and is able to keep up a continuous chase. The lack of large bones in the shoulder and collar area increases flexibility when springing on prey.

the forelimbs, and long foot bones to act as extra powerful levers. In birds the forelimbs have become modified to form wings, while in turtles all four limbs are shaped like paddles.

In addition to its roles in providing support for the weight of the body and allowing movement, the skeleton has an important function in protecting the soft internal organs from the shock of impact on the outside. The skull protects the brain and the delicate sense organs – the eyes, ears, nose and mouth. The rib cage protects most of the heart, lungs and other major internal organs, which lie above the lowest ribs. The abdominal organs are protected by the pelvis. The different shapes and sizes of necks and skulls are associated with variations in the size of the eyes and the brain, and in the types of jaws and teeth needed for particular diets.

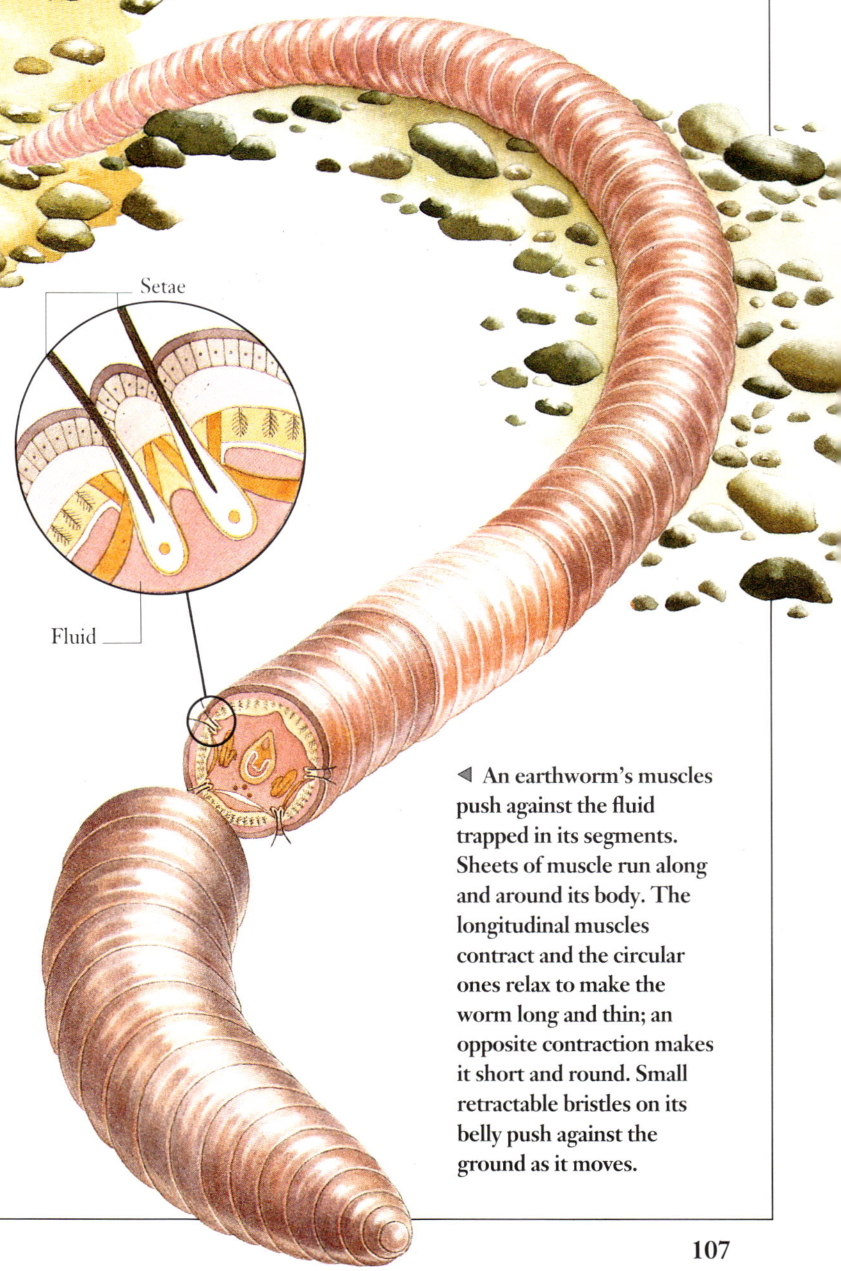

◀ An earthworm's muscles push against the fluid trapped in its segments. Sheets of muscle run along and around its body. The longitudinal muscles contract and the circular ones relax to make the worm long and thin; an opposite contraction makes it short and round. Small retractable bristles on its belly push against the ground as it moves.

WALKING, RUNNING, JUMPING

MOVING animals can achieve some remarkable feats. A cheetah can run at almost 100 kilometers per hour, while a flea can jump over 130 times its own height. In animal skeletons, the bones act as levers and the joints act as fulcrums.

During walking, the push of the foot generates an equal force, or thrust, in the opposite direction, propelling the body forward and up. The thrust is transmitted to the rest of the body through the skeleton and amplified by the leg bones, which act as a series of levers. The body must also be balanced around its center of gravity, otherwise it will fall over. As the leading foot bears down on the ground, the rear foot rocks forward, the body leans forward and the arms tend to swing in opposite directions to the feet in order to keep the center of gravity over the legs.

KEYWORDS

BALANCE
BONE
NERVOUS SYSTEM
SEMICIRCULAR CANAL
SPINE
TENDON

At slow speeds, a four-footed animal needs to have three feet on the ground to form a supporting tripod, and its center of gravity must lie between these three feet. Jumping animals such as kangaroos need to move both feet at the same time, so the center of gravity needs to be nearer the back of the body, and the animal moves awkwardly when on four legs.

Friction with the ground slows down the rate of walking and running. The shorter the time the foot is in contact with the ground, the greater the speed at which an animal can travel. In running, the feet are off the ground for much longer, and the need to be perfectly balanced is not so great.

In four-footed animals, the order in which the feet touch the ground is important for balance, and also affects the efficiency of movement. Most walking vertebrates move diagonally opposite feet in sequence. First one foot is moved forward, then the diagonally opposite one is brought forward, followed by the other front foot, and so on. Salamanders and lizards move diagonally opposite feet at almost the same time, causing their bodies to curve from side to side, which wastes a lot of energy.

As a mammal speeds up into a trot, it usually moves diagonally opposite feet together, but does not twist its body. It no longer needs the stabilizing tripod. An exception is the camel, which moves the two legs on the same side together. This makes the animal's weight shift from side to side as it moves and provides an uncomfortable ride. Faster still, all four feet come down at different times, and all four feet may be off the ground at the same time for brief periods.

Mammals and birds are efficient walkers because their legs are underneath the rest of the body. In fast-moving animals, friction is reduced by decreasing the area of foot in contact with the ground. Cats and dogs walk on their toes, and really fast animals such as antelopes, horses and ostriches have fewer toes, often fused together for extra strength. The degree of flexibility of the spine also affects speed. Cheetahs move exceptionally fast because their spines curve under as they run, bringing the hind legs in front of the forelegs to produce a powerful thrust.

Moving animals also make use of special devices such as "elastic energy" stored in tendons. In vertebrates, the Achilles tendon – which joins the calf muscle to the heel – is particularly important. As the foot hits the ground, the tendon stretches, storing elastic energy. As the ankle straightens out again, this energy is released to bounce the foot forwards. Thus the tendon acts like a spring. Jumping insects such as grasshoppers and fleas use a catapult mechanism. The flea squeezes its leg against a pad of an elastic protein called resilin. A special trigger mechanism releases the pressure as the insect flicks its legs straight, catapulting it forward and up.

All these movements are controlled by the nervous system. In insects, a series of reflexes is triggered by sense cells which can detect the degree of extension or contraction of the various muscles, but in vertebrates the brain is needed to coordinate information to allow the movement of more complex vertebrate bodies. Muscle stretch receptors send information to the brain, and the semicircular canals in the ear provide information on the body's position, helping the animal to balance.

▶ The human skeleton is adapted for a two-legged gait: the legs and spine lie in a straight line. The curvature of the spine ensures that the various parts of the body are balanced over the legs and feet. Five of the lower vertebrae are fused to form the sacrum, the back area of the pelvis, for extra strength. The knee joint carries almost half the body's weight, and locks when straightened. So does the elbow – a relic of four-footed ancestry. The arch formed by the bones of the feet forms a natural spring which acts as a shock absorber when walking. The "wings" of the vertebrae, the bulges on the end of the limb bones and the ridges on the shoulder blades and pelvis provide attachment points for the muscles.

▶ During walking, the foot pushes against the ground at an angle, so that it presses both down and back. The push generates an equal force (thrust) in the opposite direction, so the body is propelled forward and up at the same time, causing it to bob up and down slightly. While walking, the center of gravity must be kept over the legs in order to keep the body balanced. Moving the arms and legs, and leaning the body slightly, help keep the center of gravity over the legs.

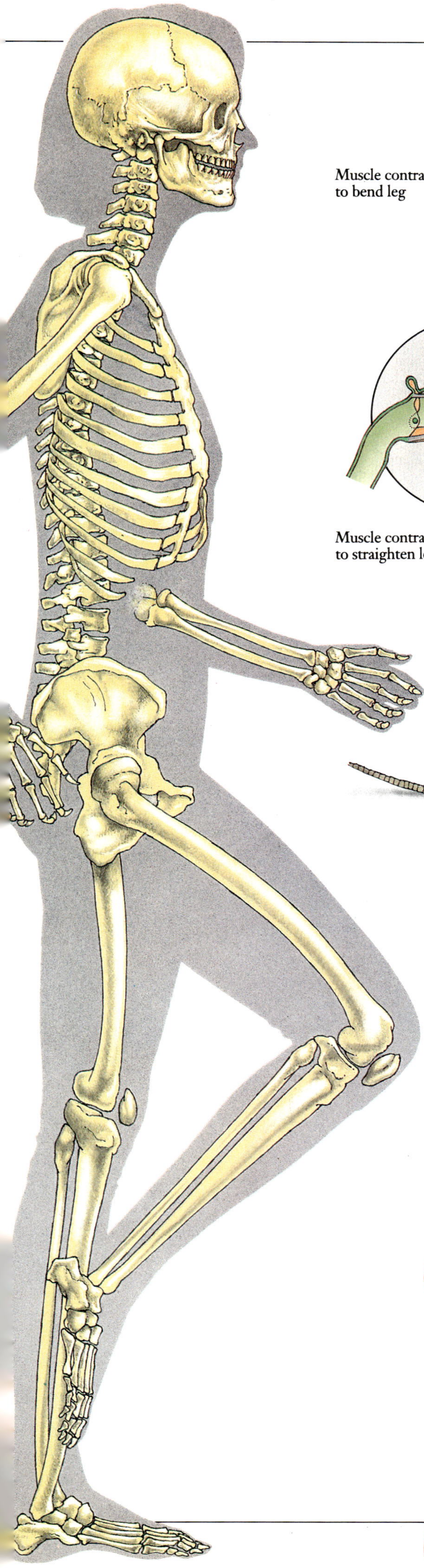

◀ The grasshopper leaps by a catapult mechanism. Energy stored in the elastic tendons of the knee extensor muscles is released on takeoff. The long back legs form powerful levers, allowing a takeoff speed of 3.5 meters per second.

◀ Lizards and salamanders move their four diagonally opposite feet at almost the same time. They tend to wiggle as they walk, which is not very efficient for moving; they can neither move fast, nor cover significant distances.

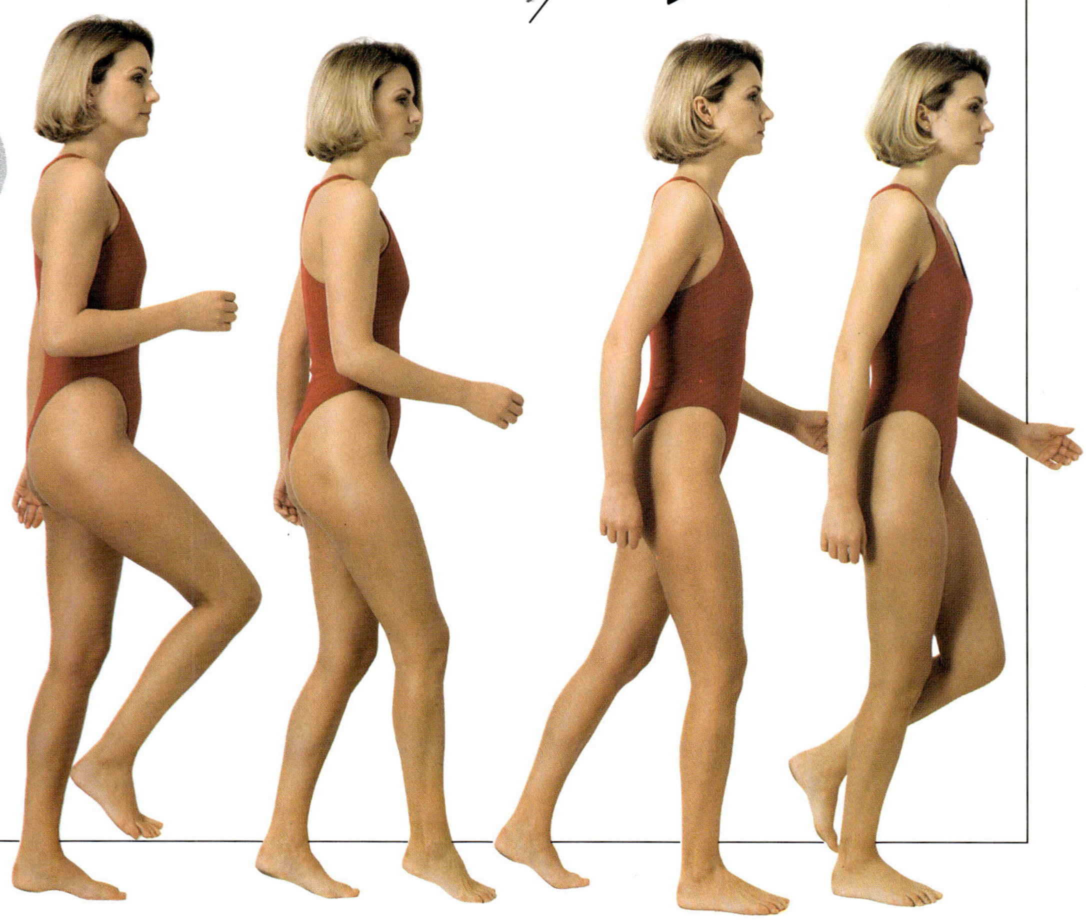

Crawling and Climbing

FOR many animals – both prey and predators – speed is an advantage and can enhance their chances of survival. However, there are many species that have survived for millions of years without moving faster than a slow crawl.

Crawling does not require bulky limbs, because the body does not have to be lifted off the ground. Many crawlers, such as snakes and worms, have long thin bodies which are able to slide into cracks and crannies not accessible to more active animals. Crawlers can weave their way between the stems of grasses and other dense vegetation, glide into underground burrows and even, on occasion, climb trees. Snakes are masters of the art of crawling, and move in a number of different ways. Because they have no limbs to push against the ground, snakes must achieve forward thrust in a different way. Some use their scales as levers, erecting them to push against tiny bumps in the ground. But most snakes simply throw themselves into a series of curves which push against stones and other small obstacles. Hot deserts present a problem for snakes, which usually drag their bellies along the sand. Some desert snakes overcome this discomfort by sidewinding: only two small areas of the body are in contact with the hot ground at any one moment.

KEYWORDS

ADAPTATION
BALANCE
BINOCULAR VISION
CLAW
VERTEBRATE

Quite a different series of adaptations is needed for animals that want to leave the ground and climb into the trees. Tree-dwellers are safe from predators that stalk the forest floor, and there is food in the form of leaves, flowers, fruit, nuts and insects to be found among the branches. To climb a tree trunk an animal needs a good grip. Tree-climbing birds often have the toes of each foot arranged in two pairs. The upper pair hook into the bark, while the rear pair provide an anchor. Birds such as woodpeckers and tree-creepers also use their tails as a prop. The tail feathers are extra broad and strong, and the birds have broad vertebrae with powerful muscles for pressing the tail down. A few birds, such as nuthatches, can climb both up and down a tree, as can squirrels, which can swivel their ankles around to act as anchors for the descent.

Some animals leap from tree to tree, while others have evolved parachute-like membranes and glide gently down. Many monkeys and apes are good jumpers. Their thumbs are opposable – they can be swiveled into position opposite the fingers in order to seize and grip branches. Some species, such as gibbons, have long hands that are used like hooks for swinging from tree to tree. Monkeys use their tails as a counterbalance when leaping. Some monkeys also use their tails as a fifth limb, curling them around the branches as an anchor. Many tree-climbing animals have such "prehensile" tails – armadillos, anteaters, possums and chameleons are examples. These aerobatics require good judgment of distance and speed, and the animals that perform them usually have their eyes placed well to the front of the head in order to have good binocular vision.

▼ In serpentine crawling, the snake throws its body into S-shaped waves. As the body curves, it pushes against the ground, aided by the scales, which act as tiny levers. The curves pass backward as the snake is thrust forward. The tighter the curves, the greater the thrust.

▶ Gibbons use their long arms to swing themselves through the treetops. This form of animal movement is called brachiation. Their long fingers and toes, specially equipped with opposable first digits (both thumbs and "big toes"), allow them to grasp the trees' branches.

▼ Geckos can walk across vertical sheets of glass. The Tokay gecko has overlapping scales beneath its toes, each with up to 150,000 hairs ending in suction pads. These grip even the smoothest surfaces, providing traction.

▼ Many mammals have claws to help them climb, but the squirrel has special equipment for climbing in both directions. Its ankle can be twisted around to point backward – behind the animal – so the claws on the hind feet can act as anchors for the descent as well as the ascent.

MOVING THROUGH THE AIR

ABOUT 300 million years ago, or even earlier, insects began to take to the air. They flew like dragonflies, with all four wings operating independently of each other. Reptiles were the next group of flying animals. The fossils of pterosaurs – reptiles with long tails and large wings formed from membranes of skin stretched between the limbs – are found in rocks that are about 220 million years old. The fossils of the earliest known birds are only 140 million years old, and the only flying mammals – bats – did not evolve until about 60 million years ago.

KEYWORDS

BIRD
BUOYANCY
CONTOUR FEATHER
FEATHER
MOLTING
THORAX

Animals that can fly can easily colonize new areas or travel around in search of mates or food. Flight provides a means of escape from predators on the ground, and an aerial view makes it easier to spot prey. Among modern flying animals, insects are the most numerous. Their wings are made of thin layers of cuticle extended by blood-filled veins, and attached to the thorax or to the flight muscles. Larger insects such as dragonflies have separate flight muscles for each wing, attached directly to the wing and fired by individual nerve impulses. Some dragonflies can reach speeds of 58 km/h over short distances. Smaller insects beat their wings much faster with muscles that distort the thorax, moving all four wings at the same time.

The largest flying species are birds. Even large birds such as eagles or fat birds like partridges can get airborne. Their skeletons have many adaptations for flying, including lightweight bones with special attachment sites for flight muscles, and a rigid structure for transmitting the forces of flight to the rest of the body. Air sacs extended from the lungs also increase the bird's buoyancy. Feathers provide a large, strong surface area and weigh very little. Despite their lightness, feathers make up some 15 to 20 percent of the bird's body weight.

Wings are specially designed for flight. A cross-section of the wing forms an elongated teardrop shape called an airfoil, which generates lift. Airflow is speeded up as it passes over the convex upper surface of the wing, causing reduced pressure that sucks the wing upward. As the air passes across the concave lower surface, it slows down, increasing air pressure and lifting the wing. The bird's body offers considerable resistance, or drag, to the air. In order to remain airborne, the bird must generate more lift than drag. Angling the airfoil so that the leading edge is lower than the trailing edge produces lift and forward propulsion. Small adjustments to the angle of the primary feathers or the tail help the bird to steer.

In order to land, the bird spreads its tail feathers to act as a brake, tilting them so they are almost vertical. It may also lower its feet well before landing. The bird changes the direction in which its wings beat, from up and down to back and forth. When it reaches a very slow speed, turbulence around the trailing edge of the airfoil can cause the bird to stall. To prevent this, the bird raises its first, feather-covered digit, the alula, so that air can pass beneath it. This reduces turbulence. A similar wing action is used when hovering. The bird faces into the wind to help it stay in one place. Only hummingbirds have really perfected the art of hovering. They beat their wings up to 50 times a second, while the primary feathers move in a figure of eight, generating lift and forward propulsion on both the downstroke and the upstroke.

The most common method of flying is by flapping. Some birds also travel great distances by gliding. They

▲ When a bird flies, the wing extends on the downstroke and the feathers spread out to increase the surface area. The front edge is lower than the back edge, pushing the air down and back. The air pressure twists the primary feathers downward, increasing the backward push. Then the bird lifts the leading edge of the wing, generating mostly lift. As the upstroke starts, the wing becomes vertical and the tips sweep forward. The wings fold close to the body and the primary feathers twist and separate. As it sweeps up, the wing flexes slightly backward, producing extra thrust.

◀ The bird's skeleton is very light. Many bones are hollow, supported by struts of bone for strength. The breastbone is drawn out into a flattened keel with flight muscles attached.

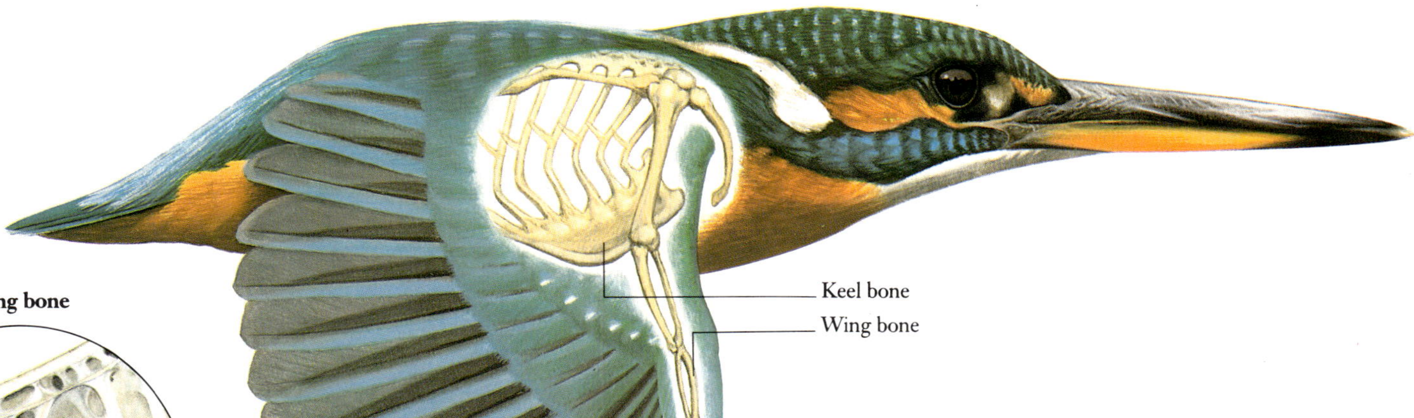

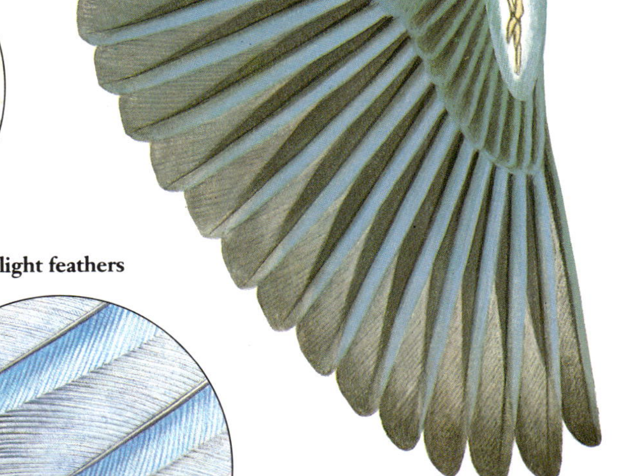

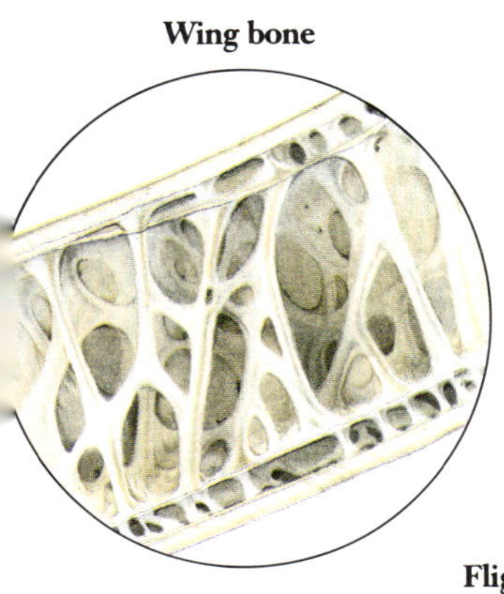

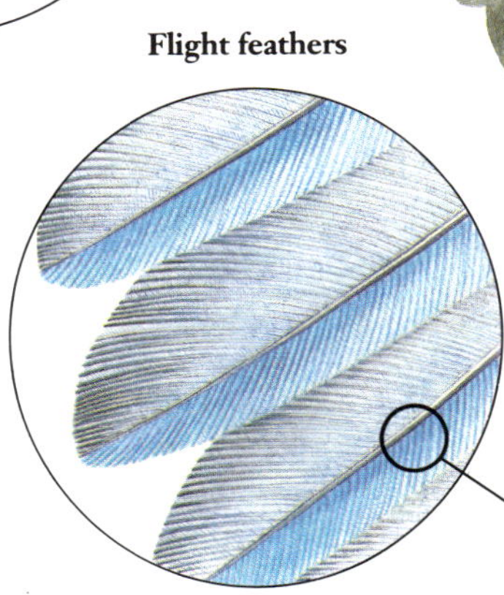

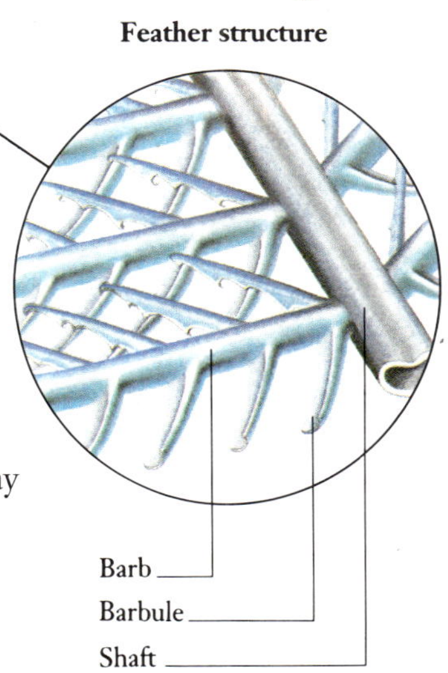

use the rising air currents that develop over warm land, or where a wind meets cliffs or waves. Gliding birds usually have long, narrow wings, which they hold almost fully extended as they glide. As long as the air is rising faster than the bird is sinking, the bird rises. Birds often circle to stay in zones of rising air. When they have risen as far as they can, they glide down without flapping their wings, often for several kilometers, until they reach another system of rising air. The albatross is the master glider, spending most of its life at sea.

Bats are less versatile flyers. The wing is supported by very long fingers, and the wing membranes extend along the sides of the body to the hind limbs. A bat has no tail feathers to help in braking and turning, nor can it fold its wings so effectively on the upstroke.

◀ The hollow quill and shaft of feathers support the vane. Each barb bears two rows of barbules. The barbules of adjacent barbs lock the structure together.

◀ The wings of dragonflies FAR LEFT operate independently of each other. In flight, each wing twists to provide forward thrust and lift. Dragonflies have flight muscles attached directly to the wings.

▲ An Australian sugar glider glides from one tree to the next. The sheet of tissue stretched like a cape along the side of its body provides a flat gliding surface to support its weight and generate lift. Many other animals – including species of snakes, frogs, lizards, squirrels and some marsupials – have adopted similar tactics. Most of these animals use trees as take-off points.

Moving Through Water

CONSIDERABLE effort is needed to swim: water is 800 times more dense than air. As in moving on land, the basic principle of swimming is a backward push against a resisting surface – water – which generates an equal thrust in the opposite direction. There are four common forms of swimming based on this principle: undulation, the frog kick, rowing and hydrofoil action. Jet propulsion, another common method of swimming, works by sucking water into the body, then expelling it with considerable force.

KEYWORDS

BUOYANCY
DIVING MAMMAL
FIN
HYDROFOIL
JET PROPULSION
SWIM BLADDER

Swimming by undulation uses the same principle as serpentine crawling in snakes. The animal's body throws itself into curves that press sideways and back against the water. The wings of penguins and some other diving birds, the flippers of turtles and the hind legs of swimming crabs act as hydrofoils. They beat up and down at an angle, generating forward thrust on both strokes. The downstroke also generates an upward thrust, while the upstroke generates a downward thrust.

The bodies of swimming animals show many adaptations to their mode of travel. Most animals that travel at relatively high speeds underwater usually adopt a streamlined body shape while swimming. Newts, salamanders, crocodiles, seals and otters hold their legs flat against their sides while moving forward through the water. In fish and amphibians a coat of slippery slime on the animal's body helps to reduce drag. In dolphins and porpoises, the skin forms tiny ripples in response to differences in water pressure. This has also been shown to reduce drag.

Arthropods (crustaceans and aquatic insects) have flattened limbs that act like paddles, or limbs lined with flat fringes of bristles to increase their surface area. In fish the main forward thrust is achieved by flexing the body, especially the tail. Fish also have fins supported by stiff rays made of cartilage and powered by muscles. The dorsal and anal fins can be undulated for propulsion, while the tail fin beats down and back at an angle on the water. Depending on the shape of the tail fin, it may be capable of altering the fish's pitch, too. This fin is also used as a rudder for steering. The paired pectoral and pelvic fins beat in a sculling action, and are used mainly for steering and for correcting the fish's position in the water. The pectoral and pelvic fins can also be used for braking. Powerful blocks of muscles along the fish's flanks pull on a strong but flexible spine.

The limbs of marine and aquatic vertebrates show various modifications for moving through water. Otters and salamanders have webs of skin between their toes to increase the surface area for swimming. Webs are even better developed in frogs and in swimming and diving birds, which have long toes that support a large area of web. The toes are spread to extend the web on the power stroke, and closed to reduce drag on the recovery stroke. This is the driving force of the frog kick. A permanently large surface area for pushing against the water is provided by the tails of fish, otters and sea snakes, which are flattened vertically to create a larger area for pushing sideways against the water. Whales and dolphins have horizontally flattened tail flukes for beating up and down.

Keeping afloat is a problem for animals whose bodies are denser than water. Many microscopic plankton have spines to spread their weight over a larger surface area. Globules of oil, which is less dense than water, may also keep small creatures buoyant. Sharks have very oily livers but need to keep swimming to stay afloat. Many bony fish have a swim bladder, whose volume can be altered to keep the fish's overall density equal to that of the surrounding water. Gas can be expelled from the mouth or absorbed into the blood, and extra gas can be secreted into the swim bladder if needed. This gas is composed mainly of nitrogen and oxygen and sometimes also of carbon dioxide. Finer adjustment can be made by changing the angle of fins, flukes and flippers. The air in the lungs of mammals, birds and reptiles also increases their buoyancy. Freshwater turtles adjust the amount of air to change their buoyancy.

▶ **Flatfish twist as they develop and come to lie on their sides, so they appear to undulate up and down as they swim, instead of moving from side to side.**

◀ Unlike fish, dolphins undulate up and down as they swim. The main thrust is provided by the powerful, flattened, horizontal tail flukes. The flippers are used for steering. The lack of hind limbs gives a streamlined body.

▼ The slow-moving platypus uses its webbed front feet as paddles. The hind feet are only partially webbed, and serve as rudders. The legs are very short, which reduces the animal's resistance to water.

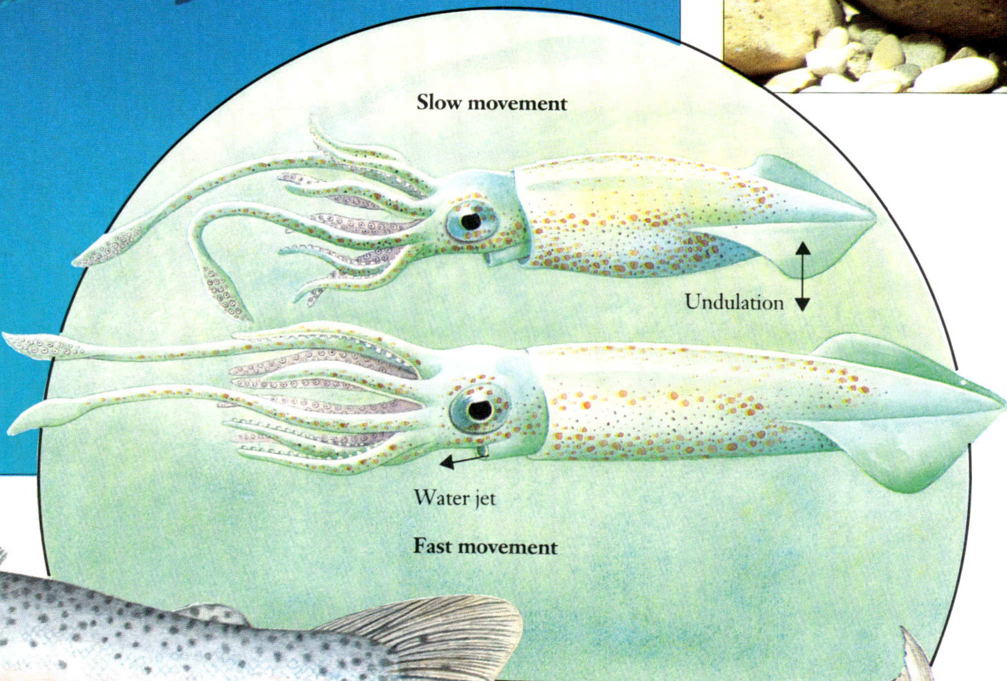

◀ Squid swim gently forward by undulating on the winglike extensions of their mantle. They can also swim rapidly backward by jet propulsion, squirting water out of the body cavity through a special siphon, which can be angled to control the direction of movement.

◀ In fish, the main power comes from the tail. As it flexes it pushes against the water. The water resistance provides a forward and sideways thrust in the opposite direction to the tail movement. The side-to-side motion cancels out the sideways component leaving the combined forward force. The vertical dorsal and ventral fins help control rolling and yawing (sideways instability) while pitching (up-and-down movement) is controlled by the paired pectoral and pelvic fins.

5

GROWTH & *Reproduction*

THE HUGE DIVERSITY of living creatures would not be possible without the appearance of new characteristics and the constant reshuffling of existing ones. Even among individual species (creatures that breed only with members of their own kind), the amount of natural variation is enormous. The human race is a good example, with its wide range of characteristics.

Because of the variation within populations, some individuals may cope better with changes in their environment and survive to produce more offspring, spreading their characteristics through the population. A similar process occurs when animals colonize a new habitat. Over many years, this process gives rise to new species. Without this variation, a species is unable to adapt to change and is likely to become extinct.

The variation between individuals of the same species arises in two ways: by spontaneous changes in the genes, and by the mixing of the genes from two individuals during sexual reproduction. Special chemicals (genes) inside the cell nuclei carry the genetic program that runs the cell's life and the life of daughter cells that result from cell division. From the first division of a fertilized egg, the outcome is preprogrammed: genes in the egg nucleus determine the development of the different body cells to produce complex organs.

Animals have evolved an incredible variety of displays and signals to help them select their mates. Females need to conserve their energy for rearing the young; for this reason, in most species it is the males that show off, and the females that do the choosing. The most dramatic displays and the most dazzling plumage – of which the peacock is a worldwide symbol – usually belong to the healthiest, "fittest" males, so the female benefits from choosing on the basis of outward appearance.

Patterns of Growth

During the last two months in its mother's womb, a blue whale fetus grows at a rate of 100 kilograms a day. Some insect larvae make even more incredible growth spurts, increasing their sizes a thousandfold after hatching. Nor is growth a simple increase in size: ducklings grow into swans and underwater larvae are transformed into shimmering dragonflies. All this growth is accomplished by the division of cells too small to be seen with the naked eye. It is preprogrammed by the genes in its nucleus. The genes determine the pattern of development of cells, producing all the complex organs that will be needed by the adult animal. The genes also control the production of hormones that stimulate certain cells to divide and become differentiated (specialized).

KEYWORDS

CELL
CELL DIVISION
DIFFERENTIATION
EMBRYO
MOLTING
REGENERATION

Most animals have a period of general increase in size after birth, called the juvenile stage. Late in this stage – called puberty in humans – hormones trigger the further development of the sexual organs. The age at which this occurs is chiefly determined by the genes, but it may be fine-tuned by the environment: humans in the 20th century have entered puberty at a younger age due to improved nutrition.

Not all animals have such a simple growth pattern. At regular intervals during its life, an arthropod sheds its cuticle – molts – and undergoes rapid expansion while the new soft cuticle expands and hardens. Later its tissues will grow to fill the new space. For other animals, the outer surface must be able to accommodate growth. In simple animals the surface cells may divide to keep pace with expansion. In land-dwelling vertebrates, however, the outer layers of the skin are usually hard and water-resistant due to deposits of the protein keratin. This outer layer of skin may be sloughed off continuously, as in mammals and birds, or the whole layer may be shed from time to time, as in reptiles and amphibians.

Birds and mammals also need to renew their outer layers of feathers and fur. Animals in cold

▶ **Lizards and snakes shed their skins from time to time to allow for growth and repair. Molting is controlled by hormones. A lizard will rub itself against stones and twigs in order to remove the loose skin.**

◀ **Many animals show spurts of growth during favorable seasons and very little growth in adverse conditions. Each of the concentric ridges on the tortoise shell represents one year's growth.**

◀ Elephants produce only one large, well-developed young at a time, after a pregnancy lasting some 22 months. But the elephant's lifespan of 60–70 years ensures that enough off-spring are produced to continue the species.

▼ A crab climbs out of its old, discarded shell. The shell cannot expand, so its must be shed if the animal is to grow. The new shell is soft at first, so the crab must keep out of sight of predators until it has hardened.

climates may shed thick, soft winter fur or feathers in spring and grow a thinner coat, which may have a different camouflage color. Ptarmigans and Arctic hares, for instance, have whites coats in winter and brown ones in summer. Birds must renew their feathers to keep them airworthy. This is also an opportunity to don bright new breeding plumage. A few species, such as shelducks, shed all their flight feathers at the same time.

The limits to growth, size and age are genetically determined, but also influenced by nutrition. At a certain age, the hormone output changes, body structures and processes become less efficient, and aging begins. In general, small animals have shorter lifespans, but not always. Many mollusks of cold polar oceans grow extremely slowly and reach great ages. Some deep-sea clams are hundreds of years old; the longest human life on record is 120 years.

Longevity is also a feature of large mammals such as elephants and humans. Larger animals tend to reproduce more slowly, with long gestation periods or a long period of learning before the young are capable of surviving without their parents' care and protection. To compensate for their ability to produce only a few young (or only one) at a time, these animals have a longer breeding span.

▼ Animals such as horses and antelopes, which live in the wild in large herds con-tinually on the move, give birth to large, well developed "precocial" young, capable of running with the herd soon after birth.

▶ The toucan produces small, helpless "altricial" young, which grow rapidly. Highly dependent on their parents, these young are easy prey to predators, but their large numbers compensate for their low rate of survival.

Getting Together

Some of nature's most extravagant experiments were designed to bring the sexes together for reproduction. Most invertebrates mate with the first member of the opposite sex that attracts them, but vertebrates – especially birds and mammals – are often more selective. For animals with bright breeding colors, meeting and recognizing potential mates is easy. But the visual displays and courtship plumage used by males to attract females may attract predators. The less bright coloring of females makes them less conspicuous when tending their eggs or young.

In most species the females care for the young and expend energy to produce well-provisioned eggs or carry the young before birth. Females cannot afford to use up their energy in multiple courtships and matings, but males court as many females as they can. Some courtship rituals recognize the female's greater expenditure of energy in mating, and the males of some species bring food to the females.

KEYWORDS

BIOLOGICAL CLOCK
ESTRUS CYCLE
HORMONE
MONOGAMY
PHEROMONE
POLYGAMY
REPRODUCTION
RUT
TERRITORY

In many species that form large breeding groups, such as deer and seals, the males round up "harems" of females and compete to mate with them. Ritualized displays establish dominance without injury. In the breeding season, called the rut, stags roar at each other, and they may fight, pushing each other with locked antlers until one gives way or is pushed away. The boxing matches of kangaroos and European hares serve a similar purpose. Other animals, such as elephant seals, may actually fight – often brutally.

Some species leave the choice of mate to the females. Female frogs are attracted to the males with the loudest and deepest croaks, which are usually also the largest, healthiest frogs. Male sage grouse, prairie hens and ruffs use communal display grounds, called leks, where they strut around displaying to the females. The males compete actively for the best site within the lek, and females tend to be attracted to the birds in the center, which are the fittest.

Many animals – especially birds and fish – migrate to special breeding grounds. Many species need a breeding territory large enough to provide food for a growing family. Birds sing to advertise their ownership of a territory, while mammals commonly use scent signals. Even fish may hold territories. Some provide the nest itself: the male stickleback builds a nest of weeds, then dances to lure passing females in.

The timing of mating is very important if the young are to be reared in a period of plentiful food. Genetically programmed biological clocks are fine-tuned to environmental signals – for animals such as deer, with long gestation periods, the shortening days in autumn. These signals trigger hormone changes that bring the animals into breeding condition and may also compel them to migrate to breeding areas. The sexual organs of birds start to increase in size with the increasing length of day in spring. At the end of the breeding season they shrink so that the bird does not have to fly with the extra weight. Desert birds can breed at any time of year. Their breeding behavior is triggered by the sound of rain falling and the sight of green vegetation. In habitats where food is abundant all year, mammals such as primates may mate at almost any time.

A few animals change sex to suit the situation. Slipper limpets can move around only when young, then settle in a heap on top of one another. The ones at the top are males, but as they become covered by other males, they change into females. Cleanerfish use the opposite tactic. They live in small groups of females in which the most senior becomes a male. When this fish dies, the next most senior fish changes sex. This economizes on the need for males, which serve no purpose other than to fertilize eggs.

▲ The spectacular courtship display of the blue bird of paradise reflects the importance in evolution of successful competition for mates.

▶ Elephant seal bulls fight over territories and females on the beach. This display is followed by lunges, as the two bulls attack each other with their teeth.

◀ A tiny male orb-web spider courts a huge female. By special vibrations of the web and tapping on her body, he hopes to persuade her to let him mate with her. She may refuse and eat him.

▲ Blue-footed boobies pair for life. As well as courtship displays, other displays help to reinforce the pair bond, especially greeting displays which take place when an absent partner returns to the nest.

ANIMAL REPRODUCTION

INDIVIDUAL characteristics are determined by genes – sections of the nucleic acid chains found in the nuclei of almost every cell – which contain the blueprint for producing every cell in the body. Occasionally, changes occur in this blueprint. If the mutations occur in the sex cells – the eggs and sperm – they become inherited characteristics.

KEYWORDS

- BUDDING
- CHROMOSOME
- EGG
- FERTILIZATION
- GAMETE
- GENE
- HERMAPHRODITE
- MEIOSIS
- SPERM

Reshuffling of inherited characteristics takes place during sexual reproduction, which involves individuals of different sex. At its simplest, in single-celled creatures, two individuals come together and exchange nuclear material. In most higher animals, it involves distinct sex cells – eggs (ova) and sperm. At fertilization, the egg and sperm of two individuals fuse. The genes are shuffled so that each offspring contains a mixture of parental genes. This explains why members of a species vary in appearance and physiological adaptations.

Early in the evolution of animals, the ova became larger and more specialized to provide a food store, and sperm were adapted to swim to the ova. Internal fertilization is the most efficient method of getting the sperm as close as possible to the ova. It economizes on sperm and allows for the production of fewer but larger eggs with large food stores (yolk).

There are many ways of placing sperm inside a female's body. Male spiders spin small triangular webs to put their sperm in, using a spoon-shaped leg to scoop it up and put it inside the female. Many other invertebrates, and some newts and salamanders, deposit packages of sperm (spermatophores) where the female will pick them up, or place them inside her. The most reliable method uses a special organ, the penis, inserted into the female's genital opening. Insects, mammals and reptiles use this method.

External fertilization is most common among animals that live on the seabed and have limited mobility, and among animals that mate in water. Mussels, clams, sponges and corals send their sperm and ova into the sea. The release of sex cells, or gametes, is synchronized by stimulating chemicals which induce all the animals in the area to release them at the same time.

Not all matings involve a male and a female animal. A few groups of animals, such as earthworms and snails, are hermaphrodite – they have both male and female organs. A pair exchange sperm, and both partners end up with fertilized eggs. This means that every worm or snail can mate with every other one, which saves time looking for a mate, but both partners expend energy growing male and female sex organs.

Asexual reproduction – which allows a single animal to produce genetically identical offspring – occurs in many simple animals. Hydras reproduce by budding off new individuals, and corals can regenerate from broken fragments. Many parasites have asexual phases which spread rapidly throughout the bodies of their hosts. However, in these same animals, sexual reproduction takes place at regular intervals to maintain the variation in the species – often under unfavorable conditions, such as food shortage, drought or the approach of winter. The resulting variation may help the species to survive the difficult period.

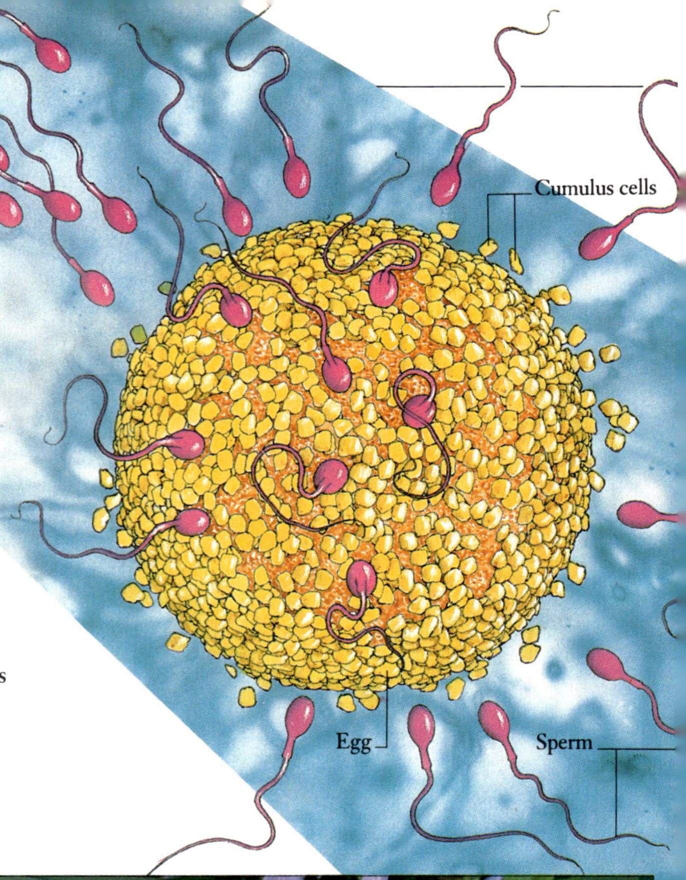

▶ The unfertilized human egg is surrounded by up to 2000 cumulus cells which make it large enough to be wafted down the fallopian tubes by cilia. The zona pellucida protects the egg from damage in transit. As soon as one sperm has penetrated the egg, the zona pellucida hardens to form a "fertilization membrane" which prevents further sperm from entering. Multiple fertilization would result in failure of cell division in the embryo.

▲ Roman snails, which are hermaphrodites, have a complex and unusual courtship ritual which begins with a "dance". Both partners rear up and press their muscular feet together. Then they stroke one another with their tentacles, and after some hours, shoot sharp "love-darts" in each other, an act that stimulates them to complete the act of mating.

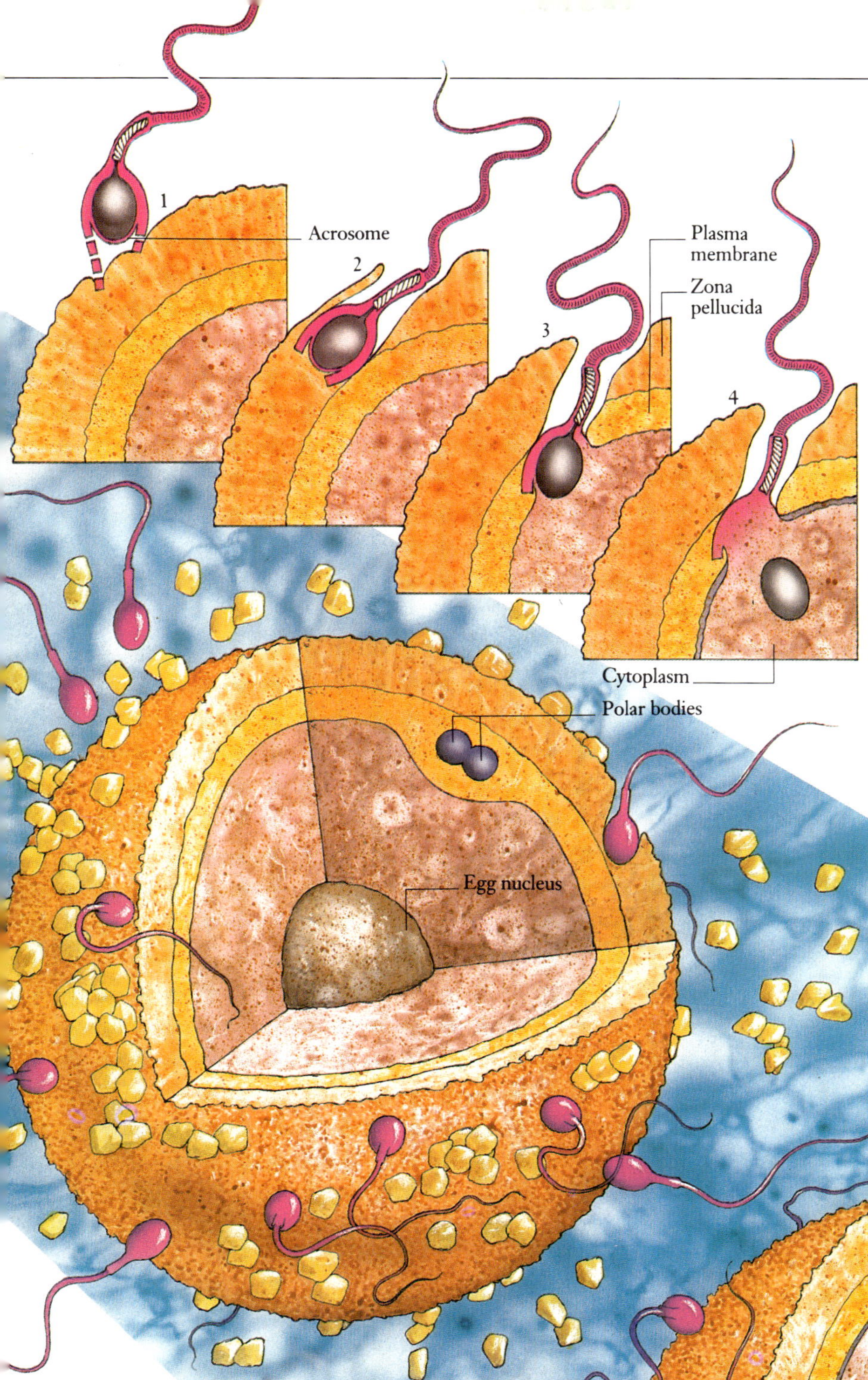

▲ Internal fertilization is essential for land-dwellers like ladybirds. Most male insects use a special organ to inject sperm into the female. This allows fewer eggs to have more chance of being fertilized.

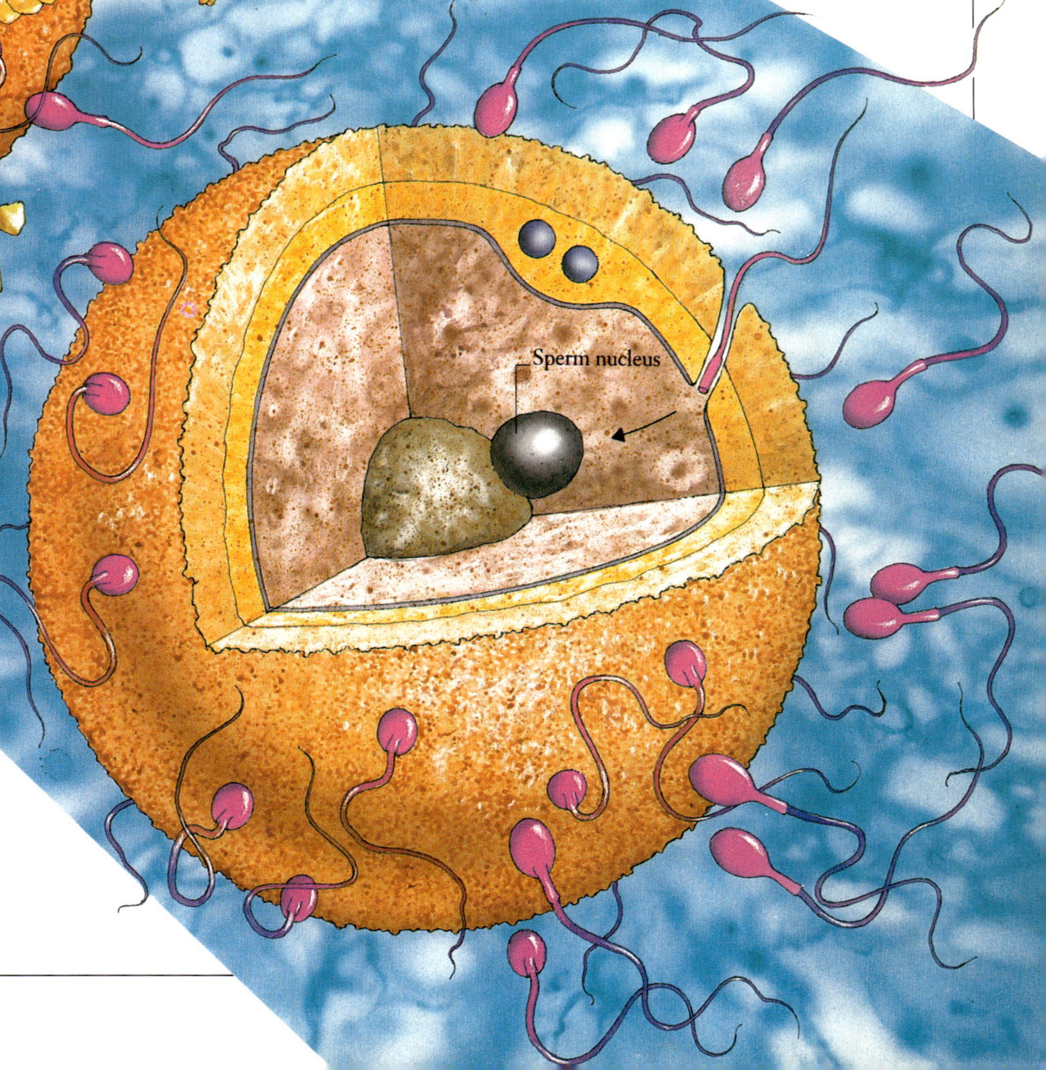

▲ When a sperm reaches the egg 1, it binds to sites on the jellylike zona pellucida. From the acrosome, at its tip, the sperm releases the enzyme acrosin, which softens the membrane covering the egg. The acrosome then forms a fine needle-like filament which pierces the membrane, allowing the sperm to enter 2. The membrane hardens and a fluid layer grows to prevent more sperm entering 3. The sperm now sheds its tail, and the head and middle section enter the egg cytoplasm 4.

▶ **Prior to conception,** the egg has divided, producing a large daughter cell, with the first polar body as a byproduct. The polar body contains extra chromosomes which will not be needed when the egg fuses with a sperm. It may divide again, as shown here; then, as soon as a sperm enters the cell, new division takes place, producing another polar body and the egg that will be fertilized. The nuclei of the sperm and egg fuse, and the cell immediately divides – the first division in the formation of the embryo.

Egg to Embryo

The early human embryo has gill slits; so do the embryos of birds and reptiles, even though the adults have lungs. The embryos of related groups of animals – in this case vertebrates – are often remarkably similar, and the very early stages of development are much the same in all animals.

In very simple animals, such as hydra, the fertilized egg divides repeatedly to form a ball of cells, which then form two main layers – the ectoderm, or outer layer, and the endoderm, or inner layer. More advanced animals, whose organs are suspended in a distinct body cavity (celom), develop three layers – ectoderm, endoderm and a middle layer, the mesoderm. In all animals, the body structures are formed from infoldings of these layers: the ectoderm forms the outer covering (epidermis), such as the skin of vertebrates, and the peripheral nervous system; the mesoderm gives rise to the muscles, heart and vascular system, skeleton, kidneys and reproductive organs, the outer layers of the stomach and gut, and the inner layers of the skin; and the endoderm develops into the inner lining of the stomach and digestive tract, the liver and the lungs or gills.

KEYWORDS

AMNION
EMBRYO
ECTODERM
ENDODERM
FETUS
GENE
MAMMAL
PLACENTA
UTERUS

The shape, position and relative size of these different body structures, and the way in which they arise, is governed by the inherited genes in the nucleus of the newly fertilized egg. Through the action of the genes, chemicals are produced in a certain sequence to stimulate particular cells to become specialized to form tissues and organs at certain stages of development. The type of mature cell that will eventually develop is determined at a very early stage by the position of the cell in relation to the embryo – whether the cell is found near the head or the tail – and by the concentrations of chemicals produced by other cells. Sometimes the external environment also plays a part: the sex of baby crocodiles, turtles and tortoises depends upon the temperature at which they incubate, though the sex organs will not mature until much later.

Some animals produce a large number of eggs with very little yolk. These eggs hatch into relatively undeveloped young with a high mortality rate from injury and predators. Other animals produce fewer eggs with larger yolks. The young that hatch from these eggs are better able to take care of themselves and have a higher rate of survival.

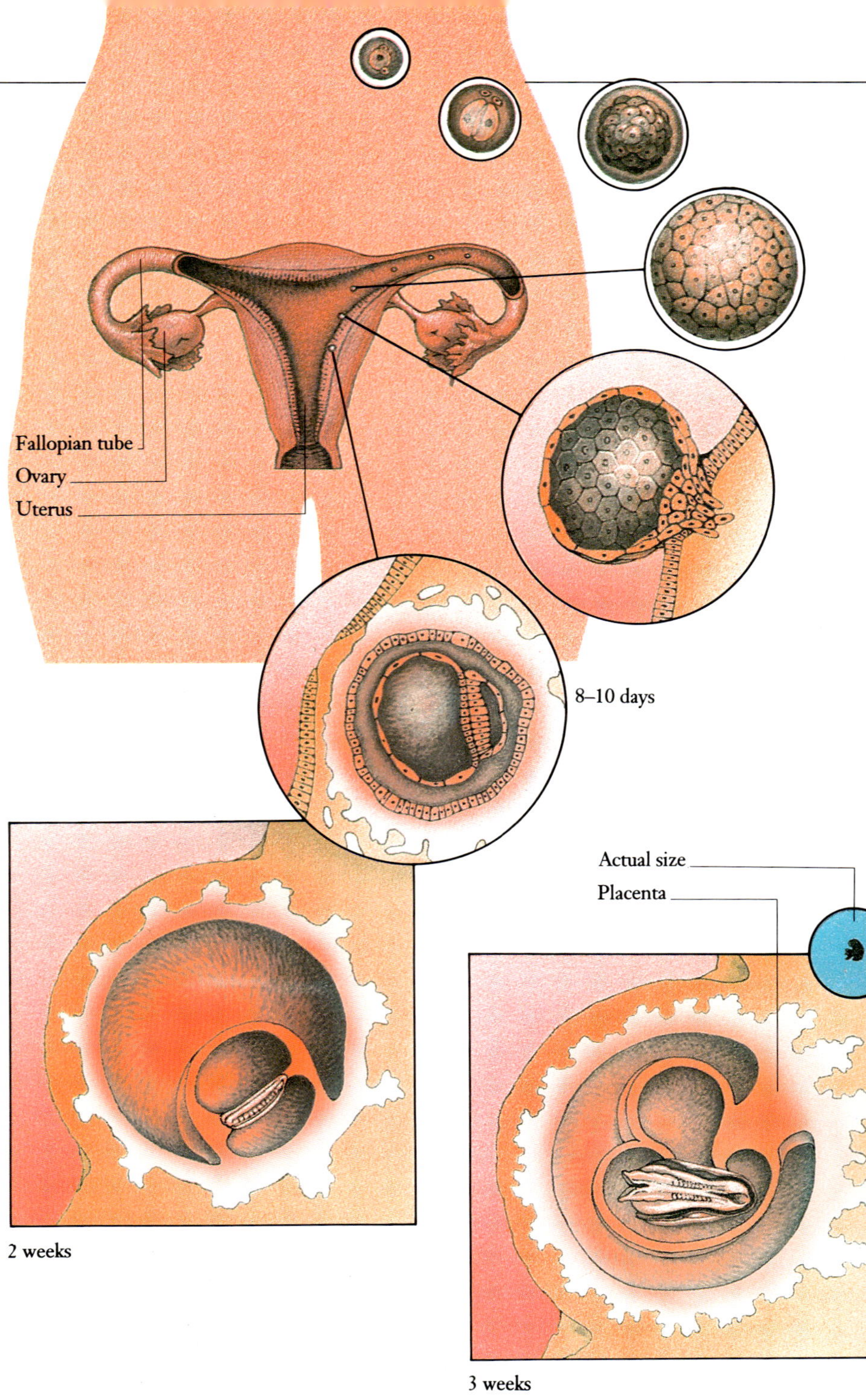

▶ **A crocodile shortly before hatching. The reptile egg contains a rich supply of yolk and protein-rich "white"; it has a special sac, the allantois, into which wastes are excreted. The embryo is cushioned in another fluid-filled sac, the amnion. The outer shell provides protection against external injury and drying out, but still allows gas exchange with the atmosphere. The evolution of such eggs was an important step in animals' adapting to life on land.**

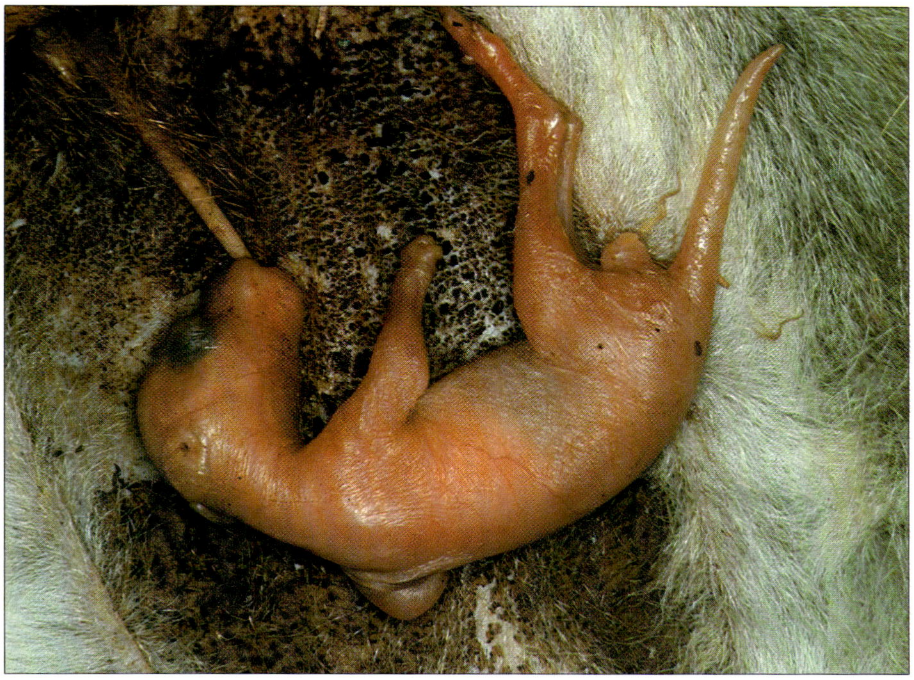

▲ A baby red kangaroo barely 2 cm long suckles on a teat in its mother's pouch. Marsupials do not form a placenta, and their young are born at a very early stage of development. They are carried in the pouch until they are larger.

Eggs that are shed directly into the water to await fertilization are limited in the amount of food they can store in a single cell. On the other hand, eggs that are fertilized inside the female's body can be surrounded with layers of food after they have been fertilized, and in some groups of animals a tough shell is secreted around them for protection against injury and drying. Frog eggs are surrounded by a jellylike substance that swells on contact with water. This sticks the eggs together into a slippery ball which predators find almost impossible to swallow. Bird eggs may also be coated with pigments for camouflage.

Many animals, from insects to mammals, keep the fertilized eggs inside the mother's body. There they are protected against predators and mechanical injury, and have a warmer, more stable environment. The parents do not have to take time out from hunting or feeding to guard them or keep them warm. Most mammals retain their embryos in this way. Marsupials (pouched mammals) give birth to a very tiny, immature young which is then protected inside a pouch, where it is fed on milk. In the placental mammals a soft pad of tissue rich in blood vessels develops, in which the embryo's blood vessels mingle with the mother's to exchange respiratory gases, nutrients and waste. This pad of tissue is called the placenta.

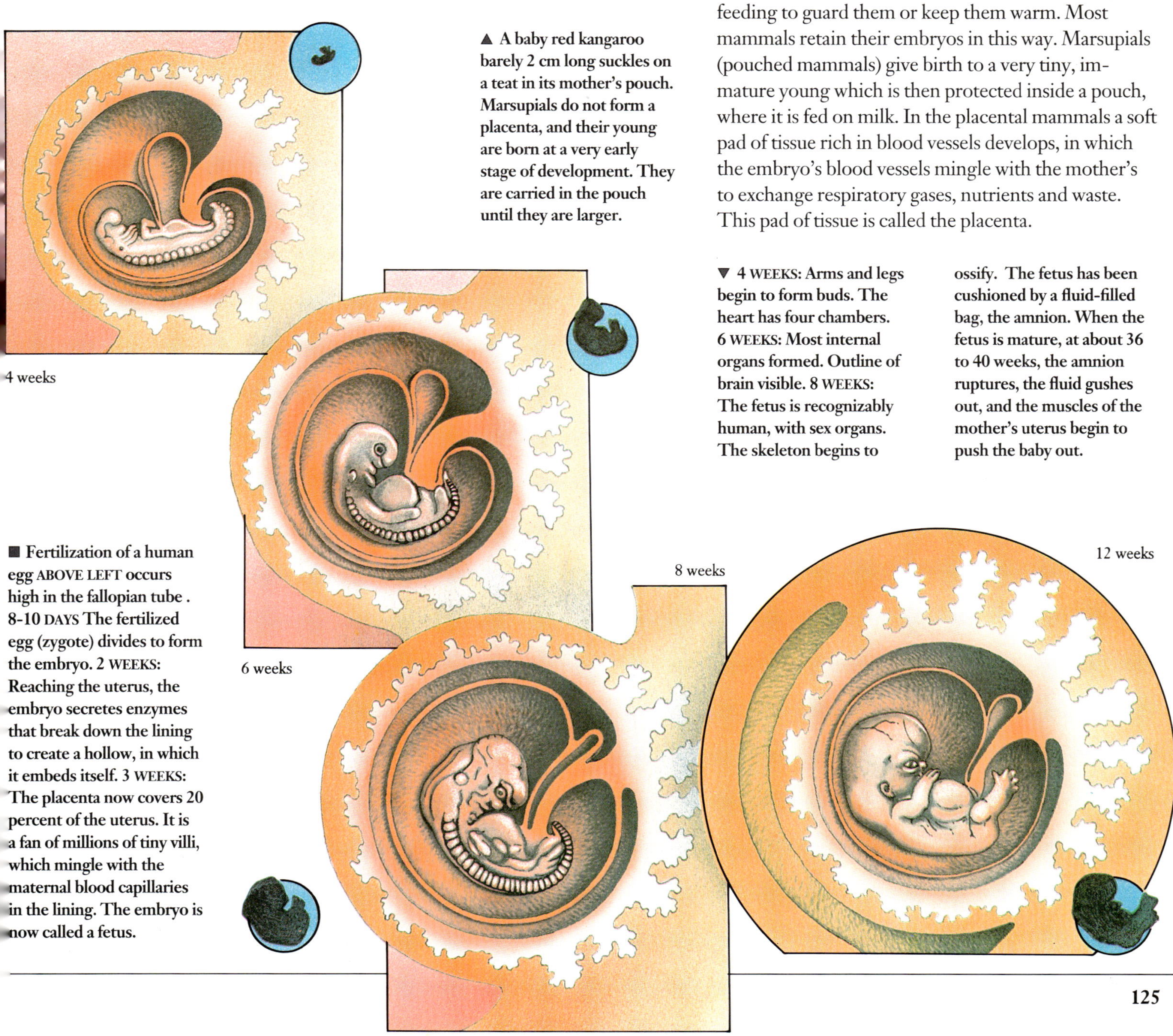

▼ 4 WEEKS: Arms and legs begin to form buds. The heart has four chambers. 6 WEEKS: Most internal organs formed. Outline of brain visible. 8 WEEKS: The fetus is recognizably human, with sex organs. The skeleton begins to ossify. The fetus has been cushioned by a fluid-filled bag, the amnion. When the fetus is mature, at about 36 to 40 weeks, the amnion ruptures, the fluid gushes out, and the muscles of the mother's uterus begin to push the baby out.

■ Fertilization of a human egg ABOVE LEFT occurs high in the fallopian tube . 8-10 DAYS The fertilized egg (zygote) divides to form the embryo. 2 WEEKS: Reaching the uterus, the embryo secretes enzymes that break down the lining to create a hollow, in which it embeds itself. 3 WEEKS: The placenta now covers 20 percent of the uterus. It is a fan of millions of tiny villi, which mingle with the maternal blood capillaries in the lining. The embryo is now called a fetus.

Growing Up

Many animals need no parental care: they are independent from birth or hatching. But examples of one or both parents caring for the young can be found throughout the animal kingdom. Among invertebrates, guarding or brooding of young is found in sea anemones, starfish, octopuses, bugs, spiders, scorpions and centipedes, but only the social insects – the bees, wasps, ants and termites – feed and groom their young from egg to adult. Parental care is more common among vertebrates, including some species of fish, amphibians and reptiles.

KEYWORDS

MAMMAL
MILK
MONOTREME
PUBERTY
PUPA
WARM-BLOODED ANIMAL

More protection is offered by building a nest. Birds are not the only animals that build nests. Siamese fighting fish make bubble nests at the water surface. In the African deserts, foam nest frogs make communal nests by whipping up a froth of saliva and body secretions with their legs. The froth keeps the eggs moist. The American alligator builds a huge pile of vegetation in which to lay her eggs. The heat from the rotting plants helps to incubate them. She helps the young out of the eggs and carries them gently in her mouth to water.

A parent's body can offer even more protection. In sea horses and pipefish the fertilized eggs are placed in a pouch on the male's belly to develop and hatch. Female marsupial toads and frogs have soft spongy tissue on their backs. The male presses the fertilized eggs into this tissue, which then grows over them to protect them from predators and from drying out. The tadpoles pass their entire development in these pockets. When they have become tiny frogs, the mother claws away the skin covering them and they escape. In "warm-blooded" birds, the eggs must be kept warm. Most build nests, and all birds sit on their eggs to incubate them. Many birds have brood pouches – patches of almost bare skin rich in blood vessels that swell and warm in the breeding season.

Marsupials and monotremes have warm pouches for their young, and all other mammals carry them inside their bodies in the early stages of development. Burrowing mammals may construct nursery chambers which they line with grasses or leaves for extra warmth. Mammals have the advantage of being able to suckle their young on milk, avoiding the need to find food for them. This has been an important feature in the evolution of mammal lifestyles: the young mammal has a set of unspecialized milk teeth, which it uses to tackle soft, often partly chewed food that its parents bring for it. Cnly when its jaws have grown larger does a replacement set of adult teeth appear. This allows for the growth of different teeth, including large molars for grinding vegetation or premolars for crushing bones. There is no room for such teeth in the jaws of young mammals.

In some birds and mammals, other members of the family or social group may help to bring up the young. These are often the young of the previous brood or litter, or non-breeding members of the group. Among wild dogs, wolves and other social hunters, several members of the group may bring food for the young or guard them while their parents hunt. Lion prides are remarkable in that any breeding female may suckle the young of another female. The females are often sisters, so their young have a lot of genes in common, which perhaps explains this unusual situation. Shelducks collect their young together into large groups which the adults take turns to guard. At the other extreme, some birds, such as cuckoos and cowbirds, leave other species to bring up their offspring. The young cuckoo ejects the foster parents' young from the nest. Such practices are not always detrimental to the host species. Oropendula young share the nest with the young cowbirds, which eat various nest parasites that would otherwise infect the oropendula chicks.

▲ Young fox cubs at play. The young of many predatory animals spend much of their time at play. The activities teach them the physical skills and quick reactions they will need in their adult life for hunting and killing.

▶ The young of many insects receive no parental care. This moon moth started life alone as an egg on a plant and had to fend for itself from the start. Its youth as a caterpillar bore little relation to its new aerial life.

▲ Throughout their early development, young orangutans learn from their mother. These include not only physical skills necessary for survival, but also the social skills needed to live successfully with other orangutans.

◄ Meerkats (or suricates) of southern Africa benefit from the protection of an extended family. Some of the adults stay behind to keep a watchful eye on the young while the others go off to hunt for food.

Changing Shape

Coral animals, frogs, starfish and barnacles all undergo metamorphosis – substantial changes of shape at different stages of the life cycle.

For butterflies and moths, the caterpillar is the main growth stage. Its role is to take in plant food and convert it to animal tissue as fast as possible, without developing complicated body structures such as the adult's wings and sense organs. Eventually it stops feeding and secretes a hard protective case around itself, or makes a silk cocoon. This is the chrysalis or pupa. In a few weeks, its tissues are rearranged to produce the winged adult. A life cycle involving such a dramatic change of form is called complete metamorphosis.

The adult butterflies feed on quite different food from caterpillars – sugar-rich nectar which provides energy for flying. Caterpillars are able to start feeding on leaves early in spring, long before there are many flowers around, allowing the insect to complete its life cycle in a year. Some insect species pass the winter resting inside the pupal case. For many – butterflies, moths, flies, dragonflies, mayflies and mosquitoes – the adult stage is relatively short-lived compared with the larva. Yet some cicada larvae take 17 years to reach maturity.

KEYWORDS

HORMONE
LARVA
METAMORPHOSIS
MOLTING
NYMPH
PUPA

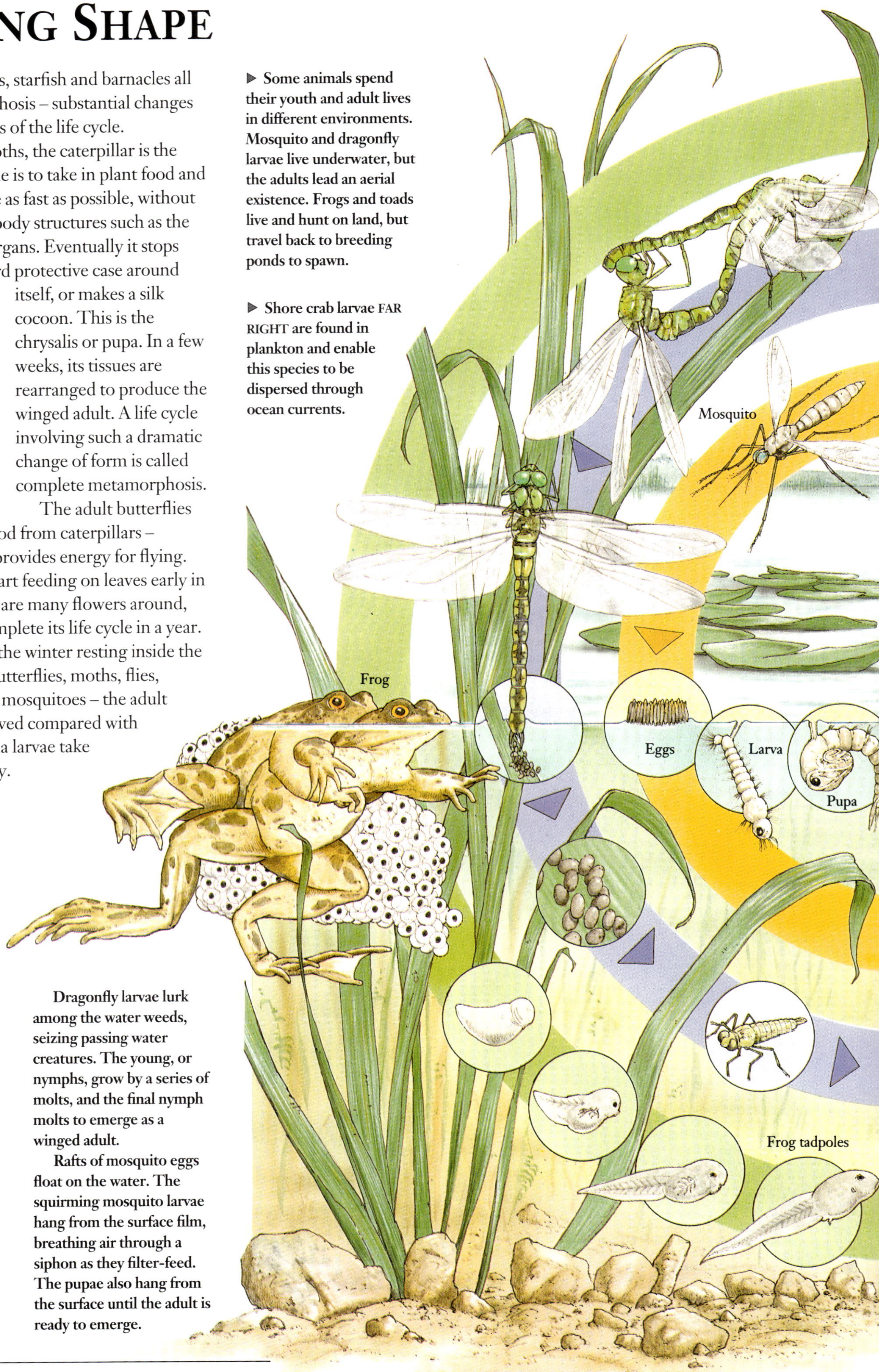

▶ Some animals spend their youth and adult lives in different environments. Mosquito and dragonfly larvae live underwater, but the adults lead an aerial existence. Frogs and toads live and hunt on land, but travel back to breeding ponds to spawn.

▶ Shore crab larvae FAR RIGHT are found in plankton and enable this species to be dispersed through ocean currents.

▶ Cycles of growth and change take different forms in many different animals, such as frogs, dragonflies and mosquitoes. Newly hatched frog tadpoles have external gills. As they grow, the gills are reabsorbed and internal ones form. The tadpoles gradually develop legs, their mouths become wider, and they change to a more carnivorous diet. Eventually, their lungs form and they gulp air at the surface before finally crawling out onto dry land (where they continue to grow for some time).

Dragonfly larvae lurk among the water weeds, seizing passing water creatures. The young, or nymphs, grow by a series of molts, and the final nymph molts to emerge as a winged adult.

Rafts of mosquito eggs float on the water. The squirming mosquito larvae hang from the surface film, breathing air through a siphon as they filter-feed. The pupae also hang from the surface until the adult is ready to emerge.

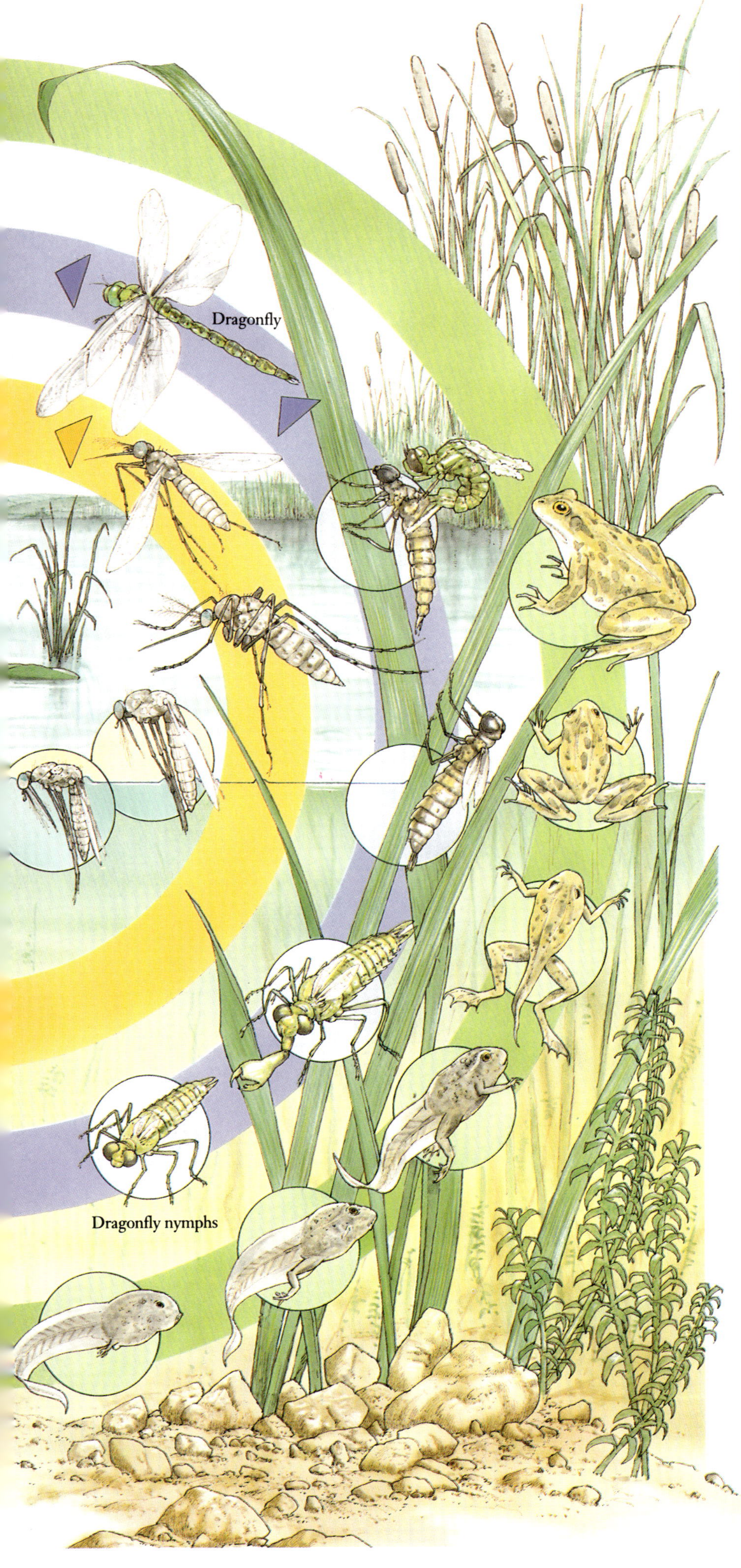

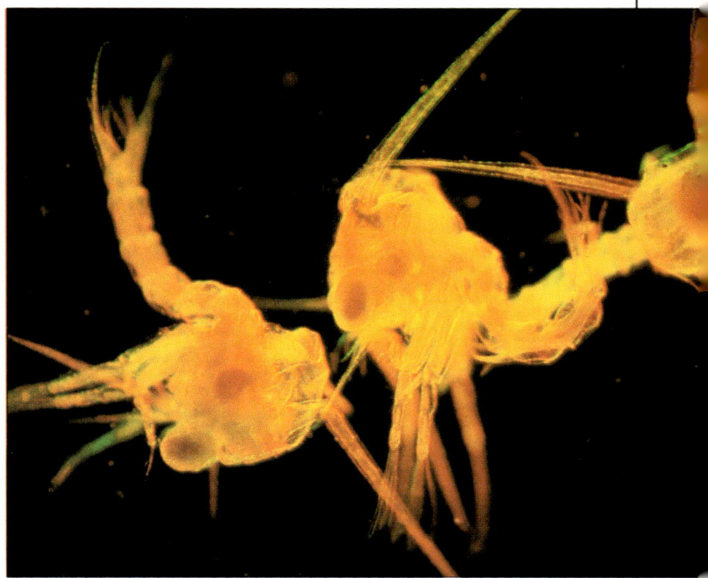

The frog tadpole is also a feeding stage. Most of its body space is taken up by the large stomach and long coiled intestines. As it grows older, its diet gradually changes from herbivorous to carnivorous.

Not all insects change shape as they grow. Many, like grasshoppers and crickets, simply grow wings: after each molt the wing buds are a little larger, until the final molt, when a fully formed pair of wings emerges from beneath the old skin. Small, gradual changes in form are called incomplete metamorphosis.

Metamorphosis is under the control of hormones. Molting (ecdysis, or casting off an old cuticle) in insects involves ecdysone (molting hormone) and neotinin (juvenile hormone). If there is enough of both hormones, another stage of larva is produced. But if the level of juvenile hormone decreases, the next molt produces the adult form. This change in hormone levels is triggered by environmental factors such as daylength, temperature or changes in food supply.

Amphibian metamorphosis is controlled by two hormones: prolactin from the pituitary gland and thyroxine from the thyroid. An increasing sensitivity to thyroxine triggers metamorphosis. Larvae typically have no reproductive organs, but in some circumstances larvae may develop sex organs and reproduce. This is called pedomorphosis (young form). The axolotl salamander is an example. The water in which it normally lives in Mexico is low in iodine and also cold, both factors which reduce thyroxine production. In the laboratory, axolotls can be made to change to the adult form by adding a little iodine to their water. In some groups of salamanders this situation has become genetically fixed, and the normal adult form resembles the tadpole, with external gills and a long tail. This is called neoteny.

6

ANIMAL *Communication*

THE SENSES ARE THE LINK between an animal and its environment, and between one animal and another. Simply to survive requires well-developed senses. Food may be located by smell, taste, sight or even sound. In a large group, or among strangers, young animals recognize their parents, and parents their young, by the calls they make or by their distinctive smell. For animals such as wolves, chimpanzees, hunting dogs and meerkats, body postures and facial expressions are vital social signals, helping to bond the group together and reduce aggression.

To make this range of nonverbal communication possible, many animals have sensory capabilities that far outstrip those of humans. The surprising feats of navigation and migration accomplished by some animals – from small birds to huge whales – often involve unexpected senses: animals may recognize such signals as infrasound and the Earth's magnetic field.

Senses are crucial in every stage of life. The earliest cells that grow to form an animal can detect gradients of various chemicals, which determine which parts of the cells develop into the different organs of the body. Some of the strongest sensory signals are sent in courtship. In competing for mates, territory and food, the animal that sends the strongest signals is usually the most successful.

Bees rely on chemical messages and touch to communicate in the dark of the hive, where up to 80,000 individuals may live and work, each carrying out a specific task to ensure the smooth running of the hive. Pheromones – chemical messages – control the tasks each worker performs, the number of queen bees produced, and the establishment of new hives. A swarm occurs when a queen, departing an old hive, secretes a pheromone that causes the workers to follow her.

Seeing the World

Light-sensitive cells are found throughout the animal kingdom, from the tiny pigment cells of protozoans to the huge eyes of the giant squid, about 40 centimeters across. All eyes work by changing light energy into the electrical energy of nerve impulses. Light rays behave like waves; the distance between pulses of energy is the wavelength. Different wavelengths produce different colors of light.

These transformations are carried out by special cells containing colored pigments – chemicals that absorb certain colors of light. The light energy they absorb causes chemical changes in the pigments, releasing some of the energy. This energy is turned into electrical energy and passed along nerve cells to the brain. Some pigment cells need more energy to make them react than others. By analyzing which cells have reacted and where they are located in the eye, the brain is able to work out light and shade and pattern.

Color vision involves using two or more different pigments which absorb different wavelengths, or colors, of light. The brain receives signals telling it which color pigments have been excited (this gives information on the color of the image), and how many pigment cells have been excited (this gives information on light and shade). From this, it works out the pattern of color and shadows the eye is seeing. The colors seen by an animal depend on the kinds of color-sensitive cells it has. For example, humans have cells that absorb red, green and blue light, whereas the eyes of bees absorb blue, yellow and ultraviolet.

KEYWORDS

ACCOMMODATION
BINOCULAR VISION
COLOR VISION
COMPOUND EYE
DIURNAL
IRIS
NIGHT VISION
NOCTURNAL
OPTIC NERVE
PIGMENT
PUPIL
RETINA
ROD
TAPETUM

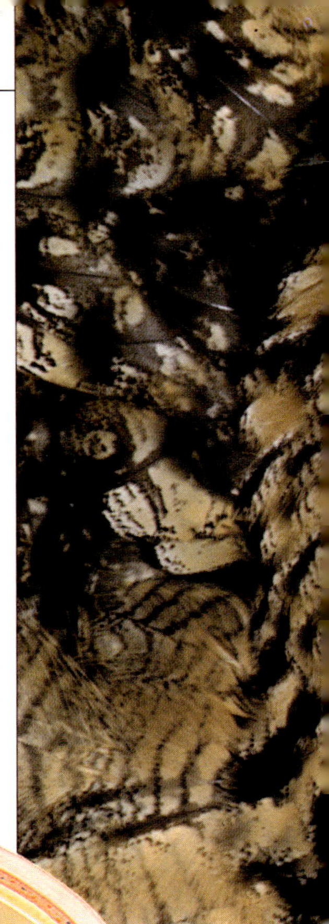

▶ Many nocturnal animals, such as owls and cats, have a reflective layer, the tapetum, at the back of the retina. This layer glows if a light, such as the beam of car headlights, is shone on the eyes at night. Light is reflected back through the retina, so the retinal cells get a second chance to absorb it. The pupils also open very wide to allow in as much light as possible.

▼ The vertebrate eye is the most sophisticated eye in the animal world, capable of sharp focus, color vision and judgment of distance and speed. The eye is held in position and moved by various external muscles. The pressure of the humors against the sclera helps to keep the eye in shape. Gases, nutrients and waste diffuse through the humors. The sclera and cornea form a tough protective coat. The conjunctiva secretes lubricating fluid and anti-bacterial chemicals. The dark choroid layer reduces internal reflection.

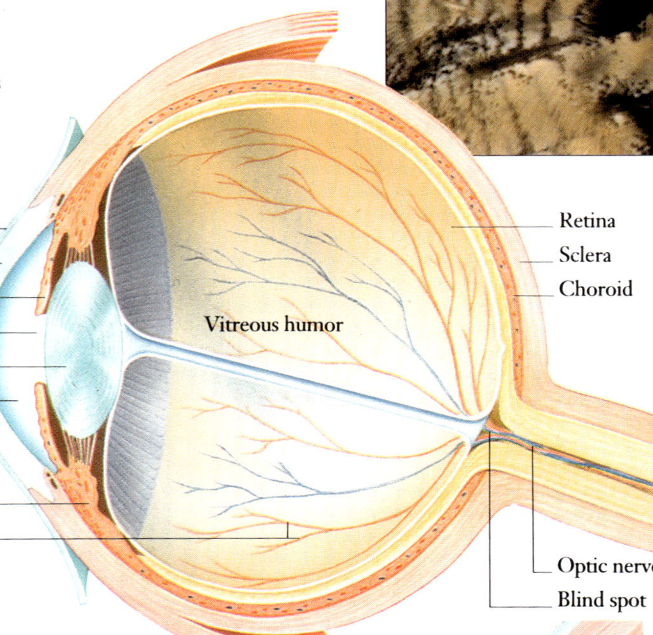

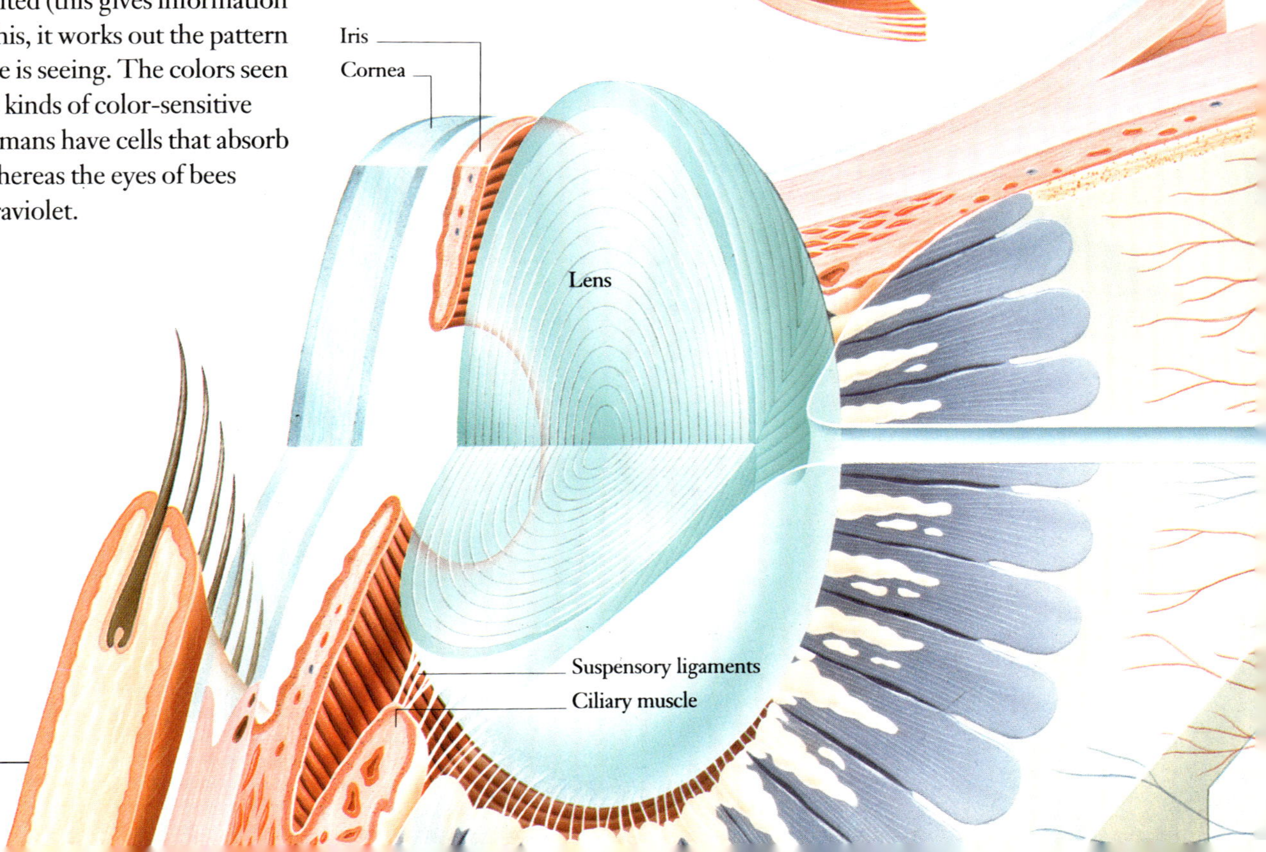

▶ Light rays entering the eye are bent (refracted) as they pass through the cornea and the humors. But the main focusing occurs when the ciliary muscles change the shape of the lens to focus on an inverted image on the retina at the back of the eye. This image is sharpest at the fovea, where the light-sensitive cells are most densely packed.

If the view from two eyes overlaps (binocular vision), the brain can compare the two images and work out the three-dimensional scene as well as the speed of moving objects. The eyes of most animals are fixed in sockets in their heads, with only limited movement. If the eyes are directed forward for good binocular vision, the animal does not have a good all-around view, and vice versa. The eyes of birds of prey and owls are so large, in order to see from great heights or in the dark, that they cannot move around in the socket. These birds, however, can turn their heads almost 360 degrees to look over their shoulders.

The simplest eyes – clusters of light-sensitive cells, as found in earthworms and in the "simple" eyes of insects – are used only to distinguish between light and dark. A similar function is performed by the pineal body, the so-called "third eye" found in the center of the head of lizards and still present in a reduced form in humans. Such eyes may be used to monitor day-length, which is used to trigger events such as reproduction and migration.

Light-sensitive cells may be grouped together to form eyes. Animals with more advanced eyes have special lenses to focus the light on a layer of sensitive cells, the retina, as well as structures that can control the amount of light entering the eye. Animals that live underwater or in dim light, or come out only at night, may have mirrorlike eyes that reflect light around the inside of the eye so that it can absorb as much as possible. The compound eyes of many insects and crustaceans are made up of hundreds of tiny eyelike facets, each with its own lens.

Vertebrate eyes have two types of light-sensitive cells – rods, which are highly sensitive but do not distinguish color, and several types of cones, each absorbing different wavelengths of light. The more densely packed these cells are, the sharper the image that can be seen. The human eye contains about 130 million rods and cones, and can distinguish more than 10 million different colors – more colors than any machine that is used to analyze light.

Special lifestyles require special eyes. The eyes of fish, for example, are not spherical but flattened, because a flatter surface is better for coping with the light bending that occurs underwater. The eyes of birds of prey – which need to be able to look down a long way toward their prey but also sideways to see where they are going – have two foveas, clusters of extra dense light-sensitive cells that give sharp focus. The cheetah needs to see clearly over a wide area in order to follow fast-moving prey; its eyes have an elongated fovea that produces a slitlike image in very sharp focus, like a wide-angle cinema screen.

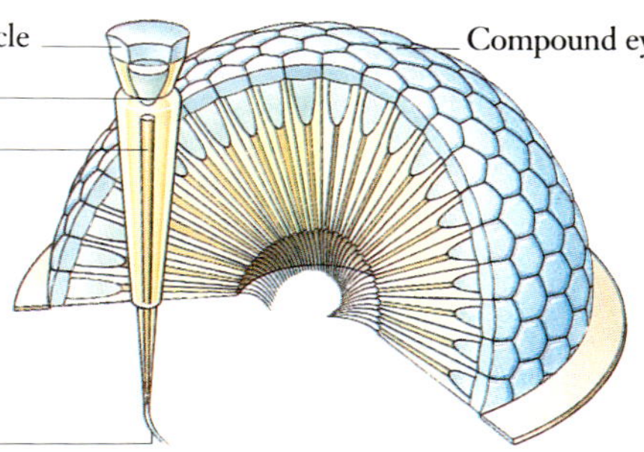

◀ The compound eyes of insects and crustaceans LEFT are made up of thousands (up to 30,000) of individual lenses in pigment-containing visual units called ommatidia. Each ommatidium has a narrow field of view of about 20 degrees, but the images from adjacent ommatidia overlap. The closer together the ommatidia are, the sharper the image they produce – rather like the cone cells of the vertebrate eye. Such eyes are particularly good at detecting movement.

Each ommatidium has two focusing lenses, a "cornea" made from transparent cuticle, and a crystalline lens. Behind these is a light-sensitive rhabdom containing visual pigment, surrounded by a ring of retina cells that send electrical signals from the visual pigment to the brain. Surrounding these cells are cells containing more pigment, which prevent light entering the ommatidium from its neighbor.

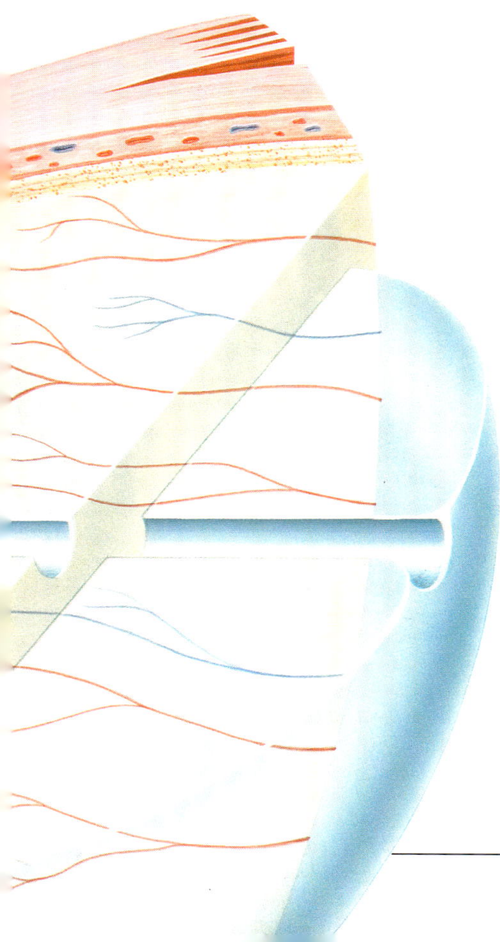

Detecting Sound

THROUGHOUT the animal kingdom, calls, songs, whistles, croaks, buzzes and thumps are used for signaling and conveying emotions such as aggression and desire, warning and fear.

Animal sound-producing and sound-receiving structures are based on the same principle as a drum – a membrane that is vibrated sets the air vibrating. Mammals produce sounds by passing the air leaving their lungs through a chamber, the larynx, across which are strung elastic ridges called vocal cords, which vibrate when air currents pass between them. The vocal cords are held in place by ridges of cartilage, forming what is known as the Adam's apple. Muscles change the tension of the cords to alter the pitch of the sounds made. Changing the speed at which the air is passed over the vocal cords affects the loudness of the sound produced. Humans also use their tongues and lips to control the escaping sounds to produce speech. The vocal systems of other vertebrates follow the same principles, but some frogs and birds use air sacs to amplify their sounds.

KEYWORDS

ANTENNA
EAR
ECHOLOCATION
LATERAL LINE SYSTEM
OSSICLES
SEMICIRCULAR CANAL

The vibrations of their wings cause bees' and wasps' buzzing, but grasshoppers chirp by rubbing a series of small knobs on their back legs against hard ridges on the forewings. Different species have different arrangements of knobs, and different chirps. Cicadas have thin disks of cuticle on their abdomens which can be buckled by muscles, producing clicks that are amplified by air sacs whose own tension can be adjusted to produce the right sound. Mole crickets make their own amplifiers by digging two trumpet-shaped openings which act like megaphones – sounds of 92 decibels have been recorded outside their burrows.

Sound receivers also use vibrating membranes. Vertebrates have a membrane called the ear drum, or tympanum, in the ear; crickets have a small membrane on their

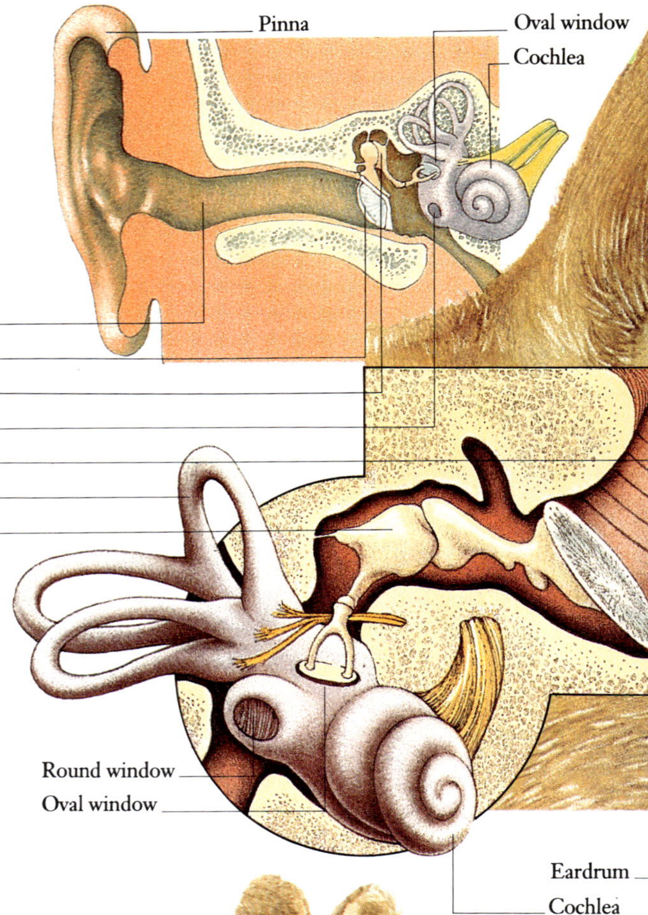

▶ The human ear and the fox ear are very similar. Vibrating air is funneled into the ear by the pinnae and sets the eardrum, ossicles, oval window, fluids of the cochlea, and round window vibrating in turn.

▶ Ossicles are small bones that act as levers, amplifying the vibrations. The oval window is only $\frac{1}{25}$ the area of the eardrum, further concentrating the vibrations. The Eustachian tube helps to even out the air pressure in the middle ear. In the cochlea, pressure waves stimulate sensitive hair cells in the organ of Corti. These are sensitive to different frequencies and send individual signals to the brain via the auditory nerve. The pressure waves are finally dissipated at the round window.

▶ The fennec fox's large outer ears (pinnae) funnel even faint sounds into the ear, helping the fox locate its prey by night. By turning first its ears, then its head, toward the noise, the fox can work out where it is coming from.

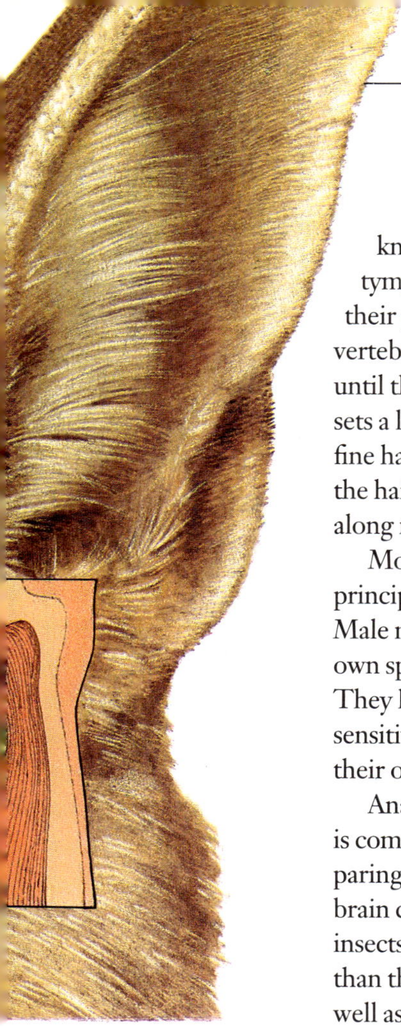

knees; grasshoppers and cicadas have their tympanum on their abdomen or thorax. Earwigs use their pincers to detect sounds. Vibrations of the vertebrate ear drum are transmitted through the ear until they vibrate another membrane which in turn sets a liquid vibrating. The sensory cells of the ear have fine hairs protruding into this liquid. Displacement of the hairs sets off an electrical signal, which is relayed along nerves to the brain to be interpreted.

Most sound receivers in animals work on this principle, but the hairs need not always be in liquid. Male mosquitoes need to recognize a mate of their own species among the many mosquitoes flying past. They have long hairs on their antennae which are sensitive to just the wavelengths of sound emitted by their own species.

Analyzing the exact direction from which the sound is coming requires paired hearing organs. By comparing the loudness of the sound in the two ears, the brain can judge the direction of its source. In some insects and birds, one tympanum is slightly higher than the other. This gives up and down information as well as side to side information. The huge cheeklike facial disks of owls are really slightly lopsided sound receptors. The ears of mammals such as bat-eared foxes and bats, which rely on sound for hunting at night, have particularly large outer ears (pinnae) that can be turned toward the sound. Dogs have over 15 muscles for twisting and turning their ears.

Animals that live underwater need to detect vibrations in water. The lateral line system of fish can detect vibrations caused by the movements of other animals nearby, and by water currents flowing around solid objects. In the deep sea, combinations of temperature, salinity and density can create sound tunnels that transmit sound over great distances. Baleen whales can communicate over distances of 80 kilometers or more.

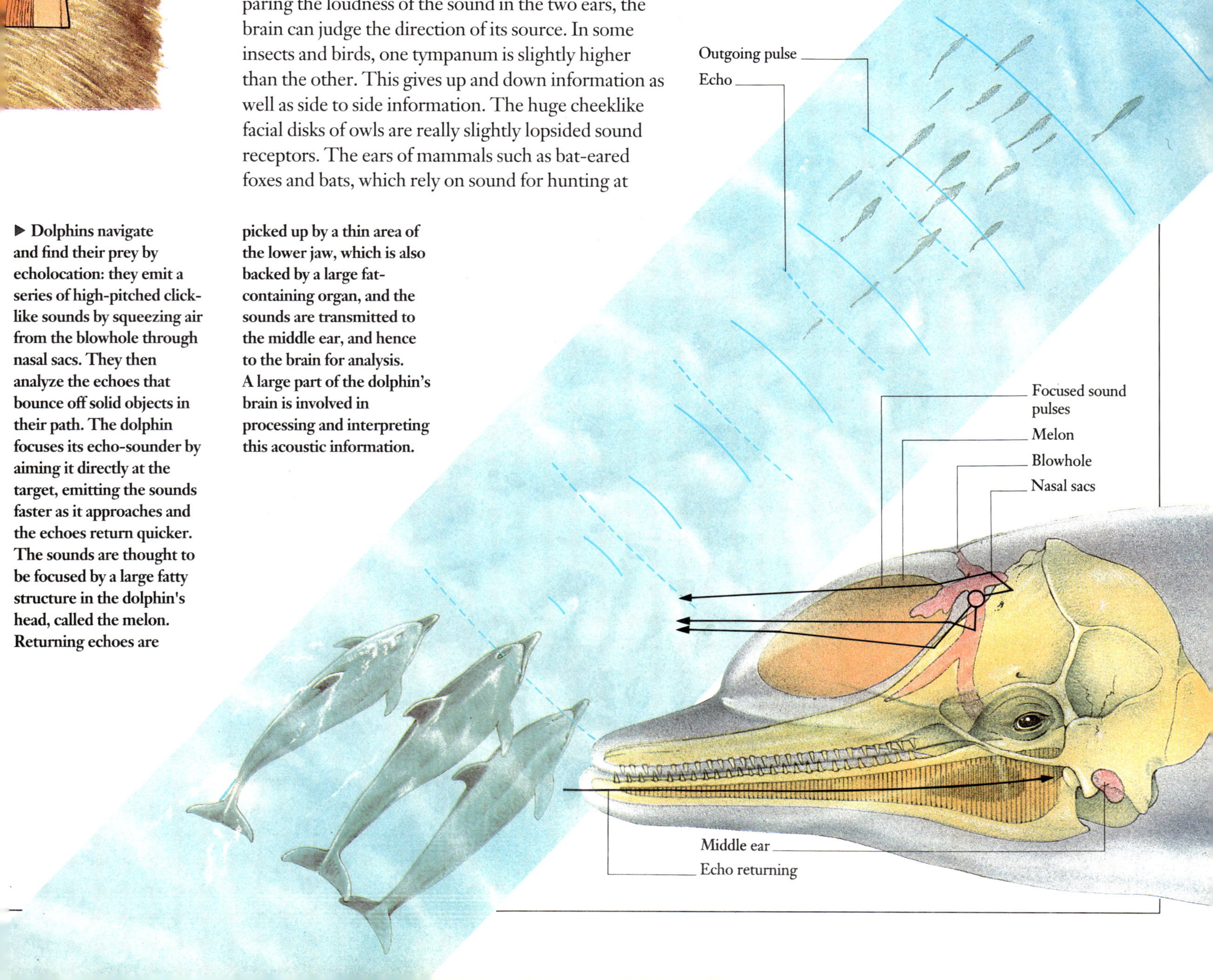

▶ Dolphins navigate and find their prey by echolocation: they emit a series of high-pitched click-like sounds by squeezing air from the blowhole through nasal sacs. They then analyze the echoes that bounce off solid objects in their path. The dolphin focuses its echo-sounder by aiming it directly at the target, emitting the sounds faster as it approaches and the echoes return quicker. The sounds are thought to be focused by a large fatty structure in the dolphin's head, called the melon. Returning echoes are picked up by a thin area of the lower jaw, which is also backed by a large fat-containing organ, and the sounds are transmitted to the middle ear, and hence to the brain for analysis. A large part of the dolphin's brain is involved in processing and interpreting this acoustic information.

TASTE AND SMELL

SMELL and taste are essential to animals, not only for finding food and judging whether it is edible, but also for recognizing other members of the same species, potential mates and rival suitors, enemies and prey; and for identifying dangers such as the approach of fire, and communicating in dense vegetation or in darkness. Much of this ability to communicate depends on the production of specific chemicals called pheromones, which have very specific scents.

KEYWORDS

ANTENNAE
JACOBSEN'S ORGANS
PHEROMONE
SMELL
TASTE
TASTE BUDS

Taste and smell are intricately linked, so that it is often difficult to tell which is which. Smell sensors (olfactory sensors) in the nose analyze airborne chemicals that have dissolved in the thin film of water coating the smell sensors. Taste sensors on the tongue analyze moistened food, while some of the scent chemicals from the food are wafted up to the small sensors at the back of the nose.

If the sense of smell is not functioning – as when humans have a cold and the nose is blocked – the sense of taste also seems to be impaired. In animals that live underwater, the nostrils are used to analyze small traces of chemicals in the water, while the taste sensors are located in the mouth and gill chambers, and sometimes also on the skin. The taste sensors sample chemicals in much higher concentrations at close range.

There are probably about seven different kinds of smell sensors. Each of these detects a particular group of chemicals whose molecules have a similar shape and size. These smells have been described as musky, floral, pepperminty, ether-like, camphor-like, pungent and putrid.

Taste sensors recognize only four groups – sweet, sour, salt-sweet and bitter. It is thought that the chemicals fit into matching-shaped sites on the sensors. Some chemicals fit better than others, and produce a stronger stimulation. These groups of chemicals form a kind of smell and taste code: it is the combination of signals from different types of sensors and the different degrees of stimulation that produce the sensation which the animal identifies as a particular taste or smell.

It is an extremely sensitive system. Migrating eels can detect chemicals in the sea that are diluted to one part in 3,000,000,000,000,000,000. A polar bear can smell a

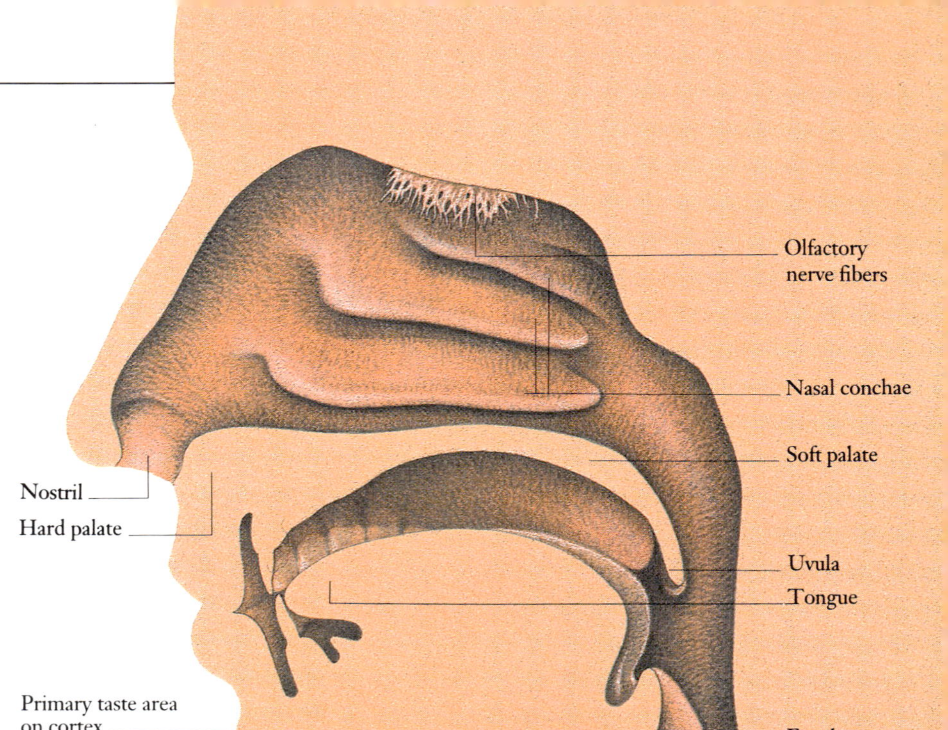

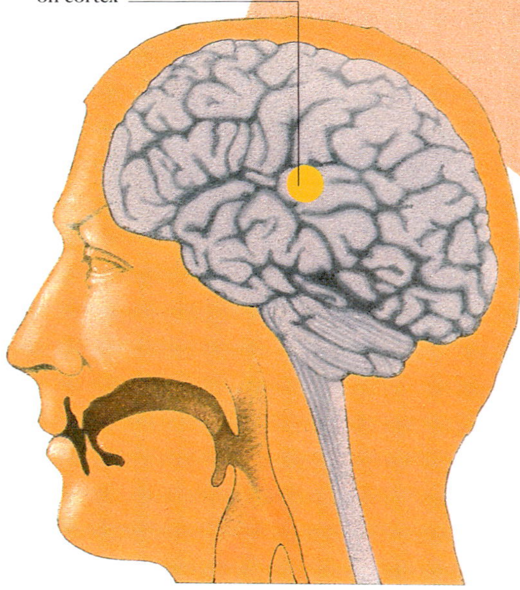

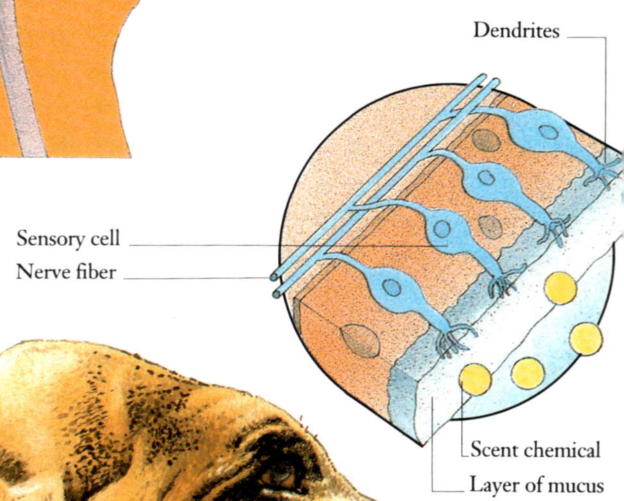

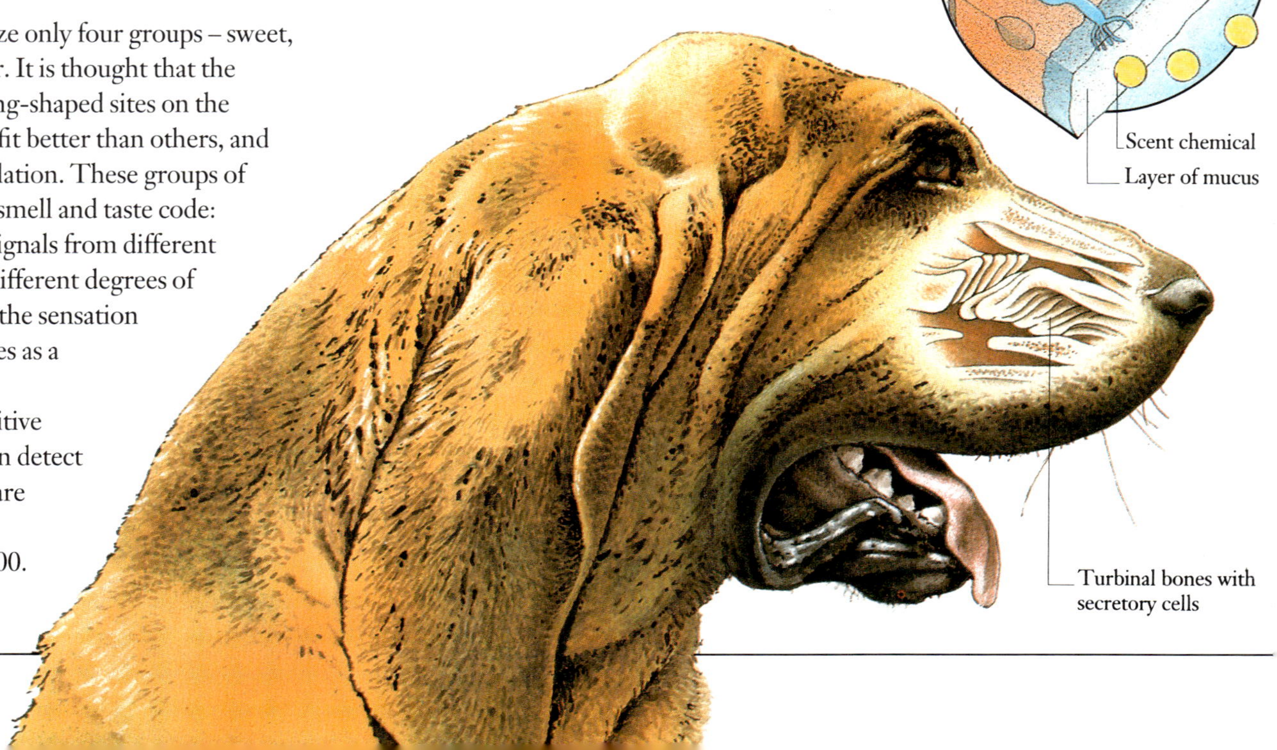

◀ **The nostrils of vertebrates contain a series of bony plates, which support a large area of membranes covered in smell sensors. The animal's breathing movements draw air containing scent chemicals through the nose past these sensors. Nerve signals from the nose pass to the olfactory lobe of the brain for analysis. Scent particles from the food in the mouth can also pass via the back of the throat to the nasal chambers.**

▼ **The taste sensors and their supporting cells are arranged in clusters, called taste buds, in grooves between the various raised bumps (papillae) on the tongue. A film of mucus provides moisture in which taste chemicals can dissolve. Each taste sensor is linked to a separate nerve fiber, which passes signals to the brain. Sweet sensors are found at the tip of the tongue, salt and sour on the sides, and bitter at the back.**

■ **The large surface area of the antennae RIGHT of a male moon moth BELOW is covered with special smell sensors, sunk in small pits for protection. Some of the sensors are so sensitive that they can detect a single molecule of a sex hormone from a female moon moth.**

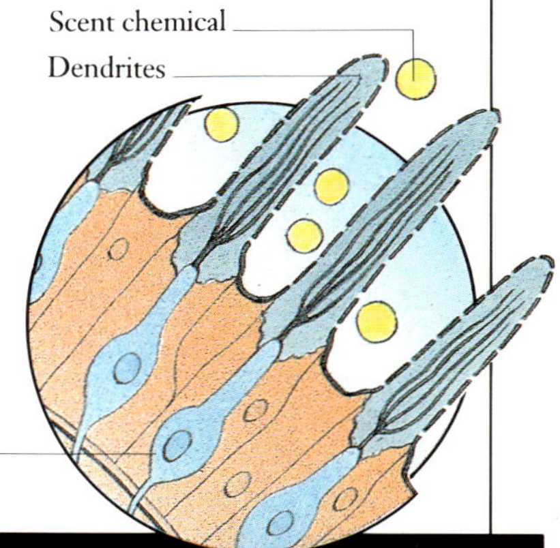

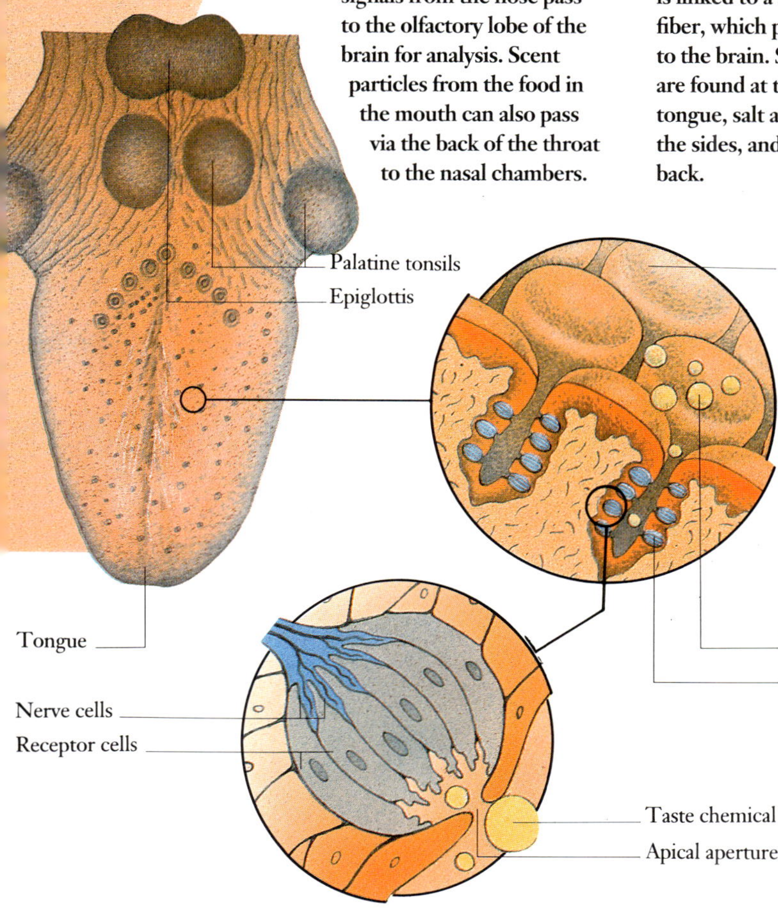

◀ **A dog, particularly a bloodhound, has a much larger area of olfactory membrane than a human, hence its better sense of smell. Each smell sensor consists of a nerve fiber ending in several fine branches, surrounded by supporting cells. Mucus secreted by the olfactory glands provides a layer of moisture in which scent chemicals dissolve. Tiny whiplike flagella on the supporting cells waft mucus toward the back of the throat to be carried to the stomach, where foreign particles can be dealt with.**

dead seal from a distance of 20 kilometers. Animals with a powerful sense of smell have a large area of sensory cells. Some male moths, which can detect a female moth from a distance of 2 kilometers, may have over 150,000 sensory cells on their antennae. Bloodhounds (a species of dog) have some 150 square centimeters of olfactory membranes in their nostrils, compared to the 14 square centimeters of the human nose, and are bred and used for this extraordinary ability to track someone or something by scent.

The organs of smell of most "advanced" animals such as insects and vertebrates are arranged in pairs – in the nostrils of vertebrates, and on the antennae of insects. They send electrical signals via nerves to the brain, which interprets them. By comparing signals from the nostrils, the brain can work out from which direction the smell is coming.

The organs of taste are not arranged in pairs, and are usually concentrated around the mouth, on the mouthparts and antennae of insects, and on the tongue and sometimes also the throat and gill chambers of vertebrates. Insects and other invertebrates often have small clusters of taste sensors on other parts of their bodies, as do fish and amphibians. Fish that feed on the seabed may have long tentacle-like barbels on their chins. These are laden with taste and touch sensors, to the extent that catfish have been described as "swimming tongues". Vertebrate noses, snouts and tongues have a large surface area of membranes rich in sensors for smell or taste. The surfaces are kept moist by mucus secreted by special glands, because the chemicals they need to detect must be dissolved in moisture before they can act on the sensors. Because it is inside the body, the whole organ is warm and moist, which speeds up the sensory reactions.

The smell and taste sensors of insects and vertebrates consist of a nerve fiber with a highly branched sensory tip. The fibers are surrounded by closely packed supporting cells. They are highly sensitive to particular chemicals, whose presence triggers off an action potential along the nerve cell. In insects, the sensory tips are protected by a fine tube of hard cuticle to form a hairlike structure called a sensillum. Air enters through pores in the cuticle.

HIDDEN SENSES

MANY animals have special senses in addition to sight, hearing, touch, taste and smell. For example, most animals have heat sensors. These may be specialized nerve cells in the skin or other outer covering which relay signals back to the brain. Pit vipers such as rattlesnakes have a pair of heat-sensitive "pits" on each side of their nostrils, which produce a kind of "heat picture" of their surroundings by feeding signals to the same part of the brain as the eyes do. As the snake closes in on its prey – whose body warmth has betrayed its presence – more heat sensors inside its mouth give it accurate information for striking.

KEYWORDS

HEAT PIT
MIGRATION
PHEROMONE
SKIN
TOUCH
WHISKERS (VIBRISSAE)

The skin of mammals contains a wide range of sensors, detecting heat, cold, touch, pressure and pain. Most of these sensors are modified nerve fibers with specialized tips. Some touch receptors are encased in capsules whose deformation triggers an electric signal to the brain. Insect sensors often use slight bending of the cuticle to prompt a signal, and often end in fine hairs, called sensilla, which can detect the slightest movements of air, the lightest touch, or the faintest traces of scent chemicals.

Touch is really a measure of pressure. In humans it is the response of special sensors embedded in the skin or pressed against the hairs. Many nocturnal mammals have long whiskers on their snouts, each with its own nerve supply. This makes them extremely sensitive to touch. Seals use their whiskers to navigate underwater, which may explain how blind seals are able to feed themselves and survive.

Scorpions and spiders have hairs on their legs which are sensitive to vibrations in particular directions. Scorpions can detect air moving at

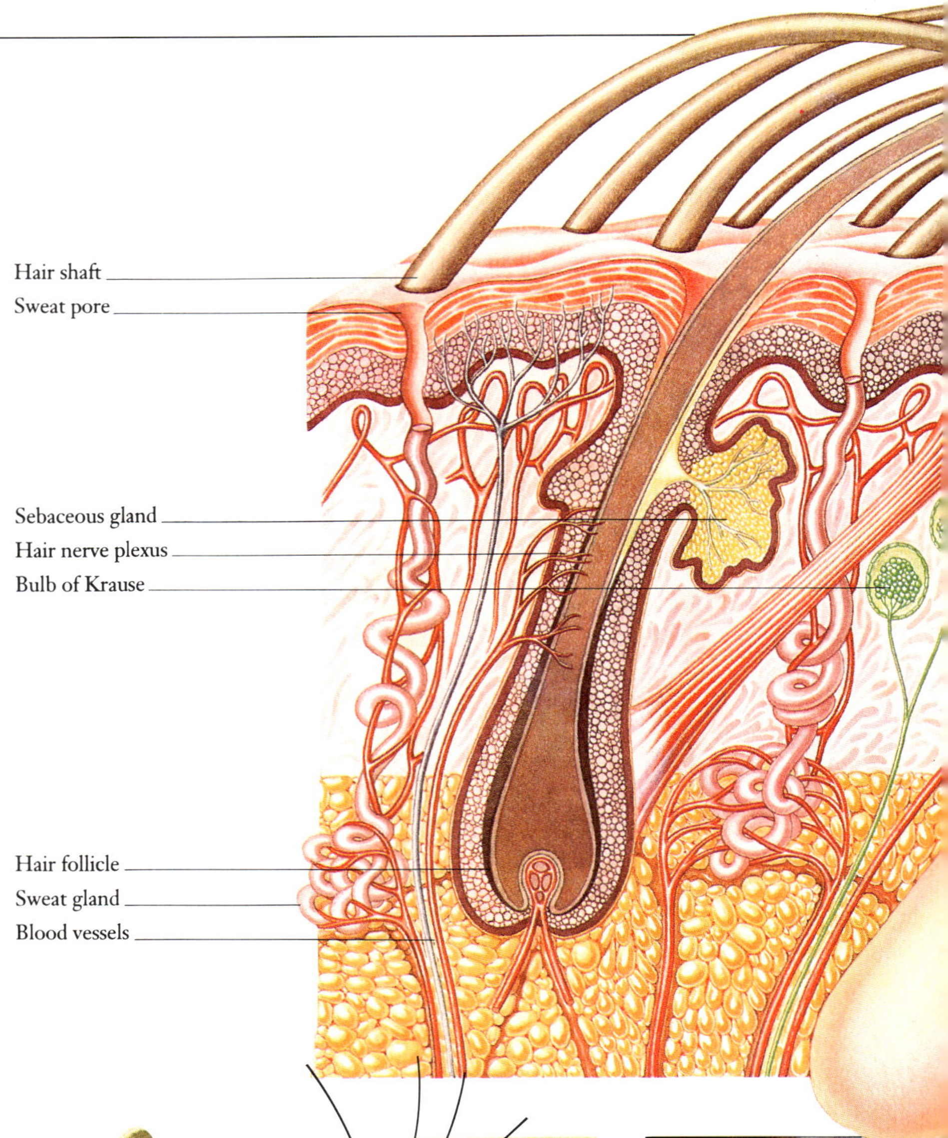

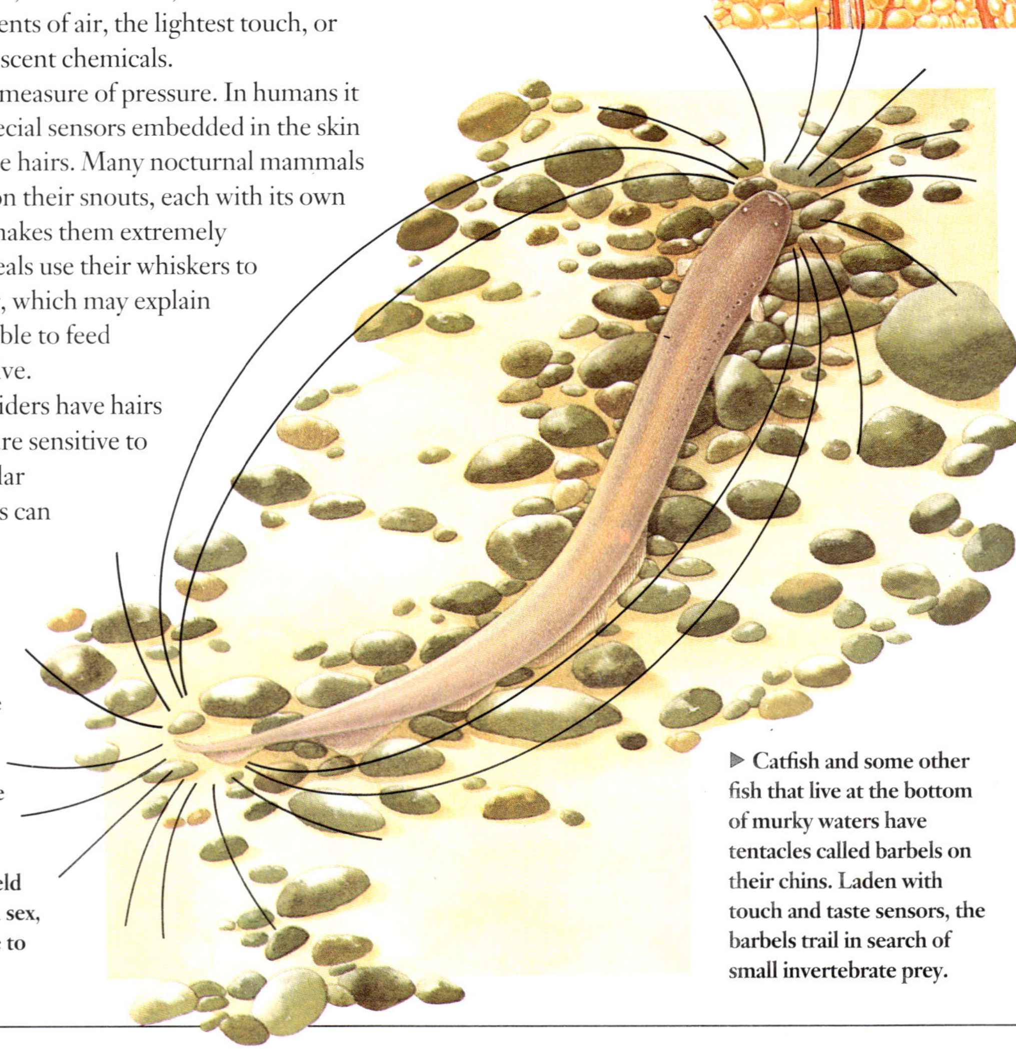

▶ **Electric fish produce a weak electric field. Objects in the water distort the field, and the changes are detected by receptors along the sides of the fish. The field conveys information on sex, age and emotional state to other fish.**

▶ **Catfish and some other fish that live at the bottom of murky waters have tentacles called barbels on their chins. Laden with touch and taste sensors, the barbels trail in search of small invertebrate prey.**

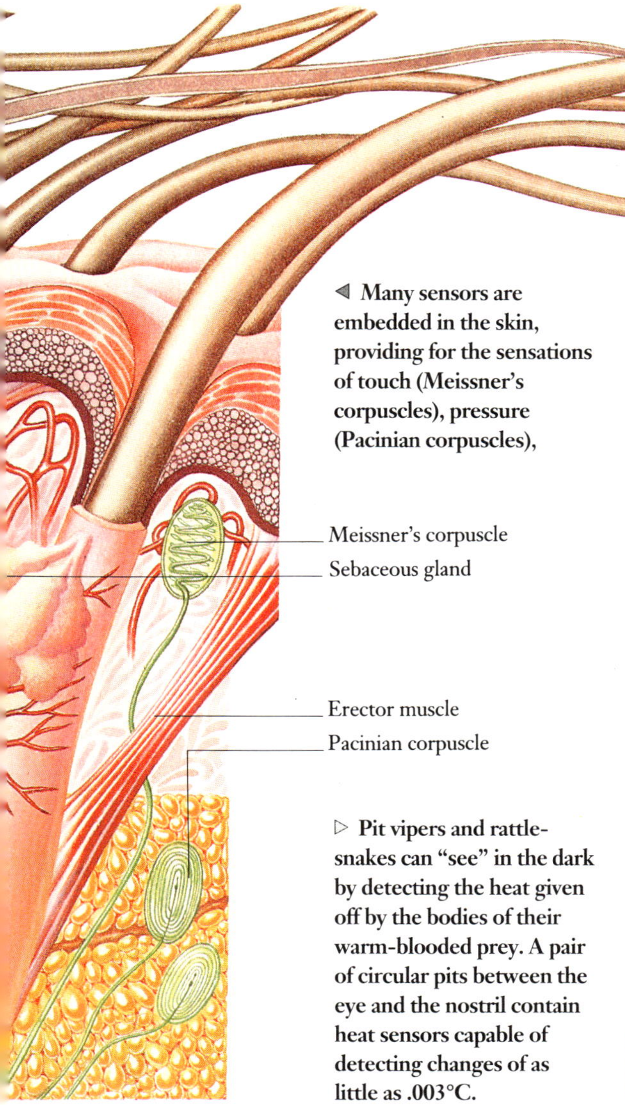

◀ Many sensors are embedded in the skin, providing for the sensations of touch (Meissner's corpuscles), pressure (Pacinian corpuscles), position (bulbs of Krause) and pain (nerve endings). The hairs trap an insulating layer of air, which helps to keep the animal warm. They can be raised or lowered by muscles to control temperature. The evaporation of sweat from the sweat pores helps to cool the skin.

▷ Pit vipers and rattlesnakes can "see" in the dark by detecting the heat given off by the bodies of their warm-blooded prey. A pair of circular pits between the eye and the nostril contain heat sensors capable of detecting changes of as little as .003°C.

0.072 kilometers per hour, one hundred times less movement than a light breeze. Pressure-sensitive hairs are used by flying insects to judge their speed –the hairs respond to the pressure of the passing air. Birds use special feathers to measure air pressure. The fine hairlike filoplumes lie alongside each main feather, and have small touch receptors at their bases to signal the position of each feather.

Magnetism is another special sense that helps animals to find their way. Some animals are guided by changes in the Earth's magnetic field. From time to time large numbers of whales run aground on the shore at certain places around the coast. These sites have been shown to occur where bands of high magnetic strength run perpendicular to the shore, apparently disrupting the whales' normal navigation system. Honeybees use magnetism not only for navigation but also for orienting the combs in their hives. Compass termites orient their mounds north-south, so that there is always one cool side.

Certain fish that live and hunt in murky water use electrical signals to sense their surroundings. The electric fish of South America and the elephant-snouts of Africa generate their own electric field, then detect distortions in the field produced by nearby objects. Sharks and rays use electric signals tosense the very small electric signals produced by the nervous systems of their prey. The faint electric signal produced by a breathing fish buried in the mud of the seabed is still strong enough to alert a shark or ray to the fish's presence. In addition to detecting external objects or substances, internal sensors control body metabolism and processes such as breathing and the pumping of blood around the body.

All sensors are specialized cells in particular locations of the body, each with a nerve link to the part of the brain designated to receive specific information and act on it. Chemical sensors in the gut can induce the feelings of thirst or hunger. Other chemical sensors in the muscles are responsible for the sensation of muscle fatigue. Balance, posture and muscle coordination depend on proprioceptors – sensors in the muscles which detect the length and tension of muscles and tendons (and cuticle deformation in insects), and relay information about the position of the limbs. Without these special sensors, the brain would not have the information it needs to control the actions of the body or even to keep it alive.

Insect Societies

COMMUNICATION has allowed some animal species to create highly complex societies based on organized labor. By far the largest societies are found among bees, wasps, ants and termites – the social insects. Some termite colonies may contain over two million members.

The structure of these insect societies is well defined. Members are organized into different castes, each specialized for a different task. Reproduction is a task in itself, distinct from all other forms of work. Some ant and termite species produce workers of several sizes, as well as "soldiers" with powerful poison-injecting jaws, glue-squirting snouts, or large heads that can block the entrance to the nest. Caste may be determined genetically or by special feeding of the young. Unfertilized eggs become drones (the male reproductive caste), while fertilized eggs produce workers (always female). If the worker larvae are fed with royal jelly, they become queens.

KEYWORDS

ARTHROPOD
INSECT
LARVA
NYMPH
PHEROMONE
SOCIAL INSECT

Colonies of social insects are ruled by at least one queen – a female whose most important function is to give birth to workers. Termite queens pair for life, and the king termite remains with the queen in the nuptial chamber. But in ants, bees and wasps, the male reproductives die once they have fertilized the queens. Queen bees and wasps remain mobile despite their large size, but ant and termite queens – which shed their wings before mating – soon swell up with eggs. They become too large and awkward to move far, and remain in their nests for life. Workers feed the queen with regurgitated food or special secretions, groom her, and tend the eggs and young. In addition to laying all the eggs, the queen bee controls the colony by releasing special chemicals called pheromones. Pheromones act as chemical messages to the hive, controlling the level of activity and preventing the development of ordinary workers' reproductive organs. Older queens produce fewer pheromones, until eventually new reproductive castes are formed.

Workers' tasks usually change with age and size. Young or small workers – who are more vulnerable – tend the nest while the larger ones go out to forage for food. Domestic tasks include feeding the rest of the colony, removing dead bodies, repairing the nest and adding new sections. Coordinated activity shared by many different castes allows the building of intricate nests. Parts of the nest may be reserved for specific purposes, such as food storage or the queen's chamber. Bees and wasps have perfected hexagonal cells which pack the greatest numbers of larvae into small spaces, economizing on the wax and paper used for construction. Some African termites' nests reach several meters above the ground, yet also penetrate to the water table equally far below to draw up water for an elaborate air-conditioning system. This ventilation prevents suffocation in the densely populated nest.

Servicing these large and complex societies depends on communication. If this breaks down, the colony will disintegrate. In the dark interior of the nest, the senses of smell, taste and touch are all used for communication. A worker may be encouraged to perform a task by being tapped with the antennae of another worker, or by a stimulating chemical deposited in the nest's tunnels, or simply by a change in her instincts as it grows older. The members of a colony all have a characteristic odor that enables them to recognize each other and to identify any strangers in their nest. Different chemical signals, as well as visual displays and tapping, are used to warn of danger or to direct other workers to food plants. Foragers create trails to sources of food by clearing tracks and marking them with scented secretions. Scouts that discover food may alert other workers by thumping on the ground, or tapping on other individuals, or by wafting chemicals into the air.

One of the most sophisticated forms of communication is the dancing of honeybees. Returning from the search for food, a forager performs a dance on the comb in the darkness of the hive which conveys not only the type of flower found, but also its direction and distance from the hive. The other workers sense the information through the vibrations and sounds created by the angle of the dance on the comb, the whirring of the dancer's wings and the wiggling of her abdomen. The dance is also adjusted to allow for the changing position of the sun and the direction and speed of the prevailing wind.

■ **Mounds built RIGHT by termites of the African savanna may be 6 meters high and 3 meters below ground. Towers with chimneys provide cooling and ventilation, aided by cellars. There are many tunnels in the nest, through which workers bring back food BELOW. Workers travel in the tunnels protected from the view of predators. Soldier ants 1 serve as outside guards. BOTTOM The queen 2 keeps tens of thousands of eggs in her abdomen. She is many times larger than the king 3 or the winged males 4. Large workers forage 5; smaller ones work inside the nest 6.**

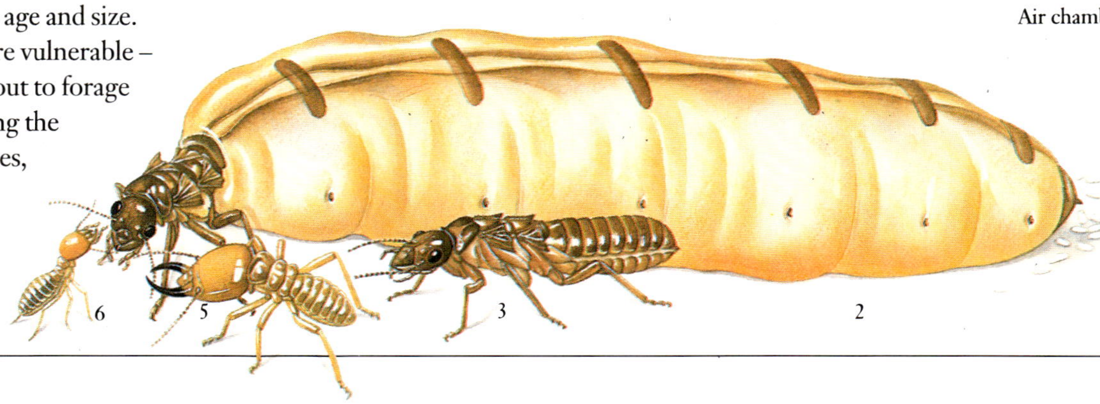

◀ One section of the termites' nest is set aside as a garden for growing a special fungus on combs made of wood and feces. The fungus thrives in the moist atmosphere of the nest. It breaks down the comb and extracts nutrients from it; the termites then eat the fungus. Workers tend the fungus garden to keep it free from weeds and other unwanted fungi.

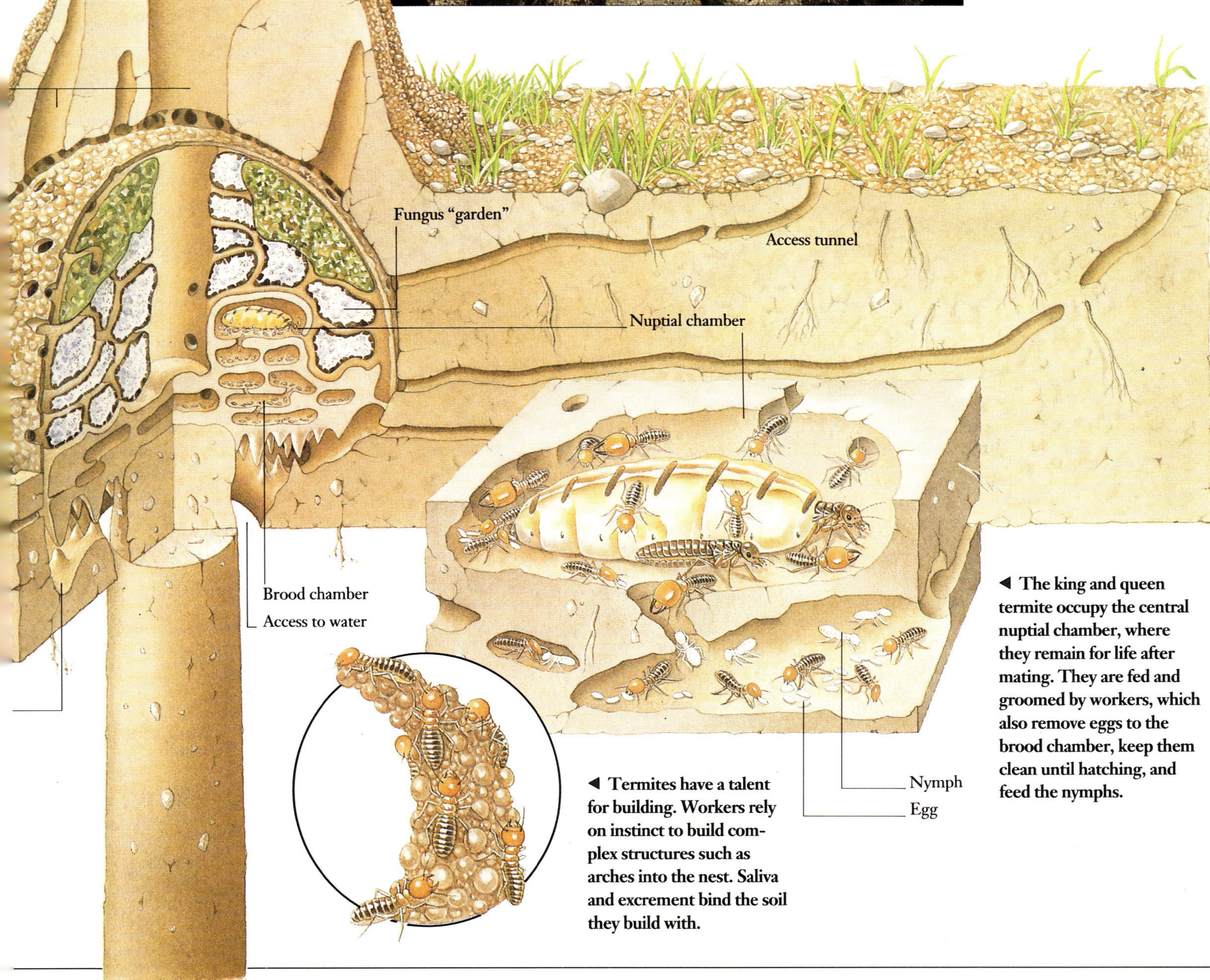

◀ The king and queen termite occupy the central nuptial chamber, where they remain for life after mating. They are fed and groomed by workers, which also remove eggs to the brood chamber, keep them clean until hatching, and feed the nymphs.

◀ Termites have a talent for building. Workers rely on instinct to build complex structures such as arches into the nest. Saliva and excrement bind the soil they build with.

Mammal Societies

The whole range of senses is used by animals to communicate with each other and with other species. Most mammals have signals for alarm, fear, aggression, attraction and invitation, and special signals for a mother to keep in touch with her young. But it is the social mammals – those that live in complex societies – that use the most elaborate systems.

Mammal societies are often highly structured, with hierarchies in which certain animals are dominant over others. This helps to reduce aggression and fighting, because each animal knows its place. Maintaining a hierarchy involves complex signals. Ritualized displays give animals an idea of each other's strength and status. For example, stags and elephant seals roar at each other: the strength of the roar indicates the animal's physical fitness. Only if an animal thinks he is a match for his opponent will he challenge him to a fight.

KEYWORDS

AGGRESSION
HORMONE
PECKING ORDER
PHEROMONE
TERRITORY

The type of signal depends on the habitat and on the size and lifestyle of the mammal. Visual signals are little use in dense forests; chemical signals do not carry far underwater. The speed with which the signals have to be detected is also important. Alarm calls work faster than scents or sights, but the flash of a rabbit's white tail enhances the alert while giving information about which way to run.

Visual signals are important in courtship and as alarms. In some monkeys and baboons, the females develop large pink swellings around their genital area when they are ready to mate. When they are interested in a particular male they approach him and display the swellings to him. Displays that make an animal look larger than it is can be useful when danger threatens. Cats arch their backs, raise their tails and raise their fur as they bare their teeth at an attacker. Rhinoceroses, deer, wildebeest and musk oxen may lower their heads to direct the tips of their horns or antlers at the enemy in the hope of frightening it off.

Touch maintains close bonding between members of a social group. Mutual grooming is particularly important among monkeys and apes. Greeting ceremonies involving nose-touching and other physical contact are used by wild dogs and prairie dogs.

Territories are an important part of mammal societies. Mammals need signals to inform other groups of the boundaries of the territory, and to threaten strangers that invade it. Most territorial mammals mark the boundaries of their territories with scent from special glands. The scent may be discharged with the urine or droppings, or the animal may rub the gland area on the ground, or on prominent objects in the area. Bears and large cats scrape the ground or scratch tree bark to draw more attention to their scent posts.

Mammals probably make more use of scents than any other animals. Some species have as many as 13 scent-producing glands. Scents produced for the purpose of communication are called pheromones. Chemicals in the scent reveal whether the scent-maker is male or female and, if female, whether she is ready to mate. Scents can also be used to recognize individual animals and animal groups, and may give clues as to an animal's last meal. The power of scent is perhaps greatest among mice and molerats. The smell of a male rat can make a pregnant female abort or resorb her growing fetuses and bring her on heat again. The smell of a female can induce hormone changes in the male to make him produce more pheromones, which in turn make the female come into heat.

▶ **Displays form an important part of courtship for gerenuks, a species of African gazelles: 1 the male turns his head sideways to display his horns, while the female raises her nose high in a defensive gesture; 2 the male marks the female on the thigh with his own scent from a facial gland; 3 finally he taps her hind legs with his foreleg. This is called the foreleg kick.**

◀ A bull fur seal is surrounded by a harem of cows. The breeding sites are crowded, and males must compete with each other to mate with the females in the cluster. They fend off rivals by displaying and by actual fighting.

▶ Like those of humans, the facial expressions of chimpanzees reveal their mood. They also vary according to the social positions of the animals involved in the exchange. Expressions 1 and 2 are often used when two chimps are calling to each other, either in greeting or to attract attention, as when food is found. 3 is used when the owner is under attack, and 4 is used when approaching a chimp of higher social rank.

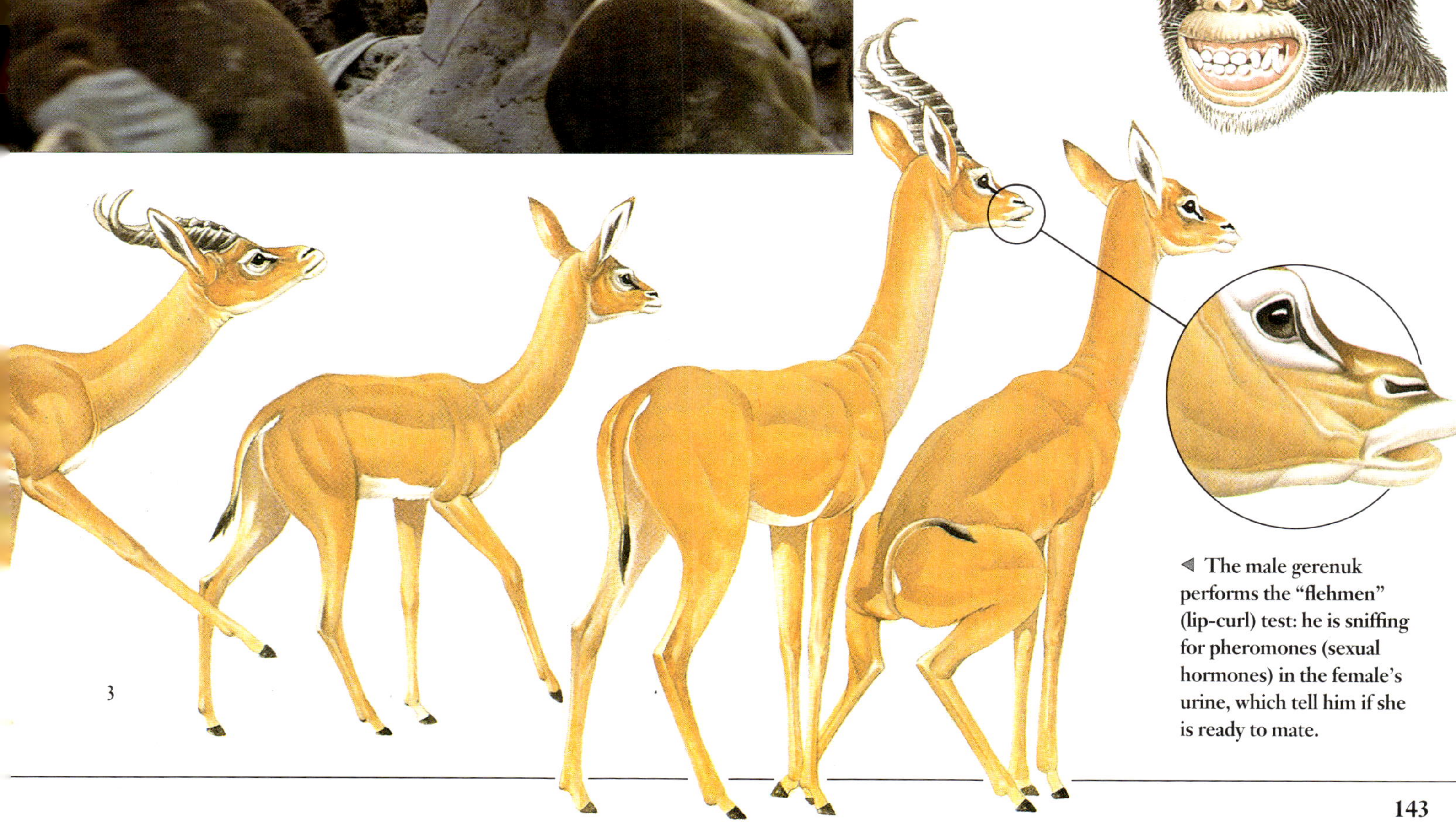

◀ The male gerenuk performs the "flehmen" (lip-curl) test: he is sniffing for pheromones (sexual hormones) in the female's urine, which tell him if she is ready to mate.

FACTFILE

PRECISE MEASUREMENT is at the heart of all science, and several standard systems have been in use in the present century in different societies. Today, the SI system of units is universally used by scientists, but other units are used in some parts of the world. The metric system, which was developed in France in the late 18th century, is in everyday use in many countries, as well as being used by scientists; but imperial units (based on the traditional British measurement standard, also known as the foot–pound–second system), and standard units (based on commonly used American standards) are still in common use.

Whereas the basic units of length, mass and time were originally defined arbitrarily, scientists have sought to establish definitions of these which can be related to measurable physical constants; thus length is now defined in terms of the speed of light, and time in terms of the vibrations of a crystal of an particular atom. Mass, however, still eludes such definition, and is based on a piece of platinum-iridium metal kept in Sèvres, France.

☐ METRIC PREFIXES

Very large and very small units are often written using powers of ten; in addition the following prefixes are also used with SI units. Examples include: milligram (mg), meaning one thousandth of a gram, kilogram (kg), meaning one thousand grams.

Name	Number	Factor	Prefix	Symbol
trillionth	0.000000000001	10^{-12}	pico-	p
billionth	0.000000001	10^{-9}	nano-	n
millionth	0.000001	10^{-6}	micro-	µ
thousandth	0.001	10^{-3}	milli-	m
hundredth	0.01	10^{-2}	centi-	c
tenth	0.1	10^{-1}	deci-	d
one	1.0	10^{0}	–	–
ten	10	10^{1}	deca-	da
hundred	100	10^{2}	hecto-	h
thousand	1000	10^{3}	kilo-	k
million	1,000,000	10^{6}	mega-	M
billion	1,000,000,000	10^{9}	giga-	G
trillion	1,000,000,000,000	10^{12}	tera-	T
quadrillion	1,000,000,000,000,000	10^{15}	exa-	E

☐ CONVERSION FACTORS

Conversion of METRIC units to imperial (or standard) units

To convert:	to:	multiply by:
LENGTH		
millimeters	inches	0.03937
centimeters	inches	0.3937
meters	inches	39.37
meters	feet	3.2808
meters	yards	1.0936
kilometers	miles	0.6214
AREA		
square centimeters	square inches	0.1552
square meters	square feet	10.7636
square meters	square yards	1.196
square kilometers	square miles	0.3861
square kilometers	acres	247.1
hectares	acres	2.471
VOLUME		
cubic centimeters	cubic inches	0.061
cubic meters	cubic feet	35.315
cubic meters	cubic yards	1.308
cubic kilometers	cubic miles	0.2399
CAPACITY		
milliliters	fluid ounces	0.0351
milliliters	pints	0.00176 (0.002114 for US pints)
liters	pints	1.760 (2.114 for US pints)
liters	gallons	0.2193 (0.2643 for US gallons)
WEIGHT		
grams	ounces	0.0352
grams	pounds	0.0022
kilograms	pounds	2.2046
tonnes	tons	0.9842 (1.1023 for US, or short, tons)
TEMPERATURE		
Celsius	Fahrenheit	1.8, then add 32

Conversion of STANDARD (or imperial) units to metric units

To convert:	to:	multiply by:
LENGTH		
inches	millimeters	25.4
inches	centimeters	2.54
inches	meters	0.245
feet	meters	0.3048
yards	meters	0.9144
miles	kilometers	1.6094
AREA		
square inches	square centimeters	6.4516
square feet	square meters	0.0929
square yards	square meters	0.8316
square miles	square kilometers	2.5898
acres	hectares	0.4047
acres	square kilometers	0.00405
VOLUME		
cubic inches	cubic centimeters	16.3871
cubic feet	cubic meters	0.0283
cubic yards	cubic meters	0.7646
cubic miles	cubic kilometers	4.1678
CAPACITY		
fluid ounces	milliliters	28.5
pints	milliliters	568.0 (473.32 for US pints)
pints	liters	0.568 (0.4733 for US pints)
gallons	liters	4.55 (3.785 for US gallons)
WEIGHT		
ounces	grams	28.3495
pounds	grams	453.592
pounds	kilograms	0.4536
tons	tonnes	1.0161
TEMPERATURE		
Fahrenheit	Celsius	subtract 32, then × 0.55556

☐ SI UNITS

Now universally employed throughout the world of science and the legal standard in many countries, SI units (short for *Système International d'Unités*) were adopted by the General Conference on Weights and Measures in 1960. There are seven base units and two supplementary ones, which replaced those of the MKS (meter–kilogram–second) and CGS (centimeter–gram–second) systems that were used previously. There are also 18 derived units, and all SI units have an internationally agreed symbol.

None of the unit terms, even if named for a notable scientist, begins with a capital letter: thus, for example, the units of temperature and force are the kelvin and the newton (the abbreviations of some units are capitalized, however). Apart from the kilogram, which is an arbitrary standard based on a carefully preserved piece of metal, all the basic units are now defined in a manner that permits them to be measured conveniently in a laboratory.

Name	Symbol	Quantity	Standard
BASIC UNITS			
meter	m	length	The distance light travels in a vacuum in 1/299,792,458 of a second
kilogram	kg	mass	The mass of the international prototype kilogram, a cylinder of platinum-iridium alloy, kept at Sèvres, France
second	s	time	The time taken for 9,192,631,770 resonance vibrations of an atom of cesium-133
kelvin	K	temperature	1/273.16 of the thermodynamic temperature of the triple point of water
ampere	A	electric current	The current that produces a force of 2×10^{-7} newtons per meter between two parallel conductors of infinite length and negligible cross section, placed one meter apart in a vacuum
mole	mol	amount of substance	The amount of a substance that contains as many atoms, molecules, ions or subatomic particles as 12 grams of carbon-12 has atoms
candela	cd	luminous intensity	The luminous intensity of a source that emits monochromatic light of a frequency 540×10^{-12} hertz and whose radiant intensity is 1/683 watt per steradian in a given direction
SUPPLEMENTARY UNITS			
radian	rad	plane angle	The angle subtended at the center of a circle by an arc whose length is the radius of the circle
steradian	sr	solid angle	The solid angle subtended at the center of a sphere by a part of the surface whose area is equal to the square of the radius of the sphere

Name	Symbol	Quantity	Standard
DERIVED UNITS			
becquerel	Bq	radioactivity	The activity of a quantity of a radio-isotope in which 1 nucleus decays (on average) every second
coulomb	C	electric current	The quantity of electricity carried by a charge of 1 ampere flowing for 1 second
farad	F	electric capacitance	The capacitance that holds charge of 1 coulomb when it is charged by a potential difference of 1 volt
gray	Gy	absorbed dose	The dosage of ionizing radiation equal to 1 joule of energy per kilogram
henry	H	inductance	The mutual inductance in a closed circuit in which an electromotive force of 1 volt is produced by a current that varies at 1 ampere per second
hertz	Hz	frequency	The frequency of 1 cycle per second
joule	J	energy	The work done when a force of 1 newton moves its point of application 1 meter in its direction of application
lumen	lm	luminous flux	The amount of light emitted per unit solid angle by a source of 1 candela intensity
lux	lx	illuminance	The amount of light that illuminates 1 square meter with a flux of 1 lumen
newton	N	force	The force that gives a mass of 1 kilogram an acceleration of 1 meter per second per second
ohm	Ω	electric resistance	The resistance of a conductor across which a potential of 1 volt produces a current of 1 ampere
pascal	Pa	pressure	The pressure exerted when a force of 1 newton acts on an area of 1 square meter
siemens	S	electric conductance	The conductance of a material or circuit component that has a resistance of 1 ohm
sievert	Sv	dose	The radiation dosage equal to 1 joule equivalent of radiant energy per kilogram
tesla	T	magnetic flux density	The flux density (or density induction) of 1 weber of magnetic flux per square meter
volt	V	electric potential	The potential difference across a conductor in which a constant current of 1 ampere dissipates 1 watt of power
watt	W	power	The amount of power equal to a rate of energy transfer of (or rate of doing work at) 1 joule per second
weber	Wb	magnetic flux	The amount of magnetic flux that, decaying to zero in 1 second, induces an electromotive force of 1 volt in a circuit of one turn

Organisms are classified by being grouped together according to the number of features they have in common. The largest group is a kingdom, which is then divided into phyla and classes, then into orders made up of families containing several genera.

While early classification systems were based mainly on easily observable features, scientists now use microscopic features and chemical analysis of the genetic material to determine the relatedness of different organisms.

Modern classification attempts to combine a recognition system with a statement of phylogeny – the evolutionary relatedness of species; the lower divisions of subphyla, classes and orders remains controversial.

The most widely accepted classification today is the Five Kingdoms system, which divides the living world into the kingdoms Monera (bacteria and cyanobacteria), Plantae (plants), Animalia (multicellular animals), Fungi and Protoctista (all the creatures not in the other four kingdoms).

KINGDOM MONERA
Prokaryotic cells
- Bacteria and cyanobacteria (blue-green algae)

KINGDOM PROTOCTISTA
All creatures that do not fall into the other four kingdoms. There is no phylogenetic relationship between these. The protoctista include:
- Slime molds
- Oomycetes
- Dinoflagellates
- Various kinds of algae (excluding the blue-green algae, but including euglenoids, diatoms and various seaweeds)
- Former members of the Protozoans, including foraminiferans, radiolarians, ciliates, amebas

KINGDOM FUNGI
Eukaryotes that never have flagella or cilia at any stage of the life cycle, that produce spores and that lack embryological development.

KINGDOM PLANTAE
Photosynthetic eukaryotes that develop from embryos, and show an alteration between haploid and diploid generations in their life cycles.
- Mosses, liverworts and hornworts
- Ferns, clubmosses and horsetails
- Cycads, ginkgoes and conifers
- Angiosperms or flowering plants

KINGDOM ANIMALIA
Multicellular eukaryotes that develop from a large egg and small sperm through a characteristic series of embryonic stages.

Phylum Poriphera
(about 10,000 species)
- Class Calcarea – calcareous sponges
- Class Desmospongiae – sponges with a network of spongin
- Class Sclerospongiae – sponges with a network of spongin and aragonite or silica

Phylum Cnidaria
(about 9400 species)
- Class Hydrozoa – hydras, hydroids, fire corals
- Class Scyphozoa – true jellyfish
- Class Anthozoa – most corals and sea anemones

Phylum Ctenophora
(about 90 species)
- Sea gooseberries and comb jellies

Phylum Platyhelminthes
(about 15,000 species)
- Class Turbellaria – freeliving flatworms
- Class Trematoda – flukes
- Class Cestoda – tapeworms

Phylum Nemertina
(about 750 species)
- Ribbonworms

Phylum Rotifera
(about 2000 species)
- Rotifers

Phylum Nematoda
(about 80,000 species)
- Nematodes

Phylum Ectoprocta
(about 5000 species)
- Sea mats or moss animals

Phylum Brachiopoda
(about 260 species)
- Brachiopods or lamp shells

Phylum Mollusca
(about 110,000 species)
- Class Monoplacophora – monoplacophorans
- Class Aplacophora – solenogasters
- Class Polyplacophora – chitons or coat-of-mail shells
- Class Pelecypoda (Bivalvia) – bivalves (clams, mussels, oysters, scallops)
- Class Gastropoda – snails and slugs
- Class Scaphopoda – tooth shells
- Class Cephalopoda – octopus, squid, cuttlefish, nautiluses

Phylum Annelida
(about 9000 species)
- Class Polychaeta – marine bristle worms (lugworm, ragworm)
- Class Oligochaeta – terrestrial bristleworms (earthworms)
- Class Hirudinea – leeches

Phylum Arthropoda
(about 1,000,000 species)
- Subphylum Mandibulata (three distinct body parts)
  - Class Crustacea – water fleas, shrimps, crabs, copepods, barnacles
  - Class Diplopoda – millipedes
  - Class Chilopoda – centipedes
  - Class Insecta – insects
    - Order Thysanura – bristletails, silverfish, firebrats
    - Order Isoptera – termites
    - Order Dermaptera – earwigs
    - Order Collembola – springtails
    - Order Ephemeroptera – mayflies
    - Order Odonata – dragonflies
    - Order Orthoptera – grasshoppers, crickets, mantids
    - Order Dictyoptera – cockroaches, mantids
    - Order Phasmida – stick insects, leaf insects
    - Order Hemiptera – true bugs
    - Order Homoptera – cicadas, aphids
    - Order Lepidoptera – butterflies and moths
    - Order Diptera – flies
    - Order Siphonaptera – fleas
    - Order Mallophaga – chewing lice
    - Order Hymenoptera – wasps, bees, ants, hornets
    - Order Coleoptera – beetles
    - Order Trichoptera – caddis flies
- Subphylum Chelicerata (two distinct body parts)
  - Class Pycnogonida – sea spiders
  - Class Merostomata – horseshoe crabs or king crabs
  - Class Arachnida – spiders, scorpions, harvestmen, mites and ticks

Phylum Echinodermata
(about 600 species)
- Class Crinoidea – sea lilies, feather stars
- Class Holothuroidea – sea cucumbers
- Class Echinoidea – sea urchins, sand dollars
- Class Asteroidea – starfish or sea stars
- Class Ophiuroidea – brittlestars

Phylum Chordata
(about 45,000 species)
Subphylum Tunicata (no brain, only larva has notochord and nerve cord, adult secretes cellulose tunic)
Class Larvacea – larvaceans (tadpole-like)
Class Ascidiacea – sea squirts
Class Cephalochordata – lancelets

Subphylum Agnatha – brain and skull, no jaws or paired appendages
Class Cyclostomata – no scales, round suckerlike mouth
Order Myxiniformes – hagfish
Order Petromyzontiformes – lampreys

Subphylum Gnathostomata (brain and skull, jaws and paired appendages)
Superclass Pisces (jawed fish)
Class Chondrichthyes – cartilaginous fish (about 700 species)
Order Chlamydoselachiformes – frill sharks
Order Hexanchiformes – cow sharks
Order Heterodontiformes – bullhead sharks
Order Squaliformes – most other sharks
Order Rajiiformes – rays, sawfish, guitarfish, skates
Order Chimaeriformes – chimaeras

Class Osteichthyes – bony fish (about 21,000 species)
Order Coelacanthiformes – coelacanths
Order Dipteriformes – lungfish
Order Polypteriformes – bichirs
Order Acipenseriformes – sturgeons, paddlefish
Order Semionotiformes – gars
Order Amiiformes – bowfins
Order Elopiformes – tarpons, bonefish
Order Anguilliformes – eels, morays, swallowers, gulpers
Order Clupeiformes – herrings, anchovies
Order Osteoglossiformes – arapaimas, freshwater butterflyfish, mooneyes, featherbacks
Order Salmoniformes – salmon, trout, grayling, whitefish, pike
Order Myctophiformes – lizardfish, lanternfish
Order Gonorynchiformes – milkfish
Order Cypriniformes – hatchetfish, electric eels, minnows, carp, suckers, loaches
Order Siluriformes – catfish
Order Gadiformes – cod, pearlfish, eelpout, grenadiers
Order Atheriniformes – flying fish, foureye fish, silversides
Order Zeiformes – dories
Order Lampridiformes – opahs, ribbonfish, oarfish
Order Gasterosteiformes – sticklebacks, trumpetfish, seahorses
Order Scorpaeniformes – scorpionfish, rockfish, lumpfish
Order Perciformes – sea bass, tuna, perch, snappers, archerfish, barracudas, parrotfish, mackerel, swordfish
Order Pleuronectiformes – flounders, soles, plaice
Order Tetraodontiformes – triggerfish, puffers

Superclass Tetrapoda (four-legged vertebrates)
Class Amphibia – amphibians (about 2400 species)
Order Urodela – salamanders, mud puppies, newts
Order Anura – frogs, toads
Order Apoda – caecilians

Class Reptilia – reptiles (about 6600 species)
Order Chelonia – turtles and tortoises
Order Squamata – lizards, snakes, geckos, iguanas
Order Crocodylia – crocodiles, alligators, caimans

Class Aves – birds (about 9300 species)
Order Struthioniformes – ostrich
Order Rheiformes – rheas
Order Casuariiformes – emus, cassowaries
Order Apterygiformes – kiwis
Order Tinamiformes – tinamous
Order Sphenisciformes – penguins
Order Gaviformes – loons or divers
Order Podicipediformes – grebes, dabchicks
Order Procellariiformes – albatrosses, shearwaters, petrels
Order Pelecaniformes – pelicans, gannets, boobies, cormorants
Order Ciconiiformes – herons, storks, ibises, spoonbills, flamingoes
Order Anseriformes – screamers, ducks, geese, swans
Order Falconiformes – vultures and diurnal birds of prey
Order Galliformes – grouse, pheasants, turkeys, quail
Order Gruiformes – cranes, rails, coots, bustards
Order Charadriiformes – plovers, gulls, terns, auks, waders
Order Pteroclidiformes – sandgrouse
Order Columbiformes – pigeons, doves
Order Psittaciformes – parrots, lories, cockatoos, macaws
Order Cuculiformes – cuckoos, roadrunners
Order Strigiformes – owls
Order Caprimulgiformes – nightjars, frogmouths, oilbird
Order Apodiformes – swifts, hummingbirds
Order Coliiformes – mousebirds
Order Trogoniformes – trogons
Order Coraciiformes – kingfishers, bee-eaters, hornbills
Order Piciformes – woodpeckers, sapsuckers, honeyguides, toucans
Order Passeriformes – perching birds

Class Mammalia (about 4000 species)
Subclass Protheria – egg-laying mammals or monotremes
Order Monotremata – echidnas or spiny anteaters, duck-billed platypus

Subclass Theria – all other mammals
Infraclass Metatheria – marsupials or pouched mammals

Infraclass Eutheria – placental mammals
Order Insectivora – hedgehogs, moles and shrews
Order Dermoptera – flying lemurs
Order Chiroptera – bats and flying foxes
Order Primates – tree shrews, lemurs, monkeys, apes, humans
Order Edentata – sloths, anteaters, armadillos
Order Pholidota – pangolins or scaly anteaters
Order Lagomorpha – rabbits, hares, pikas
Order Rodentia – rats, mice, beavers, squirrels, porcupines
Order Cetacea – whales, dolphins, porpoises
Order Carnivora – dogs, bears, raccoons, weasels, hyenas, cats
Order Pinnipedia – seals, sealions, walruses
Order Tubulidentata – aardvark or ant bear
Order Proboscidea – elephants
Order Hyracoidea – hyraxes
Order Sineria – manatees, dugongs, sea cows
Order Perissodactyla (odd-toed ungulates) – horses, zebras, tapirs, rhinoceroses
Order Artiodactyla (even-toed ungulates) – pigs, camels, deers, cattle, goats, antelopes, sheep

☐ MAMMALIAN HORMONES

Multicellular animals need some means faster than diffusion to provide communication between different parts of the body. The two main signaling systems are the nervous system and a series of chemicals known as hormones. Nerve impulses are faster than hormone signals, but usually produce much shorter-lived responses. In animals with blood transport systems, hormones are usually carried to their target organs in the bloodstream. Glands that secrete hormones directly into the bloodstream are called endocrine glands. The following table shows the main activities of the major endocrine glands in the mammalian body.

There are two master glands in the brain, the hypothalamus and the pituitary. The hypothalamus contains many sensors which monitor the internal environment of the body. It provides a direct link between the nervous system and the endocrine system, secreting hormones into the blood vessels that run directly to the pituitary, to control the release of hormones from the pituitary. The posterior and anterior pituitary glands produce hormones that have a direct effect on certain organs, and also hormone-releasing factors, which cause other endocrine organs (including the adrenal cortex and the sex glands) to release hormones.

Gland	Secretion (hormone)	Functions	Controlled by
Hypothalamus	Releasing and inhibiting hormones and factors	Controls anterior pituitary hormones	Blood chemical and hormone level feedback levels
Thyroid	Thyroxin	Controls metabolic rate and probably facilitates the action of respiratory enzymes. Promotes action of pituitary growth hormone, diuresis, breakdown of protein, milk-production and amphibian metamorphosis. Enhances action of epinephrine and sympathetic nervous system	Thyroid-stimulating hormone (TSH) from anterior pituitary
Thyroid	Calcitonin	Decreases the concentration of calcium in the blood	Concentration of calcium in bloodstream
Parathyroids	Parathormone	Increases the concentration of calcium and lowers the concentration of phosphate ions in the blood	Levels of calcium and phosphate in bloodstream
Thymus	Not known	Assists lymphocytes to develop antibody-producing plasma cells shortly after birth	Not known
Pancreas (Islets of Langerhans, beta cells)	Insulin	Suppresses blood sugar by causing respiratory breakdown of glucose, conversion to glycogen or fat in the liver, and inhibiting the creation of glucose from protein	Feedback from excessive blood sugar level
Pancreas (Islets of Langerhans, alpha cells)	Glucagon	Converts glycogen to glucose in the liver, thus raising blood sugar level	Feedback from inadequate blood sugar level
Adrenal medulla	Epinephrine (adrenaline) and norepinephrine (noradrenaline)	Prepare the body for emergency or stress reaction ("fight-or-flight" response), increasing metabolic rate, raising blood sugar level, blood pressure, heartbeat etc.	Sympathetic nervous system
Adrenal cortex	Adrenal cortical hormones (steroids): mineralocorticoid hormones (aldosterone); glucocorticoids (such as cortisol)	Mineralocorticoids control the balance of sodium and phosphate ions in blood; low blood pressure Glucocorticoids inhibit cell respiration and raise blood sugar level and blood pressure, promote protein breakdown	Adrenocorticotrophic hormone (ACTH), released by anterior pituitary gland
Pineal body	Melatonin	Thought to be involved in biological clock; causes concentration of pigment cells in frog	Centers in brain controlled by light
Kidney	Renin	Activates plasma protein angiotensin	Sodium level in blood
Duodenal wall	Cholecystokinin	Stimulates release of bile from gall bladder	Presence of fatty acids and amino acids in duodenum
Testes	Androsterone and testosterone	Promote growth and activity of male reproductive organs, and stimulate the production of sperm	Follicle-stimulating hormone (FSH) and luteinizing hormone (LH)

Gland	Secretion (hormone)	Functions	Controlled by
Placenta	Chorionic gonadotrophin	Maintains the corpus luteum in ovary, to support pregnancy	Developing fetus
Ovaries	Estrogens	Promote development of female sex organs, repair of uterus after menstruation; inhibit lactation	Follicle-stimulating hormone (FSH) and luteininizing hormone (LH)
Ovaries	Progesterone	Promotes development of lining of the uterus, inhibits ovulation and develops secretory cells of mammary glands	Luteinizing hormone (LH) from anterior pituitary
Anterior pituitary	Thyroid-stimulating hormone (TSH)	Stimulates the thyroid gland to secrete thyroxine	Feedback from thyroxine level in blood
Anterior pituitary	Adrenocorticotrophic hormone (ACTH)	Causes adrenal cortex to secrete its hormones	Feedback from level of ACTH in blood
Anterior pituitary	Growth hormone (GH)	Stimulates growth by promoting protein synthesis, and increases blood sugar level	Hypothalamus hormones
Anterior pituitary	Prolactin	Stimulates milk production and secretion	Hypothalamus hormones
Anterior pituitary	Follicle-stimulating hormone (FSH)	Causes sperm production in male, and development of ovum and release of estrogens in female	Estrogen and progesterone
Anterior pituitary	Luteinizing hormone (LH) or interstitial cell-stimulating hormone (ICSH)	Stimulates sperm production and causes secretion of testosterone and androsterone in male; and ovulation in female	Stimulated by estrogen and inhibited by progesterone; affected by testosterone level
Posterior pituitary	Melanophore-stimulating hormone (MSH)	Expansion of melanin pigment in skin, especially effective in amphibians	Not known
Posterior pituitary	Antidiuretic hormone (ADH) or vasopressin	Raises blood pressure by causing reabsorption of water in kidney	Osmotic pressure of blood
Posterior pituitary	Oxytocin	Causes contraction of uterus at birth, and expulsion of milk from mammary glands	Estrogen and progesterone and nervous system

□ THE "FIGHT-OR-FLIGHT" RESPONSE

The "fight-or-flight" response is a series of changes in the body produced in response to danger, anger or fear. They sharpen the senses, and speed the body's reactions by diverting blood and respiratory substrates to the muscles and other organs.

In the immediate response, the hypothalamus stimulates organs directly by the sympathetic nervous system, which also stimulates the adrenal medulla to release the hormones epinephrine and norepinephrine into the bloodstream.

Organ	Response
Heart	Heartbeat increases. Volume of blood pumped at each beat increases. Blood pressure increases
Blood vessels	Constricted in digestive and reproductive systems and dilated in muscles, lungs and liver, to raise oxygen and glucose levels in these organs
Liver	Glycogen converted to glucose to raise available sugar in blood
Lungs	Air passages dilate and breathing rate rises to increase oxygen intake
Brain	Sensory perception and mental awareness raised to produce more rapid reactions to external stimuli

Organ	Response
Liver	Fats and amino acids converted to glucose
Digestive system	Smooth muscles relaxed to allow diaphragm to be lowered, thus increasing oxygen intake
Skin	Blood vessels constricted, keeping blood pressure high; inflammation reduces permitting general body defenses to work efficiently
Hair and fur	Hair erector muscles contract to give impression of increased size in mammals, possibly frightening enemy
Adrenal cortex	Glucocorticoid hormones produced to carry the stress reaction on for a longer period

□ MINERALS AND DIET

Many different minerals are required for the growth and maintenance of the human body. Minerals have a variety of roles in the body. Some, such as calcium and magnesium, are components of body structures such as bones and teeth. Many are involved in the transfer of electrons at the reactive centers of enzymes, or are components of coenzymes and cofactors needed for the transfer of electrons, oxygen or hydrogen in metabolic reactions.

The balance between different mineral ions such as potassium and sodium plays a key role in membrane function and nerve excitation, and helps to maintain the osmotic balance of the blood and tissue fluids. Minerals required in moderate amounts are called macronutrients; those required only in minute amounts are called micronutrients or trace elements.

Mineral	Function	Deficiency symptom	Sources in human diet
Calcium Ca^{2+}	Component of bones and teeth; also needed for blood clotting, nerve action and muscle contraction. Enzyme activator	Poor skeletal growth, soft bones, muscular spasms, slow blood clotting	Milk, cheese, fish, hard drinking water, eggs, green vegetables
Chlorine Cl^-	Needed to maintain the balance between cations and anions, and for the activity of excitable tissue, notably muscle and nerve receptors. Formation of hydrochloric acid. Needed for CO_2 transport in the blood	Muscular cramps	Salt, bacon
Cobalt Co^{2+}	Trace mineral, a constituent of vitamin B_{12}; needed for the formation of red blood cells	Pernicious anemia	Liver and red meat
Copper Cu^{2+}	Trace mineral, needed in the formation of hemoglobin and bone. It is found in many vertebrate enzymes (such as those that synthesize hemoglobin and bone), and in the blood of vertebrates and invertebrates	Various metabolic disorders	Most foods, including liver, eggs, fish, wheat, beans
Fluorine F^-	Trace mineral, found in bones and teeth, improves resistance to dental caries	Tooth decay and generally weak teeth, especially in the young;	Drinking water (often artificially enriched)
Iodine I^-	Component of the growth hormone thyroxine, which controls metabolic rate	Goiter (abnormal enlargement of thyroid gland); cretinism in children	Sea fish, shellfish, vegetables from iodine-rich soil
Iron Fe^{2+}	Metallic ion required for many enzymes and electron carriers; a key component of hemoglobin and myoglobin in vertebrate blood, and contributor to blood pigments in invertebrates	Anemia	Meat, notably liver and kidneys; eggs, cocoa powder, apricots, green vegetables, drinking water from iron-rich soils
Magnesium Mg^{2+}	Component of bones and teeth; enzyme activator		Most foods, especially meat and green vegetables
Manganese Mn^{2+}	Activates various enzymes, and contributes to the growth of bones	Malformation of the skeleton	Most foods, including liver and kidney, tea and coffee
Molybdenum Mo^{4+}	Required by various enzymes involved in uric acid production		Liver, kidneys, green vegetables
Phosphate PO_4^{3-}	Constituent of phospholipids in membranes, nucleotides (such as ATP) and nucleic acids. Also found in bones and teeth. Needed for nerve and muscle action		Most foods
Potassium K^+	Determines the cation-anion balance in intracellular fluid, and is required for the action of excitable tissue such as nerve and muscle cells. Cofactor in respiration		Meat, fish, some fruit and vegetables
Sodium Na^+	Needed for nerve and muscle action, and helps determine osmotic pressure and the anion-cation balance	Muscular cramps; overconsumption may result in high blood pressure	Salt and foodstuffs such as salty fish and dairy foods, bacon
Sulfate SO_4^{2-}	Component of proteins and coenzymes		Meat, dairy foods, eggs
Zinc Zn^{2+}	Required to activate about 70 different enzymes, and involved in insulin metabolism and in CO_2 transport in the blood		Most foods, notably liver, meat, shellfish, fish

☐ VITAMINS AND HUMAN DIET

Vitamins are organic compounds which are required in very small quantities by living organisms for their health and normal development. Most vitamins cannot be synthesized by the body but must be obtained from food. However, vitamin D is an exception to this rule, being synthesized in the skin when exposed to sunlight. Vitamins H and K can be synthesized by bacteria living in the gut. Vitamins usually act as coenzymes which promote metabolic reactions; prolonged lack of vitamins can cause deficiency diseases.

Vitamin	Function	Deficiency diseases	Sources
A Retinol	Needed for the formation of the visual pigment in the eye. Promotes skin growth	Poor adaptation to the dark; dry skin; dry mucous membranes; blindness	Halibut, cod liver oil, ox liver, milk
B_1 Thiamin	Coenzyme in cellular respiration and metabolism of carbohydrate, converting pyruvic acid to acetyl coenzyme A	Beri-beri, neuritis, heart failure; slows children's growth	Liver, kidneys, legumes, yeast, wheat and rice germ
B_2 Riboflavin	Coenzyme in protein and carbohydrate metabolism. Vital constituent of electron carriers	Sore mouth, ulcerations, eye irritation	Leafy vegetables, fish, eggs, milk, yeast, cheese, liver
B_3 Niacin	Coenzymes (NAD and NADP) required as hydrogen acceptors in cellular metabolism	Pellagra, skin lesions, rashes, fatigue, diarrhea	Meat, yeast, liver, wholemeal bread
B_5 Pantothenic acid	Forms acetyl coenzyme A which activates carboxylic acids in cellular metabolism	Fatigue, poor coordination, muscle cramps	Yeast, eggs
B_6 Pyroxydine	Part of coenzyme A involved in amino acid and fatty acid metabolism	Anemia, convulsions, dermatitis, nervous disorders, diarrhea	Most foods
B_{12} Cobalamin	Coenzyme required for ribonucleic acid (RNA) synthesis; also required in the liver for red blood cell formation	Pernicious anemia and malformation of red blood cells	Meat, eggs, fish, dairy foods
C Ascorbic acid	Involved in the formation of connective tissues, intercellular cement for bone and cartilage, maintains resistance to infection, frees iron to make hemoglobin	Scurvy, anemia, slow wound healing, heart failure	Citrus fruits, green vegetables, tomatoes, potatoes
D Calciferol	Controls absorption and metabolism of calcium and phosphorus, and involved in the formation and hardening of bone and teeth	Rickets, osteomalacia	Fish oils, dairy produce, sunlight on skin
E Tocopherol	Poorly understood; protects red blood cells and important in muscle maintenance	Bursting of red blood cells, sterility, nervous defects; muscular dystrophy	Green vegetables, milk, wheat germ, liver, kidney
H Biotin	Coenzyme in carboxylation reactions, involved in protein synthesis	Dermatitis and muscle pains	Yeast, liver, kidney; synthesized by intestinal bacteria
K Phylloquinone	Required in the liver for synthesis of prothrombin	Prolonged clotting time, especially in the newborn	Green vegetables; synthesized by intestinal bacteria
M Folic acid	Required for nucleic protein synthesis and the formation of red blood cells	Pernicious anemia	Leafy vegetables, white fish, liver

☐ DIGESTIVE ENZYMES

The breakdown reactions of digestion are controlled by enzymes, organic catalysts specific to particular reactions. Pepsin, for example, catalyzes the breakdown of proteins into peptides, while another enzyme, peptidase, converts peptides into their component amino acids. A few digestive enzymes, such as enterokinase, catalyze the conversion of inactive compounds into active enzymes.

Enzyme	Production site	Substrate	Product
Salivary amylase	Salivary glands	Starch	Maltose
Pepsin	Stomach wall	Protein	Peptides
Rennin	Stomach wall	Caseinogen	Casein
Amylase	Pancreas	Starch	Maltose
Trypsin	Pancreas	Protein	Peptides
Chymotrypsin	Pancreas	Casein	Amino acids
Carboxypeptidase	Pancreas	Peptides	Amino acids
Lipase	Pancreas	Fats	Fatty acids/glycerol

Enzyme	Production site	Substrate	Product
Nucleases	Pancreas	Nucleic acid	Nucleotides
Enterokinase	Small intestine	Trypsinogen	Trypsin
Maltase	Small intestine	Maltose	Glucose
Sucrase	Small intestine	Sucrose	Glucose/fructose
Lactase	Small intestine	Lactose	Glucose/galactose
Peptidase	Small intestine	Peptides	Amino acids
Nucleotidase	Small intestine	Nucleotides	Nucleosides

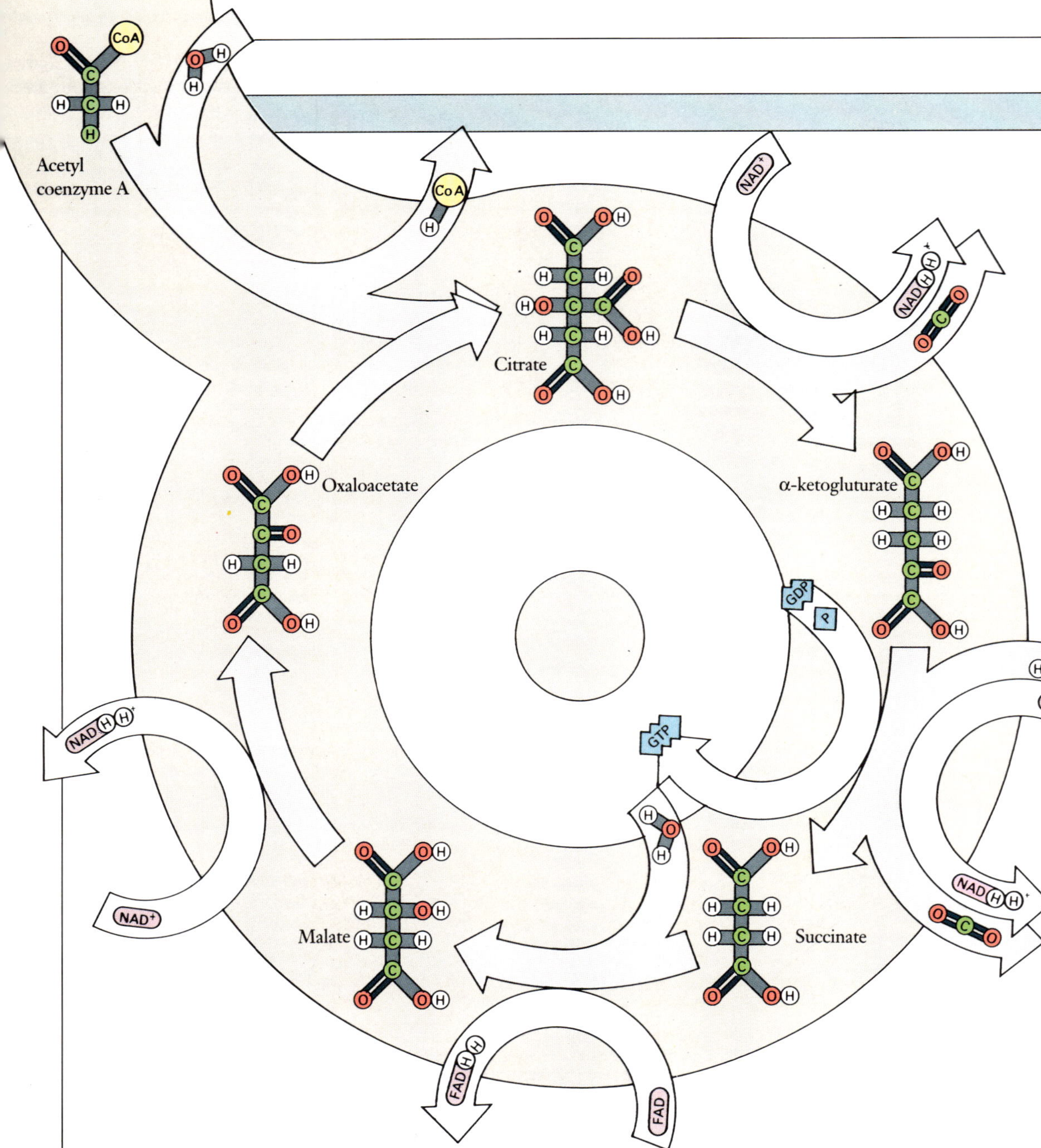

☐ THE KREBS CYCLE

The citric acid cycle, or tricarboxylic acid, also known as the Krebs cycle after its discoverer, British biochemist Hans Krebs, is at the heart of the biochemical reactions that oxidize food to provide energy to living cells. After energy is extracted from glucose through an anaerobic process known as glycolysis, one of the end-products is pyruvate. This is converted to acetyl coenzyme A, which is converted into citric acid. A cycle of catalyzed reactions results in the total oxidation of pyruvate to carbon dioxide and water. During the cycle, several adenosine diphosphate (ADP) molecules are converted to adenosine triphosphate (ATP); on returning to ADP, these release energy for use in cellular reactions. At the same time nicotinamide adenine dinucleotide phosphate (NADP) forms high-energy bonds with hydrogen atoms. NADP then undergoes a further sequence of oxidation reactions, known as the electron transport chain, which results in the storage of more energy in ATP molecules. The enzymes required for the cycle are located in the mitochondria of eukaryote cells.

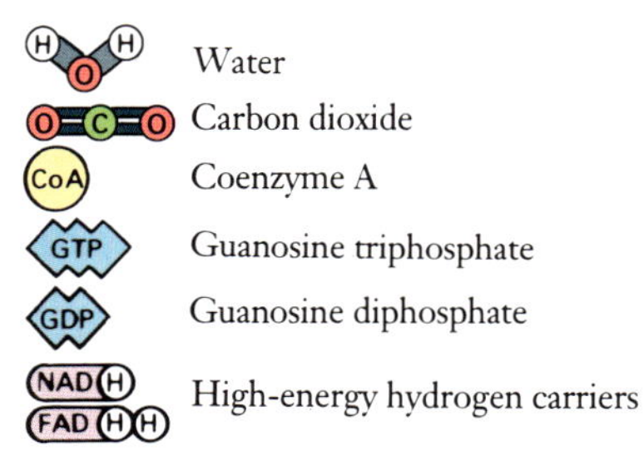

☐ FURTHER READING

Alderton, David *Turtles and Tortoises of the World* (London and New York 1988)

Allaby, Michael *Animal Artisans* (London and New York 1982)

Allaby, Michael *The Oxford Dictionary of Natural History* (Oxford and New York 1985)

Allaby, Michael (ed) *The Concise Oxford Dictionary of Zoology* (Oxford and New York 1992)

Attenborough, David *The Trials of Life* (London and New York 1990)

Banister, Keith and Campbell, Andrew (eds) *The Encyclopedia of Underwater Life* (Oxford and New York 1985)

Barnes, Robert D. *Invertebrate Zoology* (London and New York 1987)

Barnes, R. S. L. and Olive, P. J. K. *The Invertebrates: a New Synthesis* (Oxford and New York 1993)

Bright, Michael *The Private Life of Birds, a Worldwide Exploration of Bird Behaviour* (London 1993)

Brock Fenton, M. *Bats* (New York 1992)

Brooke, Michael and Birkhead, Tim *The Cambridge Encyclopedia of Ornithology* (Cambridge and New York 1991)

Brusca, Richard C. and Gary J. *Invertebrates* (New York 1990)

Buchsbaum, Ralph, Buchsbaum, Mildred, Pearse, John and Pearse, Vicki *Animals Without Backbones* (Chicago 1987)

Burton, Robert *Bird Flight* (New York 1990)

Burton, Robert *Egg, Nature's Miracle of Packaging* (London and New York 1987)

Burton, Robert *The Mating Game* (Oxford 1976)

Cooke, John *The Restless Kingdom, an Exploration of Animal Movement* (London and New York 1991)

Dalton, Stephen *The Miracle of Flight* (London 1977)

Dorit, Robert L., Walker, Warren F. Jr. and Barnes, Robert D. *Zoology* (New York 1991)

Downer, John *Supersense, Perception in the Animal World* (London 1988)

Ewer, R. F. *The Carnivores* (Cornell 1985)

Gamlin, Linda and Vines, Gail (eds) *The Evolution of Life* (London and New York 1987)

Geiser, Franz and Dossenbach, Hans *Survival in the Animal World* (London 1985)

Gould, Edwin and McKay, George *The Encyclopedia of Animals: Mammals* (Merehurst 1990)

Green, N. P. O., Stout, G. W. and Taylor, D. J. *Biological Science* (Cambridge 1990)

☐ THE MENSTRUAL CYCLE

The reproductive cycles of mammals may vary from a period of four or five days in mice, to 28 days (the menstrual cycle) in women, to a year or more in larger mammals. The release of the ovum (egg), sexual receptivity of the female and preparedness of the uterus for implantation of the fertilized egg are all controlled by hormones.

In the human cycle, the pituitary releases follicle-stimulating hormone (FSH) into the bloodstream. This causes the ovum to grow in the ovary, which also begins to release estrogen, which stimulates the lining of the uterus to thicken in preparation for implantation. The pituitary detects the estrogen levels in the blood, and reduces FSH production; this in turn triggers the release of luteinizing hormone (LH) from the pituitary. LH causes the ovum to be released. The follicle in which the ovum developed, now known as the corpus luteum, produces progesterone, which stops LH and FSH production and completes preparation of the uterus lining. If the ovum is not fertilized, progesterone production stops and menstruation begins, as the lining of the uterus is shed.

If fertilization does occur, a placenta forms which releases human chorionic gonadotropin (HCG), a hormone that maintains the corpus luteum to manufacture progesterone and estrogen and thus prevents further ovulation, and also human chorionic somatomammotropin (HCS) to stimulate the milk-producing glands in the breast.

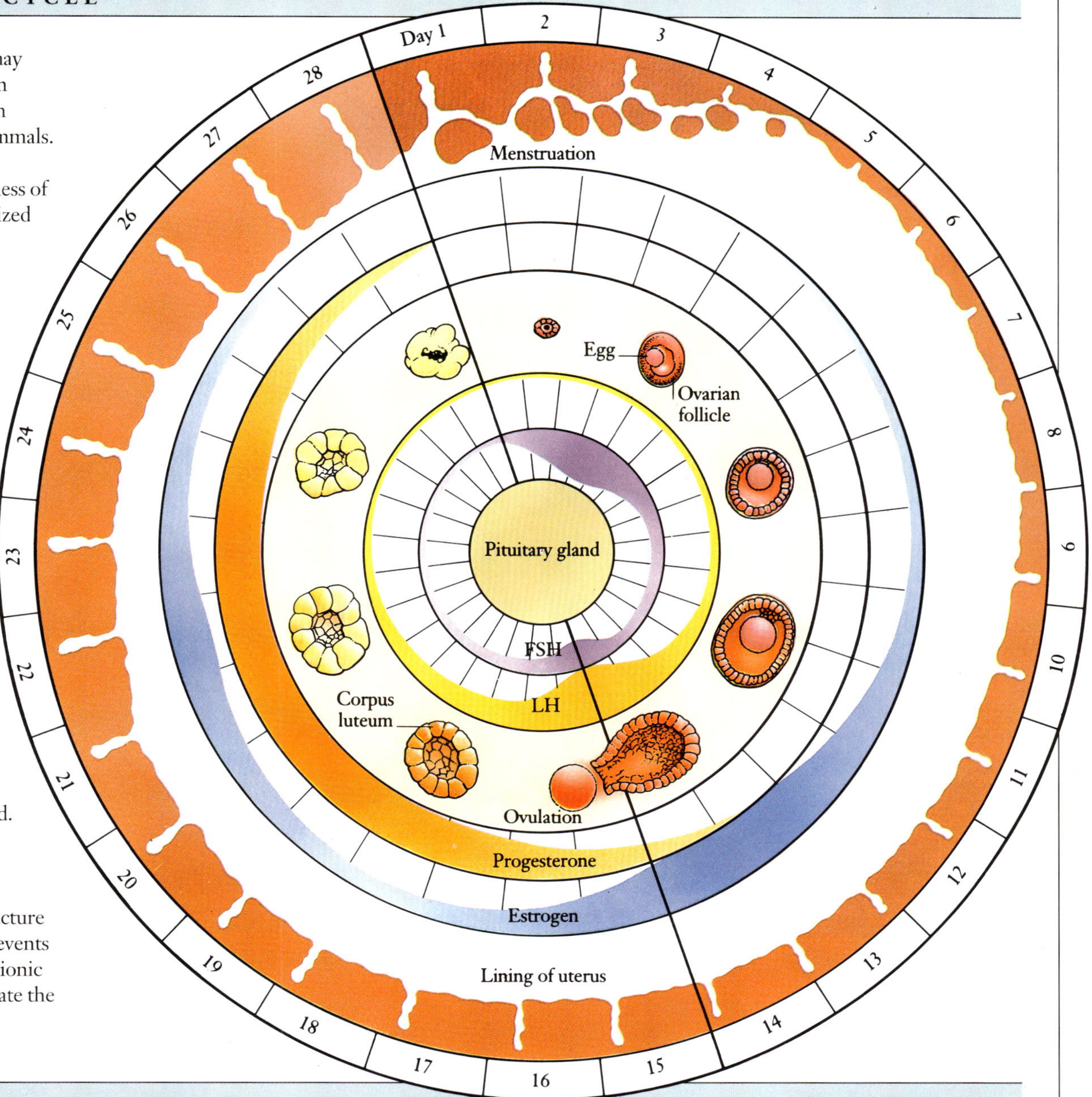

Grzimek, Bernhard *Grzimek's Encyclopedia of Mammals* (5 vols Toronto 1990)
Halliday, Tim and Adler, Kraig (eds) *The Encyclopedia of Reptiles and Amphibians* (Oxford and New York, 1986)
Harrison, Richard and Bryden, M. M. (eds) *Whales, Dolphins and Porpoises* (Merehurst 1988)
Kershaw, Diana R. *Animal Diversity* (New York 1983)
Macdonald, David (ed) *The Encyclopedia of Mammals* (Oxford and New York 1984)
Macdonald, David *The Velvet Claw, a Natural History of the Carnivores* (London 1992)
Margulis, Lynn and Schwartz, Karlene V. *Five Kingdoms, an Illustrated Guide to the Phyla of Life on Earth* (New York 1982)
McNeill Alexander, R. *Locomotion of Animals* (New York 1982)
Mattison, Chris *Frogs and Toads of the World* (London and New York 1992)
Mattison, Chris *Snakes of the World* (London and New York 1992)
Mattison, Chris *Lizards of the World* (London and New York 1989)
O'Toole, Chris *The Encyclopedia of Insects* (Oxford and New York 1986)
Parker, Steve *Inside the Whale and Other Animals* (London and New York 1992)
Perrins, Christopher and Middleton, Alex M. A. (eds) *The Encyclopedia of Birds* (Oxford and New York 1985)
Pough, F. H., Heiser, J. B. and McFarland, W. N. *Vertebrate Life* (New York 1989)
Preston-Mafham, Ron and Ken *The Encyclopedia of Land Invertebrate Behaviour* (London and New York 1993)
Preston-Mafham, Rod and Ken *Spiders of the World* (New York 1984, London 1993)
Sinclair, Sandra *How Animals See, Other Visions of Our World* (London and New York 1985)
Smith, D. C. and Douglas, A. E. *The Biology of Symbiosis* (London 1987, New York 1992)
Starr, Cecie and Taggart, Ralph *Biology, the Unity and Diversity of Life* (London 1992)
Swinney, G. and Charlesworth, K. *Fish Facts* (London 1993)
von Frisch, Karl *Animal Architecture* (London 1974)
Whitfield, Philip, Orr, Richard and Woods, Michael *The Animal Family* (Feltham and New York 1979)
Whitfield, Philip *The Hunters* (Feltham 1978)
Willson, M. F. *Vertebrate Natural History* (New York 1984)

PHYSIOLOGY OR MEDICINE NOBEL PRIZEWINNERS

The Nobel Prize for Physiology or Medicine, like similar prizes for Chemistry, Physics, Literature and Peace, has been awarded annually since 1901 as the world's most prestigious prize for outstanding work in the field, under the terms of the will of the Swedish chemist and engineer Alfred Nobel, who died in 1896. The prize for physiology or medicine is awarded by the Royal Caroline Medico-Chirurgical Institute in Stockholm, Sweden. Some outstanding achievements in biology and biochemistry have been recognized by a prize in chemistry.

1901 **Emil von Behring** *German*
Development of diphtheria antitoxin

1902 **Ronald Ross** *British*
Discovery of the mechanism of malaria transmission

1903 **Niels Finsen** *Danish*
Use of light in the treatment of skin diseases

1904 **Ivan Pavlov** *Russian*
Work on the physiology of digestion

1905 **Robert Koch** *German*
Study of tuberculosis and its transmission

1906 **Camillo Golgi** *Italian* **and S. Ramón y Cajal** *Spanish*
Study of the nervous system

1907 **C.L.A. Lavaran** *French*
Discovery of protozoan-induced disorders

1908 **Paul Erlich** *German* **and Elie Mettchnikoff** *Russian-French*
Study of immunity

1909 **Emil Kocher** *Swiss*
Study of the thyroid gland and its function

1910 **Albrecht Kossel** *German*
Chemistry of cells

1911 **Alivar Gullstrand** *Swedish*
Light diffraction by the eye

1912 **Alexis Carrell** *French*
Development of techniques for transplanting organs and blood vessels

1913 **Charles Richet** *French*
Study of allergies

1914 **Robert Bárány** *Austrian*
Study of the balancing mechanism of the ear

1915–18 No award

1919 **Jules Bordet** *Belgian*
Study of immunity

1920 **August Krogh** *Danish*
Discovery of blood capillary action

1921 No award

1922 **Archibald Hill** *British* **and Otto Meyerhof** *German*
Discovery of heat production and lactic acid formation in muscles

1923 **F.G. Banting** *Canadian* **and J. Macleod** *British*
Discovery of insulin

1924 **Willem Einthoven** *Dutch*
Invention of the electrocardiograph

1925 No award

1926 **Johannes Fibiger** *Danish*
Induction of cancer using parasites

1927 **Julius Wagner von Jauregg** *Austrian*
Treatment of paralysis using malaria inoculation

1928 **Charles Nicolle** *French*
Study of typhus

1929 **Christiaan Eijkmann** *Dutch* **and Frederick Gowland Hopkins** *British*
Discovery of vitamins connected with beri-beri and growth

1930 **Karl Landsteiner** *Austrian–American*
Discovery of blood types ABO

1931 **Otto Warburg** *German*
Role of enzymes in respiration within tissues

1932 **Edgar Adrian** *British* **and Charles Sherrington** *British*
Study of the function of neurons

1933 **Thomas Hunt Morgan** *American*
Study of the function of chromosomes in the transmission of hereditary information

1934 **George Minot, William Murphy and George Whipple** *American*
Discoveries of the use of liver therapy against anemia

▲ **F. G. Banting (prizewinner in 1923) with his assistant Charles Best RIGHT.**

1935 **Hans Spemann** *German*
Discovery of organizing centers for embryonic development

1936 **Henry Hallett Dale** *British* **and Otto Loewi** *German*
Discoveries of chemical transmission of nerve impulses

1937 **Albert Szent-Györgyi** *Hungarian*
Study of tissue respiration and the action of vitamin C

1938 **Corneille Heymans** *Belgian*
Study of the regulation of respiration through the sinus and aortic mechanisms

1939 **Gerhard Domagk** *German*
Discovery of the antibacterial effects of sulphonamide drugs

1940–42 No award

1943 **Henrik Dam** *Danish* **and Edward Doisy** *German*
Discovery and synthesis of vitamin K

1944 **Joseph Erlanger and Herbert Gasser** *American*
Study of functions of single nerve fibers

1945 **Alexander Fleming, Ernest Chain** *British* **and Howard Florey** *Austrian*
Discovery and chemotherapy use of penicillin

1946 **Hermann Muller** *American*
Production of mutations through X radiation

1947 **Carl Cori and Gerti Cori** *American* **and Bernardo Houssay** *Argentinian*
Studies of insulin, the pancreas and the pituitary gland

1948 **Paul Müller** *Swiss*
Invention of DDT insecticide

1949 **Walter Hess** *Swiss* **and Antonio Egas Moniz** *Portuguese*
Study of the middle brain and development of leucotomy as a treatment for psychosis

1950 **Philip Hench and Edward Kendall** *American* **and Tadeusz Reichstein** *Swiss*
Study of the structure and functions of adrenal cortex hormones

1951 **Max Theiler** *South African-born American*
Development of a vaccine against yellow fever

1952 **Selman Waksman** *American*
Discovery of streptomycin

1953 **Fritz Lipmann** *American* **and Hans Adolf Krebs** *German-born British*
Discovery of coenzyme A and the citric acid cycle in biosynthesis

1954 **John Enders, Thomas Weller and Frederick Robbins** *American*
Development of a method of producing polio virus in tissue culture

1955 **Hugo Theorell** *Swedish*
Studies of the nature and action of oxidation enzymes

1956 **Werner Forssmann** *German*, **Dickinson Richards and André Cournand** *American*
Discoveries concerning cardiac catheterization

1957 **Daniel Bovet** *Italian*
Discovery of antihistamines and production of synthetic curare

1958 **George Beadle, Edward Tatum and Joshua Lederberg** *American*
Discoveries in biochemical and bacterial genetics

1959 **Severo Ochoa and Arthur Kornberg** *American*
Discovery of enzymes for the artificial synthesis of nucleic acids

1960 **Macfarlane Burnet** *Australian* **and Peter Medawar** *British*
Study of acquired immunity tolerance to tissue transplants

1961 **Georg von Békésy** *Hungarian-born American*
Mechanism of sound discrimination by the inner ear

1962 **Francis Crick and Maurice Wilkins** *British* **and James Watson** *American*
Discovery of the molecular structure of deoxyribonucleic acid (DNA)

1963 **John Eccles** *Australian*, **Alan Hodgkin and Andrew Huxley** *British*
Study of the transmission and behavior of nerve impulses

1964 **Konrad Bloch** *American* **and Feodor Lynen** *German*
Discoveries concerning cholesterol and fatty-acid metabolism

1965 **François Jacob, André Lwoff and Jacques Monod** *French*
Studies of the control of the synthesis of hormones by the genes

1966 **Charles Huggins and Francis Rous** *American*
Discovery of virus-induced cancer and development of a hormone treatment for cancer

1967 **Haldan Hertline and George Wald** *American* **and Ragnar Granit** *Swedish*
Studies in the biochemistry and physiology of the eye

1968 **Robert Holley, Gobind Khorana and Marshall Nirenberg** *American*
Explanation of the genetic control of cell function

1969 **Max Delbrück, Alfred Hershey and Salvador Luria** *American*
Research concerning bacteriophages and viral diseases

1970 **Julius Axelrod** *American*, **Bernard Katz** *British* **and Ulf von Euler** *Swedish*
Discoveries concerning the chemistry of nerve transmission

1971 **Earl Sutherland** *American*
Hormone action and the discovery of cyclic AMP

1972 **Gerald Edelman** *American* **and Rodney Porter** *British*
Research on the chemical structure of antibodies

1973 **Karl von Frisch and Konrad Lorenz** *German*, **and Nikolaas Tinbergen** *Dutch*
Studies of animal behavior patterns

1974 **Albert Claude and George Palade** *American*, **Christian de Duve** *Belgian*
Research into the structure and functions of parts of the cell

1975 **Renato Dulbecco, Haward Temin and David Baltimore** *American*
Studies of the effects of viruses on cancer cell genes

1976 **Baruch Blumberg and Carleton Gajdusek** *American*
Studies of the origin and etiology of viral diseases

1977 **Rosalyn Yalow, Roger Guillemin and Andrew Schally** *American*
The role of the pituitary hormones in body chemistry

1978 **Werner Arber** *Swiss*, **Daniel Nathans and Hamilton Smith** *American*
Discovery of enzymes that fragment DNA

▲ Thomas Hunt Morgan, American biochemist and prizewinner in 1933.

1979 **Allan Cormack** *American* **and Godfrey Hounsfield** *British*
Development of the computerized axial tomography (CAT) scanner

1980 **Baruj Benacerraf and George Snell** *American* **and Jean Dausset** *French*
Studies of the genetic control of the immune system

1981 **Roger Sperry and David Hubel** *American*, **and Torsten Wiesel** *Swedish*
Studies of brain organization and functioning of cerebral cortex

1982 **Sune Bergström and Bengt Samuelsson** *Swedish* **and John Vane** *British*
Biochemistry and physiology of prostaglandins

1983 **Barbara McClintock** *American*
Discovery of anomalous intracellular cell behavior

1984 **Niels Jerne** *British-Danish*, **Georges Köhler** *German* **and César Milstein** *Argentinian*
Technique for monoclonal antibody production

1985 **Michael Brown and Joseph Goldstein** *American*
Relationship between cholesterol and heart disease

1986 **Stanley Cohen** *American* **and Rita Levi-Montalcini** *Italian*
Studies in the growth of cells and organs

1987 **Tonegawa Susumu** *Japanese*
Discovery of how genes alter to form antibodies against specific antigens

1988 **James Black** *British*, **Gertrude Elion and George Hitchings** *American*
Discovery of beta-blockers, H-2 blockers and anticancer drugs

1989 **Michael Bishop and Harold Varmus** *American*
Research on cancer-causing genes (oncogenes)

1990 **Joseph Murray and Donnall Thomas** *American*
Work on transplanting human organs and bone marrow

1991 **Erwin Neher** *German* **and Bert Sakman**
Discoveries in how cells communicate with one another

1992 **Edmond Fisher and Edwin Krebs** *American*
Discovery of a regulatory mechanism in most cells

1993 **Richard Roberts** *British* **and Philip Sharp** *American*
Discoveries in how genes are contained within DNA

INDEX

Figures in *italic type* refer to the captions to the illustrations, and to Timechart entries; figures in **bold type** refer to the Keywords and Factfile articles.

A

aardvark 96
abdomen **16**, 54, 55
absorption **16**, 66, *66*
accommodation **16**
acetyl coenzyme A 154
acetylcholine **16**, 39, 77
Achilles tendon 108
acquired characteristics **16**
acquired immunity deficiency syndrome (AIDS) *15*, 47
acrosin *123*
acrosome *123*
actin **16**, 104, *105*
action potential **16**, 37
active transport **16**, 43
Adam's apple 134
adaptation **16**, 89, *89*, 96–97, *96*, *97*, 110
  convergent evolution 96
adenine 25–26
adenosine diphosphate (ADP) 62, 152
adenosine triphosphate (ATP) **16**, 22, 26, 27, 35, 41, 43, 62, 104, 152
adipose tissue 28, 64
adrenal cortex 40, 75
adrenal gland **16–17**, 26, 30, 74
adrenal medulla 74
adrenaline **17**, 17, 44, 75. *See also* epinephrine
aggression **17**, 142
aging **17**, 119
airfoil 112
akiapolaau bird 96
alarm signal 142
albatross 113
Alcmaeon of Creton 12, *12*
alcohol *69*
aldosterone 16, **17**
algae **17**, 22, 24, 35, 53, 58, *58*, *59*, 100
  blue-green (cyanobacteria) 17, 22
  protoctist 17
alimentary canal **17**
allantois *124*
alligator 126
alternation of generations **17**
altricial young *119*
alula 112
alveolus **17**, 33, *72*
ameba **17**, *17*, 59, 66, 104
amino acid *14*, *15*, **17**, 33, 40, 46, 62, *62*, 63, 68, *69*, 74
ammonia 68, *69*
amnion **17**, *124*, *125*
amphibian **17**, 56, 126
amylase 27, 42
anabolism 34
anatomy, history of *12–15*
androgen 33
anglerfish 90
Animalia 32, 148–49
annelid worm **17**, 50, 106
ant *86*, 91, *94*, 100, *101*, 126, 140
anteater 88, 96
antelope 67, 87, 91, 100, *100*, 108, *119*
antenna **17**, 55, *55*, 135, 137
antibody **17**, 30, 63, 70, *80*
anticoagulant 42, 97, *97*, 98
antidiuretic hormone (ADH) **18**, 37, 40, 78
antigen 17, **18**, *80*
antitoxin **18**, 30, 46
antler **18**, 120
antlion 91
anus 17, 23
ape 110, 142
aphid 54, 97, 100
appendix 67, 81, 87
apterygote 31
arachnid **18**, 54, *55*, 98
archerfish 90
Aristotle 12, *12*
arteriole 46, 71
artery **18**
arthrodial membrane 32
arthropod **18**, 54–55, *55*, *70*, 71, 76, 98, 106, *106*
assimilation **18**, 67
atrium 30
Audubon, John James *13*
autotroph **18**
avocet *89*
axon **18**, 37
ayeaye 96

B

baboon 142
backbone *see* spine
bacteria 14, **18**, 22, 35, *67*, 80–81, *80*, *94*, 99
  as decomposers 94
  parasitic 99
  symbiotic 67, *67*, 87, 95, 100
bacteriophage *14*
badger *101*
balance **18–19**, *18*, 26, 106, 108, *108*, 139
baleen **19**, 92, 135
ball-and-socket joint 56
Banting, Frederick *14*, *146*
barbel 137, *139*
barnacle 54, *55*, *92*, 98, 99, 100, 128
bat *57*, *84*, 97, 112, 113, 135
bat-eared fox 135
Bayer, Karl Ernest von *13*
beak 19, 34, 86, *87*, 89, *89*
bear 84, *85*, 90, *92*, *93*, 96, 136–37, 142
Beaumont, William *13*, 14
beaver 87
bed bug 98
bee 85, *101*, 126, 132, 134, 139, 140
  dance *14*, 15, 140
bee-eater 90
beetle 54, 94
  bark- and wood-boring 95
Bell, Charles *13*
Belon, Pierre *12*
Best, Charles *14*, *154*
Bichat, Marie-François-Xavier *13*
bilateral symmetry **19**
bile **19**, 33
bill 86, *87*, 89, *89*, *96*
binary fission 18, **19**
binocular vision **19**, *19*, 56, 133
biochemistry *12–15*, **19**
biological clock **19**, 120
bird **19**, 56
  circulation *73*
  digestive system 67
  eggs 68
  excretion 68, *69*
  flight 112–13, *112*, *113*
bird of paradise *121*
birth 40
bivalve **19**, 52, *52*, 92
bladder **19**, 46
blastula 32
blinking 80
blood **20**, *20*, 50
  assimilation through 67
  B-cell *80*, 81
  circulation *see* circulation
  clotting **23**, 29, 33, 40, 80, *84*
  erythrocyte 20, 22, 30, 33, **41**, *65*, 68, *69*, 72
  hemoglobin *see* hemoglobin
  leukocyte 20, 30, **47**, 80
  lymphocyte 20, **33**, 47
  macrophage 47, 80, *80*, *81*
  neutrophil 80, 81
  oxygenation *71*, 72
  phagocyte white cell 17, 20, **39**, 47, *65*
  plasma **40**
  platelet (thrombocyte) 20, 23, **40**, *81*
  salt content 69, 78
  sugar content *69*, 75, *75*
  T-cell *80*, 81
  thermoregulation by 78
  transfusion 81
  water content 69, 78
blood pressure **20**, 46, 71, *73*, 75, 78
blood vessel system *12*, 21
bloodhound 137, *137*
bloodsucker *84*, 96, 97, *97*, 98, *98*, 99
bloodsucking fly 96
blowfly 94–95
blowhole *73*
blubber 25
blue whale 92, 118
bone **20**, 56, *65*, 95, 108
  membrane 20
  repair 80
  spongy 20
bone marrow 20, 40, 41, 47, 81
Bonnet, Charles *13*
booby, blue-footed *121*
book lung **20**, 54
brachiation *111*
brain **20**, *20*, 37, 76, *76*, 80, 108
breastbone *see* sternum
breathing **20**, 31, 41, 42, 72, *72*, *73*
breeding
  display 119, 120, *121*
  grounds 120
Breuer, Joseph *14*
bronchiole *72*
bronchus **20**, 33, *72*
brood pouch 126
brooding 126, *126*, *127*
bubble nest 126
bubble-net 91, *91*
buccal cavity 17
Buchner, Eduard *14*
budding 18, 21
Buffon, Comte de *13*
bug 126
buoyancy **21**, 44, 112, 114
burrowing 78, 110, 126
butterfly 85, 96–97, *97*, *101*, 128, 139
butterfly fish 96
buzzing 134

C

caddis fly 91
calcitonin 45
calcium 45
camel 78, 108
camouflage **21**, 56, 90, 119, 125
canine teeth **21**, 86, *89*, *93*
capillary **21**, 46, 71, 72, *72*
carapace **21**, 106
carbohydrate **21**, 68
carbon 62
carbon dioxide **21**, 68, 72
carnassial **21**, 36
carnivore 67, 84, *84*, 88–89, *89*
carotenoid 39
carrion-eater 84
cartilage **21**, 134
caste 43, 140
cat *79*, 90, *106*, 108, *132*, 142
catabolism 34
caterpillar **21**, 32, 54, *73*, 85, *86*, 128
catfish 137, *139*
cattle 67, 87, 100, *100*
cecum 52, 67, 87
cell **21–22**, *21*, 64, *64*, *65*
  absorption 16
  active transport 16
  composition 62
  connective 64
  cytosol 64
  differentiation (specialization) 118
  discovery of cells 14
  division *14*, **22**, 34, 36, *64*, 80, 118, *123*, 124, *125*
  endoplasmic reticulum **27**, 42, 64, *64*, 70
  epithelial 64
  eukaryotic 21, 22, 24, **27**, 34, 35, 36, 37, 42, 154
  membrane 21, **22**, **34**, 38, 64, *64*, 69, 104
  microtubule 64, *64*
  mitochondrion 64, *64*, *65*
  multicellular species 50, 70
  mutation 122
  nerve 64
  nucleus 21, 25, **37**, 64, *64*, 118, 122
  organelle **38**
  osmosis 69
  prokaryotic *22*, **40**
  respiration 64
  single-celled species 50, 58–59, *58*, *59*
  spindle 36
cellulose 21, **22**, 86, 87, 95
celom 124
centipede **22**, *94*, 126
central nervous system (CNS) *13*, 37, 43, 76, 104, *105*
centriole *64*
cephalopod 22, 52, *52*
cephalothorax 54
cerci 31
cerebal cortex 20, *76*
cerebal hemisphere **22**
cerebellum *13*, 20
cerebrum 20, 22
chameleon 88, 90
Chatton, Edouard *15*
cheetah 90, *106*, 108, 133
chemical control 74–75, *74*, *75*, 80
chemical reaction **22**
chimpanzee 89, *143*
chitin 21, **22**, 54, 86
chiton *52*
chloroid layer *132*
chlorophyll **22**, 32, 39
chloroplast 22
chondrocyte 21
chordate **22**, 56
chromosome 21, **22**, 25, 34, 36, *123*
chrysalis 41, 128. *See also* pupa
cicada 128, 134, 135
cilia **23**, *50*, 70, 92, 104
ciliary muscle *132*
ciliate **23**, *58*, 59, *59*
circulation **23**, *23*, 50, 70–71, *70*, *71*
  closed 20, 71
  double *71*, *73*
  hormones 74
  open 20, **38**, *70*, 71
  single **43**, *71*
  thermoregulation *71*
citric acid cycle *see* Krebs cycle
cladistics *15*
clam 52, *52*, 100, 119, 122
classification of species 12–13, *12*, *15*, **23**, *23*, 32, **146**
clavicle (collar bone) 39, 106
claw **23**, 96, 98, *111*
cleanerfish 100, 120
cleaning and symbiosis 100
climbing 110, *111*
cloaca **23**
clotting **23**
clownfish *101*
cnidarian **23**, 50, *51*
cochlea 19, 26, *134*
cocoon **23**, 128
coelacanth *15*
coelenterate *see* cnidarian
coelenteron 25
coelom 50
coenzyme 47
cold-blooded animal **23**, 45
collagen 21, 33, 45
collar bone *see* clavicle
Colombo, Realdo *12*
commensalism **24**
communication
  alarm signals 142
  bee dance *14*, 15, 140
  courtship **24**, 120, *121*, *122*, 142, *142*, *143*
  pheromone **39**, 120, 136, 137, *137*, 140, 142
  social insects and animals 140, 142, *143*
  sound 134–35
  taste and smell 136
compass termite 139
competition 96
conditioning *14*
conduction *79*
cone 28, 133
conjunction 40
conjunctiva *132*
constrictor snake 88
contractile vacuole **24**, 58, 69
copepod *55*, 59
copperhead snake 90
coral **24**, 50, 53, 88, 100, 122, 128
cormorant *69*
cornea 28, *132*, *133*
corpus luteum 27, 155
Corti *134*
coughing 72
counter-current flow **24**
courtship **24**, 119, 120, *121*, *122*, *142*, *143*
cowbird 126
crab 54, *55*, 80, 95, *95*, 99, 100, 114, *119*, *128*
cranefly 95
crawling 110, *110*
crazer *87*
crepuscular activity 25
Crick, Francis *15*
cricket 129, 134
cries and calls 45, 134
crinoid **24**, 53
crocodile 88, 90, *91*, 114, 124, *124*
crop **24**, 25, *51*, *67*
crossbill 86, *87*
crustacean **24**, 54, *55*, 95, *95*, 98
cuckoo 126
cud 42
cuticle **24**, 26, 112, 118, 129, *133*, 134, 137, 138, 139
cuttlefish *52*
Cuvier, Georges *13*
cyanobacteria 17, 22
cytoplasm **24**, 35, 59, *65*, 66
cytosine 25–26
cytosol 24, 64

D

danger 136, 142
Darwin, Charles 13, 14–15, *14*, 27
deamination 68, *69*
decapod **24**
deciduous tooth 35
decomposer **24–25**, 84, 94–95, *94*, *95*
decomposition 94
deer 67, 87, 120, 142
defense systems 80–81, *80*, *81*
deficiency disease 47
dendrite **25**
dentine 45

deoxyribonucleic acid (DNA) *15*, 17, 21–22, **25–26**, *25*, 27, 29, 36, 37
  mitochondrial 35
deoxyribose 37
dermis 43
desmid *58*
detritivore **25**, 53, 84, 93, 95
diaphragm 16, 20, **25**
diastema **25**, 87
diastolic pressure 20
diatom *58*, *59*
diet *see* food and feeding
differentiation **25**
diffusion **25**, 38, 50, 64, 67, 69, 70, 72, 74
digestion *13*, 14, **25**, 33, 42, 50, 66–67, *66*, *67*
  alimentary canal 17
  bile **19**, 33
  digestive enzymes 151
  external 66, 97
  herbivores 86, *87*
  human digestive system 66
  symbiotic bacteria 67, *67*, 87, 95, 100
digit 108, 110, *111*
dikdik 87
diploid 17, 22, **25**
disaccharide 21
dispersal of species **25**
display 56, 119, 120, *121*
diurnal **25**
diving mammal **25**, 72, *73*
DNA *see* deoxyribonucleic acid
dog 78, 88, 91, 94, *106*, 108, 126, 135, 137, *137*, 142
dolphin 56, *57*, *73*, 88, 100, 114, *115*, *135*
Domagk, Gerhard *15*
dor beetle *95*
dormouse *79*
dorsal **26**
dragonfly 54, 112, *113*, 118, 128, *128*
drone 140
drugs *69*
duck *87*
dung beetle 95
dung fly 95
duodenum 31, 66

E

eagle *89*
ear **26**, 38, *65*, 134–35, *134*
ear drum 26, 134–35, *134*
ear wax 80
earthworm 50, *51*, 67, *94*, 95, 106, *107*, 122
earwig 135
ecdysis **26**, 36, 129
ecdysone 129
echinoderm **26**, 52–53, 106
echolocation *15*, **26**, *135*
ectoderm **26**, 124
ectoparasite **26**, 98, *98*, 100, *100*
ectoplasm 24
ectotherm 23
eel 26, 88, 136
egestion 28
egg 17, *22*, **26**, 26, 29, 33, 38, 42, 43, 47, 70, 122, *122*, *123*, 124–25, *124*, *125*, 126, 155
  bird 68
  incubation *79*, 126
  mammal *13*
egg tooth **26**
egret, cattle 100
Ehrlich, Paul *14*
electric fish **26**, *138*, 139
electron transport chain **26**, 154
elephant *79*, 87, 106, 119, *119*
elephant-snout 139
embryo **26**, 124, *125*
embryology 13
Empedocles of Akragas 12, *12*
endocrine gland 16, **26**, 74
endoderm **26**, 124
endoparasite **26**, 26, 99, *99*
endoplasm 24
endoplasmic reticulum **27**, 42, 64, *64*, 70
endorphin *15*
endoskeleton **27**, 106
endothermic 78. *See also* warm-blooded animal
endotoxin 45
energy 62
  consumption and food supply 84, *84*
  elastic 108
  Krebs cycle *15*, 41, **152**, *152*
enteric cavity 25
enzyme *13*, *14*, 22, **27**, *27*, 40, 63, 64
  digestive 151
epidermis 32, 43, 44, 124
epinephrine 17, 75, *75*. *See also* adrenaline
epithelium **27**, 64
erythrocyte *see* blood
esophagus 17, **27**, **39**
estivation **27**
estrogen **27**, 27, 33, 38, 155
estrus cycle **27**
ethology 15, *15*
eukaryote 21, 22, 24, **27**, 34, 35, 36, 37, 42, 154
Eustachian tube 39, *134*
evolution **27**, 36
  convergent 96
excretion **27**, 68–69, *69*
  role of decomposers 94, 95, *95*
exocrine gland **28**
exocytosis **28**
exoskeleton 18, 21, 26, 32, 54, 105, 106, *106*
exoskeleton *see* skeleton
exotoxin 45–46
extinction **28**
eye **28**, *28*, 132–33, *132*, *133*
  accommodation 16
  binocular vision **19**, *19*, 56, 133
  color vision **23–24**, 132, *132*, 133
  compound **24**, 28, 55, *55*, 133, *133*
  cone 28, 133
  night vision **37**
  rod 28, 37, **42**, *65*, 133
  simple *55*, 133
  third 133
eyespot 59

F

Fabre, Henri *14*
Fabricius, Hieronymus *12*, 13
facial expression *143*
fallopian tube 38, *125*
fat **28**, 33, 56, 62–63, 64, 68
fatty acid **28**, 33, 62–63
feather **28**, 32, 56, 78, 110, 112–13, *112*, *113*
  contour **24**
  molting 118–19
  pressure-sensitive 139
feather star 53
feces **28**, 68
feeler *see* antenna
fennec fox *134*
fertilization *13*, **28**, *28*, 122, *122*, *123*, 124–25, *125*
  cross-fertilization 28
  external 28, 122
  internal 28, 39, 43, 122, *123*
  self-fertilization 28
fetus **29**, 118, *125*
fibrin **29**, 45, *81*
fibrinogen 29, 45, *81*
"fight or flight" response 44, 75, 153
filaria worm 99
filoplume 139
filter-feeder **29**, *52*, 53, 54, 84, 92, *92*, 95, *128*
fin **29**, 114, *115*
Fischer, Emil 14
fish **29**, *71*, 72, 126
five-kingdom classification *15*, 32, **146–47**
flagellate 17, **29**, 59, *59*
flagellum **29**, 70, 104, *137*
flame cell *see* solenocyte
flamingo 92, *92*
flapping 112
flatfish 90, *114*
flatworm 50, *50*, *51*, 80, 105
flea 98, *104*, 108
Flemming, Walther *14*
flight 112–13, *112*, *113*
flipper 25, 56, 114
Flourens, Pierre *13*
fluid, control of body 18, 38, 69, 78
fluke 50, 99
fly **29**, 66, 94, *94*, *97*, 128
flycatcher 90
follicle-stimulating hormone (FSH) 153
food chain **29**, *29*, 62, 94, *94*
food and feeding **38**, 84–85
  absorption 66, *66*
  energy consumption and food supply 84, *84*
  food stores *85*
  hunger and thirst 84, 139
  minerals 150
  processing food 66–67, *66*, *67*
  regurgitation **41**, 42, 140
  specialized diets 96–97, *96*, *97*
  storage of surplus food 67, 68, *69*
  symbiosis 100
  taste and smell 136–37, *136*, *137*
  vitamins 151
  see also carnivore; digestion; herbivore; omnivore; parasite
foot 106, 108
  false *see* pseudopod
  tube *see* tube foot
  webbed 114, *115*
foraminiferan 59
fovea *132*, 133
fox 90, 94, *126*, *134*, 135
Fricke, H *15*
friction 106, 108
Frisch, Karl von *14*, 15
frog 56, *56*, 72, 88, 90, *113*, 114, 125, 126, 128, *128*, 129, 134
frog kick 114
Fungi 32, 94, *94*, 95, *141*, 148
fur *see* hair

G

Galen *12*
gall bladder 19, 68
Galvani, Luigi *13*
gamete 17, 22, 26, 28, **29**, 34, 42, 43, 122
gametophyte 17
ganglion 50, *51*, 76
gastropod *52*
gecko *111*
gene **29**, 118, 122, 124
  adaptation 16
genetic code **29**
genetic drift 27
genetic mutation 27
genetics **29**, 30
genus **30**
gerenuk 87, *142*, *143*
germ-plasm theory of heredity *14*
gestation 119, 120. *See also* pregnancy
gibbon 110, *111*
gill 52, 54, 68, 70, *71*, 72, *73*, *128*
  counter-current flow **24**
gill chamber 137
gill-raker 92
gill slit 56
giraffe *86*, 87, 106
gizzard 25, 67
gliding 112–13, *113*
glucagon 38
glucose 33, 41, 152
glycerol 33
glycogen 21, 33, 68, *69*
glycolysis 41, 154
Golgi apparatus 34, *64*, *65*, 70
gonads 40
goose pimple 78
Graafian follicle 27
grasshopper 54, 108, *109*, 129, 134, 135
gravity 19
grazer 87, *87*
greeting ceremony 142
Griffin, Donald *15*
grizzly bear 92
groomimg, mutual 142
growth 45, 118–19, *118*, *119*, 126, *126*, *127*
guanine 25–26
guano *69*
gut *see* intestine

H

hagfish 95
hair 32, 34, 56, 78, *111*, 135, *138*, 138
  molting 118–19
Haller, Albrecht von *13*
Hamilton, W.D. 15, *15*
hand 110, *111*
Hanson, J *15*
haploid 17, **30**
hare 106, 119, 120
hawfinch *87*
hearing 134–35, *134*, *135*
heart *12*, **30**, *30*, 36, 50, 52, 70–71, *70*, *71*
heat *see* thermoregulation
heat pit **30**, 138, *139*
heat sensor 138, *139*
Heinroth, Oskar 15
hemoglobin *15*, 20, **30**, 41, 63, 72
hemolymph 20, 38
Hennig, William *15*
herbivore 25, 30, 67, 84, *85*, 86–87, *86*, *87*, *89*, 100
heredity 37
hermaphrodite **30**, 42, 43, 122, *122*
hermit crab 100, *119*
herring 92
hibernation **30**, 75, 78, *79*
hide beetle 94
hierarchy 39, 142
HIV *15*
Hodgkin, Alan 15
homeothermic see warm-blooded animal
honeycreeper *96*
honey-eater 97
honeyguide *101*
hoof 23, 32
Hooke, Robert *12*, 14
Hopkins, Frederick Gowland *14*
hormone **30**, 63, *118*
  aging process 119
  as control chemical 74–75, *74*, *75*
  digestion 67
  disposal of waste hormones 69
  genetic control 118
  mammalian hormones 152–53
  metamorphosis 129
  secretion 74
horn 32
horse 108, *119*
housefly *97*
hovering 112
Hughes, J *15*
human *57*, *71*, 119, 132, 139
  alimentary canal 17
  circulation *72*, *73*
  diet 92, *93*
  eye *132*, 133
  hearing *134*
  movement *105*, *108*
  reproduction 124, *125*
  skeleton 106, *108*
  speech 45, 134
hummingbird 85, *96*, 97, 112
humors *132*
humpback whale 91, *91*
hunger 84, 139
hunting 90–91, *91*, *126*
Huxley, Andrew *15*
Huxley, Hugh *15*
Huxley, Thomas Henry 27
hydra 69, 100, 122, 124
hydrofoil **30**, 114
hydrogen 62
hydroid 50, *51*
hyena 91, 94
hypothalamus 37, 40, 74, *75*, 78

I

ileum 31
ilium 39
imago 31
immune system *14*, **30**, 47, 80–81, *80*, 98
immunology *14*
imperial units 144
imprinting 15
incisor **30**, 86, 87, *89*
incubation *79*, 126
incus 38
infrasound 35
inherited characteristic 122
insect **31**, 31, *31*, 54, 55, 71, *73*, 89, 96–97, *97*, 106, 112, 137
instinct *14*, 15, 15
insulin *14*, 38, 63, 75, *75*
intercostal muscle 20
intestine 17, 25, **31**, 35, 47, 50, 52, *65*, 66, 67, 81, 87
invertebrate *13*, **31**, 70–71, *70*
involuntary action **31**
ion **31**
iris 28, **31**
ischium 39
islets of Langerhans 38, *75*

J

jackal 94, *94*
jackrabbit *71*
Jacobson's organ **31**
jaw **31**, *56*, 86, *86*, *89*, *93*
  see also beak; bill; teeth
jay 85
jejunum 31
jellyfish **31–32**, *31*, 50, *50*, *51*, 88
jet propulsion **32**, 43, *50*, *55*, 114, *115*
joint **32**, 33, 105, 106, 108
jumping *104*, 108, *109*, 110, *111*
juvenile 118

K

kangaroo *79*, *104*, 106, 108, 120, *125*
keratin 28, **32**, 43, 118
kidney **32**, *32*, 34, 46, *65*, 69, *69*, 70, 78
killer whale 91
kingdom **32**
kingfisher 88, *112*
koala 84, *85*
Krebs, Hans Adolf *15*, 152
Krebs cycle *15*, 41, **152**, *152*

L

lacrimal gland 44
lactation **32**
lacteal **32**
ladybird *123*
Lamarck, Jean-Baptiste *13*, 27
lamprey *98*
lancelet **32**, 56
Landsteiner, Karl *147*
larva 31, **32**, 94, 118, 128, *128*, 129, 140
larynx 134
lateral line system 19, **33**, *33*, 56, 135
leech 50, 98
Leeuwenhoek, Anton van *12*, 14
lek 120
lens 16, 28
leukocyte *see* blood
licking 78, *79*
life cycle **33**
ligament 32, **33**, 63
limb 110, 114
Linnaeus, Carl *12*, 13
lion *56*, *84*, 85, 88, *89*, 91, *93*, 94, 126
lip 134
lipase 27
lipid 28, **33**
liver 19, **33**, 46, 68, *69*, *75*, 78, 80
lizard 90, 108, *109*, *113*, *118*, 133
lobster 54, *55*, *70*
locust 86
Loewi, Otto *14*
longevity 119
Lorenz, Konrad 15, *15*
lung 17, 20, **33**, *33*, 68, *71*, 72, *73*
  book **20**, 54
lure 90
luteinizing hormone (LH) **33**, 155
Lyell, Charles 27
lymph 21, 32, **33–34**, 67, 71, 81
lymph node 81
lymphatic 33
lymphocyte *see* blood
lymphokinins 81
lysosome *64*

M

macromolecule 62
macrophage *see* blood
maggot 29, 94, *94*
magnetism, sensitivity to 35, 139
malaria 58
malleus 38
Malpighi, Marcello *12*
mammal **34**, 56, *56*, 126
  diving **25**, 72, *73*
  eggs *13*
  flight 112
mammary gland 32, **34**, 34, 35
mandible 31, **34**, 86
mantis 54, 88, 90
mantle **34**, 52, *52*
marine snow 95
marmoset 97
marsupial **34**, 34, *113*, 125, *125*, 126
mating 120, *121*, 136, 142, *142*, *143*
maxilla 31, **34**
mayfly 128
measurement, units of 144–45
medicine, time chart *12–15*
medulla **34**
medulla oblongata 20
medusa **34**
meerkat *127*
meiosis *14*, 17, 22, **34**
melanin **34**, 43
membrane **34**, *34*
memory 76
Mendel, Gregor 27, 29–30
menstrual cycle **153**, *153*
menstruation 40, 41
mesoderm 124
mesoglea *51*
metabolic pathway **34**
metabolic rate 45, 71
metabolism **34**, *62*, *62*, 63, 78, 99, 139
metabolite 34
metamorphosis 30, **35**, *35*, 128–29, *128*
metazoan **35**
metric units 144
  conversion to and from 144
  prefixes 144
microbiology 35
microfibril 22
microorganism **35**
microscope 14
microtubule 64, *64*, 104
microvillus **35**
midge 94
migration **35**, 75, 120, 136
milk 32, **35**, 126
milk tooth **35**
millipede **35**, *94*, 95
minerals and diet 150
mite **35**, *55*, *95*, 98, 100
mitochondrion **35**, *35*, 58, 64, *64*, *65*
mitosis *14*, *22*, **36**
molar **36**, 86, 87, *89*, *93*, 126
molecule 62, 62
molerat 142
mollusk **36**, 52, *52*, 86, *87*, 106, 119
molting **36**, 54, 80, 118–19, *118*, *128*, 129
Monera 32, 148
monkey 110, 142
monogamy **36**
monosaccharide 21
monotreme 34, **36**, 126
mosquito 96, 97, *97*, *98*, 99, 128, *128*, 135
moth 94, 96–97, *126*, 128, 137, *137*
motor neuron **36**
mouse 87, 142
mouth 17
movement 104–15
mucus **36**, 70, 80, *99*, *101*, *137*
mucus net 93
mullet, gray 95
muscle **36**, 63, 104, *104*, *105*, 106
  antagonistic 105
  cardiac 36
  cells *65*
  coordination 139
  flight 112
  oxygen storage 72
  peristalsis 50, 67
  skeletal 104, *105*
  sliding filament theory *15*, 104
  smooth 36
  striated 36
muscle fibre **36**, 104
mussel 52, *52*, 70, 92, 122
mutation 16, **36**
mutualism *see* symbiosis
myelin sheath **36**
myofibril 36, 104, *105*
myoglobin **36**, 72
myosin **36**, 104, *105*

N

nail 23, 32
natural selection 13, *14*, 27, **36**
nautilus *52*
navigation 35, 138, 139
nectar-feeder 85, 96–97, *96*, *97*
nematocyst **36**
nematode **36–37**, *94*, *98*
Neo-Darwinism 27
neotinin 129
nephridium **37**, *51*
nerve **37**
nerve cell 44, 64, *65*
nerve excitation *15*
nerve fibre 76, 77, 138
nerve impulse 74
nervous system **37**, 76, *76*, *77*
  action potential 16
  automatic (involuntary) **18**, 39, 44, 76
  brain **20**, *20*
  central *see* central nervous system
  damage 80
  dendrite **25**
  digestion, absorption and assimilation 67
  dorsal nerve cord 56
  electrical impulses *13*, 76
  ganglion 50, *51*, 76
  hearing *134*
  muscle movement 104, *105*, 108
  nerve cell insulation 63
  parasympathetic 18, **39**, 44
  reflex action **41**
  sensory and motor nerves distinguished *13*
  sight 132
  somatic (voluntary) 76
  sympathetic 18, **44**
nest 120, 126, *140*, *141*
net-casting spider 90–91
neurohormone **37**
neuromuscular junction 37, **44**
neuron 36, **37**, 43, 76
  sensory **42**
neurotransmitter *14*, 16, 20, **37**, 37, 39
neutrophil *see* blood
newt 56, 114, 122
nicotinamide adenine dinucleotide phosphate (NADP) 152
night vision **37**
nightjar *89*
nipple 32, 34
nitrogen 62
Nobel Prize for Physiology or Medicine prizewinners **154–55**
nocturnal **37**, *132*, 133, 138, *139*
noradrenaline 17, **44**, 75
norepinephrine *74*, *75*
nose 136, *136*, 137, *137*
nostril 39, 136, *136*, 137
notochord 22, **37**, *37*, 56
nuclear envelope **37**
nucleic acid **37**, 122
nucleotide 25, 62, 63
nucleus 21, 25, **37**, 64, *64*, 118, 122
nursery chamber 126
nuthatch 110
nutrient **37**, *37*, 70
nutrition **38**
nymph 31, **38**, *128*

O

octopus *52*, 90, 126
olfaction *see* smell
olfactory **38**
olfactory nerve 43
olfactory sensor 136, 137
ommatidium 24, *133*
omnivore **38**, 84, 92–93, *92*, *93*
operculum **38**, 72
opisthosoma 54, *55*
optic nerve 28, **38**, 42
orangutan *127*
orb-web spider *121*
order **38**
organ **38**, 45, 50, 64
organelle 24, **38**, 58, *58*, 64, *65*
organic compound 14
oropendula 126
Osborne, Thomas *14*
osmoregulation **38**, 69
osmosis **38**, 69, 78
ossicle 34, **38**, *134*
osteoblast 20, 80
osteoclast 80
osteocyte 20, *65*
ostrich 108
otolith organ 19
otter 114
oval window *134*
ovary 26, 30, 33, **38**, 75, 155
oviduct **38**, 70
ovipary 26, **38**
ovipositor 31
ovivipary 26, **38**
ovum *see* egg
owl *132*, 133, 135
oxen *100*, 142
oxpecker 100, *100*
oxygen 62, 70, *71*, 72, 154
oxyhemoglobin 41
oxytocin **38**, 40

P

pack hunting 91, 126
pain **38**
palp **38**
pancreas 26, 30, **38**, 74, *75*
panda *96*
pangolin 96
panting 78
paramecia 23, *58*, 59, *59*
parasite **38–39**, 54, 58, *59*, 84, 98–99, *98*, *99*, 122, 126
  external (ectoparasite) **26**, 98, *98*, 100, *100*
  internal (endoparasite) 26, 99, *99*
parathyroid 26, 30, 74
parental care 126, *126*, *127*
parrotfish 89
parthenogenesis **39**
Pasteur, Louis *14*
Pauling, Linus *15*
Pavlov, Ivan *14*
pecking order **39**
pectoral girdle (shoulder girdle) **39**, 106
pedicellariae 53, *53*
pedipalp **39**, *55*
pedomorphosis 129
pelican 91
pelvic girdle **39**, 106
pelvis 106
penguin *79*, 114
penis **39**, 122
pepsin *13*
peptide *62*, 74
peregrine falcon 90
peristalsis 31, **39**, *39*, 50, 67
Perutz, Max *15*
pH scale **39**
phagocyte *see* blood
pharynx 17, **39**, 52
pheromone **39**, 120, 136, 137, *137*, 140, 142
phosphate 45
phosphorus 62
photosynthesis 22, **39**, *58*, *59*, 62, 100
phyloplankton **39**
phylum **39**
physiology, history of *12–15*
phytoplankton 40
pigment 19, 30, **39**, 132, 133
pillbug *55*
pilotfish 100
pincer **39**
pineal body 133
pinna *134*
pinocytosis **39**
pipefish 96, 126
piranha 89, 91
pit viper 138, *139*
pituitary gland 18, 26, 30, 33, 38, **40**, 45, 74, 129, 148
placenta **40**, 125, *125*
placental mammal 34
plankton **40**, 95, *128*
Plantae 32, 146
plasma 20, **40**
plasmagel 24
plasmasol 24
platelet (thrombocyte) *see* blood
platyhelminthes 50
platypus *115*
play *126*
pleural membrane *72*
poikilothermic 23
polar bear 90, 136–37
polar body *123*
pollination 85
polygamy **40**, 120
polymorphism **40**, *40*
polyp 23, **40**
polypeptide 17
polysaccharide 21
population **40**
porpoise 114
posture 139
potassium 16
prarie hen 120
prawn *55*
praying mantis 54, 90
precocial young *119*
predator 19, 62, 84, *84*, 85, 88–89, *89*, *94*, 110, *119*, 120, *126*, 133, 136
pregnancy 33, **40**, 40, 46. *See also* gestation
premolar 86, 126
pressure 138, *138*
prey animal 19
primate **40**
proboscis **40**
progesterone 27, 33, 38, **40**, 153
prokaryote *15*, 22, 27, 32, **40**
prolactin 129
Prontosil *15*
prosoma *55*
protease 27
protein *14*, *15*, 17, **40**, *62*, 63, 64, 68, 104
prothrombin *81*
Protoctista 17, 32, **40**, 58, 146
protoplasm 21, 64
protozoan 14, 35, **40**, 58, *58*, 59, *67*, 70, *94*, 99, 104
pseudopod **41**
pseudoscorpion 100
ptarmigan 119
pterygote 31
puberty **41**, 118
pubis 39
puffin *89*
pulmonary artery 18
pupa **41**, 128, *128*. *See also* chrysalis
pupil 28, **41**, *132*
purine 25, 37
pyrimidine 25, 37
pyruvate 41, 154

Q

queen 140, *141*

R

rabbit 78, 142
racoon 93, 94
radial symmetry **41**
radiation *79*
radiolarian 59
radula 52, *52*, 86, *87*
rat 87, 142
rattlesnake *89*, 138, *139*
ray 139
Ray, John *12*
reactant 22
recombination 16
reflex 31, **41**, *105*
refraction *132*
regeneration **41**, 80–81, *80*, *81*, 122
regurgitation **41**, 42, 140

reproduction **41**, 122, *122*, *123*, 124–25, *124*, *125*
alternation of generations 17
asexual 18, 19, 21, 39, 122
binary fission 18, 19
budding 18, **21**
conjunction 40
fertilization *see* fertilization
menstrual cycle 155, *155*
ovipary 26, **38**
ovivipary 26, **38**
parthenogenesis **39**
sexual 28, 34, **43**, 122, *122*, *123*
vivipary 26, **47**
reproductive organs 75
reptile **41**, 56, 112, *124*, 126
resilin *104*
respiration *14*, 16, 33, **41**, 62, 68, 72, 72, *73*
aerobic 26, 35, 41
anaerobic 41
cell 64
lung *see* lung
respiratory tract 65
retina 28, **42**, 42, *132*, 133, *133*
rhabdom *133*
rhinoceros 142
rib **42**
ribonucleic acid (RNA) 37, 42
ribose 37
ribosome 21, **42**, 64, *64*
ritual 120, *121*, 142
roadrunner 90
rod 28, 37, **42**, *65*, 133
rodent 87, *87*
round window *134*
roundworm 99
rove beetle *94*
rowing 114
royal jelly 140
ruff 120
rumen **42**
ruminant **42**, 67, *86*, 87
running 108
rut **42**, 120

S

Sacculina crab 99
sage grouse 120
salamander 56, *73*, *109*, 114, 122, 129
saliva **42**
salt 69
salt loss 78
sandhopper 95
Sanger, Frederick *15*
sap-feeder 96–97, 98
saprotroph 40
sarcomeres *105*
scale **42**, 56, *110*, 111, 111
scallop 52, *52*
scapula (shoulder blade) 39, 106
scar tissue 80
scavenger **42**, 84, 93, 94, *94*, 95, *95*
scent marking and signaling 142
Schwann, Theodor *13*, 14
Schwann cell 36
sclera *132*
scorpion **42**, 54, *55*, 126, 139
sea anemone 50, 88, 100, *101*, 126
sea cucumber 52, 53, 93, 95
sea horse 126
sea lily 24
sea otter 89
sea snake 114
sea squirt **42**, 56, 92
sea turtle 100
sea urchin 52, 53, *53*, 89
seagull 84, 93, 94, 95
seal 72, 106, 114, 120, *121*, 138, 142, *143*
sebaceous gland **42**
sebum **42**
segmentation **42**, *42*, 50, *51*, 54, *99*
semicircular canal 19, **42**, 108
sense organ 50
sensillum 137, 138
sensor **42**
sensory neuron **42**
septum **42**
sex **42** *see* reproduction
change of 120
sexual organs, development 118
sexual selection 27
shark 88, 89, *89*, 91, 92, 100, 114, 139
sharksucker 100
sheep 100
shelduck 119, 126
shell **43**, *43*, 52, *52*, 54, *55*, 106
shivering **43**, 78
shore crab *128*
shoulder blade *see* scapula
shoulder girdle *see* pectoral girdle
shrimp 54, *55*, 88, 92, 100
SI units 144, 145
Siamese fighting fish 126
sidewinding 110
sight 132–3, *132*, *133*. *See also* eye
signaling 134, 142
silk 32
sinoatrial node 30
siphon 32, **43**, *52*
skeleton 20, 32, *56*, *57*, 106, *106*, *107*, 108
adaptation for flight 112, *113*
external (exoskeleton) 18, 21, 26, 32, 54, 106, *106*
hydrostatic 106, *107*
internal (endoskeleton) **27**, 106
vertebrate 56
skin **43**, 56, 80, 118, 138, *138*
skull 56, *56*, *93*
slamander 108
slipper limpet 120
sloth *62*, 84
slug 86, **94**
smell 31, **43**, 136–37, *136*, *137*
snail 86, *94*, 105, 122, *122*
snail kite 84
snake 88, *89*, 90, 110, *110*, 111, *113*, *118*, 138, *139*
social behavior 15, *15*, **39**, 91, 100, 126
social insect **43**, 126, 140, *140*, *141*
social mammal 142, *142*, *143*
social skills *127*
sodium 16
sodium pump **43**
solenocyte (flame cell) **43**, *51*
sound 45, 134–35, *134*, *135*
Spallanzani, Lazzaro *13*
spawn **43**
speciation **43**
speech 45, 134
sperm 22, 29, 42, **43**, 45, *65*, 104, 122, *122*, *123*
sperm whale 88
spermatophore **43**, 122
sphincter **43**
spider 54, *55*, 66, 80, 88, 90–91, *91*, *94*, 97, *121*, 122, 126, 139
spinal cord 37, 38, **43**, 76
spine (backbone; vertebral column) 22, **43–44**, 53, *53*, 108
spiracle **44**, *73*
spleen 81
sponge **44**, 70, 122
spontaneous generation *13*
sporophyte 17
springtail *95*
squid *52*, *115*, 132
squirrel 85, 87, 110, *111*, *113*
standard units, conversion to and from 144
stapes 38
starch 21
starfish 52, 53, *53*, 80, 97, 126, 128
statocyst 19
statolith *50*
stentor 23, 59, *59*
sternum (breastbone) 39, 106
steroid hormone 63
stickleback 120
stomach 17, 25, 52, 80, 87
stress 17
striped possum 96
stylet 97, *97*
substance P 38
subungulate 46
sucker 98, 100
suction *111*
sugar 21, *62*, *69*, 75, *75*
sugar glider *113*
sulfa drug *15*
sulfur 62
suricate *127*
suspension feeder **44**, 93, 95
swallower 88
swan 118
Swammerdam, Jan *12*
sweat **44**, 78, *138*
sweat gland **44**, 44, 78
swim bladder 21, **44**, 114
swimming 114, *114*, *115*
symbiosis **44**, *59*, 67, *67*, 87, 95, 100, *100*, *101*
obligatory 44
symmetry **44**
bilateral **19**
radial **41**
synapse 16, 18, 37, **44**, *44*, 76, 77
synaptic knob 77
synovial fluid 32
systolic pressure 20

T

tadpole 32, 126, *128*, 129
tail 106, 110, 112, 114, *115*
tapetum 37, **44**, *132*
tapeworm 50, 99, *99*
taste **44**, 136–37, *137*, *139*
taste bud **44**, 45
tear **44**, 80
teeth **45**, *45*, 87
carnivores 89, *89*
egg tooth **26**
herbivores 86–87, *86*
milk 126
omnivores *93*
tendon **45**, 108, *109*
tentacle **45**, 53, 93
termite *67*, *86*, 95, 126, 139, 140, *140*, *141*
territory **45**, 121, 142
testis 26, 30, 33, 43, **45**, 75
testosterone **45**, 45
thermoregulation 24, 33, 43, **45**, *71*, 78, *79*, *138*
thirst 139
thorax **45**, 54, 55, 72, 76, 112
threadworm *98*, 99
throat 137
thrombin 23, 29, **45**
thrombocyte (platelet) *see* blood
thrombokinase 23
thromboplastin *81*
thrush 89
thumb 110, *111*
thymine 25–26
thymus gland 81
thyroid gland 26, 30, 40, **45**, 74, 75, 129
thyrotrophin 45
thyroxine **45**, 45, 129
tick *55*, 98
Tinbergen, Nikolaas 15, *15*
tissue **45**, 50, 64
connective **24**
dead cells 81
identification *13*
regeneration 80
toad 90, 126, *128*
toe 108, 110, *111*
webbed 114
tongue 44, **45**, 97, 134, 136, 137, *137*
tonsil 81
tortoise 86, *118*, 124
toucan *119*
touch **45**, 138, *138*, *139*
toxin 33, **45–46**, 69, *69*
trachea 31, 39, **46**, 46, *72*
tracheole 46
trap 90–91
trap-line 90
trapdoor spider 90
tree snake 90
tree-creeper 110
tri-iodothyronine 45
tricarboxylic acid cycle *see* Krebs cycle
triglyceride 28
trimethylamine oxide 68
tryptophan *14*
tsetse fly 97, 99
tube foot 24, 26, **46**, 52, *52*, 53
tubeworm **46**
tuna 139
turtle 86, 90, 114, 124, 139
tusk 30
Twort, Frederick *14*
tympanum 26, 134–35

U

undulation 114, *115*
ungulate **46**
urea 14, **46**, 68, *69*
uretha 19, 39
uric acid 68
urination 31
urine 19, 32, **46**, *69*, 78
urinogenital opening 23
uterus 17, 30, 40, **46**, 46, 70, *125*, 155

V

vacuole **46**, 58, 59, 66
vagina **46**
Valentin, Gabriel Gustav *13*
variation **46**
vasoconstriction **46**
vasodilation **46**
vasopressin 18
vein **46**, 52
venom **46**, 88, 140
ventilation **46**, 72
ventral **46**
ventricle 30
venule 71
vertebra 44
vertebral column *see* spine
vertebral disk **46**
vertebrate *13*, **46**, 47, 56, *56*, *57*, 70, 86
vibrassae *see* whisker
villus **47**, 66
viperfish 89
virus *14*, 35, **47**, *47*, 80, 99
vitamin 33, **47**
conversion of food to *69*
vitamins and human diet 151
vivipary 26, **47**
vocal chord 134
Voit, Karl von *14*
vorticellid 23, 59, *59*
Vries, Hugo de 27
vulture *67*, 89, 94, *94*

W

walking 108, *108*, *109*
warbler *87*
warm-blooded animal 23, 45, **47**, 78
warning coloration **47**
wasp 54, 126, 134, 140
waste products 68–69, *69*, 70
water flea *55*
water levels 69, 78
Watson, John *15*
wax **47**
web 90–91
Weismann, August *14*
whale 19, 25, 56, *73*, 88, 91, *91*, 92, 100, 106, 114, 118, 135, 139
whalebone *see* baleen
whisker (vibrassae) 45, **47**, 138
Whittaker, R H *15*
wildebeest 87, *89*, 91, 142
Wilson, Edward Osborne 15, *15*
windpipe *see* trachea
wing 56, 112–13, *112*, *113*, 114, 129, 134
Wohler, Friedrich 14
wolf 85, 91, *106*, 126
womb *see* uterus
woodlouse *55*, *94*, 95
woodpecker 85, 85, 89, 95, 97, 110
worker 140, *140*
worm 93, 95, 99, 105, 106, *107*, 110, 122

Y

yeast 35
yolk **47**, 122, 124, *124*

Z

zebra 87
zona pellucida *123*
zoology, history of *12–15*
zooplankton 40, **47**
zygote 17, 28, 43, *125*

ACKNOWLEDGMENTS

Picture credits

1 OSF/Peter Parks **2-3** NHPA/Stephen Dalton **6** OSF/Michael Leach **7** OSF/Fredrik Ehrenstrom **48–49** OSF/Fred Bavendam **49** AOL **50–51t** OSF/Fredrik Ehrenstrom **50–51b** NHPA/Bill Wood **53** OSF/David Fleetham **54–55** Biofotos/Heather Angel **55** OSF/James H Robinson **59** OSF/Peter Parks **60–61** Agence Nature/Fritz Polking **61** AOL **63** OSF/Michael Fogden **66–67** OSF/Frank Schneidermeyer **68t** Gerald Cubitt **68b** SPL/Dept of Anatomy, Uni "La Sapienza", Rome/Professor P Motta **70–71** Agence Nature/Lanceau **73t** BCL/Jane Burton **73cl** OSF/Ben Osborne **73cr** Premaphotos/K G Preston-Mafham **78–79** NHPA/Stephen Dalton **79tr** ABPL/Robert C Nunnington **79bl** OSF/Doug Allen **79br** Premaphotos/K G Preston-Mafham **81** SPL/Dr Arnold Brody **82–83** Premaphotos/K G Preston-Mafham **83** AOL **84** OSF/Stephen Dalton **84–85** Gerald Cubitt **85** OSF/Patridge Films Limited/Jim Clare **86** FLPA/Philip Perry **87tr** PEP/Cameron Read **87tl** PEP/Jonathan Scott **88–89** PEP/Ken Lucas **89** OSF/Photo Researchers Inc/Tom McHugh **90** OSF/Kjell Sandved **90–91** PEP/Duncan Murrell **92–93** NHPA/Andy Rouse **93** Survival Anglia/Jeff Foott **95** NHPA/Haroldo Palo **96** OSF/Animals Animals/Mary Souffer Productions **96–97** OSF/Robert Tyrrell **98t** BCL/Kim Taylor **98b** Biofotos/Heather Angel **98–99t** BCL/Dr Freider Sauer **98–99b** OSF/John Paling **100–101** OSF/David Fleetham **101** OSF/David Thompson **102–103** NHPA/Peter Johnson **103** AOL **104–105** SPL/David Scharf **106–107** BCL/Stephen J Kraseman **108–109** AOL **109** NHPA/Stephen Dalton **110–111** OSF/Kathie Atkinson **111t** BCL/Dr John MacKinnon **111c** OSF/Animals Animals/Breck P Kent **112–113** NHPA/Stephen Dalton **113** NHPA/C & S Pollitt **114–115** PEP/Doug Perrine **115** OSF/Photo Researchers Inc/Tom McHugh **116–117** RF/Skyline Features/Vince Streano **117** AOL **118** ABPL **118–119** Nature Photographers/Hugo Van Lawick **119** BCL/Jane Burton **120–121** NHPA/ANT **121t** FLPA/E & D Hosking **121b** Biofotos/Soames Summerhays **122** Premaphotos/K G Preston-Mafham **123** Agence Nature/F Sauer **125** BCL/Vincent Serventy **126** FLPA/Silvestris **126–127t** FLPA/Panda Photo **126–127b** Survival Anglia/Dieter & Mary Plage **127** ABPL/Clem Haagner **128** SPL/Andrew Syred **130–131** NHPA/Stephen Dalton **132–133** OSF/Michael Leach **137** NHPA/Anthony Bannister **138–139** Agence Nature/Chaumeton **139** Michael & Patricia Fogden **141t** OSF/N M Collins **142–143** Nature Photographers/Paul Sterry

Abbreviations
b = bottom, **t** = top
l = left, **c** = center, **r** = right

ABPL Anthony Bannister Picture Library, South Africa
AOL Andromeda Oxford Limited
BCL Bruce Coleman Limited, Middlesex, UK
FLPA Frank Lane Picture Library, Suffolk, UK
OSF Oxford Scientific Films Limited, Oxford, UK
RF Rex Features, London, UK

Artists
Mike Badrock, John Davies, Hugh Dixon, Bill Donohoe, Sandra Doyle, John Francis, Shami Ghale, Mick Gillah, Ron Hayward, Jim Hayward, Trevor Hill/Vennor Art, Joshua Associates, Frank Kennard, Pavel Kostell, Ruth Lindsey, Mike Lister, Jim Robins, Colin Rose, Colin Salmon, Leslie D. Smith, Ed Stewart, Tony Townsend, Halli Verinder, Peter Visscher

Studio photography
Richard Clark

Editorial assistance
Peter Lafferty, Ray Loughlin, Katie Screaton

Index
Ann Barrett

Origination by
J Film, Bangkok; ASA Litho, UK